AF566672

OH MY GOD

OH MY GOD

The Nature of Divine Faultlines

Shashi S. Sharma

Rupa . Co

Published 2002 by
Rupa & Co
7/16, Ansari Road, Daryaganj,
New Delhi 110 002

Sales Centres:

Allahabad Bangalore Chandigarh Chennai
Dehradun Hyderabad Jaipur Kathmandu
Kolkata Ludhiana Mumbai Pune

ISBN 81-7167-745-2

Typeset in 11 pts Sanskrit-Garmond by
Nikita Overseas Pvt Ltd, 1410 Chiranjiv Tower,
43 Nehru Place, New Delhi 110 019

Printed in India by
Rekha Printers Pvt Ltd, A-102/1
Okhla Industrial Area, Phase-II,
New Delhi-110 020

To
Sadhu Baba Dayanand ji, Bhola Baba,
and
my father Dr. Sukhdeo Sharma
for showing me the way.

Contents

Acknowledgement

My gratitude is due to the elders and friends of my village Patut, who taught me the living nuances of my culture and spirituality. I learnt immensely from their stable faith in their god, their religion and their cultifual motifs.

If I can claim to understand a little of my own tradition, it is because at some point many great teachers showed me the way. Teachers like Dr. Anil Kumar, Dr. V.N. Mishra and the late Dr. R.C. Prasad have helped me immensely. Thank you Sir, for holding my hand and leading me patiently towards a path of intellectual exploration.

I am deeply grateful to my father. A man of very limited financial means, he spared no effort to provide me with whatever I wanted to read. He has been a dear friend, teacher and a comrade.

A word of gratitude is due for my uncle Mangal Prabhat Sharma for being such a dear friend and for introducing me to the music and romance of life. It is always good to sing together with him of the joys of life.

I have been able to get a lot of academic and conceptual assistance from the publications of the Kalpataru Academy, Bangalore, and my unqualified gratitude is due to Prof. S.K. Ramchandra Rao and Sri Somaya ji. I shall fail in my duty if I do not express my indebtedness to the Central Secretariat Library, New Delhi, for providing me most of the reading material.

Introduction

God is a highly protean idea. It does not have a singular, recognizable 'personality' or an identifiable spatial locus. It can only be discerned if an attempt is made to explore and understand the reality and logic of statements made about, and in relation to, this idea of god. Since time immemorial individuals and human societies have pondered over the mystery of a transcendent but very real presence of a para-human phenomenon. Different societies have formulated their own specific notion of this elusive *mysterium* in an immensely rich range of theories. Human civilization is in possession of a vast body of literature in which man's encounter with the presence of god has been recorded over the span of many millennia. Our knowledge of the history of the idea of god is based principally on the basis of the records of man's engagement with god in the form of stylized instruments of laws, rituals, theological precepts and codes of action. It is the avowedly concretized and objectified character of god expressed in the credal dogma of various religions that human beings have reposed their strongest of loyalties in.

The present examination, however, is principally focussed on the study of the religions of the Judaic family—Jewry , Christianity and Islam—and the notions of god prevalent in various spiritual traditions of India. As and when required, collateral allusions have been made to other pagan spiritual traditions, but the main idea is to examine the two prominent classes of religious doctrines that have important bearing on the socio-cultural life of contemporary India. To a large measure, the defining attitude of the religious communities of India are moulded by their theological and religious doctrines. The credal doctrines of a religion determine the cultural, social and political attitude of the adherents, and on most occasions these attitudes overwhelm the secular requirements of the life of a nation and a citizen's response to it. In the Indian context the credal doctrines of Christianity and Islam, on the one hand, and the different ritual groupings or *sampradāya* of Indian origin, on the other, form two distinct ideological categories. There are, indeed, many important differences between the individual religions within a category but the two categories share very fundamental eschatological, cultural and theological principles.

The principle purpose of this work is to delineate a broad and commonly accepted idea of god in various spiritual traditions of India. It is true that various schools of philosophy and even individual saints and teachers have developed their own idea of god whose nuances differentiate one from the other. However, there has been a solid core of beliefs on which all schools and spiritual teachers of India have agreed. This core consists of the recognition of the complete freedom of a human being in pursuing his spiritual quest, without any let or hindrance, in order to have his very own personal epiphany of god. The spiritual traditions of India accept unreservedly the truth of god's polymorphy in the phenomenal perspective and his descent in the world of men in many aeons in many forms. In its own basic nature god is inscrutably attributeless but it joins the manifested world as the latter's inherent and controlling potencies. It is possible for an individual to meet god in its attributive form as well as in its pure, formless and indescribable nature.

In the contemporary Indian scene, it is impossible to talk about god, religions, or spirituality without being misunderstood. The reason for philosophical confusion emanates from the legacy of the last two hundred and fifty years of doctrinal development and the pressure of contemporary intellectual opinion which thinks that all philosophical ideas are cult-neutral or theo-neutral. India's encounter with Europe and Western Christianity under conditions of political and academic subjugation, created an ambience in which the modern, educated Indian embarked on an enterprise of re-evaluating his cultural and religious legacy in the light of the tenets of Christianity and, to some extent, Islam. In this process, a very serious methodological and comparative error was introduced by Indians themselves in the nature of this re-evaluation. They accepted, mostly, the European critique of Indian cultural and religious practices and tried to explain and, if possible, defend India's religious heritage in terms of the concepts and the language which the West suggested. The effort to counter a challenge, by the notions on which the challenge was based in the first place, proved highly inadequate.

Modern India by and large accepted many theological notions uncritically as a self-evident given. It assumed that there was something like a body of doctrines denotable by the term 'Hinduism' to mean a religion which belongs to a class of other religions like Islam or Christianity. With the assumption of this premise, the Indian idea of god was examined in terms of concepts like monotheism, polytheism, revelation, idolatry, false-gods, objective-morality, etc. Indians diffidently accepted the theory that some religions are polytheistic while others are monotheistic and also that being polytheistic and idolatrous was somehow an inferior way of religiosity. Very few serious attempts were made to question the basic premise of monotheism, prophetism and revelation as such. It was important to examine the notion of monotheism to know that it does not mean the existential reality of a numerically singular divinity but only a nominal emphasis on a particular cultic expression of the idea of god. The theory of revelation also needed to be critically examined. It would then have been possible to see revelation also in terms of an attempt to find outward locus for what was essentially an internal vision of reality.

All religious discussion in India lands in the muddle created by the Judaic notions of god, religion and spirituality. The concepts of prophetism, revelatory ethics, monotheism and stern religious legalism of the Judaic world of discourse were accepted as *ab initio* immutable and god-given categories of assessment that were objectively and empirically knowable. That these concepts should have been examined by Indians to test their worth was not deemed necessary. Ideas that grew in the specific world of Judaic religions became the sacrosanct scales of evaluation. Its god was considered to be the standardized personal god locatable in history whose commands constitute the only basis for objective morality. Everything beyond the pale of a Judaic revelation is non-consequential. Judaic theological notions became the yardstick for evaluation of the Indian idea of god and spirituality.

As far as the religious challenge of Islam was concerned, Indian cultural and spiritual leadership waged a defiant battle against its insular and exclusive theological claims with the convictional tools forged from the precepts of indigenous tradition. Saints, poets and reformers explained god and its message in the idiom of the new age and strengthened the faith of common men in their spirituality. They criticized the non-essential harmful accretion of ritual formalism in Indian spirituality but not the core meaning of the scriptural tradition. The common Indians listened to these teachers and maintained their poise and religious pride.

A new class of Indians came to occupy the intellectual centrestage in India with the advent of the Europeans and the commencement of English education by the end of the eighteenth century. This class was trained in 'modern' educational institutions in an European environment to criticize and belittle everything that its own tradition had held to be venerable. European theoretical paradigms, emerging out of Europe's Christian religious heritage, were uncritically used to evaluate and criticize a completely different world of metaphysical discourse. It was, somehow, believed that concepts like revelation, 'one-god', divine-laws, monotheism, anti-idolatry are divinely ordained, objectively verifiable and self-proven dicta. By implication, therefore, any body of doctrines that did not answer the paradigmatic demands of Europeanism and monotheistic religious discourse was believed to be decidedly inferior and erroneous.

Indians were being taught to accept that not only does 'monotheism' mean the existence of an objectively existent supreme god but also the existence of only one type of god that lives and breathes in the dogma of monotheistic religions. Monotheism was proferred as the most important, divinely ordained, benchmark for judging all other religious traditions. The merit or decadence of a system grew or diminished *pari passu* with its conformity with monotheism. Indian spirituality was also judged and found to be utterly deficient in merit. Hindu religious doctrines were declared to be polytheistic and idolatrous and therefore decadent. On closer scrutiny it would appear that in the realm of discourse on god no hard and fast theoretical parameters apply objectively. All discourses on god originate in a particular cultural tradition and carry with it the ideological stamp of the preferences of that culture. Every statement regarding god necessarily reflects the psycho-somatic predilection of the individual speaker. Ideological concepts which determine a religious statement originate in the cultural background of the speaker. A religious statement is not a record of an objective fact. To say that 'There is no god but god' or 'Jesus is the Son of God' does not have any independent or stand-alone universal meaning. As a statement it may mean no more than saying 'Creech creech'. The pronouncements of a religion are specific, goal-oriented theological premises that emerge in a tradition to serve certain cognitive and behavioural purposes. The notions of monotheism, revelation, prophetism, messiahship, god of history, etc, are not notions of Truth but tools of religious discourse that derive their meaning only in the world of the monotheistic religions of the Judaic family. Outside that world they have no sanctity.

The nature of religious experience is such that it entails the danger of the occurrence of a great linguistic fallacy if that experience is translated into words by the indicative use of language. By using the word 'monotheism' as a descriptive epithet, a theory regarding the spatio-temporal presence of god on the basis of a purely personal experience of one man is introduced as largescale spirituality for men in general. Words like monotheism, polytheism, etc, do not suggest anything about god indicatively; they only express the preference of a society regarding the ritualistic expression of the idea of the divine. In the manner in which it is generally used, monotheism does not mean the physical presence of 'one-god' but a particular mode of apperception of the 'one-god'. A monotheist chooses a particular idea of god, a deity, and exalts it to become the only idea of god. God is fundamentally indescribable. His presence is seen by men in various states of realization. The Supreme Being becomes a *theos* when it manifests in this world and in the life of human beings as a power and a presence. As a felt presence, it is described variously in the form of many deities as the essence of a man's or a group's experience. What is described as monotheism is basically a religious group's monodeitism.

The word 'god' cannot be used univocally to convey a fixed and universally accepted pre-determined meaning. It does not have any meaning neutrally; but comes alive with semantic life in the context of its use in the ritual or spiritual experience of a communicant. It acquires any meaning only in reference to a human user. The idea of god has evolved and grown over the years in a wide spectrum of theoretical formulations. God has a history of his own to contend with. In this sweep of god's history the Judaic experience of god in the Palestine constitutes just one chapter. The Judaic experience of god by no means comprises the normative understanding of the divine persona. It is just one way of looking at the unfathomable mystery of god. The perceptional structure of monotheism cannot be made the universal yardstick to measure the merit and efficacy of every spiritual idea of man. Monotheism of the Judaic kind, that rejects all human experience of man, but its own, as spurious has not been the defining characteristic of man's spirituality.

Monotheism as a Judaic construct does not have any inherent sacrosanctity. It is not the only, much less the most important, manifestation of god's relation to man. Therefore, it is meaningless to use it as a 'master-perspective' and create a system of comparative concepts like polytheism, henotheism, idolatry, etc, around it and with reference to it. A polytheistic interpretation of the spiritual reality is as efficacious, meritorious and 'true' as Judaic monotheism. God can be 'one', and this assertion is unimpeachable as a metaphysical statement; but to qualify it by saying that god is one in the way it is enshrined in the New Testament, or in the Holy Quran, is a 'faith statement' and not a proven fact. But Judaic religions develop their 'faith statements' into standardized benchmarks and evaluate every other religion from the perspective of their own faith. Therefore, concepts like 'barbarians', 'savages', 'pagans', 'infidels', 'unbelievers', *kafirs, mushrik,* etc, are developed to characterize pejoratively those human beings who do not subscribe to the idea of manifestation of the Judaic god. Man is seen as fallen not because of unrighteous living but because of his subscription to non-Judaic theology.

Religious ideas have to be judged according to the internal perspective of the community which subscribes to them. The merit of an idea should be predicated on its purpose and metaphysical meaning and not on the calumny of the preachers of other systems. In this sense the notions of 'true' and 'false' cannot be attached to the idea of god or religious systems. But our times are witness to incessant efforts and organised movements by religious denominations declaring other religions to be false and decadent. On the basis of such characterisation they also arrogate to themselves the right of taking corrective measures by changing the religious affiliation of the adherents of the so called 'false' religions. Money, material and metaphysics are collectively showered on the societies practising 'false', pagan and polytheistic religions as an act towards inducing 'reformation' by the 'true' religions of the 'one-god'. The immensely immoral paradox of calling the spiritual insight of other human beings as false and decadent does not bother the proponents of monotheism.

One only needs to go through the scriptures of the Judaic faiths to confirm in what contempt they hold the people outside their own community on account of their religious and sacredotal ideas. The religious practices of all people, but the 'chosen' one and the members of the *Umma* or the Church, are devastated as blasphemously abhorrent. Communities that do not subscribe to the idea of the Judaic god are threatened with promises of dire and blood-curdling punishment. God promises to annihilate whole communities if they do not eschew the hallowed practices of their ancestors and fall into the cultic slavery of a 'revealed' and 'historical' god. The followers of this god would, then, most naturally, deem it their duty to carry on the commands of their sovereign as a token of their sacred duty. This has resulted in extreme hardship for every society in which these insular religions have found accommodation. History bears copious witness to it. We may like to hide instances of cruelty on the basis of religious commandments or find some unctuous non-sectarian explanation for them. But the fact that persecution as an organised and scripturally sanctioned religious tool has been the singular hallmark of the Judaic religions is eloquently testified by their own history.

The religions of the non-Judaic kind have put up with tremendous calumny, castigation and physical assault for nearly fifteen hundred years from the hands of the proponents of the Judaic faiths. History is replete with instances where serious historians, great philosophers, and venerable religious leaders have used choicest of abuses to shower on the gods and spiritual systems of India. It is a testimony to the infinite patience, catholicity and fanatical respect for religious freedom of the adherents of the *Sanātan Dharma* of India that they tolerated such a long period of brutal and overpowering threat to their way of life without themselves adopting cultic brutality as a tool of cultural response. It is a proof of the great tolerance of Indian spirituality that it has put up with, and still puts up with, so much of motivated, arrogant and malicious propaganda against its gods and its religious traditions and that it has not developed a collective sense of neurotic xenophobia. It is amazing that the followers of the *Sanātan* systems of spirituality still defend the right of the Judaic religions to not only honourably exist but prosper and grow as proud and equal members of the spiritual landscape of India. Nay, a *Sanātan dharmi* also accepts theoretically the right of the Judaic religions to continue calumniating the religions of the *Sanātan* family. After all you cannot convert a human being unless you tell him that his idea of god and spirituality is false and decadent. Any attempt at religious conversion implies a malicious denigration of the gods of other people.

But lately one sees evidence of the infinite patience, tolerance, and catholicity of the *Sanātan* religions wavering and showing signs of stress. There are evidences that the unreasonableness of the religious discourse of certain religions is causing tremendous strain in the Indian society. Many segments of society have started reacting, even violently, to the day in and day out malicious and fabricated propaganda against their religion and their gods. The arrogance of exclusive and advanced spirituality is a dangerous thing. Indian tradition has taught that knowledge leads to humility—*vidyā dadāti vinayam.* It is difficult for an Indian trained in that tradition to say a harsh word against other gods and other religions. He is naturally trained to bow before every image of god; be it in a temple, a *dargāh, a mazār* or a church. He only expects a similar and equal respect being extended by other religions to his gods, temples and shrines. There is a danger that shrill justifications or tendentious explanations of the cultic buccaneering of the past, and the present atmosphere of discourse bent on hiding proven historical facts, may further harden an already stiffening of attitude. Hiding facts solves no problems.

It is necessary that Indian citizens start pondering over the rights claimed by Judaic religions, mostly Christianity and Islam, regarding the inviolable, eternal and fundamental sancrosanctity of the truth in the dogma of their own religion, while denying the legitimacy of all other religions at the same time. What gives the authority to the supreme religious leader of a religious sect to come to India and declare with confident equanimity that time has come to plant the Christian cross on the heart of India and reap a rich harvest of the souls of its citizens? In one fell denominational sweep the revered religious leader declared that all Indians, who are not Christians, are sunk in sin and ignorance, and their souls are completely degenerate and decadent because they subscribe to a Hindu, Sikh, Jain or Buddhist system of worship. In effect he declared that the greatest Hindu or Sikh has a sick soul that needs to be cured under the benign guidance of a Christian church. That such clear affront against the spiritual tradition of a nation is seen by many as religious discourse is a measure of India's intellectual predicament.

The present study seeks to evaluate the claim of certain religions that they are the only repositories of religious and divine truth. It seeks to evaluate their claim of exclusivity and of unitary hold on truth and virtue. It seeks to evaluate every claim by organized religious bodies regarding the uniqueness and utter finality of their religious message. Simply put, the book tries to find an answer to this question: who gives the authority to the leaders of a religion to proclaim their own religion as the only true religion and declare other religions as deplorable? It tries to explore the legitimacy of the authority which confers on an institution or a religious leader the responsibility of wrecking the religious practices of other people. It seeks to impugn the premise which is believed to give to a religious group the authority to kill other human beings because they believe in a different notion of god. It seeks to seriously challenge every claim of authority on the basis of a religious revelation or the command of a god.

On the other hand the present study tries to look at the idea of god as it has grown and developed in India in the past five-six millenia. The idea of god in the Indian tradition has been completely different from that of the Judaic religions. Judaic religions insist on communal brotherhood only within the community of the believers. The non-believer is not entitled to equal social treatment or equal religious justice. The exclusive revelation of god leads to the exclusive mandate of the community of believers.

Indian religious tradition looks at the idea of god very differently. To understand that idea, many pre-conceived notions inherited from Judaic religions have to be given up. To start with one should stop equating the idea of 'god' with the idea of *devatā*. The two are different categories of a reality but are not synonymous existential entities. To understand the notion of god and *devatā* a student needs to get away from the straitjacket of revelatory prophetic-monotheism and look at the *Sanātan* idea of god on the basis of the theory and practices of its own proponents. It is necessary to discard notions of interpretation borrowed from the Judaic faiths and approach the *Sanātan* idea of god on the basis of its own systems of analysis. We should realize that there are no fixed, immutable and sacrosanct theories regarding god and religion. The ultimate test of an idea of worship and god is its virtuosity, humaneness, tolerance and truthfulness. It does not matter whether these characteristics are 'revealed' by god or realized by great teachers on their own.

God has revealed itself to man in many modes. Indians believe that god can be seen in a special manner by each individual. For this reason every idea of god has been traditionally revered by the followers of the *Sanātan* tradition. This viewpoint explains the tolerance and pluralism of the Hindu religious worldview. It explains why force and oppression has never been used in India as a holy tool for spiritual betterment, and therefore, enlightenment of mankind. If we are desirous of creating an environment of peace and goodwill in our societies we must eschew all discourse which in some manner amounts to saying, 'my religion is better than yours and I shall not rest unless I convert the whole world to my viewpoint'. Religious narcissism must give way to spiritual humility. One would do well to, at least, appreciate the maltreatment a civilization must have undergone for centuries from torrents of malicious abuse hurled at it under the labels of infidelity, *Shirk*, polytheism and idolatry.

The present volume contains some Sanskrit and Hindi textual references. The literal meaning of these references are not provided separately in parenthesis. However, in most cases the non-English references occur in the context where the preceding or succeeding descriptive propositions contain the full meaning of those references. The non-English quotations generally follow a proposition which in fact is also its core meaning. Once a reader keeps the context of the references in mind he would be able to clearly understand the meaning of those allusions. The non-English references are used only as a collateral elucidatory support for the main idea. I hope the learned readers would have no problem in going through the many non-English references in the text.

Religare

I shall bind myself to you my God

It is very difficult to assert anything about god by the use of the term 'god'. As a linguistic utterance the word is empty of any universally valid meaning and substance. It is expressive and meaningful not in a general, cohesive sense but in a utterer-specific and listener-dependent manner. It is possible for two persons to talk about god without realizing that they are talking about two completely different phenomena. This is perhaps the only word which needs to carry with itself in parenthesis its intended meaning whenever it is used. To hear from someone that 'god is one' would not convey the exact intention of the speaker unless we know the speaker's name—John or Jehangir? Without the background of the speaker, a Jai would understand the statement in the manner in which it is prevalent in his own system of worship. It is like the game of bridge in which sometimes it becomes necessary to ask a player what he meant when he made a particular bid because 'two clubs' would correspond to two different values in two different systems of bidding. The meaning would also depend on the convention which the players have agreed upon for the assignation of bid value.

'God' can theoretically have as many meanings as there are men and women who use the word. The response of a person to the word 'god' would depend upon that person's expectations and the meaning that such a person assigns to his or her encounter with god as determined by his or her respective culture. The meaning of the word materializes in the synchronisation of the presentation of the divine source and the respectful disposition of the human agent. It is the encounter between 'god' and man that provides meaning to the former. God may happen to be 'god' essentially and factually, but in human discourse it assumes many different connotations depending on the construction which different universes of discourse put on it. It is futile to look for a common literal and metaphysical meaning behind the use of the term 'god' that does not have any reference to a 'group' and their specific cognitive routine. Philosophers have not been able to come up with a definition of god that can have trans-communal acceptability in all human societies. The definitions given by theologians are in any case the cause of the recurrent ambiguity, and occasionally wars, between two different god-groups. Paul Tillich perhaps was right when he said: "God is symbol for god".[1]

To use the word 'god' is to resort to symbolic use of language in order that a highly complex and transcendent idea is centextualized in a manageable format. The word 'god' is always used in conjunction with certain cognitive predicates. The most common formulations are 'I believe in god', 'god exists', 'god has commanded me', etc, because god derives most of its meaning only in such linguistic expressions of a certain state of responsive disposition. It is in the response of a person and a group that we know something about god. Human communities have perceived god in a manner that defy standardization in a uniform pattern. However, we can broadly distinguish human response to god in three major categories: Judaic—Jewry, Christianity, Islam; the systems of the *Sanātan Dharma* of India; and pagan religions comprising all other systems of god-talk. For the present study we shall confine our attention to the categories of the Judaic religions and the *Sanātan Dharma.* There are many intra-group variations in each category, but supervening above them in a group there does exist a clear ideological compulsion which the whole group shares. The Judaic group, despite the credal differences of the constituent units, responds to the idea of god in a fairly similar manner in which a person is completely and irrevocably subordinated to the will and commands of a particular revealed god. They believe in the exclusive veracity of their own deity and regard all other deities and devotional practices as anathema.

The followers of *Sanātan Dharma* by and large relate to god in a personal and internalized manner, and their morality does not always derive from the commands of a deity. The Judaic group claims to believe in a single deity but does not agree on its common manifestation in the system of the three constitutive units, whereas the other groups draw sustenance from various divine sources but still manage to be respectful to the religion of one another. The Judaic group has a fixed and unalterable personal and communal covenant with a holy god; the followers of *Sanātan Dharma* live with their gods in a fairly open and dynamic relationship. The Judaic group is morally duty bound to preach its god to all people, whereas a *Sanātan dharmi* is happy celebrating his god in his own small world and is loath to force his god on others. These are very relevant differences and they cannot be generalized by the use of any portmanteau term equally descriptive of both the groups.

At a certain level the *Sanātan* worshipper may relate to his god in a theistic manner through various systems of worship, but this practice should not deceive an observer because the phenomenology of his theism is completely different from that of a Muslim or Christian faithful. The difference between the god-talk of the Judaic group and the *Sanātan Dharma* is fundamental and to club them together would be erroneous. The morphology of the divine and the expectations of the two group from their respective gods do not tally. If there is no consensus regarding the meaning of the idea of god then there cannot be any uniformity in the character of the structure that regulates this idea. Prof. Gerardus Van Der Leeuw believes there is an ambiguity in the god-idea of man: "But when we say that *God* is the Object of religious experience, we must realize that 'God' is frequently an extremely indefinite concept which does not completely coincide with what we ourselves usually understand by it. Religious experience, in other terms, is concerned with a 'Somewhat'."[2]

The denominational problem of human society has to a large measure arisen in the course of their reification of this 'somewhat' as their respective gods and the delimitation of its geographical constituency. Human societies have not delimited and concretised the 'somewhat' in a similar manner. But the attitude of the Judaic group is *sui generis* among all other human responses to god. It is an attitude that treats its own characterisation of god as not only unique and valid for itself but also mandatory for all humanity. The Judaic god is believed to be the only god and its adherents are obligated to obey this god to the complete negation and exclusion of the gods of all other men. Judaic religions want to make their god a singular sovereign in a unilingual world of divine discourse. What Don Cupitt says about Christianity can be happily used also to describe the attitude of other Judaic religions: "That Jesus is God's only Son; that only through him can men be saved; that God acted in him once and for all; that world history will be wound up by him; and that he is God's chief executive..."[3] This special way of seeing and understanding god is what makes a man 'religious' and constitutes his 'religion'. A *Vaishnav* does not hold a god-opinion that conforms to that of a Muslim and therefore his relation to his god cannot be a 'religion' in the manner of a Christian or a Muslim. A Muslim knows his position vis-à-vis his god as his *imān* and *dīn*. A Christian sees his relation with Christ as his 'faith'. Ask a Hindu about his god, and what does he call his relationship to this god, and you would encounter a very confused and disturbed person. If he is cajoled to answer he may hesitatingly offer to describe it as *bhakti, sākhya, prem,* and in a lot more ways leaving a very confused questioner. The reason is simple: he does not have a 'religion'. He has his *dharma* which defines much more than his god.

'Religion' is a very distinct and special way of talking of god and the positioning of man in history. According to a religious viewpoint god creates the world at a finite point in time and continues to guide its future course in an orderly fashion according to his will. Man is created by god in his own image and in order to become the correct image he is expected to mould his life in conformity with the will of god revealed by the latter through his special prophets. While revealing himself to his prophet, god confers the honour of being 'chosen' on the people amidst whom the revelation is located. The 'chosen people' under the sovereignty of a creator god deem their destiny to be the non-recurring and unrepeatable occurrence in history. The chosen people are women and men transformed in the image of their god; those outside this unique march of history are seen as disobeying god's will and therefore need to be forced to conform. The religions of the Judaic family inherited this linear and non-cyclical view of Israelite history in which every minute of man's life is a response to god's creative plan in which the world is hurtling towards a predetermined end when all men would be finally judged for their loyalty.

The god of history is the transcendent Power and Will to which entire humanity must effect complete and unquestioning surrender. This god is a terrible, powerful and judgmental god who is so removed from the inner self of men that he can be only seen as the powerful 'other'. This powerful otherness of god makes him an object of both reverence and dread; some sort of *tabu* that man should be wary of. With this one god and his revelation developed the theses of religions being 'true' and 'false'. Since the one creator god has finally revealed himself and declared his will to men, it is incumbent on all humanity to live their lives in accordance with the revealed and 'true' religion; every other way of life is 'false' and deceitful and men must avoid them on the pain of utter damnation. Righteous life means complete adherence to the dictates of god in a spirit of humble obedience. Don Cupitt has drawn attention to the fact that the English word 'true' is related to 'troth', or 'trow' and primarily means loyalty to a covenant and fidelity to a vow or word. Similarly the Latin 'versus' has an equivalent meaning of reliability and solidity. The implication is clear: God's will deserves to be followed and his will constitutes the 'true' path because it is generative of a binding loyalty in men. God's words are *eo ipso* true and all other viewpoints are 'false' inasmuch as they are not endorsed by the god of Judaic religions.

Every other metaphysical truth held sacred by humanity is negated by the Judaic religions because the former does not conform to the revelation of the god in a small geographical area of Palestine and Arabia. Judaic religions continue to talk in terms of 'true' and 'false' gods and their true and false religions even in the face of overwhelming philosophical consensus that "the categories of truth and falsity do not apply to religious beliefs."[4] We shall later talk about the 'evolutionary theory' of god in which the god of the Judaic faiths is shown as the final product of the evolution of the god of primitive humanity. Theory of evolution, according to this hypothesis, applies to the god of non-Judaic humanity but ceases to operate when the divinity metamorphoses itself into the god of Judaic monotheism. Mercifully, it has stopped being purveyed with any seriousness in academic circles. However, it remains a widely accepted belief among all Judaic faiths that the spiritual doctrines of socieites outside their own limited brotherhood are not worthy of attention.

Obviously, the religions that comprise the Judaic group have a very distinct idea of god and man's relation to it. In their exclusivism they promote a very parochial view of the unfathomable mystery of the divine truth. A localized deity is sought to be exalted as expressive of all that can be said about man and the world; an idea which is especially difficult to universalize if it has the tendency to be used as a prop for the idiosyncrasies of a group of people. In this sense the Judaic religions propagate what can be characterized as an intolerant monodeitism, that began and grew as a completely human phenomenon, and therefore carries a deep trace of narcissism with it. Judaic religions talk of 'a god' but confuse it with the idea of 'the god'. The deity of Judaic religions presents itself as a final and only option to which inescapable loyalty is due. However, adherents of other systems of spirituality may not like to subscribe to this claustrophobic display of divine narcissism. Although Hindus hold their deities in veneration, most of them desire to ultimately free themselves of the bondage of every deity and every god and roam free in the realm of the pure and blissful spirit. A Hindu may use a deity in order that some day he would transcend it whereas in the world of the Judaic faiths, "The true religion is the religion which gives believers a true experience of God, and binds its adherents indissolubly to him".[5] Judaic faiths get stuck in a singular covenant;

whereas *Sanātan Dharma* wants to break free of all limitations and bondages, whether of the flesh or the spirit.

If we use the word 'religion' to denote the faiths of the Judaic group we cannot apply it to describe the belief system of non-Judaic faiths. The nature of the two phenomena are radically different. 'Religion' as a term can be applied only to characterize a very special way of life in which man and deity are co-dependently fixed in an unchanging relationship. It would be appropriate to quote John Hick's analysis of Wilfred Cantwell Smith's theory of religion. Smith, says John Hick, "traces the development of the concept of a religion as a distinct and bounded historical phenomenon, and shows that the notion, so far from being universal and self-evident, is a distinctively western invention which we have magisterially exported to the rest of the world. It began in the Roman empire, and reached its present form, in which we virtually equate a religion with a theological system, at the time of the European Enlightenment. This notion of religions as mutually exclusive entities with their own characteristics and histories, although it now tends to operate as a habitual category of our thinking, may well be but another example of the illicit reification, the turning of good objectives into bad substantives, to which the western mind is prone and against which contemporary philosophy has armed us."[6] You cannot have a religious outlook without a god; but equally truly you do not always have a religion even if you have a god.

It is essential to keep in mind the insistence of the Judaic religions in establishing the outward and public demonstration of faith as an objective and necessary entailment of their faith. Public proclamation of the creed is considered essential to the observance of faith as they are related to the extent to which god's influence is rightfully believed to encompass a man's life. All commands of god are required to be faithfully obeyed, and all rituals are to be observed scrupulously not in the privacy of the faithful's home but in group affirmations of the final and the only true message of the one and only god. If is often repeated in learned circles of India that religion is the matter of a man's private and subjective occupation and it should not be made to become an objective intrusion in the common public domain. A

Hindu may have no problem in accepting this proposition, but a Christian, for example would never agree to it. We have the authority of Paul Tillich, one of the most respected theologians, on this count and let us hear carefully what he says: "If religion is mere feeling it is innocuous....Faith as the state of ultimate concern claims the whole man and cannot be restricted to the subjectivity of mere feeling. It claims truth for its concern and commitment to it. It does not accept the situation "in the corner" of mere feeling... If the whole man is grasped, all his functions are grasped. If this claim of religion is denied, religion itself is denied... Faith is definite in its direction and concrete in its content. Therefore, it claims truth and commitment."[7] Christianity and Islam *are* religions: Hinduism *isn't*.

The idea that is being explored here relates to the impossibility of describing the *Sanātan* perception of the divine by the use of the word 'religion'. And there are sound reasons for holding this hypothesis. Words grow within the linguistic community that uses them, and mostly owe their meaning to the socio-cultural milieu in which they originate and find their use. Functionally they work as a medium of communication within the boundaries of a pre-established linguistic convention. This convention comprises of a set of rules which the members of the linguistic community inherit as a given and accept it in use by assenting to be a part of that linguistic community. These conventions are unique for every linguistic community because they specify and determine the context and the impact of words. Every word carries with it a well entrenched historical meaning which, outside the ambit of the user community, can only become an object of linguistic archaeology but not the locus of a shared living experience. There has, nevertheless, remained a tendency among some users of a language to treat the thematic import of a word or a concept as capable of being abstracted from the contextual landscape in which it originates, and made applicable to any other landscape. This belief can cause serious perceptional anomalies for both the self-illumination of the user and the intended audience. By using words indiscriminately both would play a 'language-game' without any regard to the rules of the game and ultimately land themselves into the frustration of an inconclusive and highly unsatisfying game. '*Words*', as Wittgenstein said, '*are deeds*'.

The use of the word '*religion*' when employed to describe the Indian attitude towards the divine, suffers from a serious infirmity. A descriptive epithet designed for a completely different speech situation is used into another situation on the very tenuous ground that the notion of 'god' is the object of communication in both the situations. In spite of the untenability of translating the word 'religion' into the sanskrit '*dharma*', this practice has become so entrenched in our common perception that to suggest that 'religion' is not '*dharma*' invites opprobrium ranging from cultural cussedness to unhealthy paranoia. There have been many sane voices urging against the establishment of a correspondence between religion and *dharma* but generally they have been met with a prejudiced upper lip and an overbearing superciliousness. The popular modern wisdom in India considers it to be an established fact that the basic import of the English 'religion' is the same as the Sanskrit '*dharma*'. Don't they relate, it is argued, somehow to 'god' and worship and all the paraphernalia associated with the regulation of this relationship?

The reality, unequivocally, is that they do not, and 'religion' and '*dharma*' do not mean the same thing. The Concise Oxford Dictionary defines 'religion' as,... "*particular system of faith and worship; thing that one is devoted to or is bound to*". It also provides the information that the word 'religion' is derived from a Latin root which means,..."*obligation, bond*". The Collins Cobuild English Language Dictionary defines religion as something that , ..."consists of a belief in a god or gods and the activities that are connected with this belief". The Merriam Webster Collegiate Dictionary defines religion as, ..."*the service and worship of God or the supernatural, commitment or devotion to religious faith or observance; a personal set or institutionalized system of religious attitudes, beliefs and practices*". The dictionary also traces the origin of the word religion to its Latin root 'religare' which means "to restrain, tie back". This root developed into the more popular Latin form of 'religio' which was used to denote, "supernatural constraint, sanction, religious practice".

Various dictionaries seem to be quite clear about the origin of the word 'religion' and the subject matter to which it gives linguistic expression. Semantically and etymologically religion belongs to the European world of discourse, especially drawing its sustenance from its Latin or Roman heritage: a heritage intimately connected with the tradition that has given birth to most of the civilizational tools which the West claims to be its abiding legacy. A.C. Bouquet reached the heart of the concept when he said: "'Religion' is a European word, and it is a European convention which has led to its employment as a general term to embrace certain human interests all the world over".[8] Bouquet further suggests that religion has been derived from the common Latin use of 'religio' which, as pointed out earlier, indicated a cultic practice derived from the avowed necessity of a supernatural constraint or sanction. Indian understanding of worship cannot be expressed by the word 'religion', much less will such a use be justified to convey the idea of *dharma,* and in order to do justice to India's vision any student of *dharma* would have to break free of the Western paradigmatic rut. Nirad C. Chaudhuri underlined this aspect when he said: "In reading about Hinduism the reader must emancipate himself from the prepossession created by the current conception of religion. It is of European origin, but has been adopted even by modern Hindus under the influence of Western thought. It was shaped by Christianity, but partly also by Judaism and Islam, all of which constitute a particular family of religions."[9] In its original Judeo-Christian context religion is a body of cultic and devotional beliefs which originates in the direct commands of a deity, perceived to be the only deity worthy of worship, and finds its operational manifestation in the formation of a community of worshippers in which the devotional paradigm of a man and his god is expanded to include the whole gamut of human behaviour from sex to war. A group of men and a deity find one another and swear to enter into a mutual convenant in which the former vows to always live by the direct commands of the latter, whatsoever they may be. The deity is always conceived as an alive, active, and locatable person who defines the vision men would follow for all times to come and, in marching towards the fulfilment of that vision, leads men to fertility, war and prayer. This personalized deity watches every move of the group of devotees and intercedes to change not only the way men view their universe and its ontology—but also the way they climb into bed between sheets. To be religious is to be bound down gut, groin and gray matter.

That the word 'religion' grew out of the particular requirements of the Judaic faiths in a western environment has been recognized by many scholars. Peter B. Clarke and Peter Byrne have asserted that no customary sense can be pinned down to the concept of 'religion' because, "it is Western in Origin".[10] Edwin A. Burtt has studied religious experience of man across cultures and continents, and he believes that the word 'religion', in its essential meaning, can be assigned principally to the Western world and the Judaic faiths inasmuch as they have been characterized by cultic exclusiveness and total rejection of the belief of all other people. "The notion that religion is an exclusive affair, demanding faith in the form of dogmatic attachment to one creed and hostile repudiation of other creeds is not a universal feature of religion. In general, it is characteristics of the Western faiths—Judaism, Christianity, and Islam—but by and large it is foreign to the Eastern religions."[11] The word 'religion' was used to denote a particularly western dispositional attitude towards an object of worship and it had a limited application of defining the contours of this attitude. Ninian Smart has correctly described this attitude as very specific, particularized and limited because,... "Western traditions has been deeply acquainted only with the Judaic group of faiths".[12]

Obviously, the word cannot be divorced from the original import which it wanted to capture and convey. René Guénon writes without hesitation: "...the term 'religion' is difficult to apply strictly outside the group formed by Judaism, Christianity and Islam, which goes to prove the specifically Jewish origin of the idea that the word now expresses".[13] The Judaic description of divinity and its relation with man was to mark a complete rupture from the way in which man throughout his known history had understood divinity. On the soil of Palestine was born an idea which was to chart a devotional course never attempted before by man. It was a new and daring experiment and all the three faiths which grew in the Palestine and Arabia share very distinct and specific characteristics which can not be found in other systems. A word, religion for example, used to describe the Judaic way to god cannot be used to describe, let us say, a *Vedantic* view of god. To this end we can add, as an adequate explanatory note, the firm opinion of Mr. Girilal Jain who said: "For, religion as such is a Semitic enterprise".[14]

There is no dispute regarding the etymological origin of religion from a Latin root. However, there are two opinions regarding the actual Latin root from which it grew. Cicero is said to have believed that the Latin 'religio' grew from the original 'relegare' which meant to 'take up', 'to gather' and also to 'read signs or omens over and over'. Servius thought that 'religio' emerged from the root 'religare' which described a relationship, a clear binding, and a sense of adherence. The two meanings of the original Latin root differ only in matters of detail but at the basic level they operate in a spirit of complementarity and both, separately and in conjunction, capture the essence of what is meant by religion in its original Western or Judaic sense. Cicero's conception of gathering together in the sense of 'taking up' or observing specific signs and reading or repeating, read with Servius' meaning of a bonding or a convenant completely describe *in ovo* what the Western concept of religion essentially is. It is no surprise that St. Augustine uses religion in both these senses. There is a wide acceptance of the sense in which Servius used the word. But if one goes by the sense in which Cicero used the word one can see, as pointed out by Bouquet, that it has nearly the exact meaning as the Greek word 'parateresis', which meant scrupulous observation of omens and the performance of rituals. It is no wonder that most of Western scholarship has conceptualized religion in a way that combines the modes in which both Cicero and Servius have interpreted it. The elements that emerge out of the two interpretations can be listed as: to take up something as holy; to gather together and be counted; to observe certain specific signs and rituals; to enter into a relationship with the object thought to be holy; to enter into a binding convenant and to adhere to it through thick and thin as the sign of a final and irrevocable affiliation and surrender. James Wm. McClendon Jr. and

James M. Smith were correct when in their study of religious conviction they noted that the use of religious utterance is not to describe or assert or predict, "but to avow".[15]

It would then imply that the message of a religious affirmation can be discerned by the careful study of the thought that characterizes a particular religion and also by an analysis of the use of religious language by the followers of that religion in its right context. An examination of the Western philosophical and theological tradition would be highly useful to understand how it has conceived and interpreted the phenomenon of religion. Such an examination is possible because we have a large corpus of definitive interpretations available to us. We may as a measure of caution disregard such 'figurative definitions' as Renan Leuba's theory of religion as progress of reason, or A.N.Whitehead's representation of religion as a man's occupation in his solitariness, or Matthew Arnold's belief that religion was morality tinged with emotion; not for the reason that they are unimportant, but for the reason that they have no bearing on the typology of the Western-Semitic enterprise of religion. We may similarly leave aside the 'propagandist definitions' such as religion being the opiate of the masses. This is necessary to avoid detour through non-essential territory lying far away from the theological mainstream of Christianity and Islam and to focus our attention on the more commonly acceptable functional and substantive definitions of 'religion'.

According to R.B. Braithwaite religion and belief in God is to... "commit oneself to a specific way of life".[16] According to him, religion is more a commitment of will rather assenting to such a way of life through intellectual assent. Keith Ward believes that,... "A religion may be characterized as a social organized way of relating men to the sacred; and a person becomes a religious believer when he commits himself to such a society, accepting its disciplines and goals."[17] Keith Ward further adds that two notions are central to the life of religion, "the notions of community and of revelation".[18] Schleiermacher defined religion by saying that ... "The essence of religion consists in the feeling of an absolute dependence."[19] Schleiermacher should have added 'upon god' at the end of his definition, because that is where the whole argument eventually leads to. And when he is talking of god, he is obviously talking of the 'Christian god' who, as we shall see later, demands absolute commitment to a certain specific set of beliefs. We may be inclined to agree with Walter Kaufmann when he says, "In fact, no practice as such is at all religious: it is only religious in the context of certain beliefs and emotions".[20]

Ed.L.Miller is more forthcoming when he states that in the Western tradition to use the word religion means to talk principally of "The God", and goes on to clarify that in the West, "The word 'religion' is almost always associated with God and the supernatural".[21] Although Miller is aware of the danger inherent in pinning an exclusive meaning on religion as belief in the Judeo-Christian God, and states that holding such a view "would be to exclude a vast block of human experience which most of us simply cannot resist calling 'religious'."[22] But this is precisely the point which the Western tradition has wanted to stress, namely, that religion means belief only in a Judeo-Christian god. Anything that does not fit into this vision does not qualify as religion at all. It is outside the purview of religion in a sense that it does not exist as worthy of serious consideration. Religions other than those of the Semitic stock are generally regarded as moral abomination, and on a few rare occasions of benignity, termed charitably as 'false religion'. And if 'God' becomes an essential posit of religion, demanding unwavering commitment, it is natural that such commitment, would necessarily follow the description given by F.H. Bradley when he identified religion as a…"fixed feeling of fear, resignation, admiration or approval no matter what may be the object, provided only that this feeling reaches a certain strength and is qualified by a certain degree of reflection".[23]

Western scholarship has been very clear in its perception of what religion was in the Western and the Judaic context. A.C Bouquet felt that for a European, religion has a well defined meaning which can be characterized as a …"fixed relationship between the human self and some non-human entity, the Sacred, the Supernatural, the Self-Existent, the Absolute, or simply 'God'."[24] This analysis of the Western view of religion underscores certain cardinal concepts, interpretable in terms of the all-important idea of a God, to which human commitment is due in a fixed relationship and the determination of the principles such a relationship would be contingent on. Understood in this European sense—which is the only and the right sense to understand religion in—religion is a practical system of relating to a deity and a particular way of worshipping it and living with it. Bouquet has also indicated, in what comes out as a stark contrast to the Western idea, the view point according to which the East has never been theistic. This would entail that for the Eastern tradition a god was not necessary to make a man religious; alternatively any god in that sense would do. Bouquet further holds that the Western view of religion is characterized by man's relationship with a person and not, as it were, with a process. E.B. Tylor was of the view that "the belief in spiritual beings" constitute "the minimum definition of religion". Tylor uses the term 'spiritual beings' to denote the belief in the existence of 'spirits' that can exist independently of material things. He believed that religion began in *animism* when man became aware of the presence and existence of powerful spirits. Ritual and magic was developed as primitive technology to cope with this new reality. It is of a piece with the Judaic and Western concept of religion in which the divine has to be conceived as a person who in some way is also said to be a spiritual category.

The theme of belief in a supernatural being, a spiritual presence, a person, a God, aligned with the mandate of utmost obedience to him gets repeated with strict regularity. It was on account of this fact that Andrew Lang suggested a deity—centric view of religion: "For these reasons we propose…to define religion as the belief in a primal being, a Maker, undying."[25] George Galloway expressed the opinion in 'The Philosophy of Religion' that,… "Religion is man's faith in a power beyond himself whereby he seeks to satisfy emotional needs and gain stability of life, and which he expresses in acts of worship and service." A similar sentiment is echoed by W.T. Blackstone when he says,… "Religious beliefs provide an all pervasive frame of reference or a focal attitude of orientation of life and induce a total commitment to an object of devotion." Max Weber, while examining the phenomenon of religion from a sociological viewpoint, strikes a similar note when he asserts that,... "The relationship of man to supernatural forces which take the forms of prayer, sacrifice and worship may be termed 'cult' and 'religion'.."[26] The messages are clear: Religion presupposes the belief in a 'god' and finds its expression in a responsive regulation of man's life in terms of that belief; sometimes in prayer and rituals, sometimes in direct action. No wonder the words 'Faith' and '*īmān*' can be happily substituted, and most frequently are, for the word 'religion'. Erich Fromm, therefore, defines religion as, ... "any system of thought and action shared by a group which gives the individual a frame of orientation and an object of devotion".[27]

Another major component of the concept of religion deals with the problem of defining the terms of a group's belief and regulating its relationship with the object of such belief. Without such definition of the terms of, so to say, the contract, the Western mind is incapable of understanding what to do with its religion. To formulate the idea of a god somehow means also to pledge a certain kind of loyalty to that idea requiring the complete exclusion of the possibility of any other idea ever being allowed to pose even a whisper of threat. It may seem a strange linguistic practice, in the first place, that words like 'loyalty' can be used for religion which in fact would only mean active loyalty to one's own reified idea. The concept of religion becomes inscrutable when it enjoins that a person is not only entitled to such loyalty but also authorised to transmit his loyalty to a larger group of persons by use of persuasion and, if necessary, force. Till the time that the monotheistic experiment began in man's history, ideas of worship, if shared by majority of members, have always evolved within a community as the evolute of its common experience or through willing acceptance of the way shown by a teacher. Even in the primitive societies magicians or shamans have only symbolized or represented the communal idea; they never exalted their personal experience of god and used threats of grave nature to enforce that experience on others.

In the Western-Judaic concept of religion men are expected to enter into a fixed and immutable relationship with 'god'. In the simplest form this relationship was a straightforward *quid pro quo*—a reciprocal promise of exchange of favours. Learned theological skills have added some academic embellishment to this core idea in order to cater to the intellectual contingencies of various epochs. Essentially, however, it was a fairly simple idea: there is a god who wants man to enter into a bond with him and obey all his commands regardless of many of them being incompatible with man's natural instincts of fair-play and righteousness. The Judaic religious tradition went a step further and alongwith the necessity of complete loyalty to their own idea of god, imposed on the adherents, the additional conditionality of rejecting the gods of other peoples including their own ancestors. The Judaic tradition represents god and its prophets as obsessed with this idea of rather extreme form of loyalty. God declares in the Bible to his chosen people: "I am the Lord: there is no other God." He adds, "I am the only God there is". Moses exhorts the Israelities to, "Honour the Lord your God, worship only him, and make your promises in his name alone. Do not worship other gods, any of the gods of people around you."[28] Joshua commands to whoever was listening,... "Then get rid of those foreign gods that you have, and pledge your loyalty to the Lord, the God of Israel."[29] Moses adds his own bit of warning to the forboding words of God when he says,: "If you do not obey the Lord, then you will be destroyed just like those nations that he is going to destroy as you advance."[30] God further reiterates his decision: "If you will only obey Me, you will eat all the good things the land produces. But if you defy Me, you are doomed to die. I, the Lord, have spoken."[31]

The consequences of disobedience and disloyalty are extremely harsh; Isaiah warns people of the things that god is going to do to all the nations that do not worship him: "He has condemned them to destruction. Their corpses will not be buried, but will lie there rotting and stinking; and the mountains will be red with blood."[32] God's warning of the consequences of not offering exclusive worship to him in the manner he wants is unambiguous; he declares his intention for the unbelievers: "I myself will tear them to pieces and then leave them. When I drag them off, no one will be able to save them."[33] Those who worship gods other than the God of the Bible have no escape from the wrath of God: "No pity, compassion, or mercy will stop me from killing them."[34] The prescription for people who worship other gods is clearly laid down by the God of the Bible to prophet Hosea: "Samaria must be punished for rebelling against me. Her people will die in war; babies will be dashed to the ground and pregnant women will be ripped open."[35] Such peroration is the hallmark of the God that we meet in the pages of the Bible. Similar messages also come out from the Holy Quran: "Allah! There is no god but him, the living, the Ever-existent one."[36] There is a warning for those who do not accept the god as revealed in the Quran: "Those that deny Allah's revelations shall be sternly punished; Allah is Mighty and capable of punishment."[37] Allah has declared that He can inflict punishment on unbelievers Himself but on most occasions this duty is left to be scrupulously discharged by the community of faithful: "Fight for the sake of Allah...Kill them wherever you find them...Idolatry is worse than carnage."[38]

Further instruction to the faithful against those who were outside the ken of that particular faith is outlined in the following words, "Fight against them until idolatry is no more, and Allah's religion reigns supreme."[39] A Hindu would find these ideas most disturbing because he has been told not to accept any coercion in the matters of belief—spiritual or cultic—regardless of the stature of the exponent. A Hindu would also be alarmed at such picturisation of god because, as Nirad C. Chaudhuri says,... "the Hindu Gods, in the forms in which they are worshipped for centuries, had no tyrannical, malevolent, or fearful character for their worshippers. No Hindu god or goddess, except a minor and local goddess of third rank, has been represented as pursuing any human being with the vindictiveness of Hera, Athena or Aphrodite."[40] Chaudhury may have done better by adding to that list the god of Judaic religions whose jealousy and vindictiveness far outstrip the modest attempts of a Hera. Chaudhuri, however, goes on to say that,.. "What characterizes the god–man relationship in Hinduism is benignity on one side and devotion on the other."[41]

Visualizing god in terms of a covenant implied an inherent and fundamental duality in the idea of the human and the divine and had one important consequence for the Western idea of religion: god became completely separated from men and their world, an idea picturesquely captured by Rudolf Otto by the concept of god being the 'wholly other'. God being a person wholly other than the sphere of the world and men, necessitated the establishment of a formal relationship with him in which the terms and conditions of such relationship were proffered and agreed to by the two concerned parties. Such an arrangement required formulation of a protocol to steer and regulate this relationship. Terms of the protocol emerged within the specific socio-historical context of a community finding its voice in 'concrete ritual situations and corporate acts of worship,' later to be adopted by the society on faith. E.O. James has further emphasized this point by saying that, "Religion, however, has emerged and developed under conditions sociological as well as psychological."[42] This was in a sense the confirmation of Emile Durkheim's thesis that religion arose in a collective form of experience which was based on the relation of a group of men and the supernatural symbol of that society: its god. These experiences of the supernatural had no universal validity, as claimed by the Judaic faiths, beyond the immediate context of the faithful and the observant community. Emile Durkheim in 'Elementary Forms of the Religious Life' rightly observes that "The god and the clan can be nothing else than the clan itself." We can further hear with profit what Emile Durkheim has to say in this regard: "A religion is a unified system of beliefs and practices relative to sacred things, that is to say things set apart and forbidden—beliefs and practices that unite into one single moral community called a Church, all those who adhere to them."[43]

In the Western or the Judeo-Christian tradition religion is the experience of a god conceived as an ultimate power and purpose existing apart from human beings and eliciting their devotion. One may also add to the above postulate the words 'blind obedience', 'loyalty', 'subordination' and 'unquestioning faith'. We shall have occasions to confirm this proposition as we progress in our study. For the present, even the initial unamended proposition would do, because it sufficiently expresses the moot theme. The response of devotion to a god begins from a known historical point when a devotee agrees to fix his psychosomatic seal on the document of the covenant, God's portion of which can be paraphrased as, "I am the one God your Lord; you shall not worship any other god before me and shall be always obedient and loyal to me and my chosen prophets. The believer utters an undying faith in god and all his commands and promises to always be loyal to him. No man joins a 'religion' without making such an affirmation. Weston La Barre sums this important point in a most pithy manner when he says: "Religion demands behaviours, loyalties, commitment."[44]

Moses typifies the devotional affirmation required of the faithful when he agrees to, "Honour the Lord your God, worship only Him and make your promises in His name alone." Moses further affirms in the Bible that: "This is my God and I will enshrine Him; The god of my father, and I will exalt Him." The oath of fidelity or the *akedāh* is to be repeated by every inhabitant of Palestine to become a true Israelite. This profession is a necessary condition for his life as a religious person. The Christian confession of faith is required to be made by every person in order to become a member of the religion of Christ. This confessional, as evolved during the Council of Nicaea in 325 AD reads, in its essentials, "We believe in one God, the Father Almighty, maker of all things, visible and invisible, as in one Lord, Jesus Christ, the Son of God..." To join the religion of Prophet Muhammad a person is required to profess, "There is no god but Allah and Muhammad is His Prophet." No abstruse or complex dispositional theories are involved in these confessions which recognize the kernel of religion as belief in one god, his prophet or his son as the case may be, and following his dictates revealed via the prophet.

Once a binding between god and man is achieved the commands of god become law for the believers. They place those commands above all other concerns as the supreme guide for their moral and ethical choices. The command 'you ought' is faithfully accepted as 'I must' by the believer. God becomes the supreme lawgiver and his commands become law. These laws are generally codified, as in the Decalogue handed down by god to Moses and as a set of regulations by the prophets of Judaic religions. These are not laws whose propriety or efficacy can be questioned; they are absolute commands of a sovereign who brooks no dissent. We have the supporting authority of Immanuel Kant who believed God to be the source of all morality and also held the view, that religion is the recognition of all our duties as divine Commandment. The covenant with god becomes, in a way, a legal contract between god and the believer which requires that the latter obeys the terms of the contract and not renege on any of its articles. Once a man 'swears' or 'bears witness' to a particular idea of god and a body of commands he binds himself most solemnly on oath to follow a certain course of life. It is not possible for him later to recant. He is irrevocably committed. Any digression would suffer the penalty due to be inflicted in cases of perjury or false oath. The initial oath of fidelity would debar any modification in his attitude, as a probable result of that man's perceptional growth, on account of this divine theory of estoppel. The covenanted believer's initial fidelity is sought to be reinforced by a continuous supply of dogmatic assurances; as the keepers of the faith know he may suffer immense moral turmoil in the face of the existence of different theories of god-apprehension practised by various communities around him vis-a-vis the recognition of his initial pledge which frightfully circumscribes his own right of choice.

The community of believers view individual aberration not only as an individual infringement but also as a challenge to the authority of the law which, if allowed unchecked, shall have a highly invidious impact on the whole community. Apostasy or even the minor affront of questioning an article of faith—blasphemy—are regarded as cardinal offences and most often death is the only punishment. Dogma logically engenders the concept of heresy and the concomitant enforcement mechanisms like the dungeon, the stake, and the inquisition. For the community of believers the thought of burning a man alive because he does not believe in a particular idea of god or having once promised to believe has gone back on his promise, or because he worships other gods, has a rational explanation: he has disobeyed the divine law and committed theological perjury by breaking his oath. The ethicality of this rationality is deemed as besides the point. Has the Lord God himself not commanded, "If you will only obey Me, you will eat all good things the land produces. But if you defy Me, you are doomed to die. I, the Lord, have spoken.."[45] God conclusively revealed to Jeremiah the course to be adopted to deal with infraction: "I will punish my people because they have sinned; they have abandoned Me, have offered sacrifices to other gods..." The enforcement of this divine ratio is assumed as a prerogative by the spiritual heirs to the initial Judaic revelation. It is considered a small matter that such enforcement also effects people nowhere in the picture when the covenant was struck; people who were never a party to this divine game.

Basing our findings on the fundamental tenets only, we can discern the following constitutive principles of the concept of 'religion':

- Belief in a particular and personlized god alone.
- No quarter to be given to any other idea of god obtaining in other communities.
- Personal and group covenant of an individual with god.
- Existence of a community of such covenanted individuals.
- Obedience to a body of divinely ordained laws directly given by god.
- Belief in prophets or messiahs as media of god's message.
- Systems of punishment for breach of theologial precepts through communal institutions.
- Strongly felt obligation to propagate and convert (except in Judaism).

'Religion', then, in its proper sense does not have a universal meaning even if it is sought to be descriptive of man's view of god. It is very contextual and denotes a very specific matrix of institutions and behaviour. In Henry Fielding's 'Tom Jones', Parson Thwackum gives us a definition which, I think, is difficult to improve upon: "When I mention religion", said Parson Thwackum to Mr. Square, "I mean the Christian religion; and not only the Christian religion, but the Protestant religion; and not only the Protestant religion, but the

Church of England."[46] In the Judeo-Christian tradition one god and one specific mode of obedience to him is the necessary entailment of its religious outlook. Indians never subscribed to this exclusivist viewpoint. Vilvamangala, a *Śaiva* saint has most lyrically expressed India's staggeringly different vision by asserting that although he is a firm devotee of *Śiva*, he gets indescribable pleasure when he contemplates the countenance of *Kṛṣṇa*, so much so that the two appear to be the same to him:

> *"śaivāyam na khalu tatra vicārṇiyam,*
> *pancākṣarī japaparā nitarāṁ tathāpi;*
> *ceto madiyamatsīkusumāvabhāsam*
> *smerānanaṁ smarati gopavadhū kiśoram".*

A *Sanātan dharmi* does have his god but he does not let the deity blind him to the infinite possibilities that are continuously actualizing themselves in man's spiritual and conscious world. He does not reject any hypothesis as *ipso facto* wrong without making a rational and sympathetic enquiry into it. It is not natural for the *Sanātan dharmi* to be fixated permanently with any idea uncritically, and his ethical world survives without the assistance of a deity because he patterns his life on the basis not of a partial view of truth but of the deepest universal and human rhythms. He worships his deity differently and has very different expectations from it. The *Sanātan dharmi* relates to life and god not religiously but in a *dharmic* way.

Dharma

Righteous ways to noble truth

The great thinkers of the East have visualized the meaning of the world and man's life in it through the metaphor of a constant pilgrimage. Life's mission cannot be defined by, and does not end at, a particular religious revelation which is said to finally determine its future course of action within the confines of that religion. The East has always regarded man's life and its relationship with this universe as a continuously evolving perspective that draws on the experiences gained by man during his journey. No experience, whether mundane or spiritual, is irrelevant and they all collectively comprise the great rubric of humanity's experiential existence. At a fundamental level reality does not admit any material distinction between a man's mundane and worldly experience and his spiritual experience of the divine. They are believed to be different frames of experiencing the one, single, basic reality.

To stop at a particular experience as expressive of final reality and cease to move further and grow was considered as misplaced pride borne out of ignorance. The important mission was not to stop at a particular goal but to continue the journey—"*caraiveti, caraiveti*". Of course, there is a stage where every journey would end, but at that stage the traveller, the way, the journey, the destination all merge into one single undifferentiable unity. At that stage perhaps a new 'journey' starts, but we do not know. It is interesting to note that thinkers of the East have identified man's life and its ultimate quest for truth not as a historically determinable revelatory finality, but as a constant movement—as a 'Way'. The Pharisees used the word *hodos*, the Buddha called it the 'eight-fold path', Japanese recognized it as the way of gods or *shinto,* and to the Chinese it was fully symbolized by the pregnant notion of '*Tao*'—The Way.[1] In India, various sects based on their specific idea of god and worship were known by the name *pantha*, a word which denotes travelling on a way. *Sanātan* tradition has regarded itself as a happy family of many *panthas* or *sampradāya* that travel in mutual harmony in their own distinct way towards a single divine goal. Travellers of one path do not traduce the travellers of another path; on the contrary they respect them as fellow pilgrims undertaking the same spiritual journey.

The Indian experience has contributed the foundational basis for the emergence of the Eastern view of man and his relationship with reality. India has always seen man's life as a movement away from limiting individualism to an all-encompassing vision of universal cohesion. Man is not an isolated and detached sinful victim of an original *felixe culpa* in need of an external source of salvation but the proud progeny of immortality—*amṛatasya putrāḥ*! Man's existence is not shaped and defined by the contingency of a 'fall'; and there is no sinfulness in him that requires fixed instruments of salvation. Man is the living manifestation of the divine capable of realizing his full potential in a loving communion with all men of the world. The whole world is one's own family—*vasudhaiv kutumbakam*—which partakes equally in the profound truth of reality. The Indian way can be distinguished from others by the fact of its perennial striving to find the eternal truth which is not exclusively limited to one man or a particular group of men: it is believed to be the natural heritage of all humanity. Charging a personal lien on truth has been alien to the Indian way. Their constant striving has been to go beyond the individual and reach corporate fellowship of men. *Idaṁ nā mam*—this world is not only 'me', and it cannot be defined by and regulated in terms only of an individual's personal vision, is a principle Indians have always kept in mind while trying to evolve their civilizational ethos.

Understandably, Indians originally named the territory inhabited by them as *Bhārat.* This word is a compound of *bha* and *rat* which signify 'involved in pursuit of light and wisdom'. This striving towards light, towards truth and towards knowledge could not have been possible from the standpoint of a stringently solipsistic world-view. While it is granted that each man is capable of attaining the highest wisdom on his own, the importance of the wisdom gained by others has always been respected and revered. Men are visualized as moving in their own respective ways towards truth. All philosophies, all view-points, all wisdom of the teachers and sages are uninterruptedly flowing in a spirit of symbiosis towards the same paramount ocean of truth:

> *rucināṁ vaicitrayāt ṛju kutil nānā pathajuṣām,*
> *nṛṇameko gamyastvamasi payasāmarṇava iva*

In such a tradition there was no space for the 'other' positioned as an irreconcilable and exterminable quantity. Since the whole cosmos is one, this unitary reality reveals itself in myriad phenomenal and supra-phenomenal manisfestations—*ekastathā sarvabhūtarāntamā rūpam rūpam pratirūpobabhuva.* Transitory names and forms were just that; not having a stable kernel of reality. What profit could then be gained by intransigent insistence on names and forms? Traditionally the *Sanātan* thinkers had been loath to fix a particular name to their way of life. Scour through the huge corpus of ancient Indian literature and you shall not find a name which could be said to have been used as descriptive of their way of life in the sense we find the use of the word 'Israelite', 'Christian' or 'Muslim'. It was subsequent naming by outside cultures which pinned the words 'Hindu', 'Brahminical', etc. on India's heritage. The world view which we now call Hindu, and I henceforth propose to use it in that sense, could infact not have had any specific name when the object of its discourse was the whole human race. The only way to allude to it was to regard it as the *Sanātana Dharma* or the *via perennis.* The *Sanātan* worldview related to the meaning of reality, a way of life patterned on it and to a system of conduct that regarded the whole earth as a common mother of a common humanity—*mātā bhumiḥ putroham prithivyah*[2]—and encouraged man to regard all things in the world as reflections of his own-self—*ātmavat sarvabhūteṣu*.

For the Hindu tradition the whole Universe is a phenomenal manifestation of one single reality which underlies and supports the appearance of its kaleidoscopic variety. Although from an acosmic perspective reality is understandably one; in the cosmic perspective the apparent variety acquires an evident spatio-temporal meaning. When such a premise is accepted the concern of philosophy would become the unity and order that is inherent in the whole universe. Indian thinkers have believed that this order and reality is extremely complex and therefore can find its expression at many levels of human consciousness. A civilization rooted in such a consciousness of unity will always have a healthy regard for diversity "as a happy acknowledgement of an evident Law of Life".[3] It was understood much earlier by Indians that man's perception of reality depended to a large extent on the perspective from which he approached it and on the reach of his intellectual capabilities, and that there was always a possibility of looking at things from a new perspective. The Indian mind, therefore, was ever ready to pay attention to all aspects of reality through judicious exploration and the balancing of view points with sympathetic openness.

So, acceptance of the possibility of looking at reality from various perspectives and complete tolerance of and respect for men, views, customs and cultures became a civilizational preoccupation of India. One can browse through the teachings of her great masters to realize the universal acceptance of this principle so succinctly summed up in the theory of *anekāntavād* or *syādvād* found in the Jaina tradition. Philosophers of India realized that because of the complex nature of reality no single definition would ever exhaust its meaning. The complex nature of reality would necessarily generate many view points, and insistence on the finality or ultimate validity of one single presentation of the divine or mundane reality would have been treated by the Indian mind as a case of ignorant delusion. The principle *dhārmic* stipulation was against fostering a sense of hatred for others or getting angry with anyone for reasons of the views that the other person held: *Sarvabhūtaparivādakrośansna.* Since men are bound to subscribe to many schools of thought and learning, a *Sanātan dharmi* was instructed not to compare one with the other in order only to denigrate or castigate a particular school of thought: *vidyaya cā vidyānām.*

Of course, discussions were held to evaluate various viewpoints and to judge their respective merits, but such discussions were never held from the premise of a preordained presupposition. Very unlike the Judaic tradition where every aspect of life would mandatorily be judged from the standpoint of a religious pre-supposition, "in the Indian method of understanding man and the world, there are really no presuppositions"[4] which are held to be valid *a priori* and therefore to be accepted on faith. Everything was required to be put through the scrutiny of man's reason, and a S*anātan dharmi* would have wholly agreed with Aristotle that an unexamined life was not worth living. The only way to know truth is through enquiry and introspection—*vāde vāde jāyate tattva bodhaḥ;* it is only through analysis and examination that man reaches the crux of a matter and no dogma is sacrosanct enough not to be challenged by man. The tradition of intellectual debate was well established wherein men from diverse schools of thought respectfully sat with one another and discussed, in an atmosphere of amity and goodwill, doctrines that were even antithetical to their own world-view. The whole exercise was called *śastrārtha*, or finding the meaning of the treatises. Viewpoints may have been challenged, deficiencies may have been pointed out in a theory but the right of a man to hold his theory was inviolable. All intellectual disputations were held to understand and explore in an atmosphere of respect and openness: "The partisans of one system may and do impugn the dogmas of others … yet the lances are lances of courtesy and the blows are loving ones"[5]

This attitude was not only manifest in the intellectual life of the people but had permeated the social, economic and political life of the Indian civilisation as a broadly accepted vision of social and communal interaction. We can refer to the clear advice of Chanakya to the King regarding the latter's conduct when he seeks to establish his rule over a newly conquered territory which may be found to observe different modes of life and devotion. In a peremptory tone Chanakya says that a king must respect the customs of the people and even try to follow the rules of behaviour, dress and language of that territory: *tasmāt samāna śīla véṣa bhāśācaratam upagachet.'*[6] The Rock Edict of the noble Aśoka proclaims the policy of inter-religious conduct which the State and citizens should follow. It enjoins: "Do not quarrel about religions, concord is meritorious. Do not imagine that you have a complete hold on Truth. You may not have it; no religion has a monopoly of Truth; you must try to know the God above all gods who is expressed in different ways and different individuals".[7] The edict clearly states that neither praising one's own sect or blaming other sects should take place, but other sects ought to be honoured in every way.

Indian civilisation has kept the promise it made to its saints, savants, teachers and leaders and, except some minor aberrations, has discharged its responsibility with distinction. It should be no surprise that India never believed in the concept of heresy or blasphemy, much less in the killing of people because they did not agree with a sectarian dogma. In reality, some of the so called inveterate 'heretics' in reference to the established opinion of their times were also the greatest of men that Indians bowed before: Bhagawān Buddha, Bhagawān Mahāvira, Ācārya Śaṁkara and Guru Nānak are a few shining examples. The Judaic tradition sought to eliminate its heretics; Hindus canonized them. It was to such guiding principles of a way of life that the Hindus gave the name of *'dharma'*. The modes of apprehending, visualizing and worshipping god was a part of it but never the only or even the primary constitutive part of *dharma*. We would soon try and see that *dharma* was not a Sanskrit equivalent of the English 'religion' and, as we have already noted, the notion was far removed from the set of ideas conveyed by the latter term. Chaturvedi Badrinath was underlining this fact when he wrote,"The true identity of Indian civilization has been *dharmic,"* and that, "D*harma* is not 'religion'. Indian civilization is not 'religious'".[8] The idea of *dharma* may have occasionally incorporated the notion of god and man's relation to it but this notion was not a prominent or even a necessary component of the idea. One can understand why Buddha did not talk of a 'god' when discoursing on his idea of '*dhamma*'. A fixed 'god' was not considered necessary for a life of *dhamma*.

Dharma in the *Sanātan* world of discourse was the perception of a set of broad principles which men intended to follow in the course of their journey through life. These principles were derived from the intense experience of the sages of India. *Dharma* constituted the experiential and practical framework within which Indian civilization proposed to grow and prosper. *Dharma* had no prophet and, of course, never made any claim to finality. *Sanātan* mind was aware of the danger such claims to finality would entail and was humble enough to foresee that such claims would lead to egocentric and therefore avoidable prejudices. Truth could only be sought with an unprejudiced stance in a mood of receptive openness. The *Sanātan* mind has always been a seeker of universal vision, therefore its *dharma* could never have become a sect or a cult or a religion. The dispositional underpinning of the concept of *dharma* is the moral realisation that man shall not nurture enmity for anyone but be friendly to all—*mā vidviśava sarvamāśāmam mitraṁ bhavantu*[9]; and he shall not do to others that he does not want done to himself—*ātmanaḥ pratikūlāni pareśam na samācareta.*[10] It is amazing that a perceptive and well read person like Raja Ram Mohan Roy could say that the natural law of do unto others as one would be done by is ... "principally inculcated in Christianity". But, on this hangs a tale which we shall have occasion to hear later.

Etymologically the word *dharma* has been derived from the root *'dhṛ'* which means 'to sustain', 'to support', and also that which is 'worth adopting'. The notion of propriety was always an attendent meaning. In its essentials, the proposition, "*dhārayati iti dharmaḥ*"—that which sustains and nourishes and can be adopted as an ideal is *dharma*—sums up the principle meaning of the word. In the Ṛg Veda the word has been used in the form of *dharman* to denote cognate notions of, behaviour, system, rules governing action and also ritual practices; a notion expressed by observations like *sanatā dharmāṇi (R.V.3.3.1), Prathamā dharmā (RV 3.17.1), tāni dharmāṇi prathmānyāsan* (10.90.16). Maharshi Jaimini in *Mīmāṁsāsūtra* (1.1.2) affirms the idea that the noble characteristics and the inspiring signs and acts mentioned in the Veda are the basis of *dharma—codanālakṣanoartho dharmaḥ*. This idea was further expanded and elaborated in the *Dharmaśāstra*, the *Smṛtis*, the epics and the philosophical systems. In the 'Dharmaśāstra' the word is used in the sense of a set of action and behaviour that can be adopted by men within a socio-cultural milieu for the purpose of regulating their behaviour. Such an adoption, however, was not to be in a haphazard, chaotic and a free-for-all manner but with a clear goal in mind. This goal was the collective ascendance and supreme sublimity of man—*yatoabhyudayaniḥṣreyassiddhi sa dharmaḥ*.[11] This whole cosmos is sustained by a unifying truthful principle or *ṛta*, and human life is required to follow the underlying rhythms of the cosmos. The patterns of the Universe and the human society should cohere. *Dharma* is the correlate of the inherent physical and moral order within creation, adopted for man's mundane and spiritual welfare.

Prof. Rhys Davids' observation in 'Buddhism: Its History and Literature', comes very close to the true nature of the notion of *dharma*: "In India, indeed, the same word is used by followers of every school of thought for law and for religion—the word Dharma, etymologically equivalent to the Latin *forma* ... 'good form'... not ... legislation. It was rather custom, established precedent; and a sense of duty to the established order of things included and implied a reverential attitude towards the gods."[12] It would be very fruitful at this juncture to examine some of the prominent explanations of *dharma* available in the literature of India. A few of them are indicated below:

- *Dhṛyate lokaḥ anena iti dharmaḥ—dharma* is the means by which men achieve beneficial regulation of behaviour in the public domain.
- *Dharmo viśvasya jagataḥ pratiṣṭhā*—it is *dharma* in which is established the whole universe.[Mahānāryāṇopaniṣat]
- *Dhāraṇād dharmaityāhurdharmo dhārayate prajāḥ*
  yat syād dhāraṇsaṁsyktaṁ sa dharma iti niścayaḥ—

Dharma sustains the society and maintains social order. *Dharma* ensures the well being and progress of humanity. *Dharma* fulfils these noble objectives of human life. [Mahābhārat]

- *Ārambho nyāyayukto yaḥ sa hi dharma iti smṛtaḥ*—An action done with a sense of justice and fairplay is *dharma*.[Mahābhārat]
- *Ācāraḥ parmodharmaḥ sarveśāmiti niścayaḥ*—Righteous conduct by all class of men is *dharma*. [Vaśiṣṭha Smṛti]
- *Ahiṁsā parmodharmaḥ*—non-violence is the highest *dharma* [Mahābhārat]
- *Anṛsaṁsayam parmo dharmaḥ* [Mahābhārat] —absence of cruelty is the greatest *dharma*.

One fact would immediately be apparent from the above cited definitions of *dharma*: the complete absence of any mention of gods and man's relation to them. The presence of a deity and the determination of an attitude of worship to it is not a major part of the *Sanātan* understanding of *dharma*. *Dharma* in its myriad applications deals primarily with the guiding principles of man's conduct in his personal and social life and the setting of rules which man should observe in his relationship with other men in the commonwealth of humanity. As men and societies evolve so do the circumstances of their inter-relationship; it is therefore quite natural that the *dhārmic* principles would also evolve. Since most of these principles do not derive their authority from divine authorship, it is possible for men to use their discretion in selecting and modifying them. They are, otherwise, not legally enforceable. In a very illustrative description Āpastamba Dharmasūtra (1-I) characterizes *dharma* as a system adopted and created by wise men through their own counsel and wisdom—*samyā-carikān dharmān*. *Dharma* draws its moral efficacy from the example set by great sages—*dharmajña samayaḥ pramāṇam.*[13] Mahābhārat rightly notes that the path trodden by great men is the Way worthy of being followed—*mahajano yen gataḥ sa panthāḥ*—their cultic affiliation or divine commitment notwithstanding. If man leads a noble life he will have a noble god—no doubts about it.

The *Sanātan* tradition has always believed in the inevitability of change in the temporal setting. Indians have tried to continuously modify, upgrade and uplift their understanding of things in the light of new experiences without belittling the importance of the previous viewpoint, whereas in the Semitic tradition the past, preceding their definitive revelation, is considered a saga of barbarism and sinfulness to be completely disowned and destroyed. Indians did not abrogate or supersede the wisdom of the past; they refined it and wherever found necessary, transcended it. All human experience is valuable and worthy of respect. While improvement in man's vision of a *dhārmic* life was advocated to cater to the contingency of ever evolving human environment, a core idea was always retained as uncompromisable. Manusmṛiti *[10.63]* has mentioned non-violence, truth, complete renunciation of wrongful and illegal gains, cleanliness, and conscious control over sensual faculties as the common *dharma* of all people:

ahimsā saytamasteyam śaucamindrīyanigrah
etaṁ sāmāsikam dharmaṁ caturvarṇyer abravinmanuḥ.

Vaśiṣṭha Dharmasūtra has described the core principles of *dharma* in a breathtaking breadth of vision. Maharshi Vaśiṣṭha says: follow the path of righteousness and eschew evil; speak always truth and not untruth; seek and judge with a broad and liberal attitude and do not have a constricted vision; do not seek anything that is petty and transient; always seek the noblest and the grandest in life and keep the aim of your life pure and elevated:

dharmaṁ carat mādharmaṁ satyaṁ vadat mānṛtaṁ
dīrghaṁ paśyat mā hraswaṁ param paśyat māparaṁ.

These core ideas formed the nave from which radiated many principles of conduct to support and sustain the felly of human society. In interpreting and implementing the principles of *dharma* in the secular sphere there have occurred certain distortions from time to time but the heart of the *Sanātan* tradition never lost its noble beat and corrective measures were immediately put into place. The nature of *dharma* is such that anything against the laws of nature and interest of human weal does not square with its essential import. Maharshi Vyās in Mahābhārat has interpreted the root '*dhr*' as a compound of ethical concerns that makes *dharma* not only the principle which sustains and supports but also that which nourishes, increases and glorifies men: *dhāranaddharmamityāhuḥ dhārṇena vidhṛtāḥ prajāḥ*. Respect for the viewpoints, beliefs, and freedom of choice of other individuals was unhesitatingly recognized and even enforced. Any viewpoint which restricted or impeded the moral choice of another human being was considered to be *adharma*—unrighteousness: true *dharma* can never be anti-anything; it has to be accommodative and respectful to the concerns of others:

> *dharma yo bādhate dharmo na sa dharmaḥ kudharma tat,*
> *avirodhāttu yo dharmaḥ so dharma satyavikramaḥ.*[14]

Dharma as the foundational principle of conduct and as a way of life reflects itself in all stages and occupations of human existence by suggesting principles for observation suited for every stage and station in life. *Sanātan* tradition recognizes many applications of *dharma: rājdharma* (conduct appropriate for a king); *chātra dharma* (for a student), *putradharma* (for a son), *varṇa dharma* (occupational); and many more. Ways of life and principles of conduct are not only person or group specific but also specific to time, space and age. Even the spatio-temporal categories need to be sustained and nurtured and the Indian genius has devised the concepts of *yugadharma, kāladharma* and *āpaddharma* to address these concerns. Indians have, however, never talked of a *'Hindu dharma'* in the manner of 'Christian religion' or 'Muslim religion' because they never let *dharma* become denominational and parochial. This courtesy has been extended to them by the scholars of the Judaic tradition and the modern Indian intelligentsia that regards the wisdom of the former as sacrosanct. The reasons for this unique Indian view of *dharma* are simple. Firstly, Hindus have never categorised humanity in terms of denominational corrals and secondly, it would have looked extremely incongruous to speak of *putra dharma* and *Hindu dharma* in the same breath. The Hindu mind always considered *dharma* in terms of its application universally to individuals and similarly placed social groups, never in terms of its application to cultic or devotional groups.

Dharma is the living and dialectical means of achieving greatness and transcendent merit for all men—*abhyudayanihssreyasiddhi*—in their lives as they traverse the ways of their temporal existence. Such a *dharma* cannot be static and orthodox, it has to move along with the movement of life which it seeks to make meaningful. The choice of the motto *dharmacakra pravartanāya* - for the rightful expository turning of the Wheel of Dharma—reflects a recognition of this deep seated civilizational consciousness; and so does the motto *dharmo rakṣati rakṣitāḥ*—preserve *dharma* in order that it preserves you. This mutual preservation can only be factored on the principles of truth, mutual respect, peace, non-violence, good conduct and fanatical respect for the glorious multifacetedness and plurality of human life and thought. For the Hindu mind, humanity has not ruptured into two irreconcilable groups: a priveleged *ummā* and a decadent group of unbelievers. It nurses hatred and enmity towards none on the basis of its cultic belief: "Hinduism provides for the ultimate Truth but not for a final and last statement of that Truth."[15] Bhagawān Mahāvīr has taught them to believe that a wise man has no enemies, but only friends:

mitti meñ subb bhūye sū bairaṁ majjh na kewai.[16]

Hostile disputations regarding cultic dogma and the nature of the deity are futile and they do not quench the fire of enmity. It is only through an attitude of non-enmity that peace can be achieved, and this attitude, Bhagawān Buddha reminded us, is the *Sanātan Dharma*:

nahi veren verāmi
sammanteedh kudācan
avereṇ ca sammanti
es dhammo sanantano.[17]

God, hitherto, has not entered the discourse regarding *dharma*. The sad part is that he never will. How can god appropriate for himself and enter into a context of discourse which directly does not involve his exalted nature? The god of the *Sanātan* tradition has not reached that level of egotistical obsession with himself where every word he utters should echo the hurt, the vindictiveness and the paranoia of an extremely fragile ego. We can fruitfully return to René Guénon for some light, especially to his analysis that,... "In India we are in the presence of a tradition which is purely metaphysical in its essence... A fact which stands out much more clearly here than in the Islamic tradition, chiefly owing to the absence of the religious point of view, ... is the complete subordination of the various particular orders relatively to metaphysics, that is to say relatively to the realm of universal principles."[18]

The impropriety of labelling the Indian concept of *dharma* as 'religion' was clear to many Indian thinkers and many of them have time and again warned against such deleterious naming. Religion is too narrow and inadequate an appellation to capture even a shadow of what is encompassed by *dharma.* 'Religion' in a much whittled down version of a simple, non-confrontational 'way of worship' can be a small part of the matrix of *dharma* but not its equivalent. But of course, we are constantly told that there is a Hindu religion as there is a, let us say, a Christian religion. Textbooks on sociology, history, politics and philosophy most authoritatively tell us about a Hindu religion when they refer to the Indian way of life. Children imbibe this fiction in their schools, from their books and their teachers at the most impressionable stage in their lives. Official government literature enumerates people as 'belonging' to the 'Hindu religion'. Try filling up a Government form or making an application, and the format forces on you the most ridiculous choice of indicating the religion to which you 'belong'; which a man belonging to a non-Judaic faith is constrained to indicate as 'Hindu' or 'Sikh', etc. as the case may be. In normal discourse we ask and are asked as to what religion we 'belong' as if religion is the most important determinant of a man's personality. 'Belong', however, is the operative word in all this: 'belong' in the sense of having been dedicated to, committed to something or owned by something. We have been so used to the idea of 'belonging' to a 'religion' that we fail to see the utter violence this does to the Hindu understanding of worship and *dharma,* and the limits it places on the convictional freedom of man which a Hindu has always regarded as an article of faith.

'Religion' as a concept cannot be applied in the Indian context even to designate a system or mode of apprehension of god and conduct of worship. A Hindu's system of worship cannot be called his religion if we keep in mind the principle ingredients of 'religion' that we have ferreted out in the earlier chapter. A Hindu does not approach god or worship it in any sense that can be said to be analogous to the way of the adherents of a Judaic religion. The mood, the dispositional attitude, the data of apprehension and the eschatological concerns of a Hindu are radically different. Only a careless profligacy with language would explain such an analogy. But metaphysical degeneration through such analogy became the norm in India for the last two hundred years. Not generally given to dogmatic canonization of men and opinions, Indians accepted as irrefutable wisdom the theory that all religions offer the same message. In a sense, such over-simplification may provide strategic manoeuvrability in a society where the advent of many competing religions, have forced a reassessment of the indigenous tradition to facilitate practical concerns of coexistence. Nonetheless, a falsely-premised aesthetic satisfaction of having a liberal and superior eclecticism cannot become a substitute for the uncompromising courage to explore. In any event, even this one-sided attempt on the part of Indian Hindu scholars to associate and align with Judaic religions in same sort of an equitable partnership has generally remained unrequited. At the fundamental level Christianity and Islam still consider the religious viewpoint of other traditions as damnably erroneous precepts entailing worship of false gods in an amoral spiritual environment.

It has been mentioned earlier that even the Hindu way of worship cannot be strictly called 'religious'. It would be fruitful, in this context, to examine a concrete experiential situation to test the meaning of this assertion. The experiences a person gains during his own passage through various stages of life, and in the performance of the rituals associated with them can provide some data to build a reasonable hypothesis on. I propose, with kind indulgence of all, to cite an example from my own experience. I would not claim this personal experience to be paradigmatic of the Hindu thoughts on worship; that would be erroneous given the leeway Hindus provide to men in matters of rituals. What I would like to submit is that this experience would give a fairly representative idea of how a Hindu posits himself in relation to a ritual situation. It may perhaps provide a concrete and applied example of the vision we are trying to understand and about which Hajime Nakamura said,... "'*dharma'* is beyond the difference of established religions. It should be universal to mankind, not restricted to any particular creed."[19] Nakamura confirms that ... "among Asians there prevails a strong antipathy to the Western use of the 'ism' to represent individual religions," and also that ... "Buddhism is not an 'ism', or Hinduism is not an 'ism'. Both are just aspects of *Dharma.*"[20].

I was born in a rural family in Bihar. Within the immediate environments of the familial and the village community there was a certain way of living and worshipping that I experienced without putting any theoretical label to that way of life. There were hundreds of forms in which I bowed my head to god, myriads of locales where its presence could be felt, and immense variety of modes in which I could express my veneration or affection for it. The modes ranged from *kīrtan, ārti, pujā,* prayer to throwing mud pebbles at our very favourite *ḍhelmarwā bābā*—the deity who loved being hit by kids. I was happy and contented. But there was a minor issue which occasionally disturbed my existential equanimity. Whenever I was forced to look at my mode of worship in a more formal framework I was asked to make sectarian choices. The contrast between what I lived and felt in my heart and what I was told about my feeling in theoretical terms was unbridgeably vast and in a certain way extremely disconcerting.

My social science school books categorically and without any qualification told me that I belonged to the 'Hindu religion' which was polytheistic in nature. It meant that I as a Hindu worshipped many 'gods'—sometimes even the figure of 330 million was mentioned to prove my incorrigible polytheism—and since worshipping many 'gods' meant acknowledging the separate existence of these myriad entities my polytheism was irrefutably confirmed. The event of the Hindus being polytheists was sometimes mentioned as an isolated objective fact. More often, however, it was mentioned in contradistinction to the fact of Islam, Christianity and Judaism being a 'one-god' or monotheistic religions. Wherever I looked I found my way of worship being described as polytheistic. My books told me so, my teachers characterised it as such and unconsciously I myself started understanding that I 'belonged' to a religion which was polytheistic in nature. By polytheism we simply understood belief in and worship of a large number of 'gods'. We were also told that Hindus were idol worshippers. They worshipped many idols of various shapes, sizes and materials and treated them as gods. These characteristics of Hindu religion were mentioned in a clinical fashion but always with a covert pejorative insinuation. Such definitions usually created an undefined sense of disquiet within myself. The serenity and sublime beauty of my interaction with my god would generally come crashing on the cold descriptive certitude of polytheism and idolatry. When my Hindu polytheism was juxtaposed, with the faith of the Christians and Muslims in their one and only god without the practice of idolatry, I had a feeling that my practices were subtly being portrayed as inferior. As I grew up the method of labelling the Hindu idea of god remained the same. But at a later age there also came a clear change in the analytical nuance. We were told on the authority of great scholars that polytheism was decidedly an inferior way of worship than monotheism, and idolatry, of course, was the pits of sacrilege.

So I grew up, and I have reasons to believe that many more like me grow up, believing that there are many categories in which man's approach to god can be unambiguously assigned. The most important categories were monotheism and polytheism on the one hand and idolatry and non-idolatry on the other. We also believed that a hierarchy of merit and efficacy can be assigned to various ways of knowing god. The theoretical premise of polytheism stood auto-justified if I looked around my social environment. My grandfather was an ardent follower of *Śri Rāma* and his life revolved around the holy verses of *Rāmcaritmānas*. His elder brother was celibate and a scholar of Upaniṣadic literature. He was also a great devotee of *Śiva* and invoked him by praying before a brass *triśūl* strung with a garland of *rudrākṣa* seeds. My grandmother was completely devoted to her assortment of *kuldevatā* and *grāmdevatā* and the daily ritual of her obeisance to the family *tulsi-caurā.* My mother doted on Śri *Kṛṣṇa.* My father had no fixed preferences but I felt he enjoyed praying to all of them. Did my family have a religion or was it multi-religious?

The small family in which I was born was clearly believing in and worshipping many 'gods'. As a part of the family I was in love with all the 'gods'. Nobody forced me to pledge my allegiance irrevocably to the god he or she was partial to. No member of the family ever told me the relative merits of the various 'gods' nor I remember to have undergone a ceremony which once and for all made me the frightened vassal of a particular god. What most surprised me was the underlying reverence which every member of the family had for all other 'gods' irrespective of their apparent and manifest preferences. In the stories of the Purāṇas and Mahābhārat narrated to me by my grandparents various gods appeared to change places and names in a highly complex but understandable pattern. There was no rivalry, no rancour, no competition at all. In a strange sense my family members appeared to be worshiping the same god under various names.

I was happy growing in my polytheistic cultural milieu. *Rāma, Kṛṣṇa, Śiva, Durgā, Gaṇeṣa*—there were so many of them to adore, worship and even play with. My polytheism knew no bounds, and it most naturally extended to circumambulating the three *karbalās* in the village during moharram in the company of my Muslim friends with a belt of small bells tied around my waist. The world seemed to be so full of god that one could meet it anywhere one wanted to in any form one liked. It seemed rather unimportant whether there was one god or there were many 'gods'. It was besides the moot point whether I dedicated myself to one god or to many of them. In fact, in my days of early youth I used to seriously wonder whether I had a god whom I can call my own. I now know about a Christian's assignation to Christ through his baptism and a Muslim's clear surrender to one Allah through witnessing the Islamic *śahāda*. These are rites of bonding between man and his god. It appears that once this bonding is made, a man is compelled to recognize and worship a particular god unwaveringly in only one particular way. Was I ever given to any god in such complete surrender or was a god given to me in exclusive fiduciary arrangement? Such were the questions that occasionally disturbed me. What then is the meaning of my personal sacrament?

It is only now that I have been able to grasp some meaning out of these dilemmas of religiosity. The questions which bothered me earlier, seemed intractable owing to the fact that I was trying to find their answer in a frame of reference to which they were unrelated. I wanted to find a parallel to the god-man covenant observable in other religious traditions into my *dhārmic* heritage. The right area to explore, however, would have been the area of the various rites of passage or *saṁskāra* that I as a *Sanātan dharmi* Hindu was expected to undergo. These *saṁskāras* are important to understand the value which the Hindu way of life assigns to various stages in the life of a human being. These *saṁskāras* are the recognition and celebration of the important stages of life on the one hand and the reminder of the *dhārmic* duties of that particular stage which one is expected to discharge on the other. Hindu tradition recognizes the performance of sixteen important *saṁskāras* of which birth, *upanayan*—(sacred-thread ceremony), marriage and death are the most important ones.

The Hindus view their *saṁskāra* as the corner stone of their physical and moral life. The Hindu śāstra define *saṁskāra* as the process by which a person is exhorted to acquire moral, physical, mental and intellectual felicities—*saṁskurvantyanen iti saṁskāraḥ*. A *saṁskāra,* on the one hand, becomes a reminder of the phase of life to which it is associated and, on the other, it symbolically gives man a new birth as reflected in his resolve to remove the dross which his mind and body have accumulated. While performing a *saṁskāra* an individual is encouraged to reiterate his commitment to a righteous way of life. He is invited to invoke noble thoughts and virtues to descend on him. A *samskara* is a psychosomatic affirmation by virtue of which a thing or a person can claim to have any value or meaning:

> *saṁskāro nām sa bhavati yasmin jāyate padārtho bhavati yogyaḥ kasyacidarthasyṁ.*
>
> [Mīmāṁsā sūtra, Śabara Bhāsya 3.1.3]

These *saṁskāras* are the intermittent reminders of man's position in this universe and the high task with which he is entrusted while he performs his worldly chores. As we grow in our life we are frequently required to be purified and made worthy. In the *Sanātan* tradition human worthiness is achieved neither by their surrender to a god through the unseverable assignation to a cult, nor by following a particular way of worship; it is achieved by resolving to become an exalted human being through intense moral discipline. These *saṁskāras* have two facets: *saṁskāras* as mentioned in the *dhārmic* treatises and *saṁskāras* which grow out of the practices of a particular local community and also from the practices prevalent in a particular family. The *saṁskāras* prescribed in the Śāstras and the folk *saṁskāras* are intended to complement one another. Of the latter type, it is said in the Āpastamba Dharmasūtra, that their determination is the right of the women of the community: '*yat striya āhustatkūryuḥ*'.

I distinctly remember some of the *saṁskāras* that I had personally undergone, while regarding others, specially of birth, I had heard from my mother and seen them being performed for other children in the family. Women of the family sing various songs of benediction and blessing for the expectant mother and for the child which is soon to arrive. In song after song the mother is addressed as *Yaśoda* or *Kauśalyā* or *Rukmaṇi* or *Pārvati*—all mothers who have brought 'gods' into this world. Every expected child is addressed by the name of some divine personage. It is amazing how simple women have realized that every child has the potential to be a *Rāma* or a *Kṛṣṇa* and through their folk songs the child is blessed and reminded of its true destiny. After the birth of a child the ceremony of *Jātkarma Saṁskāra* is performed for which some of the important mantras are provided in the Pāraskar Grihyasūtra. According to one *mantra* the child is exhorted to be strong like a rock, sharp like a scimitar and radiant like gold. The child is declared by the father to be latter's own *ātmā* in a new form and with a new name. He is blessed to live for hundred springs:

aśmā bhava paraśurbhava hiranyamsutaṁ bhava,
ātmāvai putranāmāsi so jīva śaradaḥ śatam

The child is not straitjacketed into a divine particularism. This becomes more clear when one examines the rituals associated with the sacred-thread ceremony. This is the occasion when the child is reminded of the duties that he is to follow throughout his life. The ceremony is designed in a manner that necessary mental disposition gets inculcated into a child. Throughout the ceremony not a word is uttered regarding any specific god to which a child should pray and to whom he should pledge his loyalty. In fact even the teacher conducting the ceremony does not appropriate the child as his own pupil. He wants the child to go beyond the confines of a particular school of teaching or a teacher and unravel the mysteries of the whole universe. He is advised to seek the mysteries of *Indra* and accept the cosmic intelligence, the *Agni,* as his teacher:

indrasya brahmcāryasi agnirācāryaḥ.

After guiding the child through the goals that he should pursue as a student, the presiding priest at the end of the ceremony makes a dramatic sacrifice in which the child's life itself becomes a sacred oblation. The teacher offers the child to the whole world, to all the gods that be, to all plants, to all elements, to the earth and the skies, and to life *qua* life in its wonderful multiplicity:

"*prajāpataye tvā paridadāmi devāyātvā savitre paridadāmi adabhyastvauṣadhibhyaḥ paridadāmi, dyāvāprithivibhyām tvā paridadāmi viśvebhyastvā devebhyaḥ paridadāmi sarvebhyastvā bhūtebhyaḥ paridadāmi.*"

The incantation is extremely humbling and makes a person completely open to the whole world as one cohesive source of inspiration and knowledge. I can remember the awe with which I heard these words although I was too young to understand its full implication. So, there I was clad in a cotton loin cloth vowing to pursue my learnings in a state of complete modesty with the realization that henceforth all my actions are to be as pious and holy as a *yajña,* in which the first thing I always should be willing to sacrifice is my own interest. Here I was, in my semi-nude humility trying to fathom the responsibility of having been dedicated to the whole universe. When I now look back, I wonder what religion was I initiated into, which god was I to declare as my supreme lord, which ritual was I expected to perpetuate? I 'belonged' to the supreme divinity of life and to the whole community of the created universe. I was given to all and all was mine. I was bound to be a proud polytheist.

No existential choice goes without determining the course one should set for one's life. I was asked to take certain vows that were to define the way I would conduct myself in life. One of the most important vows was that I shall try to be the protector of whole mankind as my own kith and kin; that I shall strive to acquire knowledge from all sources and also take required steps to preserve and nurture that knowledge:

asmevamadaṁ manuṣyaṇam vedasya nidhi yo bhūyasām

I was asked to promise that I shall always try to be wise and virtuous, and seek glory through a life of righteousness and spirituality; and only after making such a daily sincere effort shall I be justified in taking my food:

medhavyaham sānyanirakarisnuryaśasvi tejasvi
brahmvarcasyānn ado bhuyāsaṁ, svāhā.

Had I continued my studies according to the traditional Indian system in an *aśram* my teacher would have given me the final touchstone for judging all my action: to speak truth and to always act in a righteous way—*satyaṁ vada, dharmaṁ cara*

It surprises me today that throughout my life I was never categorically told what or who my god was. I did not know which form of god or school of worship did I 'belong'. Nobody ever told me to worship 'a god' in 'a particular way'. There was a complete freedom to choose and worship my god in any manner that I liked. It included the absolute freedom to find a god for myself on my own without recourse to a special revelation. God, in fact, seemed to materialize where the head of a man bowed. The problem of 'one god' and 'many gods' or the abstruse question of the unity or multiplicity of god never came into our universe of discourse. God seemed to be too intimate or, at times, too unapproachable to be subjected to any dispassionate and wholly objective analysis. Whether one god was better or worse than another god was simply not a subject of debate. According to the Judaic religions the mystery of the universe has finally been unravelled by them and the locus of god has been pinpointed with complete accuracy. Those who hold a confirmed opinion about the nature of god are naturally inclined to pass verdict against all other deities that can then be categorised as 'no-gods' or 'false gods'. It is considered as a logical imperative that the wisdom of one man becomes the measure of the foolishness of others. It may perhaps be a matter of irritating detail proffered by the victim of such divine calumny when it is pointed out that the definitions of wisdom and foolishness may vary according to the parameters that are chosen. The fact, however, remains that some schools of thought claim that the divine character of god's domain has finally been charted by man and doctors of religion have more or less reliable information on his nature and dispensation. We can not only mathematically enumerate his person but also clearly hear him instruct us through his chosen prophets.

Be that as it may, my 'religion', I was told by my society, was Hinduism, which was one among other religions, like Islam or Christianity. It was another matter that the adherents of the Judaic religions never seriously considered the Hindu way of life worthy enough to be called a religion. It remained a false religion worshipping false and execrable gods. What led to the obscuring and obfuscation of the clear message of the *Sanātan dharma*? What made Indians forget the pure message of their *dharma* in the labyrinth of alien interpretative concepts? It seems something, somewhere has seriously gone wrong in all this. It appears that the adoption by Indians themselves of the word 'religion', and the consequential evaluation of the Hindu way of life with European or Judaic yardstick, was a result of India's encounter with Islam and the West. That majority of the Indian followers of a non-Judaic way of life were the followers of 'Hinduism', that Hinduism was a 'religion' and that as a way of worship it was a decidedly inferior system were some of the insidious conclusions drawn by Indians from their encounter with the West and Christianity. Nirad C. Chaudhuri provides a possible explanation when he says: "Moreover, Christian religious notions brought to them the idea, utterly foreign to Hinduism, that monotheism and polytheism were mutually exclusive, and also its corollary that polytheism was a corruption of religion....In its place those modern Hindus who take an intellectual interest in their religion have become disciples of the Western specialists on Hinduism. Naturally, those Hindus who write on their religion have also adopted the method of the Western scholars"[21]. Therefore, it is this method which has to be examined. Perhaps history may give us some clues.

Close Encounter With The West

It should be borne in mind that India did not reach out to Europe; Europeans came seeking her for their own interests. For our current purpose we would concentrate our attention on the Indian-European interaction that started during the sixteenth century and further evolved till the end of the British rule. It was only in the years of this era that the full force of European material, intellectual and spiritual weight was brought to bear on India and her people. This encounter had very pervasive and lasting impression on every walk of the national life and determined, to a large extent, how Indians were going to look at themselves and also deal with the culture that was confronting them. Europe had not come to India to initiate a mutually beneficial and enlightening cultural and spiritual discussion. It had come here to appropriate India to itself and to subordinate her economic and intellectual resources to the larger interest of the European people. The language and manner of inter-cultural discourse that was brought to India was radically different from the discourse Indians were used to. As a result, wherever the European probe felt her it left a mark of branding on the soul of India. India was to be converted, in more than one sense of the word, by Europe.

Europe's initial and thereafter continuous basic interest in India was for "Christians and Spices"[1]; an expression which can be translated to indicate European material and denominational interest in India. Europe wanted to gain wealth and conquer heathen souls in India; all their efforts were geared towards these two fundamental goals, and European chroniclers have themselves admitted to these concerns in a very clear-headed manner. Revered Samuel Purchas (b 1577) wrote an account of European travellers in India which was a digest based on the travelogues of Linschoten, Sir Thomas Roe and Dr. John Fryer, and was published as "Purchas' Pilgrimage" in the year 1626. This was first serialized in a London newspaper and was reportedly well received. Reverend Samuel Purchas informed the English readers of the 'Saturday Evening's Englishman' that "the grand charm about India was its wealth,"[2] and believed that this wealth was enough, "to inoculate the gravest London citizen with a desire to do a little trade with such wealthy idolaters"[3] either directly or through the agency of an assortment of carpetbaggers, adventurers and sea-captains who "in those days were as much pirates as they were traders"[4]. It were not only the merchants and traders who sought India for her wealth. These military and mercantile classes had great co-travellers and collaborators in the various denominations of religious proselytizers who were not only interested in the enrichment of the soul of the heathen Indian but also saw in their Indian mission a great opportunity to make wealth for themselves and their Missions on the sideline. Reverend Purchas describes the enterprise of the peripatetic Jesuit preachers in India in the following words: "as to answer the ordinary brags of that World-Wandering Generation, pretending Mortification to the World, strictness of their Vow, loue to Religion and compassion to the poore Pagans, when as they have such Golden-chains to draw them thither."[5] Traders and priests, kings and merchants, had one clear agenda of harvesting the mineral, material and spiritual resources of India.

The interest of trade, administration, spiritual endeavour and research converged at a single point and moved in concert towards one unifying goal of exploitation. Most European trading companies carried a posse of priests and chaplains with them which was much in excess of the needs of the European factors. The Dutch East India Company in its Charter of 1602 was instructed by the holders to take spiritual interest in the pagans of the East apart from doing trade. The Charter of William III given to the East India Company enjoined: "Ministers…shall apply themselves to learn the native language of the country where they shall reside, the better to enable them to instruct the Gentoos that shall be the servants or slaves of the same Company, or of their agents in the Protestant religion."[6] St. Paul circumcising Timothy to destroy circumcision!—a strategy that shall be replicated in India with enthusiasm. Anyhow, religious preachers and churchmen were treated as natural collaborators in the commerce of India. The Jesuits and other Christian preachers and proselytizers were found necessary "to their Nation for the establishing of their Trading and ciuill affairs, vnder colour of Religion, winning estimation with the Pagans and remaining there as well for Intelligencers, and as it were Leeger Embassadoure with their Kings, as for Conuersion of the Heathens."[7] While the men in the cloak discharged highly secular functions for the king, the merchants and traders in all possible manner contributed to the evangelical efforts of the Churchmen. Prof. Ram Chandra Prasad has done a scholarly research on the early English travellers in India and has come to the conclusion in his erudite book that in those early years the merchant adventurers "took an interest in missionary activities, regarding the conversion of the natives as an important step towards the realisation of the Christian ideal."[8]

Priests belonging to England and Portugal were stationed at the Mughal and other royal courts to convert the kings as well as to wrest commercial concessions from them. Father Jerome Xavier was a member of the third Jesuit mission sent by the Portuguese to Akbar's Mughal Court and stayed there for twenty-three years. He sums up the burden of his office as, "working sometimes for the spiritual conversion of Emperors, at other times for the material advancement of his compatriots…"[9] Reverend Father Emmanuel Pinheiro was dispatched by the Portuguese to the court of Akbar "to counteract the influence of English travellers who visited the Mogul Court."[10] Likewise, Sir Thomas Roe's decision to go to the Court of Jehangir was impelled to a large extent by his desire, "to prevent any plots that may be wrought by the Jesuit to circumvent our trade..."[11] European preachers found the prospect of converts along with the hope of material gain, as a far more satisfying enterprise. That Christianity came to India because of her concern for the poor and for purposes of charity is a thesis propagated more by modern Indians than by the Christians themselves. Service to the poor became a concern for the Missionaries very late in their Indian career and most early Missionaries preferred the rich Indian pagans to the poor Mozambiquean when it came to set up their house of service and charity because in Mozambique "there is no profite to bee had"...[12] Van Linschoten confirms this when he records: "And therefore the Jesuits are warie not to make any Houses ... for they see no great profite to be reaped there, as they doe in *India*... where they find great quantity of Riches".[13]

The description of Europe's advent to India as a great civilizing mission that propelled India out of its sloth, poverty and material stagnation was so much of poppycock. Conversion and colonialism were two tactics of a single strategic enterprise of exploitation. India was to be bled and her wealth drained out to the vaults of the European merchants, bankers and the Churches. Samuel Purchas records the financial interest of the Jesuits in India and sees them as "enrichers of their own Societie in Europe with Gold, Pearle, Spice, and other Indian wares, then of those Asian Proselites.."[14] Men after European men that we encounter in the literature of that period, regardless of their profession, seem to have been awe-struck by India's wealth, material prosperity and her social and technological accomplishments. Such reaction would not have been possible to emerge had Europe been highly advanced compared to India and was reporting an encounter with a relatively savage and primitive people. India's material prosperity and also her superiority in many technical and economic disciplines was acknowledged by the Europeans. It was only for her cultural and spiritual heritage that choicest of abuses were reserved. For equally legitimate reasons Europe wanted to benefit from India's wealth but also sought to denigrate her culture. It was not only the European merchants and soldiers who were using various types of force to secure their interests, even the holy fathers and brothers of Christian Missions left their European abbeys not with the self-effacing solemnity of men of grace and charity but as warriors and conquerors for Christianity; and their departures to pagan lands were generally seen as the spiritual equivalent of the dispatch of a naval armada. It was going to be a long cultural crusade in India, and those pious men were aware of the nature of the mission of Father Thomas Stephen in India when they bid him adieu at the port of Lisbon in 1579, "with trumpets and shooting of ordnance"[15] all "in the manner of war."[16]

What emerges out of the European description of India of the sixteenth and seventeenth centuries are the details of a civilization which had achieved astounding material prosperity but had a highly frivolous and decadent religious, cultural and spiritual tradition; barbaric and bloodthirsty stories that pass for mythology, and practically no serious philosophy and system of morality. Europe was describing a unique civilizational paradox not attested in the history of other civilizations. We shall soon try to untangle the paradox and see that there has been a highly prejudiced motive behind such a characterisation. The laudatory reports of India's wealth were recitations of a matter of fact, and they were prepared with a view to encourage the royalty and the wealthy merchants to invest money, men and material for acquiring a share of this much more promising Asian El Dorado. The European man of religion, besides facilitating the process of exploination of Indian wealth, came to India with a religious conviction that only his specific faith was the exclusive path towards salvation, and every other group of people outside that faith were necessarily fallen and worthless; an attitude, incidentally, also shared by a majority of the merchants, armymen and administrators. In India, however, they encountered, unlike the Americas, a highly evolved social and political structure which could not have been subdued by the logic of force. The logic of cultural opprobrium was then used as the required instrument. Since the European man of religion was offering a superior spiritual truth he had to prove that Indian spirituality was highly degenerate. Moreover, if reports of a decadent society reach the European community of the faithful they shall be moved by concern for the poor heathen and contribute generously to the coffers of the Churches whose pious servants were seen to be undertaking such an onerous but holy assignment. In their own ways the merchants and the priests were seeing in India what they needed to see, and their reports were intended also to serve as promotional literature on Enterprise India addressed to their respective shareholders back home; ergo, India was wealthy but spiritually degenerate.

It is not the occasion to examine in detail the material progress of the people of India at the time when Europeans started spreading across the entire country. That is not the principal purpose of the present study. Nevertheless, we can allude *en passant* to some of the references of India's material stature available in the literature of that period which confirm that Europe in the sixteenth and seventeenth century encountered a nation clearly considered to be ahead of her in many respects. John Hüighen Van Linschoten who came to Goa from Portugal in the sixteenth century records that the "Heathen Physicians" of India were very good and "the Portugalls also, for the Vice-roy himself, the Arch-bishop, and all the Monkes and Friers do put more trust in them than in their own Countrimen"...[17] Linschoten appreciates the general state of health of Indians and the salubriousness of her environment, and he found it surprising, that,... "The Plague hath never been in *India* neither is it known unto the *Indians*."[18] James Bryce (1810) in his journal about India records, "the variety and excellence of its natural and artificial productions, have bestowed upon it an importance, in the eyes of the mercantile adventurer, which has led him to surmount every obstacle that nature or art has thrown in the way of their acquisition."[19] Maria Graham writing in 1814 about her experience of India's riches and its material prosperity, which of course, would not have been possible without adequate scientific and technological competence, records: "I might go on to quote all his descriptions of Paradise and all its bowers before I could exhaust the resemblances"[20]. She was alluding to John Milton's description of Paradise in his *Paradise Lost*.

The strength of India's material civilization was universally accepted. That India needed an external civilizational impetus is clearly subsequent imperial propaganda. The White Man's discharge of his civilizing burden in the economic and technological fields, therefore, could only have been disastrous. History is witness to the fact that Indian economy and enterprise were systematically destroyed by the European mercantile interest. Contrary to the trend witnessed in Europe, India's urban trade centres were being ravished and technicians and craftsmen were forced to move towards their villages; a phenomenon sometimes described by students of economic history as 'de-urbanisation'. However, the lyrical encomiums heaped on India's riches are generally missing in the early European description of Indian culture, way of worship, her 'gods' and her spiritual practices. In describing India's cultural heritage the general trend has been to denigrate it in all possible manners. The Catholic Church was fighting to save its ecumenical empire against a resurgent Protestantism in Europe. The two Churches had fought brutal wars to defend what they thought was the correct way of interpretation of the Christian faith. And wars have a tendency to draw hardlines of righteous conviction in the hearts of the protagonists. Although warring with one another on matters of ritual details the two Chruches were, however, completely convinced of the veracity of the universal and the only true message of their faith. The religious struggles had, in fact, further hardened their intolerance and the sense of exclusivity for their respective faiths and filled the minds of Europeans with an indignant sense of superiority. Europeans began to evaluate alien cultures from the standpoint of a self-assumed superiority. As Christians, they had inherited the cultural belief that anything outside the ken of the Christian faith was utter falsehood; as colonial pioneers they also developed a firm belief in their material superiority. With the prospect of an empire opening up in Asia, Africa and the Americas, the material and ecumenical interests of Europe gradually began to collaborate. How can an enlightened and advanced Europe, then, let such vast multitudes of India remain mired in idolatry and superstition when it was possible to make them the saved sheep of the Lord? The report of traders, merchants, priests and lay travellers regarding Indian culture underscored the sense of urgency of the European agenda of modernisation. And to this task Europe was to devote her total commitment. The construction of the theoretical premise in support of this commitment was wholly ecumenical, and the language used to express them was propositional.

"They are most subtle and wicked people, and are esteemed the worst slaues of all India; for that they are all theeues; and the Women, Whores; although this fault is common through all India, no place excepted"[21] This was the final verdict on Indian men and women that Reverend Purchas passed on to the English public drawn on the basis of the study of the travel reports of early travellers to India. Such being the disposition of the people of India it was most logical that their religion and culture would necessarily partake of this degradation. Reverend Purchas informs us about the most sympathetic analysis done by Linschoten of the cultural practices of the Indians: "Vaine Rites, stinking sinks and smoakes, Vgly Idols, conspiring with Iternall *Darknesse* of the Mindes, and External *Darknesse* of their Temples, to bring an Eternall Darknesse to the Followers ..."[22] We have on the authority of Linschoten that Hindu worshipped gods as "Idols in most devilish and deformed shapes... all shapes are made of the most ugly and deformed manner that possible may be devised."[23] These are some of the first utterances in which we hear Europe talking to other cultures and, what they assumed to be, other religions from the standpoint of her own religious and cultural conviction. As for the nature of the language, in case it is found obnoxious, we can always ascribe it to the superior morality of the visitors. Civilizational burdens are not discharged by the meek of heart and the hesitant of tongue. If one goes through the travel literature of the late sixteenth and early seventeenth century one would realize that the above mentioned opinions were not idiosyncratic; they were quite typical of Europe's perception of the Indian way of life. There were also to be found occasional flattering description like the... "*Bramenes* are the honestest and most esteemed Nation among all the Indian Heathens."[24] wherein not only were the Brahmans found to be a 'Nation' but they were also declared the Popes of India—"Bramen Pope". The general trend, however, was on the lines suggested by the earlier references. As late as the 1830s, we find J.W. Massie informing us that. "Brahmins celebrate their licentious and midnight orgies before the goddess Kalee"[25] and that the worship by women of Krishna, "will suffice to exhibit whether their worship has any claim to devotion or spirituality".[26]

It is a matter of fact that these perceptive early European observers rarely talked about Indian culture with any degree of seriousness and sobriety and limited their observations to distorted portrayal of events they did not understand. Their interest was limited to the exotic, to the frivolous, to the *avant garde,* and all that was peripheral in the Indian scene. To them Indian civilization found its supreme manifestation in the mountebanks, charlatans, esoteric rituals, idolatry—which they did not understand—and the stray incidents of Sati. Their perceptions were not based on a deep study of the Indian philosophical tradition and systems of worship. It was more a result of ad hoc and selective interpretation designed to serve a purpose. India of the fifteenth, sixteenth and seventeenth century was a land of great cultural and spiritual effervescence. Teachers and saints like Tulasidās, Surdās, Meerabāi, Raidās, Nānak and many more were causing great spiritual renaissance in all corners of the country. There was an all pervading sense of convictional stability and renewed confidence in the country's heritage which had its initial stirrings in the teachings of Kabir, Rāmānand and other saints. The country was witness to a pan-Indian cultural awakening and spiritual renaissance. It is surprising that the European travellers, preachers, and traders traversing across the length and breadth of India failed to even seriously notice and understand this phenomena. That this omission was a part of a continuing trend can be seen from the accounts of John Mckenzie, erstwhile Vice-Chancellor of Bombay University, who failed to notice these great saints and teachers even in the 1940s and wrote the typical diagnosis: "There were no great religious teachers with a message capable of lifting the minds of ordinary people above the minutae of ceremonial requirements or the puerilities of popular religious belief and practice. One of the effects of the preaching of the early missionaries was to stab awake many of the finest souls of the time. In their hearts there was created a great revulsion against the things that disfigured the Hinduism in which they had been brought up".[27] Was this learned academician ignorant or plain mischievous? Wilhelm Halbfass' theory of "tradition of silence and evasion"[28] can more suitably be applied to the European attitude towords Indian culture and spirituality. Such reliance on marginal and exotic data to the exclusion of a serious study of Indian thought was to characterize the method of many scholars even in the later years. It goes without saying that it was an unjust methodology. An Asian would not be doing justice to the USA if he characterized her culture solely on the basis of his impressions gained at the striptease bars or the Bronx, or about the Ku Klux Klan.

Europeans, however, generally continued to look at India in a very superficial manner, concentrating more on the unimportant rituals and stray incidents of social violence as indicative of India's mainstream way of life. Dutchman Abraham Rogers published his book in 1651 in Amsterdam in which he dwells mostly on the burning of widows and people throwing themselves in front of the car of 'Juggernaut'. J.Z. Holwell's account of India… "is both crude and full of mistakes."[29] Henry Lord was an English clergyman who published a book in 1630 in London which went by a rather longish title but became popular as 'A Discoverie of the Sects of the Banians". He believed, along with many early reporters, that Hindus were followers of Pythagoras. After great deal of research into the '*Shaster*' of the Banias, Lord came to the following conclusion regarding the crux of their religion: "Thus, worthy reader, thou hast the summe of the Banian religion, such as it is; not voyd of vaine superstitions, and composed of forgery, as well may be judged by the precedent discourse, wherein, as in all other heresies, may be gathered how Sathan leadeth those that are out of the pale of the Church, a round, in the maze of errour and gentilisme. I might leave the particulars to thy censure, as well to thy reading".[30] On being informed by such erudite scholarship, Europe would have naturally tended to censure rather than appreciate a 'religion' that was superstitious and composed of 'forgery'.

Later scholarship has seen through the erudition of these early commentators on Indian philosophy and religion for what it really was. Nirad C. Chaudhuri was generally inclined towards Europeanism, but even he could not help notice the motive and method of European reports on India: "Apart from serious works on Hinduism from both administrators and Missionaries there were also a fair number of books on it to cater for the popular interest in the religion in the West, which was ready to fasten on all that was curious, sensational or charlatanesque in the religion. These books do not deserve serious considerations. Unfortunately, however, it was such accounts rather than the scholarly works which moulded the popular idea of Hinduism in the West. The stories of the car of Juggernaut, the Suttee, the bloody sacrifices, the lechery of Krishna and of his worshippers, etc., travelled far, even to the United States."[31] There were indeed some European scholars who were reading Indian culture the way it was and were not loath to admit its great achievements; nonetheless the general drift was on the lines of censure recommended by Fr. Henry Lord.

Prof. Ram Chandra Prasad after examining important early English sources is of the considered opinion that: "Not only Terry but other early European travellers as well evinced only a superficial interest in the religions of India".[32] He further adds that these travellers never made "sustained investigations" into the life and culture of the people of India. This would not seem to ever have been the intention of these early European scholars on India, and we have on authority from Rev. Fr.Teixeira from Goa (1558) who reports that: "Sometimes we spend our time making fun of their gods, of their eating and drinking habits, and of the error in their religion".[33] Abbe Dubois while recording his impression of the attitude of the Europen missionaries in India says that on their arrival in India, the Missionaries continued to look at Indians, "with European Eyes, and European prejudices and to act accordingly; but finding themselves disappointed in all their attempts to make an impression upon them on the score of religion or otherwise, they, in their fiery zeal, or rather in their despair, avenge themselves by lavishing every kind of abuse and insult not only on their religion, but also on their institutions, both public and private, sacred and profane."[34]

As things would turn out, the preachers most often were

"disappointed in their attempts" because, "The gentiles, and especially the Brachmanes ... exhibited the greatest resentment,"[35] and that "their hostility on this account was the most formidable obstacle which the Fathers encountered in their efforts to extend the boundaries of the Kingdom of Jesus Christ in the territories of the Mogor."[36] Fr. Terry's (1616) report of the Indian reaction to such evangelical personages and their behaviour can also very well be a self-portrayal. Sick of the perpetual calumny heaped by votaries of the Christian religion on Indian gods and modes of worship the common Indian was exasperated and even his famed patience ran out in view of the moral nature of the Christians. Terry tells about the general behaviour of the Christian fathers when he reports Indians as believing: "Christian religion devil religion; Christian much drunk, Christian much do wrong, Christian much beat, Christian much abuse others".[37] Much philosophical effort must have flown down the Ganges of the Indian mind to make it believe only after two hundred years that the future of India was to be "harmonized, developed and shaped under the influence of Christianity." If we follow Abbe Dubois' suggestion we can see the reason and the motive behind such rabid characterisation of Indian culture and her institutions by the European pioneers. The general intellectual trend of portrayal was one of castigation, calumny and innuendo. Those chroniclers who had no immediate interest could "only see the extraordinary, the quaint and the marginal," which was inevitable because, given their attitude, their interface with people in general would have been very limited; "But most of these travellers had very little contact with the Indians."[38] O.P. Kejariwal holds a similar view regarding the Western attitude towards India: "In the first stage, scholarship was of little consequence; the emphasis was on the exotic, the mysterious, the fantastic..."[39]

Back home in England, Portugal, and France these reports were received with a fair degree of receptivity and formed the initial data on which many of the European theories regarding India were forged. Europe, especially Britain, assimilated the data and devised political, theoretical and pedagogic tools to deal with India in a manner that could serve imperial interests. The data on India was interpreted in two ways: firstly, that Indian culture was hopelessly fallen and needed to be reformed, and secondly, that such fallenness could be a result of its secession from the great Biblical root of humanity; a disruption which had spawned devilish gods and filthy rites. A philosophical enterprise for showing India her reflection in an European mirror, therefore, began. India was to be dissected, evaluated and judged by Europe, which was also to decide the agenda for her future. The trends were soon to emerge. Scholars have now indicated that it was Thomas Roe's observation regarding the Mughal Court which led to the theory of 'Oriental despotism'. Confronted with the manifest antiquity of Indian civilization and philosophy, serious scholarly research was undertaken "to explain the gods and reduce the Indian chronology to the limits set by Genesis."[40] Indian mythology was interpreted very creatively to suggest identification of cultural figures like Manu with Adam or sometimes with Noah. Francois Bernier was one of the few who recognized that the Hindus did essentially talk about 'One God' but even this talk according to him was a ruse Hindus have used to "suit the tenets of Christianity".[41] Indian civilization was interpreted as stunted and fallen, but of the original Biblical provenance. Is it any wonder that early Christian writers used to refer to the nobler pagans as "Christianus naturaliter", inclined naturally to incipient Christianity, requiring only the formal training of the sacrament to be fulfilled. European Christians even believed that India was once ruled by a Christian king called 'Prester John'. What went to Europe as immature and frivolous data came back to India synthesized as philosophy. The second phase of India's evaluation was to begin systematically from the last quarter of the eighteenth century. Some scholars believe that the second phase can be said to have begun with the writings of Charles Wilkins (1750-1836) and Alexander Dow (1735-79). And it is to the flourish of this new theme in the eighteenth century, and continuing thence unabated, that we may now turn.

Eighteenth century saw the consolidation of European commercial and administrative interest in large parts of India. Economic and political interests dictated that Europeans take a closer and systemic look at India's socio-cultural ideas and institutions. It was realized that pursuit of a long term political ambition cannot be successful in the absence of a firm grip on the minds of the people. Moreover, Europe at that point of history was supremely self-confident of her own accomplishments. Europe was on a path of great prosperity. Her sciences were growing, her economy was booming, her art was flourishing and her humanities were acquiring intellectual maturity and depth. In association with a growing empire such success further reinforced the belief in civilizational inerrancy. It is not to say that every European student of India had motives other than scholarly, or that they were studying Indian culture to strengthen the empire. The fact, however, remained that the broad framework of intellectual pursuit was determined by what Europe thought to be true from their own viewpoint. Perhaps in a sense it is also natural; civilizations tend to interpret one another from their specific perspectives. The minor innovation of mixing prejudice and motive with that perspective was, however, deemed four square with the urgent requirements of the new empire: "It was Europe and Christianity that weighed on their minds even as they wrote about the newly-discovered lands, peoples and cultures"[42]

Supplanting the traditional system of administration and jurisprudence by a system suited more to European ideas of administration would be one aspect of the strategy and a concomitant reinterpretation of India's cultural heritage would be the other. If India was to ever accept what Europe was offering as a better substitute then she had to be convinced that European science and civilization was superior to those of India. This would require the following urgent measures: establishment of European philosophical, historical, social and cultural paradigms as the most efficacious; establishment of an atmosphere of intellectual discourse through various fora to propagate the new pedagogy; and a critical study of India's socio-cultural heritage including her *upāsanā* and *dharma*. Europe needed to acquaint itself with the foundations of Indian culture to be fully prepared should an occasion present itself in the future requiring the expediency of finally destroying that foundation. That the foundation was weak and fragile was an idea that every explorer implicitly believed in and it was in such a state of mind that Europe embarked upon her mission in India. Max Muller was anticipating these early pioneers when he said in 1873 that Hinduism was dying, because it represented a school of thought, "which was long buried beneath the feet of modern man."

Since India's interface was most intense with England, we shall principally focus on the British experience, while alluding to other trends as and when required. We shall also limit ourselves to what the British scholars had to say about India's 'religion' and 'culture', because that is the aspect which principally concerns us here. We must also keep in mind the fact that many of the commentators of late eighteenth and early nineteenth centuries were not academicians by profession. Most of them, later termed as 'orientalists', were missionaries, travellers, judges and administrators and their work cannot be understood without a reference to the compulsions of the station they occupied and the tradition they inherited. Modern scholarship has identified the motives of control, hegemony and dominance in the concept of 'Orientalism' to the extent that Edward Said saw in this discourse an effort to manage and even produce the Orient. The historian Arnold Toynbee has also classified as an "uncritically accepted intellectual *cliche*" the use of the term 'Oriental' to denote decadence, stagnation, corruption, despotism, etc, of the Eastern societies. At a most fundamental level Orientalism *was* the ideology of European dominance in Asia. The Boden Professorship of Sanskrit at Oxford was instituted with the possible purpose of serving the cause of conversions in India. This purpose would necessarily have been the principle motive for which the great encumbents to the Chair-William Jones, Monier—Williams, et al.—laboured in the archives of Indian culture. They were endeavouring to create a new picture of Indian religion, philosophy and history. There is no reason to believe that an important purpose of the Boden endowment was allowed to be diluted by its beneficiaries while pursuing scholarly vocations in India.

One of the basic premises from which the European scholars proceeded was the utter infallibility and incomparability of the Christian faith and the superiority of the European civilization. Every other faith and civilization was to be judged according to the standards set by them. The venerable William Jones set the tone when he said: "The tenents of our church cannot without profaneness, be compared with that of the Hindus..."[43] At the very outset any objective or impartial assessment of Indian culture was thus overruled by him and his Asiatic Society. The Orientalists were not studying Indian culture and spirituality to appreciate and understand but to compare and traduce. The undoubted premise that reality was finally captured in the Biblical history and the teachings of the Christian gospels, produced the inevitable conclusion that everything else was either an aberration from the original or a falsehood. Jones and the 'Asiatic Society'—that venerable institution which was to set the agenda for India's self-perception—pursued both the themes. Jones believed in the veracity of the Biblical story of the deluge and proposed that he has found the confirmation of Moses in the Vedas and Purānas. Hindus, according to him, were descendants of Noah through Ham, and all Indian mythology was a distorted version of the Biblical stories. Even Indian gods were corrupted versions of the sacred history of the Bible. His idea was to establish on the one hand India's supreme religious error and to "put Indian mythology in line with biblical tradition" [44] on the other . He assured his English and Indian audiences that, "the dawn of true Indian history appears only three or four centuries before the Christian era, the preceding ages are clouded by allegory or fable."[45]

Ecclesiastical opinion in England was naturally excited by the preliminary results of the Orientalist scholarly labour. Here was a nation of fallen humanity that had forgotten its true heritage and was taken up by erroneous religious and cultic practices. These miserable heathens needed succour and, as the British pioneers were readily available on spot, their efforts were completely supportable. Intellectual opinion in England and Europe was agog with expectation and hope. The learned professor of Divinity at Cambridge, and Bishop of Llandoff, Dr.Robert Watson, while commending the birth of the 'Asiatic Society' commented that, "He was concerned to find confirmation of the biblical tradition in Hindu literature," and wanted Jones to confirm if there were any marks of Judaism among the castes of India or any reason to believe that,

"Indians are not derived from the same Noaic stock with ourselves."[46] Dr. Watson could not have been subtler in hinting for a search to find common Indo-European ancestry of the Indians. The clue seems to have been picked up. Jones' effort later proved that Oriental and Indological scholarship, did not disappoint Dr. Watson and Britain.

Study of Indian 'religion' and culture was also necessary for the purpose of propagation of Christianity. Such study provided valuable data to prove the inadequacy of Hindu scripture and the superiority of the Christian doctrine. William Jones understood the value of these studies for conversion of Indians and suggested translation in Sanskrit and Persian of "such chapters of the Prophets, particularly Isaiah, as are indisputably evangelical" [47] not for the sake of language or scholarship but for propagation of Christianity. He not only wanted these works to be translated but suggested, "quietly to disperse the work among well-educated natives"[48]. If they converted well and good, if they did not, well, Jones was a picture of Christian humility: "we could only lament more than ever the strength of prejudice and the weakness of unassisted reason"[49]. His clue was picked up with enthusiasm. The Mission at Serampore in 1785 applied for funds to the Asiatic Society to enable them to translate and publish some Sanskrit religious works; an intention not infused with any respect for the text which, let us be clear, they thought *a priori* was dictated by Satan. However, the Serampore Mission found some merit in studying and translating works dictated by Satan for evangelical reasons: "He certainly did not intend when he dictated those vile and destructive fables, that the publishing of them to the enlightened world, should supply a fund for circulating the oracles of Truth."[50] We have here an example of superior evangelical ethics according to which propagating the word of Satan is deemed virtuous to secure the religious loyalty, of a group of people. That Indian scriptures were 'vile and destructive' was never doubted by majority of the scholars of Orientalism, and the respectable judge Mr. Charles Grant was representing the general sentiment of that class when he characterized the whole Indian civilization as rotten to the core.

The unbridled humiliation of Indian civilization, her scripture and her 'gods' was not coming from ignorant fly-by-wire theoreticians and intellectuals, but from very capable and respectable minds of that time. Modern British scholarship, bureaucracy and Christian missions arrogated to themselves the right to hurl choicest abuses on Indian religions and cultural practices as a matter of moral right. Even to this day a body of opinion in India still accords natural right to the Judaic religions to criticize and trivialize Indian religions. But woe betide an Indian who challenges these dangerous claims and tries to stand up and assert. British Civil Servants were far more refreshingly candid in their narration and awesome in their understanding of Indian tradition. William Henry Sleeman, a senior officer of the East India Company, in an erudite commentary on the Ramayan explained the kernel of that great epic in a subtext as, "Rumaen, or history of the rape of Seeta, the wife of Rama..."[51] the Mahābhārat and the Bhāgawat, according to that learned gentleman, "describe the wars and amours of this god in his last human shape," and "Krishan, *if born at all,* must have been born on the 7th of August AD 600 but was most likely a mere creation of the imagination to serve the purpose of Brahmans of Ojeyn, in whom the fiction originated."[52] Ignorance *simpliciter* cannot stoop to such depths without the pressure of malice. Mark Twain joined the chorus when he informed audiences in the USA about temples of Banaras being some sort of an Ordnance establishment by describing them as "admirably stocked and wonderfully systemized Spiritual and Temporal Army and Navy Store."[53] A nation under political and military thraldom of Britain was unlikely to disregard these thoughts as unimportant; after all they were coming from an avowedly more civilized, and superior race.

British historiography and social thought, especially the more dominant school of Utilitarians and Protestant theologians, was constructing a view of history from a Eurocentric viewpoint. James Mill's "History of British India" became a highly regarded source of information on India. Mill took a very dim view of Hindu religion and metaphysics, and described them to be barbaric. He thought that Vedic cosmogony was of "fantastic and senseless forms"[54] based on the thoughts of a people "whose ideas of the Divine being were grovelling."[55] Our *ṛṣis* were men "whose ideas of the divine nature are mean, ridiculous, gross and disgusting".[56] The teachings of the

Rāmāyan and the Mahābhārat were "extravagant, unnatural, and out of touch with the physical and moral laws of the Universe".[57] Such ideas were used to great effect by the Evangelists in 1813 when the Charter of the East India Company came up for renewal. The pressure to introduce Western education and English Language in India was earnestly mounted because it was felt that such an education would ensure, as believed by Charles Grant, that "the Indian character would be receptive to the light of the Gospel".[58] and conduce towards an end when, inter alia, Indians would lose faith in their ancient culture and "would then be converted".[59] This was the moral aspect of the reconstruction of Indian life to which Macaulay was to subsequently contribute the theory of intellectual and volitional conversion. It was an agenda for all round development.

Even as time passed and British rule entrenched deeper in India the basic characterisation of Indian culture and spiritual heritage did not change. The tactics of achieving this end—whether through English or vernacular language—may have been the subject of dispute but on the intrinsic fallenness of India there was no quarrel. Macaulay characterized heathenism of India as a cruel and licentious worldview which observed idolatrous practices of the most pernicious kind. Sir Charles Trevelyan believed that Hinduism was full of gross immoralities and physical absurdities and that it would succumb before the light of European science and education and clear the way for what he picturesquely described as the placing of the Christian locomotive on the Indian cultural rail. Sir Richard Temple believed that India did not have a faith; she at best had a bunch of wild superstitions. India, according to these pioneering men, was culturally and morally fallen. Let us not forget that these were not ordinary men. These were men who commanded authority and, to a large measure, shaped the policies of the British rule in India. These were honourable men charged with the authority to govern India and their views greatly influenced important programme initiatives in the field of education, social sciences and public policy. These men understood the value of investment in the minds of the people. They proceeded accordingly to infuse British ideological and religious equity in, what they believed was, the ailing and depraved cultural enterprise of India; a liquidity which we have not yet fully off-loaded.

It was in such a universe of discourse that the minds of 'modern' Indians were being shaped. That universe spouted a torrent of Oriental research that sought to academically prove the falsehood and ordinariness of Indian religion and culture. Modern India was being systematically disabused by European scholarship regarding the antiquity and greatness of her culture. The thin line between scholarly criticism and purposeful recreation of tradition was blurred everywhere. The minds of Modern Indian leaders, scholars, and intellectuals were sought to be moulded in those British institutions, where teachers were mostly European laymen or missionary preachers and the curricular proclivity was the product of the Eurocentric viewpoint that went into the design of the typical European educational system for India. It was not possible for these men to have been impervious to the flippant critique of their culture and religion. The pressure of criticism on the one hand and the attraction of the European alternative on the other was most tellingly evident in some of the finest minds of modern India. It would be most instructive to examine the viewpoints of some of these great men on their ancestral 'religion', and other cultural practices. Such an examination may give us a clue to the attitude of educated men and women regarding their *dhārmic* tradition and point out to a general evaluative tendency which was to broadly characterize the response of modern Indians towards their own cultural heritage.

The responses of modern educated Indians have been studied by scholars of cultural interaction in a great variety of complex theoretical constructions. Wilhelm Halbfass while evaluating the Indian xeneology drew the conclusion that for the Indian mind there were no 'others'; it suffered from no bias and its cultural response was not an instance of ethnocentricity but "theoretical structure of self-universalization".[60] Clifford Geertz believed that acculturation responses should be studied primarily as reactions to modernization along Western lines and as an outcome of a process of 'disorientation'. Such responses were viewed as entailing the reinterpretation of traditional cultural features by giving them fresh meaning through, what Geertz called 'symbolic strategies'. Rajni Kothari agreed with those theories that characterized India's response to Europe as the construction of a tradition, and calls this process as an effort to legitimize the imitation of Western ideas and practices by presenting them as analogous to elements of indigenous tradition or to have been contained therein.[61] E. Hobsbaum draws a similar conclusion and describes the process as 'invention of tradition' and emphasizes on the capacity of this process to establish, what he thinks is, a fictitious continuity with the past. C. Jaffrelot describes the Indian cultural response to the West as an instance of simultaneous stigmatization of the other and emulation of those features of the other which were regarded as prestigious and efficacious in order to gain self-esteem.[62] One noticeable feature of these theories is that they generally judge the nature of the responses abstractedly, without any reference to the legitimacy and propriety of the provocations that occasioned these responses.

Another important feature of these evaluative theories is that they confine the study of the nature of Indian response to the English educated, Western-oriented elite of India. These studies by and large do not examine the phenomena of the vast and powerful traditional Indian response to Islam and Europe since the beginning of the fourteenth century. The response being asserted throughout India in her innumerable villages and *qasbās* under the leadership of revolutionary saints and warriors, who taught India to be proudly firm in her cultural and spiritual traditions and be critical of those practices which were contrary to Indian ethos and injurious to human dignity, was completely disregarded. The criticism of social evils and malpractices by the saints was not a result of any foreign influence; it was the legacy of a proud and hoary Indian tradition of self-criticism. Evidently, in its encounter with Europe and modernity, common India held its cultural and civilizational nerve; modern and educated India cracked. Modern theories regarding India's response to Europe show the impossibility of picking up a single modern Indian response to the European encounter without falling prey to the inbuilt negative presupposition of one or the other theory. The rules of the game are such that the onus of providing bonafides is on the respondent. Nonetheless these theories point out certain features of the Indian response to which we need to pay fruitful attention.

By the end of the eighteenth century we start getting copious material produced by Indian scholars. A large portion of this material is devoted to the elucidation of Indian culture and religious tradition. A study of these early responses by well educated and learned Indians elicit certain typical features. Most of them believed in the superiority of the British civilization over their own. Most of them developed a very high regard for the Christian doctrine, especially the doctrine of, what they thought, One God or monotheism and a concomitant belief in the deficiency of the Hindu concept of polytheism or belief in 'many gods'. They were generally ill disposed towards major Hindu rites, rituals, *sankalp,* and *saṁskāras* and exhibited an inveterate antipathy towards use of idols in worship. It was generally accepted by them that 'ethical' monotheism of Christianity was decidedly superior to the welter of substandard gods which the Hindus invoked and propitiated in their ignorance. A shadow of credulity regarding the suspect morality of most of the Hindu 'gods' quitely lurked around their intellectual input.. In a nutshell, the European and Christian criticism of 'Hindu religion' became paradigmatic and many modern Indians accepted them uncritically as true. As a spin-off, these views also legitimized and sanctified the claims of superiority of Christianity and other monotheistic faiths over a polytheistic Hinduism.

A study of the thoughts of Raja Ram Mohan Roy, the stalwart of the Indian renaissance, would confirm that as far as the basic picture of the Hindu *upāsanā* was concerned, his ideas were roughly in accordance with the drift of British scholarship. He implicitly accepted as true the Judaic concept of god as a single monotheistic entity. He interpreted the Hindu scriptural sources in such a way that their purport would seem to conform to the theistic interpretation of a single personal god of Christianity. Commentators have noted this fact, and Stephen Hay has observed that Roy, while translating the Upaniṣads in Bengali, so worded it as, "to emphasize the unity and power of God—a monotheistic emphasis quite different from the monism in the original Sanskrit texts." [63] Inspite of the intellectual vicissitudes that Roy underwent in his life, his faith in the morality and theism of the Christian godhead remained unshaken. During his later career he would criticise many of the dogmas of Christianity and also pick up the defense of Hindu religion in the face of mounting slander; nonetheless he always accepted the superior veracity of the monotheistic conception of god found in the prophetic religions. This tendency partially explains his desire to incorporate "Christian ideas and practices"[64] in Hinduism. One major reason for such inclination was his belief that the system of education based on Sanskrit and Indian subjects would be harmful for Indians and "...calculated to keep this country in darkness".[65] Many observers have recognized this emphasis in Roy's message. Cromwell summed it well when he said: "Ram Mohan was saying that monotheism should be the national religion of the Hindu".[66] Roy was wrong on both counts as he not only missed the essence of monotheism and religion but by talking about a 'national religion' imposed from above was proposing to do something which India has consciously avoided trying in her whole history. However, the Baptist Mission of Serampore was happy and recommended Roy for special praise because he had, "brought to the crucible of public investigation, doctrines which have received the implicit credence of his countrymen from the remotest antiquity".[67] They further hoped that this investigation would lead to Raja's "adoption of Christianity".[68]

Sophia Dobson Collet records that Roy from his early days "had then ceased to cherish any religious veneration for his family deity", [69] for the ponderous reason that "the idolatrous life-style of his father's home took its toll of Ram Mohan's endurance"[70]. In fact he wrote a manuscript during his early youth criticizing the practice of idol-worship. Roy himself was far more categorical in his assertion when he said, "I have forsaken idolatry for the worship of the true eternal God!" [71] How was the true and eternal god incompatible with Hindu idolatdry but compatible with the idolatrous veneration of the Cross, Mother Mary and Jesus Christ, Roy never convincingly elaborated. He assumed with the Europeans that the use of images for worship was bad. Such sentiments were received in the European academic circle with great expectation and 'The Missionary Register' of London perceived great hope for the evangelization of India and saw Roy as a man who may help "accomplish the overthrow of idolatry".[72] The 'Calcutta Monthly Journal' of 1818 reviewed Roy's translation of Māndukya Upaniṣhad and wrote: "He seems to have just views of the absurd and wicked practices of his countrymen in their religious ceremonies" [73] and hoped that his efforts would contribute "to wipe out so gross a stain in the human character".[74]

Roy was eventually to become critical of many practices of the Christian missionaries and write vigorously in deference of the Hindu system of worship. His misplaced belief, however, in the inherent superiority of what he conceived to be the Christian message remained intact. He believed that Jesus Christ was the best prophet that had come to mankind and his personality revealed the greatness of god in his fullness. Taking a literal clue from the Christian talk of monotheism and charity he transliterated and transposed them in the Indian context and claimed that the essence of Hindu religion was belief in 'One Being' and 'Daya'. These were very promising developments and they were received with great commendation in the interested quarters. The Baptist Missionaries Society of Serampore, led by the venerable William Carey noted with obvious satisfaction that... "many who heretofore reposed the firmest belief in the dogmas of that faith which their ancestors have credited for ages, have now began to waver".[75] The Serampore Baptists were hoping that the next logical step in Raja's life would be "the adoption of Christianity".[76] This was a hope never to be fulfilled because Roy was too learned a man with a deep sense of attachment to his roots, to finally renounce his faith. Nevertheless his characterization of Hindu religion, heavily borrowed from the paradigms of Christianity, set the trend for the young men and women of modern India to emulate. Efforts of the Indian reformers were reinforced in institutions inspired by European and Christian ideals under the guidance of people like Henry Derozio, David Hare and Alexander Duff. These teachers and their institutions were not only producing a generation of educated Indians who concocted "wretched English verses which no Englishman can read without a smile",[77] but who in order to prove their Anglophilia also took such absurd steps like removing their hats and wishing the goddess *Kāli* good luck. And within the very body of modern Indian intelligentsia was growing a conviction that believed, "Hinduism as productive of an effete culture, which they renounced by receiving Christian baptism or joining beef-eating and beer-drinking clubs."[78]

This was a cultural ghost dance which Englishmen watched with contented amusement. After a sustained effort of about two hundred years India was finally biting the bait. The years of intellectual brainwashing had started to pay dividends and educated Indians were now evaluating their 'religion' in terms of the standards set by Christianity. Roy went a step further and collaborated with the Unitarians and the Presbyterian Church in their effort to establish a Church in India. He keenly urged the Church of Scotland to divert its attention "to British India as a field of missionary exertions".[79] Roy's was not the lone voice; Devendranath Tagore and other *Brahmos* warned their countrymen against the worship of god through idols, Hindu polytheism, and even the concept of god's descent in this world as *avatār*. The spirit that guided them sprang "from the same blend of Upanishadic and Christian imperations that we find in the writings of Rammohan Roy".[80] Devendranath Tagore had no hesitation in declaring that,... "we are Brahmos first, and Indians or Hindus afterwards".[81]

Keshub Chandra Sen further radicalized these sentiments when he declared that India prior to the British was "sunk in ignorance and superstition and hopeless jejuneness"[82] and it was "a land where superstition and prejudices prevailed to an alarming extent".[83] Christianity, of course, was without blemish and error. Sen observed with palpable pride that, "The spirit of Christianity has already pervaded the whole atmosphere of Indian society, and we breathe, think, feel and move in a Christian atmosphere. Native society is being roused, enlightened, and reformed under the influence of Christian education."[84] He was not only stirred by the virtues of Christian education and divinity, he even conceived of the British rule in religious terms: "Assuredly the record of British rule in India is not a chapter of profane history, but of ecclesiastical history"[85] and it was, "Providence that rules India through England".[86]

Such perception did not, however, go completely unchallenged. Swami Dayanand Saraswati mounted a strong defense of the Indian culture and checked the doctrine of despair which was being purveyed by the English educated modern Indians of his age who were completely unaware of the fountainhead of India's spiritual heritage. We can get some clue if we realize that most of the initial diatribe against Indian religion and culture came from the intellectuals of Bengal, a majority of whom were Brahmins. It was believed by the people of upper India that Bengal was not very proficient in its understanding of the original scriptures of *Sanātan dharma* and the former taunted the Bengalis for their ignorance of the Veda. This deficiency of a strong base in the *śruti* is attested by the fact that the Brahmo Samāj frequently had to invite South Indian pundits to recite the Vedic hymns during their prayer sessions because finding a competent Bengali pundit to do the recitation was difficult. Cromwell quotes Prof. Dilip Kumar Biswas as saying that the Bengali Brahmans were "traditionally deficient in the Mantra portion of the Shruti" [87]. This analysis may perhaps provide a clue to the interpretation of the Indian tradition by early Bengali intellectuals more in a ritualistic fashion rather than by systematically deciphering its philosophical core. This trend was reinforced by the European Vedic scholarship, led by Max Muller, which based its interpretation of the Vedas mostly on the ritualistic and cultic commentaries of Sāyan and Mahidhar.

Swami Dayanand was perceptive enough to understand the viewpoint of the modern intellectuals, especially the Brahmos. He was fully aware that educated Indians led by the Brahmo Samāj, the Prārthanā Samāj, etc, were not conscious of the Vedic lore and in an apparent lack of pride in their culture they had borrowed heavily from Christianity. He wrote that these new men of India think... "Indians have all along remained ignorant, and that they never made any progress".[88] The Swami was quick to point out that the books of the Brahmos and the Prārthanā Samājis include the precepts of Moses, Christ and Mohammad but they do not mention our own rishis and sages and our own great treasure of the wisdom of ancient India. Swami Dayanand wrote: "Instead of praising their country and glorifying their ancestors, they speak ill of them. In their lectures they eulogize Christians and Englishmen. They do not even mention the names of old sages, Brahma, etc."[89] Swamiji was certain that these modern intellectuals were not going to make any serious dent in solving the real problems of India, and their claims of reform were without the possibility of fruition because according to him: "No permanent sort of reform is expected from those who, in their pride for English education, are ready to launch a new religion".[90] Swamiji said this because he believed that,... "Copying is not a sign of wisdom".[91] To a great extent the response of the early Indian intellectuals was mimetic and it sought to judge Indian culture by putting it on the procrustean bed of European culture and religion. They thought with the British that Hinduism was an idolatrous and polytheistic religion and salvation lay only in the movement towards the religious idea of monotheism and non-idolatrous prophetism.

Inspite of his revolutionary transformation of the Indian society of his time Swami Dayanand himself, however, could not resist the impact of some core European ideas regarding evaluation of the Indian system of worship, and evinced the same critical attitude which was characteristic of the attitude of the English scholars, theologians and philosophers. These ideas showed in some of the important tenets of Swamiji: his insistence on worship of god in just one way, his rejection of post-Vedic Hinduism as evil, his criticism of the *avatārs* of *Rāma* and *Kṛṣṇa* and his virulent castigation of worship through the medium of an idol or image. In a certain way it tended to strengthen the sense of apathy and revulsion of the educated Indian towards Hinduism and reinforce their superficial critique—an attitude which Swamiji was so keen on correcting. However, in his assessment of Indian spiritual tradition and assertion of its legitimacy and pride Swami Dayanand was far ahead of his other contemporaries, much to the gratitude of this nation.

The reaction and responses of some of the finest minds of the late eighteenth century and the nineteenth century show a degree of fundamental similarity of approach. They implicity accepted the European castigation of various aspects of Indian culture and Hindu 'religion' as true. Some of the modern Indian leaders did strenuously try to unravel the European motive in their writings and speeches, and sought to establish the intrinsic virtues of the *Sanātan Dharma*. However, it remains a fact that most leaders and scholars accepted the critique of the indigenous tradition without seriously examining the nature of the criticism with reference to its underlying theological motivations. They regarded the worship of god by the use of idols, worship of god in many forms, the concept of *avatārs* and the prevalence of various community rites and rituals as vile *ex hypothesi*. Many of these great men in a sort of intellectual panic devoted their energies to disinter a strand of Judaic monotheism within the Indian tradition in order to claim some amount of respectability for it. An intellectual exercise to define Indian thought in terms of Western paradigm was seriously undertaken and whatever did not conform to the European standards was not recommended. The modern Indian diatribe against imposition of European religious value on Indian society was only partly due to the reason of the suspect machinations of the European empire; the other part was due to their own belief that the religious doctrines being propagated by the Judaic faiths already had its counterpart in the original Indian thought. They had a point, no doubt, but it was made at the cost of the grave allegation of simulation.

The Indian response was seen as a reactive justification because the clarifications were not given from the internal perspective of the *Sanātan Dharma* but from a completely different and alien perspective of prophetic monotheism. It is impossible to judge the merits of a particular idea of the divine by using the yardstrick of another idea. Mostly the two yardsticks are different, and as far as Judaic religions are concerned, we should always bear in mind that their most fundamental precepts are based on utter and implacable hostility to polytheism, pantheism, monism, worship through images and a general attitude of pluralism in man's relation to the divine. Prophetic monotheism grew on its hostility to paganism; therefore trying to understand any other faith from a monotheistic standpoint is futile and unfair to the other religion. But this is precisely what happened at the dawn of India's interaction with the West and modernity. The educated opinion of modern Indians facilitated the entry of an European wedge in the philosophical technique of India.

One cannot improve on the intellectual prognosis of that age which Swami Vivekanand has made in his memorable words. We may hear it straight from the great man: "On one side New India is saying: 'If we only adopt Western ideas, Western language, Western food, Western dress and Western manners, we shall be as strong and powerful as Western nations... Whatever ideas, whatever manners the White man praises or likes, are good; whatever things they dislike or censure are bad!" [92] Swamiji was correct in understanding the new attitude of educated India—'New India'—when he wrote: .... "the Westerners condemn image worship as sinful—surely then, image worship is the greatest sin, there is not doubt of it ! ... The Westerners say that worshipping a singly deity is fruitful of the highest spiritual good—therefore, let us throw our Gods and Goddesses into the river Ganges".[93] That Indians did not throw their gods and goddesses irretrievably in the river Ganges or Cauvery, is due largely to the efforts of people like Swami Ramkrishna Paramhans, Swami Vivekanand, Sri Aurobindo, Ramana Maharishi and the others. Swami Vivekanand recounts an incident when an English educated person known for his criticism of the tenets of Hinduism happened to praise the Bhagwad Gītā before Ramkrishna Paramhans. Ramkrishna was not taken aback, he understood the psychology and is reported to have said: "Methinks some European pundit has praised the *Gita* and so he has also followed suit".[94] Swami Vivekanand was talking about the modern Indian reformist attitude when he said that many of those reformers wanted, "to pull the whole edifice down to the ground and seek to build another in its place, after a sordid modern plan whose permanence has yet to be established."[95]

A civilization which always prided itself on its rationality, on critical assessment of doctrines, suddenly became unsure of itself. Indians have never revered a tradition because of the singular virtue of its age or localness; that would be foolish:

> *tātasya kūpoyam iti bruvānāh kṣāraṁ jalaṁ kāpuruṣā pibanti.*

It is amazing that such a civilization would become so uncritically credulous of European talk on religion and culture. Perhaps a civilizational phenomena similar to the one that characterized the Greeks of the later axial age was occurring and one can borrow the phrase from Gilbert Murray to describe it as a 'failure of nerve'. Chaturvedi Badrinath is aware of this sad trend which is reflected in his analysis that "English educated Indians accepted with ease the very universe of discourse in which British had mounted their challenge."[96]

Perhaps the pedagogic, academic and intellectual assault was too overbearing and all-pervasive. European philosophy and political science was defining the agenda of not only the future of Europe but also setting the parameters against which a body of thought was to be judged as serious philosophy or political science *per se*. The compulsions of education were such that in schools, colleges and universities a new Indian generation was growing under the shadows of Mill, Bentham, Hegel, Heidegger, Marx and Max Muller. Academic, curricular and pedagogic tools were designed to ensure that the necessary theoretical slant towards European paradigms was achieved. Studies of Hindu divinities were not undertaken in modern institutions as a serious subject, but the theologically oriented philosophy of Kant, Heidegger, Kierkegaard and Karl Barth was expected to be a necessary part of the philosophical curricula. The burden of the task was stupendous but clearly understood: "We require to raise up a whole generation—perhaps two or three generations—of really educated men—men, not only well instructed in scientific truth, but well imbued with moral and religious truth—with the spirit, if not with the letter of Christian teaching—and with European views on all social subjects."[97]

Indians started believing their own destiny to be linked to what Heidegger called the universalizing "destiny of Europe". The great philosopher Hegel believed in the superiority of European civilization and his thoughts contributed to the pervading European narcissism that "European thought has to provide the context and the categories for the exploration of all other traditions of thought"...[98] Wilhelm Holbfass thought that the same cultural vision was shared by

E.Husserl, the founder of the phenomenological school of philosophy, when he propounded to the effect that "Europe alone can provide other cultures with a universal framework of meaning and understanding".[99] Wilhelm Holbfass further depicts Husserl as believing that Indians will have to "Europeanize themselves," because Europeanization of all mankind is the destiny of Europe. Such sentiments were only a philosophical counterpart of the soteriology of the Biblical religion which believed that no salvation is possible outside the dogma of the Christian faith. Indians were encouraged to Europeanize in order to come out of their infirm cultural adolescence and become mature monotheistic humans. Europe proceeded to discharge this duty towards India; a land which Max Muller believed to be the land of "our childhood".

But, of course, Europe was not returning to the India of its childhood to partake in its prelapsarian innocence and purity because Hegel had confirmed to it that the Oriental civilization has finally been superseded by the Occidental. That "the Orient provides the prehistory of the Occident",[100] was a belief firmly held not only by Hegel but by a majority of Europeans, if not all. Europe believed Indian civilization to be a dead civilization which has become past and gone forever; a civilization stuck in stasis and decay without any scope of evolution on its own; a sort of "national equivalent of the dodo bird",[101] to use a phrase from Prof. Robert P. Goldman. As a result, Europeanization and Westernization of Indian mind through academia and the control of intellectual discourse was undertaken in a manner in which "historians of philosophy generally followed the lead of the Hegelian school and excluded India from the history of philosophy."[102]

The labour expended on this strategy bore fruit. Swami Vivekanand noticed the impact such strategy was having on the Indian mind and he warned his generation in anguish: "The spell of imitating the West is getting such a strong hold upon you, that what is good or what is bad is no longer decided by reason, judgement, discrimination or reference to the shastras... "[103]. Many British scholars have also noted with satisfaction the outcome of the British endeavour in India. Monier-Williams was happy that,

"Education is indeed, causing a great upheaving of old creeds... and the ancient fortress of Hinduism is in this way being gradually undermined... In fact the present condition of India seems very similar to that of Roman Empire before the coming of Christ. A complete disintegration of ancient faiths is in progress in the upper strata of society."[104] Monier-Williams believed indoctrination through education to be the necessary method to achieve complete psychological subordination of India. He encouraged the British Raj to work vigorously in this direction: "We must do more than inform their minds—we must form their whole characters and cast them in a high mould; and if we cannot convert them to the dogmas of Christianity, we must instill into them Christian ideas and ways of thinking".[105] He believed that such a result... "will be principally effected, and far more slowly, gradually, and insensibly than is commonly expected through impressions made on the minds of children by a process of education like that which our missionaries are carrying out in their schools."[106] Sir Richard Temple noted in the year 1883 the success of English education which, for all practical purposes, had distanced the educated classes from Hinduism: "It is no longer the religion of those who have either theoretical enlightenment or practical knowledge. It is being gradually dissipated, like the mist, before the science of the nineteenth century..."[107] That the 'ancient fortress of Hinduism' was tottering and ready to fall and, for the masses of India, 'Christianity is their true home' was preached as a self-evident truth. It appears that this thesis was also accepted unquestioningly by large body of the educated Indians. As it happened, this very same educated class was to set the tone for modern India's understanding of her spiritual tradition.

It was inevitable that the educated class of Indians applied these wonderful hermeneutical tools forged in the philosophical tradition of Europe and Christianity to the urgent task of defining Indian spiritual tradition. Every geography lesson in college was to make the Indian smile at the Hindu mythology. Indians were becoming, believed Sir Charles Trevelyan, more knowledgeable of the Bible than most Christians and he was sure that a vast secession from Hinduism was about to take place. Important public opinion of India was now talking of the divine as 'One-God' of the monotheistic kind and preparing to condescendingly suffer, if not abjure, the polytheistic spiritual tradition of their ancestors. A spiritual tradition that worshipped god in so many forms and adored and venerated images and idols was considered decidedly inferior to the 'One-God' religions of the Judaic family. Has god not revealed himself in the noble scriptures of the Judaic faiths to be the one and only god who personally works in history and human life? How can god be so many as Hindus seemed to believe? How can rites be so barbaric, and how can scripture be so frivolous as to evoke laughter in the girls of an English boarding school? This was the line of thought which was being extended by Western philosophy and educated opinion of India swallowed it up hook, line and sinker.

The situation obtaining among the vast majority of common and 'uneducated' Hindus—the real India—was, however, completely different. Their faith in their tradition and culture was firm and unshakable amid the cataclysmic cultural events that were causing so much of neurosis in the 'educated' classes. Monier-Williams notes that … "the chief hindrance to the progress of Christianity among the people of India is their intense pride in their own supposed moral, religious, and even intellectual superiority".[108] Monier-Williams was obviously not talking of modern Indians. English scholars had no hesitation in identifying Hinduism with the faith of the common man. Richard Temple noted with unambiguous clarity: "Hinduism is still the religion of the million, no doubt, but only of the uneducated million."[109] The representative views of the educationally well endowed Indians we have already examined. The contrast could not have been starker. Moreover the 'uneducated' Indian was not immersed in his religious tradition because of his ignorance and his superstitious deportment. He was proud of his tradition because he fully knew its essence and lived that tradition in his everyday life. The meekest of Indian would still tell you that all universe was the function of the Supreme *Brahman*. That man was not essentially different from the *Brahman* was a well understood precept, so much so that in villages when a very respected elder died the family cherished and venerated his memory as, "*Brahma Bābā*"—the elder who has become the *Brahman*. The *samādhis* of elders and venerable teachers were called '*Brahma Sthāna*'. The source of common Hindus' spiritual education and learning was not European philosophy and social science. They did not believe in man's innate fallenness and his separation from the divine. These men had learnt from their saints and teachers like Shri Ravidās to sing, with audacious self-confidence, of man's unity with the divine:

tohi mohi mohi tohi antaru kaisā kanak katika jal tarang jaisā.

The common Hindu was listening to these great saints and sages and imbibing the universal message contained in the sustaining principles of his faith, a message that carried the essence of the Veda, the Purāṇa and the Upaniṣads in the voice of the simple saints:

jaltarang aur fen budbudā jalate bhinna na koi
yah prapanch parbrahm ki leelā aur vicārat anna na hoi.

[Namdev]

His teachers asked him to believe that the supreme reality was one but manifests itself in infinite forms:

pranve Nāmdev ihu karanā,
anant roop tere Nārainā.

[Namdev]

Such being the nature of reality how can one stick to only one way of apprehending that reality? How can then one say that worshipping that reality with the aid of images was profanity? The supreme divinity in its final analysis is, of course, indescribable, but men apprehend it in their own specific ways; and any specific description can only inadequately describe him:

jas hari kahiye tasi hari nāhin, hai hari bas kuccha aisā.

[Raidas]

These teachings were not confined to a limited circle of people; these teachings were spread across the whole length and breadth of the country and common Hindu men and women sang them in their temples and homes and during their many festive occasions. These thoughts were part and parcel of the intellectual and existential world of the common 'uneducated' Hindu who, faced with the conceited theological arrogance and resentment of a religious denomination, would have laughed at it as an instance of delusion born from *maya:* "The veriest coolie, if hard pressed, will tell you that even your Honour's anger is all *'Maya'* or illusion, and that the reality lies elsewhere…"[110]. To the uneducated Hindu his spirituality was woven in his life. The most humble Hindu was steadfast in his cultural belief and treated the superior pretensions of European religions with disdain because he knew what they actually were. John McKenzie records an incident which he experienced while preaching to Hindus in a village of the Deccan with two other evangelists. After the sermon was over the men described the preaching exercise as a stage managed episode and Mckenzie felt as if the men have "been talking about the *sarkari Guru.*"[111] McKenzie records the reason why vast majority of Indians saw Christianity as a *sarkāri* enterprise, "I became very familiar with the belief that the missionary movement was nothing more than the ecclesiastical wing of the imperialistic movement."[112] In most instances it was the common Indian students of a Kabir, a Dādu, a Nāmdev, who stood firm and even fought back; the educated Indian generally wavered or collaborated.

Educated India, however, was not listening to these indigenous voices. Even when these voices made themselves heard they were not taken seriously. Such an attitude ensured that the proper Indian message was either stifled or perverted. Misinterpretation of India's spiritual message therefore became quite fashionable. But let us comeback to the tone set by modern western philosophical discourse regarding god and India's spiritual tradition. The trend was set to belittle Indian heritage in the harshest of words. Indian polytheism and idolatory was castigated for its decadence and the purer and 'advanced' concept of monotheism or the belief in one god, was accepted as the only way in which god can effectively be apprehended. Indian intelligentsia was made to live constantly under the pressure to accept that god can only be a singular person who should be worshiped somehow in a way that emphasized his singularity. The worship of god in multiple forms and with the aid of images was not found to be compatible with this purer standard of divinity. The inspiration for such perception came from the monotheistic god of the Judaic faiths. That the god of the Judaic faiths was 'one' and that it represented the necessary truth of godhead in being an advancement over defunct polytheism or pantheism was accepted without doubt.

This belief has perpetuated to this day and it would be in the fitness of things to re-examine the metaphysical underpinnings of this belief and ask a few questions. What is meant by the theory of 'One-God'? What does the term monotheism actually mean? What is the validity of the claims of exclusiveness in religion? Has monotheism in the Judaic sense been the only and most important strand of human discourse on god? Was that the way humanity has always seen its god and is it the divine denouement towards which humanly is necessarily heading? What is the nature and source of that authority which empowers the followers of certain religions to go round the world denouncing the religion of other people and causing untold misery to human societies should they not readily agree to embrace their faith. It is important to ponder over the question whether a revelation attested by an individual confers on that individual and his followers the authority to grievously injure other individuals in order to enforce the contents of that revelation on them. It is necessary to question the sacrosanctity and validity of every proposition that claims superior merit to an extent of appropriating the right to vulgarize the culture and faith of other people along with the power to cause material and physical injury to them. Let us see what exactly is the burden of the exclusive religious claim of monotheism.

I Your Lord Am One

Monotheism as a descriptive epithet is used by the three Judaic religions to convey the idea that there is only one valid idea of god as the creator and ruler of this universe. Various subsidiary ideas like the 'Unity of God', 'Unitariness of God,' etc, are also used as explanatory of the principle idea of the singleness of god. The onehood or singularity of god can mean two things: one, that god is 'one' in the manner of enumeration; second, that there is only one way of talking about that which is god. The first idea is most commonly understood and propagated by the adherents of various religions as descriptive of the one god. The lay adherent is reminded by the religious teacher that god is a singular person besides whom no other 'gods' exist. It is the practice of monotheistic thought to see god as a 'person'. When it is asserted that there is no god besides 'god', the hearer can be excused for treating it as tautologous unless he happens to belong to a community in which such assertions make perfect sense. But if the assertion 'there is no god besides god' is not self-evident tautology then it can only be the establishment of a spatio-temporal entity in an enumerable mathematical sense. To say that there is only one god is to confirm that anything that can legitimately be called 'god' cannot be conceived of apart from the only god who is actually 'The god'. Since god of monotheism is also a 'person' it would mean the existence of an identifiable entity with a combined spatial and metaspatial locus.

We can approach the issue from another angle also. To say that there is 'no god but god' would imply a few logically necessary theoretical emanations. Had there been just one god in this universe, an utterance would only be 'God is', without postulating the rather superfluous negation of other gods. The assertion that there is only one god and there are no gods besides him can lead to another problem; it raises the question of a hierarchy of divine efficacy. To say that there is only one god and other gods are not gods, is to only assign various degrees of merit to a multiplicity of divine beings. It can be, and it most certainly is, argued by the monotheists that they only wish to state that there is just one god in the whole universe and none else; but if that be the case the near compulsory attachment of some such assertions like 'there is no god like Him', or 'there is none besides Him' with the principal assertion 'god is one' does not make any sense. Nor does the peremptory denial of other gods make any sense if there were actually no other gods to deny; the need to deny the non-existent seldom arises. Another possible way of understanding the monotheistic singleness of god is to believe that the concept of one god negates the tendency to elevate other beings or objects to the level of godhood. But, is it not impossible to elevate anything high enough to ever become a god or 'the god', and even if such an elevation is theoretically assumed how can it conceivably ever detract from the existence and majesty of the only god. All such elevations would be *ab initio* inefficacious. The negation of this tendency as a tendency was possible to do straightaway, rather than resorting to the complex manoeuver of denying the non-existent gods by first posing their possible existence. If there is only one god, so be it, and all one should say is 'there is a god'. The requirement of saying there is 'The God' should not be logically necessary, unless one intends to also particularize that 'one god'. The assertion that there can only be, and is, just one god in the universe does not need any subsidiary linguistic support in order to be made intelligible, especially when it is believed to be a 'person'. This should be so *a fortiori* in view of the assertion even of the 'polytheistic' religions that god is one! If every religion says there is 'one god' then the ontology of god should not cause a problem—it would then only be the name and form of god which could be a matter of dispute, and it is precisely the name and form of god that monotheism fights for.

The second major way to understand monotheism or the belief in 'one god' can be to understand it to mean that irrespective of the ontological numerariness of god, he can only be understood in one particular way. In other words, there is only one possible way of visualizing the nature, station and the message of god. God is one because a particular faith believes that their conception of him is the only valid way of his conception. This standpoint would inevitably point towards nominalism implying that the oneness of god is just a theoretical construction to support the perpetuation of a particular name of god. God is one because he is only *Yahweh*, only *Āllāh*, or only Jesus Christ. But then any other nominalist construction—*Rāma, Kṛṣṇa*—can be equally legitimate. However, monotheists do not grant this multiplicity and insist on the exclusive veracity of the name as much as they insist on the exclusive veracity of the god. Even if we disregard the issue of the merit of the various competing claims we cannot overrule the metaphysical and linguistic possibility of making many claims about god. To still say that there is only one god is to subscribe to the thesis that .... "gods of one religion can only exist if the gods of another do not..."[1] But other gods remain to be contended with, and to continue to say there is one god is to disregard the warning that "commitment to the truth of claims about the sacred must be avoided at all costs, on pain of destroying the study of religion as an academic discipline."[2] God can be, and most assuredly is, 'one': he becomes many in the various realms and modes in which his power and majesty is discerned. God in the grace of allowing himself to be perceived by men becomes a deity. Deity is the power or spirit of 'god' that men encounter in their devotional life and attach a name to it. The moment a name is uttered to denote him, god becomes a deity. In his supreme reality and infinite essence *per se* god is unfathomable and indescribable, he is *neti, neti* or *ehyeh asher ehyeh;* when man tries to utter a name to designate or describe the supreme divinity he becomes a deity—a *devatā* . God in relation to man is the deity.

The singleness and oneness of god in the monotheistic doctrine is explained and elaborated by the use of such doctrine as the 'unity of god', 'unitary nature of god' or the 'unitariness of god'. We may do well to examine these concepts. Let us understand the concept of unity in its normal linguistic use. We use the word 'unity' not to emphasise the absence of constitutive elements in an entity but, on the contrary, to emphasise the singularity of purpose and cohesiveness of the constitutive elements within a composite entity. The dictionary describes the word 'unitary' as an adjective, which is descriptive or characteristic of something and defines its meaning as characterized by units or unity, in a sort of undivided whole. The use of the term 'unity' is then not to make any ontological statement but to make a descriptive statement, which includes the possibility of multiplicity howsoever synthesized and sublimated. It can then be argued that to proclaim the unity of god is to emphasize the unity or unitariness of a god-idea which, in turn, can mean that many concepts, many ideas, and many visions regarding god can be superimposed on the idea of the 'one god', including perhaps the thought of all other gods. There is no reason why this ordinary language usage cannot be understood to mean the same in the divine sphere unless we want to assert that the use of religious language is exclusive and different; in which case talking of god as 'one' or 'unitary' would of course not denote an established fact.

We have several examples in the scriptures of the monotheistic religions which support this viewpoint regarding the 'unity of god'. Prophets have reportedly been seen warning people not to compare other deities as gods with the 'one god' of their proclamation. Bringing anything at par with god, or associating any partner with him—*shirk*—or conceiving any other god or deity as equal to him has been completely ruled out. Unity of god in this sense may perhaps mean that powers of all other gods and the essence of all divine theories and practices have finally been merged into this particular 'one god' and the former, thereby, stand superseded. It would in this sense be possible to understand why the powerless gods and worthless theories of other religions are characterized as 'false-gods' and 'false-religions' by monotheistic prophets. But powerless or otherwise these ideas do exist and other men may have reasons to venerate them as holy and sublime. 'Unity' of god would then mean the unity of an idea of god alongside the utter sacrosanctity of the unified body of a particular religious dogma attached to that god. The vision of monotheistic god is the finality of the monotheistic idea of a specific god and in this sense it can definitely be the only 'one god'. Monotheistic faiths claim to have finally unified and merged the metaphysics of the entire universe and posited it in the unitary conception of the 'one god'. He is henceforth to be venerated in his exclusive unitary majesty. Rafiq Zakaria while clarifying the idea of the oneness of god as expressed in the assertion, 'There is no god but God' has this to say: "It is both negative and positive. Negative because it signifies the renunciation by its believers of any other deity; positive because it asserts that, 'Your God is one'."[3] This clarification is very revealing of the idea of the oneness of god. It asserts that for the believer his god is just that 'one god' who is proclaimed in his religious creed; in other words, a true believer should worship only 'one' deity or god and other deities or 'gods' are to be renounced. This assertion by no means proves that there is only one god. Renunciation of the other does not prove the *ab initio* non-existence of that other: it in fact serves as a constant and painful reminder of the other which the faithful hopes to someday obliterate. Moreover, if the renunciation is the denial of other notions of deity then it is just that: such renunciation does not disprove or deny an existential 'other'.

There is a world of difference between the god of the philosopher and the god preached from the monotheistic pulpit by the monotheistic preacher. The philosopher and the theologian strive to convince the intellectually inclined; but the pulpit is expected to preach the raw essence of the one personal and historical god. The core and fundamental message which is preached from pulpits across the world—repeated profusely in religious literature and glorified in mainstream theological discussion—is very simple: god is one according to the proclamation of a particular religion and the scriptures and laws of that religion are the only one way of knowing, obeying and worshipping him. Theologians and philosophers subsequently join hands to prove that their 'one-god' is the only truthful idea of divinity and therefore its laws should provide the compulsory legal framework for every human being. All mankind must be brought under the sway of the laws of this 'one-god' and his prophet. This is the core idea of monotheism and religious philosophy only provides intellectual justification in terms of the idioms that are academically fashionable during a particular period. Irrespective of what a school of philosophy and mysticism says, an adherent of monotheism never forgets, transcends or even questions a fundamental and core idea of his orthodox dogma. All discourse and behaviour of monotheistic religions should be understood in the background of this fundamental premise.

The lay faithful is made to understand that the 'one-god' exists in the universe as some sort of a 'person' whose location in the heaven and whose personal attributes have finally been known by the monotheistic faiths. Erudite theological conceptions are neither discussed with the common believer, nor are they emphrasized in the sermon from the pulpit. The common man's source of religious knowledge is only the preacher *ex cathedra,* the *khutbā,* the *fatwā* and the ecclesiastical publications, which purvey the credal injuctions of the 'one-god' in its intrinsic purity without the extenuating gloss of philosophy. Learned theology has never denied the core idea of the pulpit; theology, on the contrary, has tried to assist the pulpit and make its message acceptable to the knowledgeable and sceptical classes. Walter Kaufmann and other scholars of religion believe that theology is essentially denominational and it is generally used as a defensive mechanism to justify what is preached as a dogma by the mainstream religious establishment. We shall do well to follow the understanding of the mainstream religious authorities, the scriptures and the practices of the vast multitude of monotheistic believers to truthfully perceive what is meant by the monotheistic theory of 'one-god'. It is in the perception and actions of the mainstream religious establishment and the life of the general believer in his unrestrained milieu that we would get the core meaning of monotheism.

Monotheism is an exclusively Judaic construct that subscribes to the *theistic* doctrine of divinity. According to this doctrine, god creates this universe out of nothing—*ex nihilo*—and controls and directs it. God's will is revealed by him to his chosen prophets who are entrusted with the holy duty of enforcing this divine will on all human beings. The faithful are enjoined to recognize and worship the god as revealed to them in the scriptures of the Judaic faiths through the aegis of the prophets. Monotheistic exegetists have always asserted that monotheism has been a fact of man's spiritual life since the dawn of civilization. Nineteenth century anthropologists and scholars of religion, taking a clue from Darwin's theory of evolution, have proffered various theoretical models to attest the verity of the monotheistic claim. We must realize that Darwin was not only the father of biological evolution but was considered by many as also the biggest influence behind the growth of anthropology. His thoughts formed a source of inspiration for various theories of spiritual evolution. We should also realise that some of the important early anthropologists had Christian missionary affiliations. Father Coddrington and Father Wilhelm Schmidt have made important contributions to the study of primitive societies. A theological slant to the interpretation of anthropological data was not impossible to happen in such circumstances. Like much of primitive anthropology, the nineteenth century scholars of religion led by E.B. Tylor believed that man's idea of the divine has had a fixed beginning, like the beginning of man himself, and grew in a nearly linear fashion from lower to higher forms. Dim intimations of divinity available to the primitive man gradually evolved towards an ever higher station till it reached its natural and necessary apogee in Judaic monotheism. Since European man was assumed to be the highest evolution of mankind, his religion—monotheism—was logically perceived to be the highest evolution of god.

About the same time, Andrew Lang discovered the presence of a 'High God' in the religious practices of many primitive societies independent of the influence of Christian missionaries. This discovery created some problem for the theory of divine 'evolution', but European theology was supple enough to adapt to this new challenge. Fr. Wilhelm Schmidt provided a new prespective. He proposed that men had the idea of a single, sublime and creator god, and a high order of morality since the dawn of human history. According to him primitive man was aware of some sort of an incipient monotheism that degenerated in due course by acquiring accretions of mythical and magical concepts. Taking the clue from the thesis of Andrew Lang many theologians placed the concept of 'one-god' at the beginning itself and declared every departure from this idea a polytheistic degeneration. It was then claimed that Christianity has finally restored the truth of the 'one-god' which was there with man since creation. It was a perfect theological trap. Evolution or degeneration; heads polytheism loses, tails monotheism wins, because all roads either lead to, or originate from, the monotheistic Rome. Professor E.O. James quotes Andrew Lang as saying—"Our conception of God descends not from ghosts but from the Supreme Being of non-ancestor worshipping peoples."[4] This monotheistic idea of god is believed to have been corrupted in the course of history by pagan polytheism, and the monotheistic religions of the Judaic stock were finally restoring that 'one-god' by removing the accumulated dross of those dark ages. Whether through the scheme of linear evolution or through the theory of temporary degeneration and then final reassertion in the Judaic concept of god, early anthropology and theology attempted to prove that the monotheism of the Judaic faiths was the principal focus of man's spirituality down the ages and all other religious forms are only dubious charlatanry. It is only in Judaic monotheism that the real character and nature of god has been revealed. Mercifully, these early theories of historical evolution and degeneration of religions have now been completely discredited. Except in the works of preachers, sectarian scholars and some obdurate theologians, serious scholars do not agree with these claims of monotheism. Prof. E.O. James writes that: "Anthropomorphic deities from the Australian All-Fathers to the Greek Olympian Gods are no more animistic in origin and nature than the Holy One of Israel or the Sovereign Ruler of Islam..."[5]

As far as the theory of evolution of religions and the refinement of ideas of god in a linear fashion is concerned, it has been summarily rejected and discarded by the most enlightened and serious scholars.

We can have it on the authority of Prof. E.O.James that..."evolutionary interpretations of religious development could not be maintained in the light of the accumulating evidence."[6] Prof. Gerardus Van der Leeuw has pointed out the complete inadequacy and untenability of the evolutionary theory that sees the idea of a Western God retrospectively being evolved through many religions of man. He is critical of what he thought was "the dominant but shallow Evolutionism of the nineteenth century"[7]. He characterised the degeneration theory as "equally superficial according to the ideals of the Philosophy of History."[8] Van der Leeuw further points out that both the evolutionary and degeneration theories were informed by a theological motivation that sought to propagate that..."'God' can be applied only to what a modern Western European, descended from the Christianity of the age of 'Enlightenment', is accustomed to designate by this name without further philosophical or phenomenological reflection."[9] Van der Leeuw categorically states that... "it is absolutely wrong therefore to conceive the history of religion as a development leading up to 'Monotheism'."[10] Prof. James has refuted the very dubious theory of evolutionism on the ground of major differences in the idea of god that had obtained in various societies at various points of human history. He says: "Animism cannot be derived spontaneously from animatism, and monotheism from polytheism, any more than indiscriminate promiscuity can be made to pass into polygamy and thence to monogamy, because religious beliefs and human relationships are not subject to metamorphoses of this kind."[11]

In view of the philosophical burial of the idea of aforementioned evolutionism leading to the Judaic notion of a monotheistic god, Mr. Rafiq Zakaria's latest endeavour to disinter the theological ghost by labouring the thesis of evolutionism appears to be an act of courage. Mr. Zakaria still talks about... "progressive development of the notion of the one and only Supreme Being from the earliest to the present times"[12] and about the ... "history of the evolution and progress of monotheism."[13] Mr. Zakaria's recent work tries to find the trace of the monotheistic god in all religious and spiritual traditions of man since the beginning of history. His analysis is not value-neutral but appears to be inspired by a deep theological motivation. The goal of his scholarship is soon apparent when we are informed of Mr. Zakaria's wish to unite all men under the control of 'one-god': "If everyone of us were to have faith in the one and only God, then the unity of His creatures, drawing sustenance from Him, becomes inescapable."[14] But Mr. Zakaria, like all proponents of this thesis, avoids answering directly the question as to which 'one-god' is being alluded to by him as the 'one-and-only god' under whom all humanity should unite—the God of Quran or the God of Śrimad Bhāgawat? The followers of Śrimad Bhāgawat also believe their god to be the 'one and only Supreme Being'. But if one remembers the cardinal premise of Mr. Zakaria's faith—there is no god but *Allāh*—then the identity of this 'one-god' does not remain very obscure. It is also a fact that there have been many teachers and schools of thought that accepted the fact of human unity as a natural outcome of creation without the complex necessity of a theology. Did many like Pindar not naturally believe that: "Single is the race, single/Of men and gods" [15]. The epithet 'one-god' is never used by its proponents in a theologically neutral and abstract way without the limiting characteristics of a name and form. It is used always to mean god-as-the-god-of-the-religion of the monotheist speaker. Uniting humanity through some divine principle can be a noble goal and one should not take any umbrage to the idea in principle. The best way is to let men decide on their respective ways to reach this 'one-god', because all ways will logically only reach him. To hint that men should unite under one-and-only-god as *Allāh* or Jesus Christ is to purvey and promote an exclusive religious ideology which would ultimately threaten every pluralistic human striving.

Even if one assumes that mankind has always believed in only 'one-god', it cannot follow from this assumption that every talk regarding this 'one-god' has been the talk of the 'one-god' of prophetic monotheism of the Judaic group of religions. The 'one-god' of monotheism and the god of non-Judaic religions are morphologically and functionally completely different. The Watja Negro of Africa prays: "O divine power, I know thee not. But thou knowest me; I need they help."[16] The Papuan prays: "Compassionate father, here is some food for you. Eat it, and be kind to us on account of it."[17] Are the Papuan or the Watja addressing the same one-god as invoked in the Gospel when Jesus says: "I am He...Before Abraham was, I am." They are not. The non-monotheistic one-god is freely available to all who seek him in their own special ways. He does not prescribe a method of worship, he does not seek obedience, is not paranoid about how he is addressed, is not bothered whether he is worshipped or not; and definitely does not seek to destroy those who do not obey Him. The character of the two gods in the two traditions are worlds apart. God may be one but he is not so as the 'one-god' of Judaic monotheism. Few serious scholars today consider, unlike Mr. Zakaria and others who are dreaming of the whole human race under their own notion of 'one-god', the notion of one-godism to be a very laudable goal and many think that: "This view is at once the climax of universalism and particularistic intolerance."[18] And further that: "What is important in the present context, however, is the fact that exaltation of the One made it possible for cruelty to develop on a religious basis."[19]

The fundamental idea of monotheism revolves around the inviolate principle that man should '*worship only one god*', and not that '*there exists only one god*'. This idea would sound a bit paradoxical but is fundamental to the concept of monotheism. The singular object of worship of a group or nationality is also asserted to be the only authority that needs to be universally obeyed and worshipped in a particular way. Worship of god in any other form is decried. This monotheistic idea of god as the spiritual thought of a specific group of people, grew in a particular historical circumstance in a given socio-political milieu. We cannot understand the true import of monotheistic assertions regarding god in isolation. They can only be understood in their specific milieu because, as Ninian Smart says, ... "it is by an understanding of the *situations* in which a sentence might be used that we come to appreciate its 'logical style'..."[20]. It would be revelant, therefore, to bear in mind the fact that every concept or discourse regarding god evolves in the minds of people in a given society based on their specific encounter with divinity. The monotheistic concept of god was also the product of a specific historical situation and had no reference to the ontological reality of god as the one and only existent being. Prof. Arnold Toynbee believed that the Judaic notion of god is a product of the Judiac view of history which sees the functioning of all aspects of the universe as identical and in accordance with the rhythms in the career of an individual being. This volitional view of history leads to a sense of self-importance of being the 'chosen people' under the protection of a jealous and intolerant deity: "The affirmation that 'there is no god but god' is deemed, by the adherents of the Judaic religions, to entail the commandment: 'Thou shalt have none other gods but Me'..."[21]

For the follower of a monotheistic god only that area of human history matters which deals with the activities of the chosen people and their god; other nations and their gods are regarded as phases of dark and ignorant aberrations. Followers of the Judaic faiths wish to mete the same treatment to other people which their god desires to mete to other gods: ... "and what God is believed to feel about false gods sets the standard for what God's 'Chosen People' believe themselves entitled to feel about heathen human beings."[22] Since the chosen people believe their god to be the best god, they proclaim him to also be the 'only god'. Other people and other gods do not matter, because a personal and limited vision is converted into universal reality by the logic of distorted religious Descartesism. That the concept of the monotheistic god can be understood only in the specific tradition of the monotheistic religions is confirmed by Ninian Smart: "Again, to gain an inkling of the nature of the concept *God* it is surely requisite to look to the worshipping activities that surround, so to speak, belief in the divine".[23] Monotheism does not establish or prove the existence of one god; it only establishes the workability of a particular idea. There was, however, a major innovation, which prophetic monotheism introduced in man's idea of the divine: the cataclysmic doctrine of the denial of the gods and scriptural traditions of all other peoples. Karen Armstrong has no doubt that, "The human idea of God has a history, since it has always meant something slightly different to each group of people who have used it at various points of time. The idea of God formed in one generation by one set of human beings could be meaningless in another."[24] The meaning of an assertion regarding 'god' cannot be understood without positing it in the historical milieu in which it emerged and grew. To appeciate the idea of a monotheistic god we must look at the circumstances of its growth and the ideological tools by which it is propagated and sustained. It may perhaps be useful to devote some time in examining this history.

The idea of monotheism is intrinsically bound with the concept of 'prophetism'. We cannot understand the monotheistic idea of god unless we relate it to the concept of the 'prophet' through whom all god-talk originates. Without a prophet or a messiah there would not be any monotheism. The brilliant idea of one chosen-people under the control of a single theology originates in the vision of a leader. The consuming passion of an individual, ignites and then uses the group's collective megalomania to build a structure of existential satisfaction that battens on the continuous reassertion of the group's superiority over others. Self-centredness of a group—political or theological—needs the presence of an 'other' against which every idea and action of the group would be proclaimed as justified. The leader becomes the originator and also the subsequent focus of the group's behaviour. Fanatical adherence to a belief-system is more a characteristic of human phenomena rather than divine; the self-belief of the leader compels the group to acquiesce in the uniqueness of his vision. Every discussion of a monotheistic god generally begins with a prophet and it is the prophets' vision and effort that finally determines and gives shape to the group's idea of god. Monotheism has, therefore, been also described as 'prophetic monotheism'. A monotheist's idea of god is limited to the concepts said to be revealed by god to the prophet. It is not possible for any man to ever know anything of god without the aid of a prophetic revelation. It is through the prophet's words that god is said to self-reveal himself. It is the prophet who appropriates the spiritual function of the entire community of believers and divests the individual believer of the right to pursue his independent path towards the divine. A prophet's view becomes the final spiritual light for all men and women who join his religion unalterably for all times to come. In the world of prophetic religions an individual's spirituality is limited to second-hand attitudinizing regarding the prophet's original vision and finding sustainable theories to support his own devotional surrender to that vision.

The prophet becomes the only medium between man and god and also the custodian of god's will. Since the prophet becomes the medium for god's message he performs, in a sense, shamanistic functions on behalf of the community of believers. On a closer examination the prophets of monotheism would, indeed, be seen to emerge from the ancestry of the *shaman*. The only major difference is that as a 'prophet' the *shaman* claims infallible religious and secular validity for his vision in a trans-communal manner. An individual or a community is invited to unconditionally accept the authority of the prophet and his message. Once they do so, they surrender forever their individual and collective rights to ever see and seek god separately from the message of the prophet. God, then, is only what the prophet reveals him to be. Prophetic monotheism was a new experiment in human history in which a prophet growing from the protoype of a *shaman* reversed its original role by claiming exclusiveness and finality for his vision. Wellhausen maintains that prophecy was the fountainhead of Israelite monotheism and both were the creation of Israel's literary prophets like Amos, Hosea and Isaiah.

A prophet, however, was different from the *olonistic* or *shamanistic* personages which have been found in the ritual and cultic history of many human societies. Anthropologists have found the presence of people resembling the *shaman* in diverse cultures across the world. The presence of the *shaman* is not limited to any particular age but has been witnessed in many historical periods. These personages may vary in certain external details, but the essential function of the *shaman* appears to be the same, whether he be the Tungusic '*reindeer-shaman'*, the priests of Dionysus or the dancing *shaman* of Lascaux. They were the leaders, spiritual spokesmen, healers and purgers of the anxieties of their society. They were also believed by their communities to be the "impresarios of god",[25] who had the powers to communicate with the spirits and intercede with them on behalf of their society. But the *shaman* was not an infallibe authority, he was only a man who had magic powers and performed culturally important functions. The world which he professed to work in was limited to the territory which his community occupied and his concerns were limited to the concerns of his community: "The shaman was the intermediary between his group and the supernatural unknown, the intermediary between man's needs and anxieties, and the world he lives in and only partly knows." [26] In his limited world the *shaman* performed an important religious function. Every time his society needed an answer to a problem or the clarification of some intractable dilemma, the *shaman* drew on the power of the 'spirits' and when he spoke, it was believed that the 'spirit' spoke through him. Mircea Eliade believes ecstatic possession of a human medium by an alien spirit or power as characteristic of a shamanistic phenomena. La Barre quotes A. van Deursen as suggesting that the *shaman,* besides working as a culture-hero, also occupied a religious position and acted as...."a mediator between God and man....one who originated in a historical hero, chief, medicineman or prophet".[27] The religious position of the *shaman* is also indicated by Gilbert Murray in his study of Greek religion where he has suggested that religion may have had its naturalistic origin in the *shaman.* Prof. Yehezkel Kaufmann, while describing the prophetic ministry of Moses, confirms that ... "The ancient Hebrew *kahin*—clairvoyant—was the social type that served as the vehicle of his appearance as prophet and leader."[28] Prophets of monotheism emerged in Palestine out of the old *shaman* by emphasising the primacy of their religious function. Nevertheless, the early Israelite prophets remained closer to their shamanistic pedigree by generally adhering to their own community and its territory and not transcending the "cultic-territorial limitation of monotheism."[29] The Judaic god only came to the prophets of Israel and had no validity outside the holy land until very late. In the prophetic tradition, "There were shamans before there were gods."[30]

What we should be concerned with, for the present purpose, is the communicative and divinatory characteristics of the *shaman* and other similarly situated categories who, while differing in certain details, essentially performed functions which can be said to have incipient religious import. Such functions involved divination, reading of omens, telling of fortunes and the interpretation of the commands and messages of gods. *Shaman* and their likes were people who claimed to receive insight into the mystery of life through messages received from superhuman sources. The ancient Semitic society was not ignorant of the existence of such people; diviners and clairvoyants of various types existed in ancient Israel. We have references in the Bible of temple priests practicing the art of divination with the use of *Urim* and *Thummim.* Saul and David are shown to have consulted diviners in order to interpret the messages of god and the fate of men. King Ahab had four hundred prophets (*navi)* attached to his court and he used their services to receive the message of 'gods' and to decide the fate of men. The diviners were considered to be able to contact the world of the spirits and 'gods' and receive such messages from them that enabled them to perform divinatory functions. These men were known by various appellations in the Semitic world: They were called *nabiim* (prophet), *bene-neviim* (sons of prophets) or *ro'eh* (seers). Men with divinatory powers were also referred to as *Kohen* in Hebrew and *Kahin* in Arabic. Irrespective of the terms used, these men were decidedly shamanistic in their social and religious purpose.

The presence of a class of people who can see and predict future events, unravel hidden worlds and communicate with spirits and gods has been found in many ancient socieites. In the Greek culture we find references to the priest of Dionysus, to Apollo, to Orpheus, to Proteus and to Apollonius of Tyana as human prophets and prophet-gods. In ancient Canaan we have evidence of organized clans of hereditary prophets who used music and ritual celebration to invoke divine vision and were said to have inhabited the mountains and the hills. On many occasions the phrase 'men from the mountains' was used as a synonym for *nebiim* or the cultic prophet. Perhaps Moses was deferring to the antiquity and reverence of the tradition of 'men from the mountains' when he chose to go to the mountain to receive his message from his god, hoping that when he came down to the waiting Hebrews he would be regarded, through subtle association, by them as a *nabiium*—a man from the mountains. This small measure also helped the Biblical authors to relate the god of Moses to *El Shaddai*, the 'god of mountains' worshipped by the patriach Abraham and lent to the former traditional respect and validity. Ninian Smart has traced the later monotheistic prophets to the line of *shamans* and *nebiim* prevalent all over the primitive world. He also believes in the existence of a strong kinship between the old Semitic *nebiim* and the later prophets. Ninian Smart has found the prevalence of ecstatic prophecy among the Nuer of Sudan.... "which compare in certain ways to early prophecy in the Old Testament."[31] We have evidence of the existence in ancient Israel of many classes of prophets dedicated to various 'gods'. The prophets of *Yahweh* were only one of them because *Yahweh* was only one of the many deities worshipped by the Hebrews. Prophet Amos was described by the temple priest as a 'seer' or *hozeh* belonging to one of the guilds of hereditary prophets; a charge which Amos is shown in the Old Testament to refute with much indignation. Early Jewish prophets like Samuel are called *roeh* by the Hebrews and they were believed to perform shamanistic oracles for the Kings and commoners alike. Likewise, we come across the strong presence of a class of popular shamanistic seers in the pre-Islamic Arab society. These *shamans* were known as *Kahin* and were believed to have special friends or 'spirits' that spoke to them and revealed many secrets. When the *Kahin* spoke he was believed to speak the words revealed to him by his 'spirits'. This understanding of the office of a *Kahin* continued even when the term *'nabi'* came to be used; a term which literally meant one who 'speaks out', 'called out' or spoke on behalf of something. It is for these reasons that La Barre believes that .... "Hebrews used their prophets as social olonists...".[32]

It would thus appear that in his mantic function the monotheistic prophet drew on the experience of the cultural milieu of divination and prophecy in which he grew. Yehezkel Kaufmann has shown that prophets gradually..."took the place of Semitic *Kahin*,"[33] and in this process created an unique office which has led many scholars to believe that... "Apostolic prophecy is an Israelite creation."[34] However, there was a great difference in the claims that the later monotheistic prophets made regarding the nature of their divination as compared to that of the earlier prophets. Yehezkel Kaufmann has analysed the differences between the pagan prophets and the prophets of Judaic monotheism. He believes that: "The distinctive feature of apostolic prophecy is that it champions a religious and moral doctrine."[35] He explains that pagan prophecy is a result of the use of special knowledge and power by the prophets which enabled them to know the hidden meaning of things; a power which was rooted in the nature of the soul and in the deep spiritual effort of the seer. Kaufmann believes that pagan prophecy or divination.... "involves an organic, natural law; it has nothing to do with the will of the gods."[36] Monotheistic theologians generally agree to this characterisation and believe like Kaufmann that pagan "prophecy is thus not a revelation of the will of the gods, but a perception of hidden things by means of a special sense."[37] The pagan seer and prophet used his personal vision to come to a probable solution to an inscrutable problem, the monotheistic prophet claimed god's unimpeachable authority for his own vision. The words and deeds of a monotheistic prophet became the commands of god.

The differences pointed out by Prof. Kaufmann is important and we would do well to keep them in mind. He has suggested that the pagan *shamans*, diviners, prophets and clairvoyants attempted to interpret reality of the mundane, spiritual and divine world through observation, special techniques and by virtue of being endowed with special knowledge and power. The prophet of monotheism on the other hand was a man of no special skills to recommend him but what he revealed was claimed by him to be the holy words and commands of god coming directly from the latter. The monotheistic prophet claimed to be privy to the will of god. We may fruitfully read what Yehezkel Kaufmann has to say on this matter: "In place of the diviner and interpreter of signs appears the messenger of God who proclaims his will. This change is coeval with the monotheistic transformation of ancient Hebrew religion."[38] The *shaman* became the prophet and the advise of the friendly spirits was substituted by the revelation of god when attempts were made to establish the notion of 'one-god' in religion.

This view of the station and office of a prophet was to have far reaching consequences. The pagan prophets held highly diverse views depending on their own perception of the world of men and 'gods', but none of them claimed those views to have been derived from a divine person whose commands, once issued, are valid for all times to come. The pagan prophet acted either on his own or for and on behalf of his society; the monotheistic prophets were acting for and on behalf of god. The pagan prophet's attitude was not hortatory; he gave his opinion only when men sought it. Men sought a clairvoyant or a diviner or a prophet on their own accord if they were faced with a problem that needed a higher level of analysis. The monotheistic prophets, on the other hand, went about their lives declaring, in an unsolicited and hortatory manner, the will of god revealed to them, and urging others to submit to that will. There was an element of compulsion in their message. A pagan teacher generally does not claim to have received an unsolicited wisdom from god; what he professed was the result of his own spiritual quest. In India a wise man usually tended to become reticent and humble when he reached a higher stage of apprehension of truth; a monotheistic prophet tends to become opinionated and garrulous. Indian seers would have wholly agreed with Rudolf Otto's view that, "The numinous cannot be 'taught'—it must be awakened from the spirit."[39] Monotheistic prophets were not content with their own perception of god's nature and will. They undertook to propagate that knowledge with full vigour among all humanity till the time everyone consented to adopt the prophet's vision. When the monotheistic prophets, compelled by the intensity of their personal vision, projected that vision in an extra-terrestrial locus and declared it in turn to be the source of a valid epiphany for all other men, the 'one-god' of prophetic monotheism was born. In order to understand the belief in one god one must always keep in mind the deportment and the compulsions of the monotheist prophet. History is witness to the fact that god became 'one' only when he had a crusading human agent to propagate and enforce an exclusive vision of a particularized deity. Un-enforced monotheism has a tendency to attain the initial state of its polytheistic inertia.

Historians of religion inform us that the monotheistic experiment in religion had its initial beginnings in the innovations of Hammurabi in Mesopotamia and Ikhnaton a.k.a. Amonhotep in Egypt. In order to properly understand the nature of these initial innovations we must know the state of affairs of the societies in which these innovations first took place. The cultic situation obtaining in the Egyptian and Babylonian societies before the monotheistic innovation was similar to the general pagan way of worship and devotion obtaining all over the world. Since time immemorial, men have experienced the divine in a variety of numinous representations. Sometimes the mystery of the universe was conceived in the form of an animal-familiar, sometimes as a *mana* or an impersonal force. Some group of men believed in the existence of spirits or *anima* that pervade the phenomenal world, while others found the mystery of life capable of being explained through various totemic representations. Idols, images, cults and rituals abounded in a festive celebration of life and men were happy to visualize god to the best of their perceptive capacities. The questions of finality or intermediacy of their belief did not cause undue bother to men and they were able to graduate to a different viewpoint without any traumatic experience, should an earlier viewpoint prove to be inadequate. Human socieities applied various reflective tools to capture the glory of a boundless mystery that seemed to defy every single attempt to fully grasp it. Men may have believed in a High God or a Supreme Being but they never believed in its *kenosis* in one particular cultic or religious vision; a very crucial difference which all theorists of *Urmonotheismus* have tended to gloss. We have no evidence that man's conception of divine followed a linear evolutionary path and Weston La Barre, among others, confirms this view when he says that…"*Mana* and *anima* are types of concepts, not stages of belief."[40] The propagation of the theory of religious evolution towards monotheism, therefore, had other motives than scholarship. Some hint of these motives can be gathered from Ninian Smart's diagnosis that the attitude of

Western scholars towards Eastern religions has been marked by a tendency to…"interpret them as lower form of Christianity…"[41]

The Judaic world was situated geographically and culturally close to the civilizations of Egypt, Greece and Mesopotamia. The religious practices of these three cultures can provide the background for understanding the real nature of the monotheistic thought. The three cultures of Egypt, Greece and Mesopotamia were decidedly 'polytheistic'. The term 'polytheism' needs to be understood in the sense that these cultures venerated all the names and forms in which they believed the fundamental reality or the supreme being could be glimpsed by men. 'Gods' worshipped in many forms were not multiple realities but a version of reality having meaning and efficacy in certain specific situations. At a deeper level all of them believed in one fundamental creative and sustaining principle from which this whole universe and even the 'gods' have emanated. The Sumerians believed in *Nammu* to be the primeval principle behind all creation; the Babylonians named it as the primeval waters of *Enuma Elish* and the Egyptians believed it to be the *Nun*. All creation, all men and all the 'gods' were believed to have come out of this single unitary reality. This process has enabled the created phenomena to capture in their specificity an element of the divine spark and inspite of its apparent diversity the world partook fundamentally in the one single creative and sustaining force. Yehezkel Kaufmann was describing the theogonic understanding of the pagan world when he said, that most pagan cultures have held the "idea that there exists a realm of being prior to the gods and above them, upon which the gods depend, and whose decrees they must obey."[42] He further elaborates the point and says: "The god is thus a personal embodiment of one of the seminal forces of the primordial realm… It is not the plurality of gods per se, then, that expresses the essence of polytheism, but rather the notion of many independent power-entities, all on par with one another, and all rooted in the primordial realm." [43] Most of the philosophers of Greece believed in a single unitary principle which informed and sustained the phenomenal universe. The analysis and the description of the nature of that principle may have varied from man to man, but the unitariness of the cosmic principle was never in doubt. Pagan polytheism was aware of the reality that even... "in the welter of gods the unity of divine power and will is resolved into a sacred world of many potencies."[44]

A study of the Egyptian or Babylonian pantheon would elicit a very remarkable phenomenon. Various gods are seen to be swapping names and functions with such regularity, that clear assignation of a particular name, form or function to a particular god seems to be very difficult. In the Egyptian pantheon the gods *Re, Ptah,* and *Amon* are each represented severally as the creator. The god *Re* is the father of *Nut* but *Nut* is also said to be *Re's* mother. Most of these 'gods' also assume various descriptive forms. *Amon* is represented as a ram whereas *Apis* assumes the form of a bull. On some occasion, gods are represented in purely animal forms where as on other in half man-half animal form. The distinction between various gods further blurs when one encounters the phenomenon of gods having multiple or hyphenated names made from two or more names of god: *Amon-Re, Ptah-Sokar-Osiris,* etc. Not only their names but even the forms of these gods keep on changing: *Osiris* in human form adopts the characteristics of a bull and becomes *Osiris-Apis*. When *Isis* gets identified with the cow goddess *Hathor* she grows horns.

A similar phenomenon is observable in the pantheon of the Babylonians. They worshipped *Marduk, Nergal, Nebo, Enlil and Ninib* besides many other deities. However the physical and formal characterisation of these 'gods' is so nebulous that ascribing any fixed nature and function to them becomes an unreliable venture. The position of *Marduk*, was however, supreme and he is said to have mastery over all other 'gods'. We have descriptions in which *Marduk* is portrayed as identified with all the 'gods' separately and collectively. *Nergal* is called the *Marduk* of war and *Nebo* was addressed as *Marduk* of property; indicating clearly the idea that various divine manifestations are only spatial and functional potencies of the one and the only *Marduk*. The same syncretic phenomenon occurred when two or more separate pantheons met. The gods of one pantheon built up syncretic associations with the gods of the other pantheon and sometimes even merged with the alien gods. It was a smooth and happy theocrasia in which one god acquired sometimes the name and sometimes the function of the gods of the collaborating pantheon. Men rarely seemed to unduly bother about a particular name or form as long as the primary purpose of approaching the mystery of the divine nature was facilitated. Many people have mingled with one another in the course of their history and learned to live together by creating a composite society that drew from the cultures of the participating groups. It was very natural that human mingling should also lead to the respectful and happy mingling of divinities in an eclectic process of *sunoi kismos*. One gets a feeling that these ancient civilizations were playing around with various names and forms of god, positioning them in various perspectives and formats in order to get a picture of reality with improved reliability. Since no final solution appeared possible, the verbal and the plastic game of representation continued unabated. Numerous deities were just so many pieces of the jigsaw puzzle of one basic reality.

The pagan polytheists never attached any dogmatic sacrosanctity to a particular name or a particular form of god because they probably believed every name and form to be a possible mode of apprehension of the same god viewed differently because of man's disposition and mental stature. They all believed in one supreme reality and one primordial divine being but did not buy the theory that reality should only have one particular name or one particular form. Proponents of monotheistic faiths characterise the practice of representing the unitary reality through a plurality of expressions as primitive deformity over which the insular theory of 'one-god' is treated as a self-declared advancement. Monotheism does not provide a reasonable answer to the question as to why the fundamental belief of the pagan cultures, that divine truth can only be the one 'High God' as the unitary 'Supreme Reality' or the 'Supreme Being', can not be treated as a belief in the unitariness of god? Can there be anything more eloquently expressive of the pagan idea of divine unity than the declaration of goddess *Isis* in the '*Golden Ass*' of Apuleius: "I am she whose godhead, single in essence, but of many forms, with varied rites and under many names, the whole earth reveres".[45]

The burden of the monotheistic conception of god is not related to the ontological oneness of god but to the preoccupation with 'names' and 'forms' of god. It is not enough for god to be god *tout court*. God would not please the good monotheist by being single in essence and existence *tout court*. To pass the theological muster for his divine unity and oneness, god must also become 'God as *Yahweh'*, 'God as *Allāh*' or 'God as Christ' depending on the school of monotheism that has asked god to line up. As we would soon see, there are many kinds of 'monotheism', and there are many kinds of 'one-god'. But let us, for the time being, come back to the initial stirrings of monotheism in Hammurabi (1792-1750 BC) and Ikhnaton (1367-1350 BC), a religious stirring that has been recorded by many monotheistic scholars and historians with much satisfaction. It may be borne in mind that any move made by man towards a dogmatic and insular theology has always been depicted as a self-evident spiritual advancement over tolerant pluralism of the pagans. The force of this presumption has been so strong that even the pagans seem to have accepted it as truth. As a result, a major portion of their intellectual effort goes in trying to demonstrate that pagan religion is also basically monotheistic.

Pagan religion did believe in divine singularity but not in the idea of a god akin to the monotheistic god. The 'one-god' needs to be a jealous, and exclusivist god to fit the phenomenology of a monotheistic deity. Besides, there is no reason, apart from cultic assertions, to accept that belief in one deity is better than the belief in many deities: "In an age of unbelief, however, just why monotheism should be an advance on polytheism is not immediately apparent. If the one God is no less a fiction than the many gods were, wherein lies the gain?... What counts is that, in one way or another, moral value shall have been placed above the other values that human beings properly recognize... Monotheism achieves this result by denying reality to all gods but one and then ascribing to that one god a supreme concern with morality. Polytheism typically achieves the same result by denying supreme importance to any of the gods, however many they may be, and assigning it instead to an impersonal necessity of some kind whose workings favor and enforce morality and affect gods and men alike."[46]

What exactly was the innovation that the two worthy pioneers of monotheism introduced? We have seen the nature of the pantheon of the Babylonian worship and also observed how the names of gods and their functions were interchangeable. Babylonian mythology talks of an era, before the creation of the cosmos, when the entities of *Apsu* and *Tiamat* existed prior to the beginning of time and space. *Marduk* is said to have created the world and all other forces from the body of *Tiamat*; therefore, *Tiamat* was either prior to or co-present with *Marduk*. *Marduk* may have been a great god but he most certainly was not the primally antecedent reality as a 'one-god'. What Hammurabi, in fact, had done was to elevate *Marduk* over all other deities for purposes of worship. Hammurabi only chose a specific deity from amongst many in the Babylonian pantheon and emphasized its supreme ritual importance. Elevation of *Marduk*, however, cannot be seen as conferment of oneness on him in the monotheistic sense. We have seen *Marduk* receive the title and function of all other gods in such a way that he has been identified with them collectively. The elevation of *Marduk,* therefore, would mean elevation of all other gods and the negation of none. The cultic preference of Hammurabi in no way proves either the oneness or the 'onlyness' of *Marduk* in monotheistic terms. Mr. Rafiq Zakaria has very succinctly summed up the essence of monotheism while describing the Hammurabian experiment: "And still the precedence given to one deity among the many and confining worship to only One was a great advance over polytheism. Hammurabi not only showed his indifference to all other deities but even contempt."[47] According to this amazing theological argument a pagan polytheist is invited to believe that the preference or contempt of an individual can serve as conclusive and objective proof of a spiritual theory or proposition. We may all continue, in the meanwhile, to struggle with the noble assertion that giving precedence to one deity from a pantheon of many is a great religious advancement.

We may keep Mr. Zakaria's above formulation in mind whenever we encounter the word monotheism in the course of our study. Monotheism was an advancement over polytheism because it showed, inter alia, contempt for other deities! In view of this formulation the operative qualifications of monotheism are: precedence given to one deity among the many (the existence, however, of many is implied); confining worship to only one deity and utter contempt for other deities. These qualifications are believed by many scholars to constitute an advancement over polytheism which permits man to venerate many deities unquestioningly because all deities are believed to ultimately lead him to god. One would have liked to rest the case but for the important matter of alluding to the monotheistic advancement of Ikhnaton. Egyptians, as we have seen, worshipped god in many forms and invoked his attributes through various names. However, the Supreme one and the creative reason behind the world known as *Re, inter alia,* was also worshipped as the life giving sun. Ikhnaton picked up just one aspect of this solar-deity in the form of a sun-disc called *Aton* and, after elevating it high above other attributes, offered his devotion to *Re* in the image of *Aton.* The fact, however, remained that Egyptians were never in doubt that both *Amon* and *Aton* were the same supreme *Re.* A change of name or emphasis does not change the nature of reality and a dozen to one can always be twelve to another. But in view of Ikhnaton's royal preference for this one deity, he has been hailed as a great monotheistic reformer. We may again seek the help of Mr. Rafiq Zakaria to understand the essence of Ikhnaton's monotheism: "He was, in fact, aggressively involved in it. That is why he banned in his kingdom the worship of all gods but Aton and ordered the destruction of all images; gods in plural were erased from monuments; the singular was inscribed everywhere."[48] This formulation of Mr. Zakaria provides a very eloquent definition of monotheism and its methods. The crux of the thesis is that the forceful proscription by a human agent of the deities and the images of worship of other people is an overpowering evidence of the existence of the 'one-god' of the monotheistic innovator.

Hence, it would appear there is lot in a name than we normally think. It is surprising that such cultic brutality can be hailed as an act of virtue and spirituality. In monotheism, perhaps the paths of spiritual merit can only pass through the rubble of pagan idols and their venerable shrines. This very Ikhnaton is believed to be the model and inspiration for later prophetic monotheism of Bible. It should also be remembered that both Hammurabi and Ikhnaton were great Kings and their monotheism was as much a product of their spiritual yearning as their political motive for power. Apart from the great spiritual yearning for glorifying the one-god, these royal innovators had clear secular motives impelling them to embark on a monotheistic enterprise. Ikhnaton not only worshipped *'Aton'* above all deities but also allowed his own person to be worshipped as a god by his court. Hammurabi used a name for himself that meant 'Marduk his uncle, be exalted' and tried to trace biological lineage with his 'one god'. These early monotheistic attempts were designed to appropriate, to the king's jurisdiction, the prerogative and authority to determine the mode of worship by his subjects. God was sought to be taken out from the spiritual sphere of an individual religious observer. These moves represented an attempt to subject god and man's spirituality to the complete control of a strong human authority, which in this phase of the monotheistic experiment was a king: "Attempts to impose, by political authority, a religion that has been artificially manufactured for *raison d'etat* seem, indeed, always to have failed to win the necessary allegiance from the subjects of a ruler who has sought to obtain a sanction of this artificial kind for his tottering political authority."[49]

Historically, the emergence of a monotheistic deity has generally been accompanied by the growth of the power of a state and monotheism has grown and spread on account of the sustaining support by strong secular instruments of state. La Barre believes that... "under many patriarchs the Habiru had many fetishes; under one king the Hebrews began to worship one God...A monotheistic god is the product of a later and different political milieu, the kingly state."[50] Prof. E.O. James also believes in the political provenance of monotheism and categorically states that Hebrew monotheism consisted of the fact that the Hebrew... "rescued from oblivion a widely dispersed West Semitic High God, sometimes known as *El*, at other times as *Ya, Yau or Yawe*...Under the influence of their leader Moses, he was made the jealous god of the tribes when they were consolidated into a nation..."[51] Prof. Yehezkel Kaufmann has no doubt that... "the Israelite tribes were heirs to a religious tradition which can only have been polytheistic..."[52] Monotheism emerged as the doctrine of a priestly and prophetic elite at a later age and in forging this new doctrine..."the prophets were in an important sense creating a god in their own image."[53] The issue of selecting a deity with ulterior motive has also been recognized by Ninian Smart who suggests that..."it is characteristic of religious people to project their own feelings onto the Deity: personal indignation and arrogance get confused with the activity of god, and the assurance faith provides can result in unself-critical denunciation of the wickedness of other people."[54]

Let us keep the Egyptian and the Babylonian experiment in mind when we return to Palestine where the idea of pure monotheism was being worked upon by various prophets. The land of Palestine at the time of the arrival of the Hebrew was inhabited by many pagan people—Canaanites, Midianites, Kenites, Moabites, etc. These people were of a cognate stock. This was the land in which the wandering band of Hebrew nomads and warriors started pouring from Mesopotamia in around the fifteenth and fourteenth century B.C. The people of ancient Palestine worshipped god in many forms as all other pagan people of the ancient world did. '*El*' was the High God of Canaan who had *Asherah* as his wife. *Asherah* was believed to be the mother of all the gods. *Baal* as a male deity and *Anat* as a female deity, were regarded as the progeny of *El* and *Asherah* and received due veneration from people as emanations of the High God *El*. *El* was traditionally represented by the image of a bull. Bible also records the worship of *Chemosh, Ashtoreth, Milcom, Bel, Nebo and Amon* by the people of Palestine. Besides these deities, there was also *Yahweh*, an obscure sort of a deity of Midianite or Kenite extraction said to be popular among the metal workers of Sinai. In the early life of the Hebrew in Palestine *Yahweh* was just one god among many and, till the time of Moses, he showed no promise of divine greatness, much less of unique oneness. It has been suggested by some scholars that *Yahweh* and *El* were separate appellations used for the same deity. On many occasions, *Yahweh* was also assigned the epithet of *Baal.* Palestinians discerned god's presence not only with the aid of images and idols but also through the worship of many living gods. Apart from *Yahweh* and *El, Baal* was one important deity of the latter kind who was much venerated by the Canaanites. Image worship, sacrifices and cultic rituals were very popular. Ancient Hebrew also knew of the existence of superhuman beings and 'sons of gods'. The Hebrew infused the rudimentary idea of a 'personal god', brought from their own ancestral land of Mesopotamia into the culture of Palestine, and proceeded to live and share the religious life of a country which, they believed did not have a radically different idea of divinity. Many ideas were exchanged between the immigrant Hebrew and the local cultures and gods passed from one group to another as objects of the common religious experience of Palestine.

Hebrew worshipped all these gods and partook in their established cultic practices. It is not clear at this early stage of their life in Palestine whether any one god among the many available was treated by the people of Palestine as the 'only god'. We can, however, say that *El* had the status of some sort of a *primus enter pares.* Of the four Biblical sources of the Pentateuch,we find "J' adressing his god in the genesis as *Yahweh*; whereas 'E' refers to him as *El.* No scholar suggests on the basis of these differing appellations of god that Bible recognizes and accepts the existence of more than one god. It is said that the same god of Genesis was addressed by two different group of authors of the Bible by two different names! The early Hebrews, like rest of the pagan world, worshipped god in a multiplicity of forms. The early patriarchs of the Hebrew—Abraham, Issac, Jacob—were undoubtedly polytheistic and it would be..."more accurate to call these early Hebrews pagans, who shared many of the religious beliefs of their neighbours in Canaan".[55] Karen Armstrong further suggests that... "it is possible that the god of Abraham, the 'Fear' or 'Kinsman' of Issac and the 'Mighty One' of Jacob were three separate gods."[56] Abraham is shown to have addressed his god as '*El Shaddai'* and it appears that he did not know about *Yahwah* at all.

Abraham's god '*El*' was the same deity also known in Canaan as '*El Elyon*' or the 'most High God'. The character of this god was completely different from the character of *Yahweh* who subsequently became the chosen god of Moses, Israel and all succeeding protagonists of monotheism. '*El*' was also a part of the pantheon of Phoenicia along with its other divinities like goddess *Anat* and god *Mot*. Karen Armstrong has described *El* as a mild deity who was specially solicitous of Abraham, and as his friend, companion, or advisor frequently met him even in human form. The primitive anthropomorphism of *El* clearly breaks through the narrative of the Bible. We see Jacob meet *El* at Luz and wrestle with him the whole night and thereby earn for himself and his nation the name of Israel—one who fought *El*. Jacob renamed Luz as *Beth El* and raised an anointed stone symbolizing *El's* memory for respectful worship. Obviously, Jacob was drawing from his cultural heritage of erecting a symbol—an idol—as a representation of the nature and memory of the god he had encountered. It was to this local god *'El'*, a popular deity of Palestine and Phoenicia, that later Hebrews would attach their *'Yahweh'* and give it the power and authority to suppress and deny the existence of other deities and images. With an evolving monotheism *El* a.k.a *Yahweh* would become a deity uncomfortable with fellow deities of the common pantheon and strive to cast all of them out and reign in solitary and unitary majesty as the divine ruler of Israel. With the political and military supremacy of the Hebrew in Palestine, their chosen deity *Yaweh* became the only accredited god of Israel.

Early Jews believed that divinities dwelt in nature and in the regions of the sky. Every tribe and community had their own special gods. The leader of a clan was at liberty to select his own deity in the name of the group. The Hebrew also believed in the existence of living personal gods who acted in history and made a difference to man's life. We find Jephthah [Judges 11.24] speak of the god *Chemosh* who has bestowed the land to the Ammonites; In I Kings 18:21 we find a reference to *Baal* as an active god who was treated as an option to the Lord. It was much later, under the influence of the prophetic monotheism of the literary prophets that the Jews would start decrying those gods whom their ancestors venerated with esteem. It was then that *Milcom* would be called the 'abomination of the Ammonites' and *Chemosh*, would become the 'abomination of Moab'. But for the people of Palestine the existence of these gods, apart from the prophet's favourites *El* and *Yahweh*, was an indisputable fact. Early Hebrew religion shared the cultic belief of its pagan environment and accepted the sacrificial cults, the veneration of the celestial spirits, fear of the demons, and the worship of the departed ancestors as some sort of divine beings. They used many epithets like *El, Elyon, alon, melek*, etc, to characterize god in different ritual situations. At a fundamental level Israel believed that various deities ultimately…"belong to the suite of the One."[57] *El, El Shaddai, Baal, Chemosh, Yahweh,* etc, were the various names of the deities that the early Jewes used to apprehend, identify and address as their god. It was with Moses that the typical monotheistic insistence surfaced in the syncretical and eclectic religious world of the Jews, alongside an intolerant ethnic nationalism. It is possible that this exclusivism was ascribed to Moses by later Biblical narrators in order to gain historical validity. In any case Moses was only following the pioneers like Ikhnaton when he proclaimed that henceforth *Yahweh* shall be the sole god of Israel, and she shall neither acknowledge nor countenance any other name or description of god. But as late as the time of Elijah we find '*Baal*' being seriously considered by the Israelites as an option to *Yahweh*. That the name and form of the deity was of vital importance, was recognized by Elijah when in I Kings 18:24 he says:"Then you call on the name of your god, and I will call on the name of the Lord. The god who answers by fire—he is God."

The High God *El or Baal* had never claimed any such exalted and exclusive status for itself. Moses and later monotheistic prophets claimed this status for their *Yahweh* and applied alacrity and dispatch to the task of establishing the exclusive worship of this one god. Let us see what Moses does as his first affirmative action for establishing the supremacy of his god *Yahweh*. He has just come down from the top of Sinai with the tablet of the Decalogue received by him in a direct heirophany. He sees people worshipping their deity in the habitual manner of making images of it as a calf. In a sacred religious mood after his just concluded epiphany at Mt. Sinai, Moses decides that those idol-worshipping violators of spirituality be punished, and with the assistance of the priests of the clan of Levi, he supervised the slaughter of thousands of men, women and children whose destiny, it seems, was to escape the slavery of Egypt, to be butchered in the promised land. [58] Israel's, and perhaps humanity's, tryst with monotheism had now begun, and we can understand why Moses described his new god as *'Yahweh Sabaoth'*—the God of Armies. It is possible to get from this fearful pogrom a premonition of the religious consequences such monotheistic god-talk would certainly lead to. Scholars have recognized how such…"dangerous conceptions of the divine and a vengeful theology"[59] culminate in the…"fearful theology of election",[60] and in turn foster a violent fundamentalism in the chosen people. Since *Yahweh* was chosen from among many gods worshipped by the Jews to be exalted to the level of the one and only god, it was natural that from the very beginning…"Yahwism demanded a violent repression and denial of other faiths…"[61] Amazingly, the exaltation of *Yahweh* as the one-god never seemed to have automatically caused the demise or negation of the other gods of Israel; the latter continued to bother the all—powerful one-god and its prophets for many more centuries.

Egyptians and the Babylonians, after the lapse of the royal decrees of Ikhnaton and Hammurabi, eschewed their intolerant monodeitism and started worshipping god in the most natural way they knew, while showing no malice even to *Marduk* or *Aton* in whose names so many of their deities were humiliated and their shrines desecrated. People of Israel also showed a similar tendency of reverting to the worship of their traditional deities the moment the pressure and threat of a King and the prophet was removed. The natural spiritual mood was inclined towards polymorphous conception of the deity and a monomorphous worship seemed like an artificial contretemps unsuited to man's innate spiritual urge. Israel had to be forced, over many centuries, to accept the idea of one god: "One God was not coming as easily to the Israelities as Buddhism or Hinduism to the people of the subcontinent."[62] A study of the Biblical literature would indicate that in the ages prior to the dominating influence of

Yahwism, people of Israel worshipped many deities and they were free to choose a deity of their liking and devote themselves to its worship. A concept similar to the Indian idea of *iṣṭadevatā* seems to have been in practice among the people of Palestine. Most of the pre-Yahwistic references to the Hebrew deities depict the deity to be person-specifc, and the Old Testament is full of such allusions as 'god of Abraham', 'Champion of Jacob' or 'Kinsman of Jacob'. La Barre has quoted W.F. Albright as saying that…"each patriarch is represented by Hebrew tradition as choosing his god for himself." [63] The patriarchs had a sense of personal loyalty—a 'covenant' with the chosen deity. But such loyalty was not sought to be extended to and enforced on other men. By alluding to an Indian analogy, one can say that Rādhā's *Kṛṣṇa* could always have been Meerā's *Giridhar Gopāl.*

Yahweh chose Moses on the smoke filled mountain top of Sinai as his prophet and this divine choice changed the course of not only Jewish history but the religious history of mankind. The first and foremost command *Yahweh* issued to Moses was: "I, your God, am One and thou shall not worship any other gods". This Yahwist assertion of exclusivity was a completely new theology and it caused much consternation to the Hebrew when Moses first declared it to them. This assertion of exclusiveness of *Yahweh* gave a completely new direction to the way Israel had traditionally conceived of god. *Yahweh,* we have noticed, was one of the many deities that were venerated by the people of Palestine. It has now been generally recognized that *'Yahweh'* was a god foreign to the Hebrew and they borrowed him either from the iron working Midianite or the Kenite people of the Sinai; a theocrasia perfectly natural to the pagan way of life. The syncretic element in the nature of *Yahweh* has been noted by many scholars. Weston La Barre and Jack Miles believe that the growth of the idea of *Yahweh* as a deity was the result of a long process of syncretism during which he acquired the attributes of many other gods. The important characteristics of the fertility god *Baal,* the volcano god of the Midianites, the Mesopotamian sky-god, the Babylonian *Tiamat* and the neolithic bull entered into the personality of the developed *Yahweh;* the projection of Mosaic monotheism on Him is a later extrapolation. Jack Miles confirms this observation when he writes: "The God whom ancient Israel worshipped arose as the fusion of a number of the gods whom a nomadic nation had met in its wanderings."[64] Miles has referred to scholars like W.F.Albright, Frank Moore Cross and Mark S. Smith who have also attested to the genetic hybridization and diversity in the personality of *Yahweh.*

The practice of worshipping god and apprehending the divine in many forms through invocation of various deities was also the prominent feature of the pre-Islamic Arabian society. Meccan Arabs shared the cultic and religious practices and beliefs of their pagan neighbours of Arabia and the Levant and drew from a very similar heritage that sustained the peoples of Palestine, Phoenicia, Egypt and Babylonia. Among the Arabs—also the Pheonicians—god was indicated by the use of generic common names like *el, elohim, eloah* and *al lah.* To the Arab pagan the epithets *al-lah, al-Lat, al-Uzza, al-Manat*—the last three also known as *'bint al-Lah'* or daughters of god—signified the idea of the divinity which could have been worshipped in multifarious ways in the actual cultic practices of men. Arab society worshipped many tribal gods and goddesses and some of the more important ones were known as *'Hubal', al-Manat, al-Uzza, al Lat,* etc. *Al-Lah* was a male deity whom, perhaps, the Quraish of Mecca worshipped as their special tribal god. *Hubal* as a deity was the most venerated among the Meccan Arabs. He was placed prominently inside the temple at Mecca—the *Kabah*—in the company of many other deities and priests were dedicated to him. It has been suggested by some scholars that *Hubal* was not an original deity of the Quraish of Arabia and was adopted in the Arab pantheon from outside. It is said that god *Hubal* was borrowed by the Quraish from Hit in the land of the Euphrates. This affiliation to the land of Euphrates may perhaps also point to the borrowing from the original Hebrew mythology if we recall that later Arab Muslims were of the opinion that they were descendents of Abraham through the line of Ishmael. And we know that the patriarch Abraham along with the original Hebrew came from Ur, a place situated in the land of the Euphrates in Mesopotamia.

One of the important characteristics of god *Hubal* was his power for oracles; a very common shamanistic trend shared by many deities and personages of the ancient West Asian world. It is possible, and scholars have pointed it out, that *Hubal* as a deity gained greater prominence among the Arabs after the social and political ascendence of the Quraish in the Arab society of Mecca. Anyhow, *Hubal* had a place of importance among the deities of the older Arabian tribes and it was proclaimed that the latter deities had been 'associated' with the former in a syncretic, symbiotic and divine partnership—*shirkat.* It has been suggested by Julius Wellhausen that there might have been a connection and correspondence between the deities *Hubal* and *Allāh. Allāh* might have been the family deity of the Quraish because the latter are said to have been known as 'Allah's family'. Prophet Mohammad belonged to the clan of Quraish, and the formative influence of these connections may not have missed a man as perceptive and intelligent as him. When Quraish became supreme they gave to *Allāh*, their deity, "a place beside the deities of the older tribes, such as *Al-Uzza*, *Al-Lat*, *Manat*, and others; a process described in the Koran by the commercial term of associating or "taking into partership"..."[65] But once the Prophet proclaimed and finalised the monotheistic creed of Islam, the old practice of identifying any other deity with *Allāh*, or 'associating' any other deity in divine partnership with one another and with *Allāh* was completely forbidden. All other deities of Arabia existing hitherto in comfortable and, in many ways, seamless association with one another were banished, and their idols and images were destroyed. God of Islam henceforth shall only be *Allāh*, brooking no associates or partners whatsoever.

To the monotheistic belief of Islam the religion of *Yahweh* propagated by Moses in Israel was to provide the immediate precedent. *Yahweh* of Moses was certainly not the universal Hellenistic god. This was the station he was to acquire after centuries of sustained prophetic and statal effort. In the beginning it was as much a case of Moses choosing *Yahweh* from the national pantheon of gods to be his sole god, as it was a case of god choosing Moses to be his prophet. The original conception of *Yahweh* was very much like the conceptions of *El, or Baal,* or *Chemosh,* and the former shared many anthropomorphic features with the rest. The anthropomorphism of the early days in the divine career of *Yahweh* has been noted by E.O. James in the description that... "in origin, Yahweh was essentially an anthropomorphic Supreme Being..."[66] It was Moses who first proclaimed the oneness and supremacy of *Yahweh* to the complete supersession of all other deities, and evolved a doctrine of coercion to enforce his vision on those men who would not willingly accept that vision. It nonetheless remains a fact that people of Israel continued to worship their many gods, much after the time of Moses and his successors to prophetic office, and monotheism was not fully accepted by all the Jews till the socio-political circumstances compelled them during their exile and the post-exilic period. Monotheism of the prophetic kind was not the natural disposition of human societies and men reverted to the worship of their gods once the monotheistic vigil imposed under the peroration of a prophet's words slackened or was withdrawn. Old Testament is full of the lamentations of god and his various prophets regarding the neglect which characterized the attitude of the Israelite society towards the prophetic vision of one god. One of the most important grievances of *Yahweh* related to the refusal of men to accept him as their sole god. The Bible is full of instances of prophets cursing whole nations for their reluctance to recognize *Yahweh* as their only god. People of Israel were having problems in agreeing to the prophetic version of *'Yahweh—as—god'* also being the 'only-god' fit for all men, inspite of the trauma and torture that they suffered for centuries on account of this refusal.

The final acceptance by Israel of *Yahweh* as the only god came after her frightful *rites de passage* through centuries of blood, death and destruction in cyclical epochs of tragedy. *Yahweh* became one god of Israel after a very humbling national experience under special historical circumstances. However, what worried the early Israelites was not the exaltation of *Yahweh* by the prophets, but that they were exalting him over all other deities under the express demand that other deities may be banished from the lives of men. Human societies had never encountered such theological attitude in the past. Pagan polytheism was by nature tolerant, and provided scope for any number of deities to be accommodated in a particular pantheon. The control of a deity extended only to the person or the group that believed in it, and beyond its specific cultic environment the deity had neither any meaning nor power. The prophets of monotheism, however, were preaching the power and merit of their deity not only over other men but also over all other deities.

The prophetic belief in the supremacy of *Yahweh* over other deities is clearly captured in Psalm-82 of the Old Testament. A council of gods was held in the presence of *'El'* in which *Yahweh* conclusively proves the failure of other gods and assumes leadership of the divine pantheon as well as the function and position of 'El'. With the forcible assumption of the divine leadership of the Israelite pantheon *Yahweh* begins to discredit other gods. He begins not only to push them out of their respective divine office but seeks to finally exterminate them. He was not the one-and-only god naturally; he worked hard to become one. *Yahweh* declared before the Council: "I once said, 'You too are gods, sons of El Elyon, all of you;' but all the same, you shall die like men, as one man, gods, you shall fail."[67] To establish his superiority *Yahweh* wages many battles with gods of the nations: "I shall punish Bel in Babylon"; "Bel is shamed Merodach dismayed." The Prophets of monotheism after receiving such categorical clue to the intent of their god declared all other, but their own, deities to be powerless and dead. Once *Yahweh* accomplishes the task of subjugating his divine colleagues to nothingness, he turns his attention to those societies that worshipped them. Henceforth, no human being was to worship any of those gods that were overcome and defeated by *Yahweh.* If he continued to do so he shall suffer intolerable pain. With these basic measures *Yahweh* was able to proclaim and prove his triumphant unitariness and divine oneness to all men for all times to come. We can refer to many instances in the scriptures of the Monotheistic religions where the monotheistic deity is shown as reciprocating the sentiment of the prophet and declaring all others, but the faithful or the 'Chosen People', worthy of being banished and punished.

The correspondence between the facts of a prophet's life and the divine revelation of god's will has been noted by many scholars. Scholars have assigned various socio-political and psychological reasons for self-centredness to grow as religious philosophy in a society. Many historians believe that exclusivist prophetic and millenarian tendencies emerge in the societies of the *deracine* or such other societies that are under various levels of cultural stress. It is suggested that self-centredness results from a community's sense of acute anxiety and gets prompted by and reflected in the prophet's *soi-disant* attitude. This self-centredness leads to the concept of a god whose will is supposed to run the universe, and also to the concept of a 'Chosen People' who are charged with the duty of enforcing god's will on other people and other gods. Prof. Arnold Toynbee believes that the intolerance and anger of the monotheistic prophets is a result of the shifting of the "centre that lies in themselves and not in god", from whose fiat their uniqueness derives: "Thus in the Judaic societies, Human Nature's innate self-centredness is consecrated by being given the blessing of a God who is held to be not only almighty but also all-wise and all righteous".[68] Prof. Toynbee believes that all religious self-centredness... "is consequently infected with the intellectual mistake and the moral sin of treating a part of the Universe as if it were the whole..."; [69] an occurrence that is more likely to happen in a society in turmoil and strife when men want to transfer their allegiance to a god which would unite them by itself being declared as unitary and universal. Prof. Toynbee alludes to the idea held by the Judaic faiths that at a certain "peak in time-space" god reveals himself and chooses a prophet or a people to be his exclusive medium, judge and executor, in which a capricious god is just the prop for the devotees' wish-fulfilment. We may listen to Prof. Toynbee on this: "Any such idea of mine would seem less likely to be the Truth than to be an hallucination conjured up by my innate self-centredness....Does not any creature stand convicted of megalomania if he allows himself to imagine that God can have committed Himself in an annunciation to one or more of His creatures, or, still more preposterous, in a covenant with one or more of them, at a particular point in Space-Time, to making this particular encounter of their with Him into the supreme moment in the history of His creation?"[70]

The monotheistic prophet was doing two things: firstly, he was proclaiming his own preferred deity, chosen from a host of deities, to be the single most powerful deity; and secondly, he was ascribing the source of all his actions to that deity, interpreting them in turn to be the deity's absolute commands. Apart from reducing the infinite god to the nitty-gritty of a prophet's life, such claims of uniqueness deriving from the will of an abstract and unverifiable deity can also be seen as a sign of surrender. Prof. Toynbee has characterised this psychology of prophetic revelation as the... "craving to escape from the burdensome responsibility of having to take decisions for oneself."[71] Apologists of monotheistic religions have mainly alluded to the special historical circumstances of the Jewish or Arab nation as the unique reason contributive to the growth of monotheistic idea and have generally tried to downplay the dispositional, the attitudinal and the political elements. However, modern scholarship has started looking at the prophetic phenomena in all its manifestations and scholars like La Barre, for example, believe that, "A man's religion is what he *feels* about the Unknown; and what he feels is based on what he has experienced in his emotional growth and individual life history, his own positive and inescapable 'truth'...Religion is what a man thinks and feels concerning this unique unknown, and what he does with his ignorance."[72] In the monotheistic world of the prophet, religious and moral utterances are said to come from the command of his god and in that sense they are more phatic than semantic in nature. In the light of the demands made by these prophets of monotheism, one wonders whether their idiosyncratic deportment and behaviour, sometimes bordering on what many observers have described as insane, is not a mantic characteristic typical of this special class. These prophets are found cavilling about the ills of society, the depravity of people, the scourge of god and the arrival of some sort of a new 'kingdom' under their leadership. P. Bayle in his 'Dictionarie' has found a parallel to this phenomena in the technique of those ecclesiastical movements that seek to incite their followers: "A very potent mechanism for mounting great revolutions is to prepare the peoples for them by interpretations of the Apocalypse, uttered with an air of inspiration and enthusiasm."[73] Prof. Toynbee has quoted Leonardo da Vinci as saying, "Anyone who conducts an argument by appealing to Authority is not using his intelligence; he is just using his memory."[74] The only caveat one would have suggested to the da Vinci formula in reference to the divine claims of the prophets is that the latter used memory selectively by altering its contents in a purposive manner. They did not use the human memory of tolerance and plurality, but drew mainly on its violent atavism. This is a tradition that has continued unabated till our times in many societies that live under the dispensation of the monotheistic faiths and we can find the arguments of a Moses or a Hosea being reiterated, in ever new theological dialects, in the disciplines of logic and philosophy. We can find it, for example, in Wittgenstein: "It is often said that a new religion brands the gods of the old ones as devils. But in reality they have presumably by that time already become devils."[75] The votaries of the old religions, however, may differ on the definition of 'devil', and one really does not know how *'El', 'Baal', 'Hubal', 'Al-Manat'*, etc, had become devils and whether *Yahweh*, etc, are really a great moral improvement upon the old gods. One can understand Wittgenstein's viewpoint only if one shares with him his reliance on faith and not on intelligence: "Go on, believe! It does no harm."[76]

The great spiritual cultures have experienced the divine reality in a wide variety of perceptional modes. Prophetic monotheism gets snared in one particular mode of frozen experience. Reality becomes the final word of the prophet as depicted in his single-frame expression which all followers are expected to watch and contemplate till eternity. Coercive tools were always at hand to punish any wavering of attention of the believer. The realm of spirit is equated with the realm of the mundane. Humanity is allowed to experience only a spirituality determined by the limits set by the 'one-god' and his Prophet. In a sense prophetic monotheism is an example of a surrogate and vicarious spiritualism. Man's personal search of the divine are forfeited. Men are expected to experience spirituality on the basis of their faith in the veracity of the prophet's vision. In the monotheistic tradition man's individual search for truth has always been perceived by the mainstream orthodoxy with grave suspicion. Some of the finest spiritual seekers had to tread a very careful path lest they disturb the main contours of their revealed religion and incur the wrath of the establishment. As long as mysticism and spiritualism operated within the boundaries of the dogma and provided esoteric support to it, they were welcome. Those seekers who went beyond the orthodox religious frame of monotheism met the brutal fate of an al-Hallaj, or a Bruno. Has god and the prophets not warned man of grave consequences if he dared to probe the divine mystery beyond the revealed word? Were Adam and Eve not thrown out of Eden in eternal shame for evincing legitimate human desire for knowledge? Are god and his prophets not pathologically afraid of a situation when men may stop believing in them? God of monotheism seems to have been born in insecurity and it subsequently battens on the fear and timid hope of the faithful: "*Primus in orbe deos fecit timor*". Fear is a very serious factor in the religions of the monotheistic god. In such a world faith, naturally, becomes the most important attitudinal response in spirituality and also serves as a handy survival technique. Hobbes believed that the fear of invisible things is the natural seed of religion. Auguste Sabatier recognized the value of fear but found its amalgam with hope far more efficacious: "In order that fear become religiously productive, there must be mixed in it, from the beginning, a spark of hope…"[77] Man can be cajoled to abdicate his personal spiritual experience and accept the prophet's revelation on the basis of fear and faith.

Coming back to Israel, we see the prophets pinning their faith in *Yahweh* as their exclusive god. To begin with, however, the post-exodus Hebrew were not certain that *Yahweh* of Moses was *the* god who led them out of Egypt. After crossing the Red Sea the Hebrew are seen camping at the foot of the mountain waiting for Moses to return from the top. Meanwhile with the help of Aaron, they started worshipping and thanking god for having delivered them from slavery. The god they are seen worshipping is their old familiar deity in the form of golden calves. There was no doubt in their minds that the god they were worshipping with the aid of the bull-image was the same god who delivered them from Egypt. In Exodus 32:4 and I Kings 12.28 the 'golden calves' of Aaron and Jeroboam are depicted as the gods of Israel who brought then out of Egypt. Israelites were rudely shocked when they were informed by Moses that it was not their familiar god who rescued them from slavery, but the feat had been accomplished by a god called *Yahweh*. The Hebrew were generally incredulous and suffered slaughter for not accepting this divine novelty. The words of the monotheist prophets were generally received with amusement and surprise because they contained ideas that were new and alien to Israel's spiritual tradition. Yehezkel Kaufmann puts the prophetic struggle against other gods in right perspective when he says: "The struggle against, idols, calves, pillars, divination, and magic may be said to involve not monotheism but monolatory; at issue is not belief in one God, but the exclusive worship of him".[78] One does not know whether the worshippers of *El, Baal and Chemosh* did likewise accord to their deities exclusive worship as the 'one-god', but if they did, which is most likely, then the problem boils down to a question of relativistic monolatory, and it would imply that in order to take complete hold of the people, monotheism would have had to fully exterminate their ancient faith. This is what monotheism always strove to do, albeit unsuccessfully: "What is important in the present context, however, is the fact that exaltation of the One made it possible for cruelty to develop on a religious basis...Precisely because of its exclusiveness monotheism can be ruthless."[79] Jozff Tischner believes that totalitarianism grows as a corollary to the monotheistic insistence on one deity: "In this way totalitarian sacrology and ethics emerge alongside totalitarian ontology... the totalitarian principle has an identity with the relationships of the transcendental and the sacred."[80]

There was, however, a very significant feature of the Jewish monotheism which was forsaken by Christianity and Islam. This feature related to the belief in the territorial and racial affiliations of *Yahweh*. He was only the god of Israel and the areas beyond her boundaries were areas of *shedim* or 'no-gods'. *Yahweh* was to be worshipped by Israel in Israel, and it was believed, till the time of the exile, that those who dwell outside Israel are the damned and that they will not receive his grace. What happened, therefore, to the damned was not to be the concern of history. A consequence of this national and territorial affiliation of *Yahweh* was that missionary tendency never grew in the religion of the Jews in a manner it became characteristics of Islam and Christianity. Prophets were sent by god only to Israel and not to the *nations.* Inspite of Second Isiah declaring the whole world to be the people of Yahweh, Jews never took to ecumenism with any sense of urgency and it remained just a dormant thought. The association of apostolic prophecy with Israel was so deeply ingrained in the Hebrew thought that it has found clear enunciation even in the attitude of Jesus. We have been told by Matthew (15:21-24) that when a Canaanite woman beseeched Jesus to heal her ailing daughter, Jesus refused, telling that he was a messiah sent only to the people of Israel: "I have been sent only to those lost sheep, the people of Israel." It was under the post-Easter Church that, a historical break was made and god's light through the prophet was to become also a light to the gentiles. Later, the organised Church declared conversion of the whole world to be a great religious duty. This proselytizing theme was also picked up by Islam which made spreading the message of the one god an important article of faith.

Prophetic monotheism that emerged with the Apostolic prophets of Israel concentrated on the worship of *Yahweh* as the God of Israel. At a fundamental level Hebrews did not deny the possibility of other nations having their own gods but as far as Israel was concerned *Yahweh* was their only god. The god of Christianity and Islam are said to be this very god of the Old Testament. However, in the hands of the gospel writers, St.Paul and Prophet Mohammad the nature of this god underwent a complete change. His name changed from the tetragrammaton of *YHWH* to 'Father' of Jesus Christ and then to *Allah* of Prophet Muhammad. Not only did the name of the one-god change in the other two monotheistic religions, the nature of the person and the message of this one-god also underwent radical alteration. One important point stressed by all monotheistic religions relates to the assertion that every word spoken by the prophet or written in their scripture came straight from god. The signature claim of prophetic monotheism predicated itself on the revelation of god to his chosen prophet. It was on the basis of divine authorship of the message that 'prophets' distinguished themselves from the *nebiium* or the *kahin* of their times. But facts point to a piquant situation. In the three monotheistic faiths the same 'one-god' speaks differently on all important matters relating to salvation and god's soteriological plan for humanity.

The three Judaic faiths deny the veracity of the claims of each other. Jews believed pagan religion to be idolatrous, false and obnoxious. Christians believe that Jews have doctored their scriptures to deny god's true revelation regarding the messiah and his divine sonship. The Christian gospels dispute the authority and divine sanctity of the Judaic laws of the Old Testament god. Islam denies the central claim of Christianity that Jesus was the only Son of god. Prophet Mohammad believed that Hebrews and Christians had falsified the original message of god and it was in the Quran that god's message was purified and truly revealed. Acceptance of this logic of falsification raises grave uncertainty regarding the original and pure message of god. The upshot of this logic is that all we have today as words of god are allegedly falsified and redacted documents designed to serve a particular religious purpose. By this logic the Quran would be the final word of god according to the Muslims; a claim Christians and Jews would scoff at as plain grandstanding. However, Prophet Mohammad was aware of the dangers of such claims and counter-claims and his god closed the doors of prophecy for all times to come. We may recall, however, that this was not a new position and Jews had proclaimed the end of prophecy—on the authority of the same god—nearly seven to eight hundred years before Prophet Mohammad. So, the problem of god's revelation does not get resovled. The claim of each monotheistic religion to have god's personal authorship for its scripture is not four square with the denunciation by the same divine author of a part of his own revelation enshrined in the scripture of other religions. In view of the mutual denunciation of each other's messages by the three monotheistic religions it is difficult to logically believe that all their scriptures are the work of a single authority.

It is worrying that this divine and morally blemishless 'one-god' delivers such disparate and contradictory messages to his prophets. How else can the chosen prophets, who receive messages directly from god, get their messages so wrong? Especially when we are told that prophets are personally chosen by god to be the media. Where does then the veracity of the prophethood and the uniqueness of the message stabilize and rest? One wonders whether the three monotheistic faiths are talking of a single 'one-god' or three separate 'one-god(s)'. Perhaps what they are saying is this: god is 'one' in the sense of being either only *Yahweh,* or only *Jesus Christ, or* only *Allāh,* and the truthfulness of the message of a prophet depends on its complete acceptance on faith by the group of communicants. There isn't an objectively verifiable original divine message. If you have faith, the message of the prophet is true and the nature of god in that message is also true. And once these premises are accepted, the god of that particular message becomes the 'one-god' for the faithful. Without reception in faith there is no revelation nor an exclusive god. *Yahweh* is aware of the difference between him and the god of Abraham and he repeatedly assures Moses and the Hebrew that he, indeed, is the god of Abraham. Faith in the dogma of one religion becomes a sacrilege in the perspective of other religions of the same god. "'Yahweh *ehad*'", says Karen Armstrong, "did not mean that God is one but Yawheh was the only deity whom it was permitted to worship".[81]

Monotheism as the concept of 'one-god' is not, then, a question of numeration but of nominal preference. Yehezkel Kaufmann in his erudite analysis has commented on this issue and said, "it is not a question of number that distinguishes the Israelite idea of God. Belief in 'One Marduk' or 'One Re' or 'One Aton' is, for all that, no less pagan. It is not an arithmetical diminution of the number of gods, but a new religious category..."[82] This analysis points out to a very fundamental character of the concept of monotheism. And, therefore, the need to find an answer to a very legitimate question has haunted the monotheistic religions throughout their history:

why should it be believed that someone is a prophet in direct communion with the one-and-only god and that what he says are the words, and what he does are the commands, of that god? If one recalls the varied and often mutually antithetical descriptions of the nature of god and the inconsistency of his commands as revealed to different prophets on the same issue, the relevance of this question becomes apparent. The answer of the monotheistic religions is simple: the mystery of god's revelation, has to be accepted on 'faith' without trying to fathom it by the use of reason and intellect. All other religious doctrines other than the behiever's own dogma are false and forged precepts. The philosophy of monotheism can be summed up as follows: when it is said that god is 'one', the ontology of god is not being indicated in terms of mathematical numeration; that *Yahweh,* or *Jesus,* or *Allāh* are the only gods and that there are no gods besides them is just a matter of preferential description. What a prophet says about his god is just what he says—empirically neutral—and the message becomes valid co-dependently with the inclination of the faithful to believe it.

There is no objective, confirmable fact regarding god being 'one' and regarding a person being the son or prophet of god: if someone believes it to be true, *it is.* The assertion that there is only one supreme being in this universe as its final basis and explanation, no one would quarrel with. In this sense monotheism is unexceptionable. The problem occurs when this one supreme being is captured and made the prisoner in the person of a deity. The problem is not the idea that 'god is one', but the idea that god is one only as Jesus or *Allāh.* This is precisely what 'monotheistic' religions have done. The Judaic religions in this sense do not insist on monotheism; they insist on monodeitism. They propagate not god but the cult of their specific deity along with social and ritual doctrines that go with the notion of that deity. Very few monotheistic utterances assert that there is 'only one god in the whole universe', which in fact should have been the correct linguistic assertion in keeping with the theory of a universally valid one-god. What we find instead are statements to the effect that, "there is no god but Allah,' there is "no god but Yahweh" 'or that "Jesus is the only Lord". The revealed scriptures of Judaic religions do not favour such arsertions that simply state god to be one without the defining qualifications of a deity or a prophet. If god is one then all men only seek it regardless of the names used to address it. Monotheistic religions do not accept this definition. The one-and-only-god is believed to be omnipotent and omniscient; but this god is not expected to listen to the respectful and focussed address to him by a righteous man simply because the name used was *Śri Rāma,* Buddha, or the *Akāl Puruṣa* and not Jesus Christ. This conclusion would make the just, merciful and omnipresent god appear pretty clannish. If the 'one-god' does not hear the prayers addressed to Him as *Nārāyaṇa,* his omniscience and unitariness stand seriously eroded. A loving mother hears the cry of an infant and rushes to its assistance without bothering whether the child has called her *ammā, mom,* or *māi*. The cry of the infant is meant just for the mother and she knows it. 'One-god' as an ontological reality, and the same 'one-god' as the exclusive theological premise of a particular religious tradition, are logically and epistemically dissonant. God is 'one' because he is to be known in a singular manner as 'Christ' or *'Allah'* on the basis of faith. This assertion makes monotheism problematic.

The monotheistic doctrine of 'one-god', and his revelation through a chosen prophet, is based on the firm belief of all the Judaic religions that ultimate knowledge can only be derived from the Will of God through the means of revelation. "Behold, the fear of the Lord, that is wisdom..." we are told in the Old Testament. Aspiration of knowledge and wisdom has been looked at with suspicion in all monotheistic faiths. The fall of man into sinfulness was caused by man's desire to know things on his own without the assistance of divine revelation. And we know how swift and ferocious was god's retribution in throwing Adam and Eve out of paradise and cursing their progeny till eternity. The pagan desire to know, and their pride in their wisdom, is roundly condemned by monotheistic prophets. Man should never aspire to know the final things on his own because all wisdom is but god's and there is no other source of knowledge outside his will. The Bible has no character like a Prometheus, or a Naciketā who dare to unravel the mysteries of the world and are ready to pay the price for it: "What offends the Bible is the heathen confidence in human wisdom, the heathen aspiration to metadivine knowledge."[83] The Biblical attitude—also reflected in all monotheistic scriptures—is summed up in the story of Job. Job, a completely righteous man, suffers such unspeakable misery that he is forced to question the justice of god. He is advised not to challenge the divine will and accept his fate with humility; but Job is not convinced and laments the absence of a moral providence in the world. Elihu unsuccessfully tells Job to be patient and accept the limitations of human wisdom. Finally god appears before Job and castigates him for trying to understand what is not in the province of human capacity. Man should accept the "fear of god" in lieu of humanly acquired wisdom as a better acquisition. Monotheistic religions insist that the wisdom of man… "subjects itself to the fear of God, and its expression—the moral law—as the end of all wisdom and understanding."[84] What god has revealed to his prophet should be accepted as the true measure of truth. Every reality, every knowledge beyond the corpus of god's revelation is false, and the faithful are advised to be wary of them. Man should accept god's revelation and put all enquiries to rest about his justice and providence. The revealed words of god should be accepted on faith.

We may also remember that revealing his will to a chosen prophet or a chosen people was the vocation which started pretty late in the career of the 'one-god'. In the pre-Mosaic period '*El*', '*Yahweh*' and '*Hubal*' do not reveal their will in the manner the 'one-god' started doing in the time of the later prophets. The monotheistic 'one-god' is highly loquacious, and provides detailed operational guidelines for man's moral and physical upliftment. The divine and the prophet become one in a concerted movement towards the inevitability of a centralized administrative structure supported by a unified community of believers, under the banner of a unitary god. Religious message was to be accepted on faith. Real knowledge of god is not achievable through man's own spiritual effort and discipline but, 'cognitio Dei evangelica'—through Christ and his word. God is present only in his word in the 'Gospel' and in Christ on the Cross: *Extra-Christum* there is only darkness and ignorance. Propositions of religion are to be accepted because they are the words of god; a fact which, in turn, one has to accept on faith. Truth of natural reason cannot contradict the truth of scripture because the latter is to be accepted as the final explanation of everything on the authority of god. We seem to have forgotten that eschatological arguments of the prophets were not trusted by the people of their own times, and it was only with the aid of temporal authority that men's heart were moulded to receive the message of the 'one-god'. The Quran records: "When it is said to them: ' Believe as the other believe': They say: 'Shall we believe as the fools believe?" [2:13] And St. Paul tells us in I Corinthians: "But we preach Christ crucified, unto the Jews a stumbling block, and unto the Greeks foolishness"[1:23]. Besides the impact of their spiritual message, it is a strange but irrefutable fact of history that no monotheistic faith has succeeded in establishing itself without the faithful assistance of a state, a king or a *khalifa*: "The imposition of a new religion upon an entire people always involves the assistance of and promotion by the temporal power".[85] Many societies have found spiritualism of the monotheistic kind difficult to resist when it was propagated by conquering armies 'demanding signatures'.

Xenophanes of Colophon is quoted very profusely by monotheist philosophers if they want to decry anthropomorphism or idol worship found in a particular religious tradition. What is not mentioned that Xenophanes did not make any appeal to the authority of a prophet or a teacher in spiritual matters, much less of a personal revelation. He believed that god can be known by man through man's own personal quest. There cannot be a god who is believed to rule over, or be greater than, other lesser gods. Xenophanes, would have been critical of later prophetic monotheism and would have equated the logic and psychology of their portrayal of god with those of the Ethiopian or the horse. One is reminded of the poet Wallace Stevens who said that god and the human imagination are one. This fact was recognized by many perceptive men and we have the authority of Nicholas of Cusa who said that god was the totality of possible subjective visions, and in that sense he is the mirror of the personality of the proclaimer. Tolstoy believed that God as preached by the Church was nothing but the reification of a man's desire. A plausible psychological backdrop of monotheism has been provided by Weston La Barre in the following words: "Behind each God is only a paranoid messiah, the shaman and false wonderworker; he has somehow retained everyman's infantile omnipotence... God is the Pronoun whose antecedents differ with each individual and society. The locus of the subject matter, obviously, is somehow in societies and in men's minds, not in the outside physical universe."[86]

The ontological arguments regarding god do not prove the singularity or plurality of god, they only try to deduce god's objective reality through an analysis of the concept of god as the most perfect being. These theories are only a philosophical legerdemain and seek to demonstrate something that they already believe in. St. Anselm told his congregation that he believes in order to understand, rather than vice versa. Proving or disproving the existence of god abstractedly was considered no big deal as long as the sacrosanctity of god as *Yahweh*, Jesus or *Allāh* was not questioned. Without taking these hallowed names one can go about discussing god's nature and characteristics in millions of ways and a great variety of philosophers have done that over the centuries. It is difficult to believe that St. Augustine and Aquinas, Ibn-Rushd, Ibn-Sina and Imam Ghazzali talked about the same god. If they did, then that god cannot be 'one-god' but a complex of many gods who can be interpreted in the manner of a man's liking. Keith Ward has said: "The Thomist concept of God vacillates between a pantheistic identification of all attributes with God and an atheistic denial that God has any particular form of existence."[87] Judaic religions agree that one may talk about 'god' in any manner one liked as long one did not question the person of Christ, or the message of Prophet Mohammad. God existed as 'one' only within the framework of the message of his prophet or his apostle.

In picking up a deity from a pantheon and moulding it in accordance with an exclusivist theology, monotheism seeks to establish a religious monopoly in the great civilizational bazaar of mankind. To accept the logical existence of many deities but still claim uniqueness about one's own can be a case of solipsism but not a mature statement of fact. Therefore, a monotheistic assertion is not an ontological, but a dispositional, assertion. We have already seen that the talk of one or only god is not a matter of number but of being a new religious category. One would have hoped that the three monotheistic faiths would have the same idea regarding this new religious category of the monotheistic god. But we are told on the contrary, and the three monotheistic religions are a testimony to the diversity of god's idea. Ninian Smart tells us that: "Briefly, then, belief in god involves adherence to a number of doctrines; and it is not an ordinary empirical belief."[88] We are now confronted with a situation where monotheism not only does not mean numerical existence of 'one-god', but also means three different gods to the three monotheistic religions. The most amazing thing is that this 'one-god' does not mean the same to even all Christians, and the god of the Jerusalem group of disciples is different from the god of St. Paul: "It seems that there has been no single, determinate, concept of god shared by all Jews and Christians … or for that matter, by all Christian theologians throughout the centuries."[89] Evidently this term God is "more protean than Zeus" [90] God of monotheim is 'one' only in the denominational world of religious discourse and in this manner gods of all religions can be said to be one.

Still we are told that, of course, there is no god but God—who is One. But, of course, monotheism is an advancement over polytheism. In one sense the monotheistic god was decidedly an improvement over the polymorphic conception of god: the self-importance of being one god made him hostile to all other gods and the arrogance of being a 'chosen people' converted the pious believers into a parochial community having one single centre of ego. Prof. Toynbee says…"Collective ego is a more dangerous object of worship than the individual ego is." Let us, however, come back to the theory that a monotheist believes in 'one-god', whereas the polytheist believes in many gods and that the former god being one has a unique personality that is manifested in his interventions in history and hear what Paul Tillich has to say: "These religions of justice, history and the expectation of the end could not accept the mystical tolerance of India. They are intolerant and can become fanatical and idolatrous. This is the difference between the exclusive monotheism of the prophets and the transcendent monotheism of the mystics."[91] To the reality of this personal and historical god of monotheism, who appears and acts in history as divine *dramatis personae,* we can turn now. The life and ministry of Jesus Christ and the God of Christianity can provide us with a model to examine one of the representative views of the living god of monotheism.

The Living God

"It is a fearful thing to fall into the hands of a living god"
—Hebrew 10:31

The pagan and polytheistic traditions have a very different idea of divine reality and the deity. The first and fundamental divine person or the primal reality is believed to have existed prior to the existence of the world of material phenomena, and all deities are seen as rooted in the existence of that primordial reality. 'Gods' are not understood as judgemental lawgivers and commandants, but forces of the world-order in which the supreme reality manifests itself, and who are apprehended by men in a state of sympathetic exploration. Most of the important non-semitic traditions believe that there exists a realm of being prior to all the 'gods' and the latter are within the influence of the universal principles of that divine realm or existence. The 'gods' are seen as emanations and embodiments of certain aspects of the primal reality. Final reality, however, was believed to be meta-divine. God is not an exterior agent detached from the intrinsic reality of the world and men; he is not an outer reflection of man's inner desires and anxiety. Men offered their adulation to deities because in some way the deity was believed to be related to their lives and which creatively determined the direction their lives would take. The abundance of the divine person made it possible for man to actualize ever new spiritual possibilities within the rubric of the unitary reality. To the pagan mind polymorphism of the visible world was an evident reality but he could discern a unity of purpose behind this phenomenal multiplicity. He could understand the many-sidedness of reality, while never losing sight of its basic ineffable oneness. Yehezkel Kaufmann characterises pagan polytheism as follows: "It is not the plurality of gods per se, then, that expresses the essence of polytheism, but rather the notion of many independent power—entities, all on a par with one another, and all rooted in the primordial realm."1 In nearly every major non-monotheistic civilization we come across a creation myth in which the phenomenal world and all the gods are shown as being created out of a primary cosmic essence—the *Nammu, the Enuma Elish, the Nun,* or the Canaanite cosmic egg. Hesiod believed that the cosmos and the gods came out of an undifferentiated primal chaos. The whole world was believed to be divine because it came from a divine source. The monotheistic faiths posit 'god' *before* creation, but in the pagan culture 'god' is believed to be *behind* creation.[2]

There were, however, major differences between the one supreme power or the High-God of the primitive pagan societies and the god of monotheism. The supreme power, or the 'High God', of primitive socieites was far beyond the immediate life and environment of men. It was seen as too remote and impersonal to interfere in the day to day life of the devotee. In fact it was too 'high' to even be invoked in any cultic or ritual situation. The 'High God' transcended worship and ritual and also the limitations of name and form. It may have been an object of erudite contemplation but it was not accessible to men in mundane ritualism; and men generally believed it had withdrawn to become some sort of a *deus absconditus.* The High God was impossible to know in its entirety and the futility of invoking it as it was, through a ritual, was well understood. It is only in the form of some of his powers or attributes that he could have been made the subject of worship and prayer. The Supreme Being of primitive paganism, according to Van der Leeuw, was a static immanence. The one-and-only-god of judaic monotheism, on the contrary, is very much a god of the social almanac of the adherent. he calls men out and commandeers societies to do things that are required in order to fulfill the purpose of his creation. The first thing he does after coming down from his high station and revealing himself as a *deus revelatus* is to order the renunciation and annihilation of all the divinities hitherto worshipped lovingly by men.

Monotheism hypostatised divine presence into a jealous and irascible supreme god. The supreme god becomes an active 'person' who interacts with men and gives orders that would become the supreme temporal and spiritual law for the believer. *Yahweh,* for example, is completely different from the Supreme Being of pagan societies: "Yahweh, on the other hand, is not only a power but also a will, not only a person but also a personality, a live personality, a live god operating on and ever present to man, a hostile and jealous god, not without something of the demonic."[3] It is possible that the concept of a harsh god was back projected into ancient history of Israel to bring the old god of the patriarchs into conformity with monotheistic ideas. But once the literary prophets selected a deity as the 'only-god', theology became absolute and was available for use as an accomplice to non-religious volitions. The monotheistic god of the Judaic faiths, unlike the pagan 'High God', became malleable and subject to invocation for secular assignments. The 'High God' of pagan civilization could not be manipulated by men but... "a personal God like Yahweh can be manipulated to shore up the beleaguered self in this way, as an impersonal deity like Brahman can not."[4] The monotheistic god was not like the 'High God' of pagan religions.

Judaic, Christian and Islamic theologies have borrowed much of their jargon from neo-Platonism and Aristotle. They have profusely used Aristotelian logic to prove the existence and nature of their god. It is also claimed by European philosophers and theologians that European civilization and Christianity are basically an offshoot of the Greek civilization. It would, therefore, be fruitful to stop for a while and meet the Greeks in their native pre-Christian devotional milieu. The Greek idea of the divine was neither static nor monotheistic. The gods of Homer and Hesiod were very manlike and differed from humans only in possession of higher powers and immortality. Gods and men were both subject to the far more potent power of *anangke,* or fate—a power that recognized no claims of privilege by a theistic divinity. Hesiod in his *'Theogony'* provides a unified geneology of gods wherein gods are seen begetting one another through a process of recurring emanation. While Xenophanes denied the efficacy of Homeric anthromorphism, he never advocated characterisation of god in a unilinear way, although his own general inclination was to regard the final truth as singular and unitary. The Milesians believed that a single boundless and powerful divinity encompassed and controlled the universe. The Milesians described the supreme unfathomable divinity as the 'Unbounded'—*to apeiron*—and believed it to be the material as well as the causal substratum on which many *Kosmoi* were dotted about. Most of the pre-Socratic philosophers agreed on the premise of a supreme divine existence that bears and holds the universe onto itself and manifests its creative abundance in a wide variety of emanations. Aristotle has approvingly quoted Thales as saying that all things are full of gods.

Greek philosophy, generally, did not separate god from the created world. It was believed that in a certain way the worlds of phenomena dissolve into and were retained in a virtual state of possibility in the divine realm. It was difficult to conceive of a divinity standing outside time and space and 'creating' the world *ex nihilo*: The divine was both the material and efficient cause of the universe. The cosmos came out from the unbounded and would finally be reabsorbed in the unbounded at the end of the its lifecycle. Anaximenes was of the view that the contents of the world emerged from the unbounded and were interconvertible with it and with each other. Heraclitus believed that although there was a single all-powerful being in control of the universe this reality was concealed from men by an impenetrable veil of 'seeming'—*dokos*. Most of the presocratic philosophers considered the reality behind and within the manifest world to ultimately be One; it was only the representation of this fundamental unitariness that varied from philosopher to philosopher. Some believed that the pervading reality can be apprehended as the '*nous*', some said it was fire and water, while others believed it to be '*psuche*', or a cosmic mind. Xenophoanes said that this One pervasive reality was god. Heraclitus wrote in his 'Fragments' that the whole manifested world was a modification of the One: "God is day night, winter summer, war peace, surfeit famine; but he is modified, just as fire, when incense is added to it, takes its name from the particular scent of each different spice."[5] Parmenides believed that the universe was immutably one and in its pure suchness could only be described as "that which is". This 'that which is' was received as a unity that was unique, complete, unchanging and homogenous. There was no contradiction between 'that which is' and the world of ordinary experience: the latter was not treated as false but "strictly meaningless".[6] Reality was perceived to be one at the most fundamental level. Pagan Greece believed this one reality to be 'god': a belief that found apt representation in Heraclitus: "Having heard not me, but the *logos*, it is wise to concur that all is one."[7] Judaic monotheism completely reversed this Greek analysis that the unitary and all pervasive 'One-is-God', and declared, instead, that 'God-is-one". This reversal gave a completely new meaning to the oneness of the Supreme Being. For ontological non-duality of the Greeks, it substituted a cultic non-duality reflected in the worship of a single deity. The god of monotheism had nothing to do with the god of Greek philosophy and religion.

Greek philosophers, like most of the pagan philosophers of the axial age, believed in the eternity of the principle of creation and did not posit a personal god who created the world of phenomena from non-existent nothingness. Heraclitus tells us that, "This world order was made neither by god nor by man, but it was and is and shall be; fire ever-living, being kindled by measure and being quenched by measure."[8] All things according to him, however, are in continual change and flux. Anaximander described 'time' as a name for god in the same manner as it was used by Heraclitus to describe the creative providence of god: "Time is a child at play, playing draughts; a child's is the kingdom."[9] The Indian mind would recognize in these descriptions an allusion to the *Līlā* of the supreme *Brahman* in actualizing this phenomenon-world of appearances. Empedocles accepts the Eleatic thesis that *what is* cannot come into existence nor pass away. We can say that the world is only the eternal *līlāmaya* rearrangement of the ever-eternal possibilities of ever actualizing elements. We create a new world of perceptions everytime we want to participate in some phenomenal reality. The world was not created on a fixed day by a known person who conjured it up from nothingness.

In the Judaic cosmogony the world was conjured up from nothingness by god day around 4000 BC and, as a result of this fixed historical creation, the world and the men in it did not share one bit of the essence of the divine. Man's sinfulness was not only a result of his separation from god as a consequence of his disobedience: man was and will remain forever ontologically separate from god for the simple reason of his creation from the gossamer threads of phantasmagoria. Orthodox establishment of the Judaic religions has, therefore, never taken kindly to the odd mystic in their ranks who believed man to be a part of divinity and considered it a legitimate spiritual aspiration to seek merger with the reality of the divine existence. For such heresies retribution has been harsh. The Judaic religions seem to have tolerated some spiritual mysticism, partly because they were philosophically fashionable and gave respectability to their theology and partly because of the personality and prestige of the mystic or the *sufi*. But the mystic and his mysticism was accepted if he did not question, challenge or repudiate the official dogma. Pragmatism could have been another important reason for this tolerance. Some scholars have pointed out that Sufism and mysticism prevented individual religious dissent from turning into heresy, and the institutions run by the mystics might have been seen as an instrument for amicable management and channelisation of protest. The mystic and his seminary was later used as a potent instrument for the conversion of those societies in which Christianity and Islam entered. However, on the most fundamental aspects of their theology the gap between the later mystics and the orthodox priest did not exist. Judaic monotheism does not suffer a rebel. Liberty regarding *god qua god* was permissible if it did not mention or impugn Jesus as the Christ, or challenge a Quranic injunction. For the mainstream of religious belief the god of monotheism is completely different and distinct from his world. Robert Oakes underlines this fact when he says: "The Judaeo—Christian idea of god is theistic because god has created the world and so affects it, *yet it* is decidedly distinct from it."[10] Humanity, according to the Judaic religions, is completely separated from divinity and lives perpetually in a 'Metaphysical Hell'.

Another prominent contribution of the monotheistic religions was their emphasis on 'faith' and 'revelation', and not on human effort, as a source of knowledge. Greeks believed that man could apprehend reality by the use of his spiritual and rational faculty. Man, and not a revelatory assertion, as Protagoras believed, could have been the measure of all things. It was the factor of later, post—Reformation, theoretical necessity that made Europe appropriate Greece as the fountainhead of European culture. Christianity, which effectively became the fountainhead of European culture for nearly one thousand years before the Renaissance, was completely different from every cultural and spiritual paradigm of Greece. The Greeks were fiercely independent, rational and non-dogmatic in matters of knowledge and spirituality. In the Greek culture we find culture-heroes like Prometheus and Sisyphus fighting all odds, including the wrath of gods, to unravel and pry open the mysteries of the world. The seeker of Christianity, in comparison, is a Job whose incipient intellectual quest was nipped in the bud by a malevolent theophany and a dubious theology. Greeks could not have provided any model for Christendom and Europe; not at least till the late Reformation.

It is a matter of fact the early Christian Church was very wary of Greece and tried its best to shield the nascent Christian community and its dogma from their probing and inquisitive spirit. Christianity preached everything that many Greeks found foolish and puerile. Was it not Tertullian of Antioch who exclaimed in anguish: "What has Athens to do with Jerusalem; the Academy with the Church?" Was it not the European emperor Justinian whose political instincts realized the dangers of Greek philosophy and science for the new religion of the empire and who ordered the forcible closure of all Greek academies? Was it not the European Christian Church that sabotaged the Hellenic seminary and library of Alexandria? These are a few samples of the love Christianity and Europe bestowed on Greece. One would not have expected the roots of a culture to be so summarily mauled if a new age and continent wanted to emulate and learn from that civilization. The fact is that Christianity always saw Greek individualism and its love of knowledge as a serious threat to its theology and tried to ward it off in the way of a Justinian, or subvert it in the manner of a Thomas Aquinas. For many years Aristotle was unwelcome in the universities of Catholic Europe. The stern Plato, among the Greeks, was, however, more popular with Christianity. Europe looked at Greece when it needed an intellectual ally and a worthy history to fight the decadence of its own culture led by a moribund Church. Otherwise, Europe sounds hypocritical when it talks of appropriating Greece as its cultural bedrock. Arnold Toynbee characterised this pattern as 'archaic, infantile and crude'; as some sort of a theoretical flotsam drifting up from the European subconscious, and believed that some... "Samples of these uncritically accepted intellectual *cliches* are the conventional terms 'Europe'; 'the European heritage from Israel, Greece and Rome..."[11] The civilizational core of Greece had always been 'non-European' and closer to its Eastern legacy. Greece was culturally, spiritually, and philosophically closer to its Oriental neighbours and this fact was recognized by the early fathers of Christianity: "Church fathers like Clement and Hippolytus suggested that philosophy itself, the Hellenic reliance on reason, might have its origin among the 'barbarians' of India and Egypt."[12] By claiming Greece, Europe was unconsciously claiming its non-monotheistic, pre-Christian, pagan past that it had repudiated and disclaimed for nearly thirteen hundred years. It were the attitudinal and dispositional tools of their pagan past which, coming via Greece, again helped Europe free itself from the thralldom of an antediluvian theological dispensation and an unscientific frame of mind and helped her pursue a path of intellectual freedom. It was perhaps the pagan daring that converted a grovelling Job of an Europe into a Prometheus.

Platonism was far more to the liking of the monotheistic faiths. It was Plato who first developed a serious dogmatic theology which the State was expected to enforce on all its citizens. Plato proposed that the State should legislate on man's belief and all citizens should accept such legislated spirituality on faith: a thought Judaic religions have adopted with alacrity. A.E Taylor in his 'Plato' writes: "Plato appears as at once the creator of natural theology and the first thinker to propose that false theological belief—as distinguished from insults to an established worship—should be treated as a crime against the State and repressed by the civil magistrate." [13] These Platonic ideas were found very useful and efficacious by all monotheistic religions. The Christian Church picked up the Platonic theory of dogma, heresy and punishment and implemented them with utmost seriousness. Walter Kaufmann commenting on this proclivity of the Church says: "Christian Churches have been and still are, fountainheads of anti-intellectualism and opposition to critical thinking".[14] A huge portion of Church literature is *post dicto* justification of the dogmas of faith, and St. Anselm's prescription that he first believes in order to understand is typical of the anti-intellectualism of monotheism. Such an attitude would sire a great tradition in which noble saints, scholars and theologians would devote a lifetime of effort to 'prove' beliefs of a faith that obviously did not seem to have any natural basis to compel the unforced assent of a reasonable man. Walter Kaufmann raises a valuable point when he asks, why should we believe in what some prophet says, unless we believe *a priori* that the man was god's prophet, which begs the question. The monotheistic religions are aware of this weakness in their theological superstructure and evince uniform obsession with the maintenance of the faith of their laity through discouragement of their intellectual propensities. In case of a man's frail reason refusing to grasp the truth of the monotheistic message on the basis of the scriptural testimony and the proclamation of the Church there were other ecclesiastical measures available: fire, sword or the stake. If early Europe under Christianity learnt anything from Greece it was a highly selective reading of Plato's extreme theology.

We have seen in our study that, through a process of elimination, merger and selection, the deity called *Yahweh* became the 'one-god' of the prophets of Israel. We would soon see *Yahweh* changing his metaphysical nature from a god given exclusively to Israel, to the god of all people. It was during the despondency of the exile that Second Isaiah took a remarkable leap of imagination and declared *Yahweh* as the god of all people. Second Isaiah did two unique things: he extended the suzeranity of *Yahweh* over all nations and, as a corrollary, suggested equivalence between *Yahweh* and the gods of other nations. He declared that deeds performed by gods of other nations were in effect performed by *Yahweh* himself. In his hands *Yahweh* got identified with *El, Marduk and Baal* by a process of ascription of their feats to *Yahweh.* Second Isaiah depicts *Yahweh* as splitting *Rahab* into two and piercing the dragon *tannim*—feats which the god *Baal* had performed much before him in the Canaanite creation myth. Karen Armstrong says: "He calmly assumed that Yahweh—not Marduk or Baal—had performed the great mythical deeds that brought the world into being...Yahweh had finally absorbed his rivals in the religious imagination of Israel..."[15]. *Yahweh* not only assumed the role, function and character of previous gods but also transcended his national boundaries for the first time in his short career and embraced other nations as his people: "Blessed be my people Egypt, Assyria my creature."[16] It was roughly in such expansive mood that Jews returned to Jerusalem from the exile. It was believed that the era of prophecy has ended and there could not be any direct contact with god; god's presence could be felt only through His activities in the world and through the scripture. One hopes to meet the same god in the New Testament and also the Quran: a god whose singleness, majesty and existence is now taken to be fully established and proven; a living god! If *Marduk* and *Baal* are *Yahweh* then logically *Yahweh* should also be *The Father* of Jesus Christ and *Allāh.* Nobody denies theologically that the god of the Old Testament, the New Testament and the Quran are one and the same. Let us see what the facts are.

The first thing that strikes us in the New Testament is the near obliteration of all references to the one-and-the-only god as *Yahweh.* It is amazing that a god, who struggled for centuries to ensure that his name, fame and reputation are established among his worshippers, suddenly drops his name and nearly withdraws personally from the turmoil of man's secular and spiritual concerns. He is now addressed as the 'Father', the 'Lord' or just plain 'God'. The god of the Old Testament never allowed any other god or man to share his glory and power. His obsession with himself was complete. All humanity was required to utter and glorify his name. In the New Testament his character undergoes a surprising change and he allows a person other than himself to be revered—his son! God took a very radical decision to sire a son through the Holy Ghost on a virgin named Mary. Jews thought this was a blasphemous slander by the Christians on the character of their god *Yahweh* who was above sexuality and could not have sent a human child on earth to be tortured and killed. Jews, who lived with *Yahweh* for centuries and were privy to many details of *Yahweh*'s life, seemed to have somehow missed the clandestine Yahwist design to beget a son. *Yahweh* did many things for Israel—crossed the Red Sea, helped them escape Egypt, saved them during the Babylonian exile—in course of his association with her without ever eliciting any dynastic proclivities. However, *Yahweh* as god of the New Testament decides to have a son who is charged with a mission on earth. The 'one-god' it seems has joined history in a direct manner through his son.

Before we proceed further in our exploration of god's ministry on earth as a Son, we must be clear that our information on this subject comes to us from two sources: first, the scriptures and other orthodox sources of the Church; second, the writings of early fathers, philosophical and theological exegeses and historical criticism. The dogma of the church and the analysis of various Christian philosophers sometimes speak in different voices on the nature of god in his career as a man and a 'Son of God'. The views of the official Church would be more important inasmuch as these affect the daily life of the community of the believers and determine the ritual framework of the religion. That the god of the Old Testament is also the god of the New Testament, that he begot a Son to live and suffer in this world, and that Jesus Christ was resurrected and physically taken to heaven, and that he lives in heaven at the right hand of god, his Father, and intercedes on behalf of men, are the cardinal principles of the Christian religion, and every Christian—lay or scholarly—

accepts these principles as self-proven facts. These principles are also the staple fare of the ecclesiastical preachings of the Churches. Since these doctrines are preached as historically and objectively true and the believers receive and accept them as such one would assume that there should be no hesitation or confusion regarding such facts on the veracity of which the whole edifice of the Christian religion stood: "It is Christ that died yea rather, that is risen again, who is even at the right hand of god, who also maketh intercession for us."[17]

The faith statement in Romans 8.34, quoted above, presents a fairly simple and straightforward picture one would say, but for the small matter that none of these assertions were ever made earlier by god in his long and chequered history, and their declaration baffled both the Jews and the Gentiles in great measure. Pauline doctrines consisted in declaring Jesus to be the only begotten Son of God sent on earth for his redeeming mission. We know god never had a son by the name of Jesus. In his early days as the mighty *'El'* god is shown to have *Baal* as his son and *Anat* as his daughter. When the office, functions and even the person of *El* was taken over by *Yahweh* the latter is not shown to have any sex life and therefore no progeny. Assertions of god having a son through a human mother would have sent *Yahweh* in a fit. The claim of divine sonship for Jesus was not palatable, therefore, to most people. To say that all previous gods have accepted Jesus' supremacy and glorified him is not only scripturally unsupportable but completely against all evidence in Jewish history. Such assertions can only be called 'faith-statements' which do not need logic, history, semantics or reality to lend any credence to them. They are truthful by virtue of their utterance. So we see Peter declare with certainty: "The god of Abraham, and of Issac, and of Jacob, the God of our fathers has glorified his Son Jesus..."[18] There is not a single reference in the entire Old Testament where gods of the Patriarchs mentioned in Peter's assertion have ever mentioned Jesus as their son and praised and glorified him as such. The god of the Old Testament is so obsessed with himself that he concedes prominence to no one; glorifying somebody else was simply out of the question. Regarding the nature of Jesus, the Gospel has this to tells us: "Concerning his son Jesus Christ our Lord, which was made of the seed of David according to the flesh." [19] This assertion without any authority of the scripture or tradition came out of the blue and caused great anguish in the contemporary Jewish society. They thought Paul and the Apostles were preaching blasphemous falsehoods in which not only was God declared to be the father of Jesus but god's sovereign functions were given to him as well. According to Paul the righteousness of god was now to be achieved via Jesus: "Even the righteousness of God which is by faith of Jesus Christ unto all and upon all them that believe: for there is no difference." [20]

God caused further turmoil when he inspired the declaration that the sacrosanct laws promulgated by him earlier are now superseded by the requirement of faith in the Son of God: "... therefore we conclude that a man is justified by faith without the deeds of law"[21] It is further added: "But now we are delivered from the law, that being dead wherein we were held; that we should serve in newness of spirit and not in the oldness of the letter."[22] These assertions by Paul had only Paul's word to back them up; no support is available for them either in the scriptures or in the intelligence and common sense of man. To cope with this problem a novel epistemic technique—'faith'—was introduced in Christianity and later in Islam. This technique implied that the words of a prophet were to be accepted on faith because they were received by him directly from god and contained salvific value for men. There is, however, no logical or linguistic relation, intrinsically, between an assertion and the inevitability of inducement of faith in someone.

The New Testament gives a clue as to how Jesus could be proved to be the son of the 'god of Abraham and Moses', without God ever having said so. How is one to believe something that was so momentous for the Christians, although the Greeks thought it to be foolishness and the Jews a stumbling block? The New Testament informs us that the sonship, the salvific life and death of Jesus are attested by Jesus himself! In other words Jesus is the proof of Christ. Scripture records: "For who hath known the mind of the Lord, that he may instruct him? But we have the mind of Christ."[23] We have some idea of a historical Jesus and in his words and deeds as reported by the apostles we can now understand the nature of god. What comes to notice is disturbing. God has not only forgotten what he had said in the Old Testament, but shockingly he has now started self-contradicting himself on many vital issues. St. Paul claims to have read the mind of Christ and found out that the most sacrosanct of god's epiphanies in which Y*ahweh* reveals his nature and his covenant with Israel is basically a saga of blindness: "But their minds were blinded: for until this day remain the same veil untaken away in the reading of the old testament; which veil is done away in Christ".[24] There is a theological logic, behind this attitude: "I do not frustrate the grace of god for if righteousness come by the law, then Christ is dead in vain."[25]

Christ's death is postulated as a theoretical requirement for disproving the validity of the Jewish scripture revealed by god and not as a divine plan intrinsically. Christ should not be seen to have died in vain, and in order to allocate some meaning to his death it is necessary to deny god's previous words. Moreover the castigation of law as inefficacious and the emphasis on pure faith caused the severence of a man's moral life from his life in faith; as long as a believer believed in Christ, his moral behaviour *per se* was unimportant. God sends his only and beloved son to earth with a view that he may proclaim the majesty and glory of god. As the messianic character of the son unfolds, god watches in dismay the Son declaring that the divine creativity of the Father in the last thousand years or so has, in fact, been a purveying of doctrines based on falsehood and unrighteousness. Since Jesus was a man who lived and preached as a respected teacher, the effect on men of such words ascribed to him would be very telling. However the great puzzle regarding god's own son Jesus, similar-in-essence, declaring god's previous deeds and words as blasphemously wrong left most men dumbstruck. Such capriciousness and unreliability was understandable in the ill-developed details of the false gods of primitive men of pagan nations—an important charge brought by the monotheists against them - but in the character of the most high and only god this trait juts out as a pathological condition unless we have a higher-order explanation for it. And we have an higher order explanation coming: these are deep and divine secrets which mortal men should just accept on 'faith' without trying to understand them. Monotheistic assertions become divine and final verities only on account of their reception in 'faith'. The 'foolishness' ascribed to Jesus is divine because it has been accepted on the basis of a Christian epistemic tool—'faith'. The New Testament exhorts believers to eschew any attempt to understand the deep mystery of the revelations: "Knowing that a man is not justified by the works of the law, but by the faith of Jesus Christ... for by the works of the law shall no flesh be justified."[26]

We have another problem at hand. What we hear in the New Testament are not the direct and first person voices of either God or his Son Jesus; they are the recorded accounts of various apostles, especially of Paul. Paul is an interesting person. In his earlier avatar as Saul he persecuted the followers of Jesus. As a Jew he was convinced, on the authority of god, that Jesus' ministry was an arrogant and blasphemous attempt to falsify the true words of god. Following a psychological experience on the road to Damascus he suddenly had a vision of Jesus being the Son of God and the Messiah. As a sequel to the vision, Paul repudiated his ancestral god and his message and picked up the apocryphal stories of Jesus' life to construct a theology. Paul's repudiation of his old religion is hailed as a great spiritual act. Here we have the notice of a peculiar disposition of the monotheistic faiths: if a man rejects his old religion and accepts a monotheistic god he performs an act of merit, but if a man questions the religion of a monotheistic god he deserves death. Spiritual progress of man is a one-way *cul de sac* towards some monotheistic god of a Semitic prophet. Paul made another peculiar claim. Paul was not known to Jesus and his close early disciples. We have no evidence that Jesus or the Jerusalemic community had ever given any apostolic authority to Paul. Paul simply declared himself to be an Apostle of Christ and demanded obedience to his words: "Paul, a servant of Jesus Christ, called to be an apostle"[27]. Jesus was made to proclaim himself the Son of God; Paul proclaimed himself "an apostle of Jesus Christ by the commandment of God our Saviour, and Lord Jesus Christ...", an assertion the faithful were to accept on faith, as revelatory. There was no legal or spiritual authority which could have chosen Paul as the apostle; we have to accept this auto-election as such on faith. The revelation of the god of the Old Testament was to be taken on faith; the radically different New Testament revelation of the same god had to be accepted on faith, and the far more distinct message of the same God in Quran was also to be accepted on faith. The New Testament tells us that the death and resurrection of Jesus has to be accepted on faith because of the very surprising reason that it has been so preached by Paul: "Now if Christ be preached that he rose from the dead, how say some among you that there is no resurrection of the dead? ...And if Christ be not raised your faith is vain; ye are yet in your sins." [28]

Jesus as a preacher and miracle worker may have lived and died in a historical context but Jews never believed that he was god's son and that he was killed and then resurrected from the dead for man's salvation. Recourse to resurrection appears to have been taken for theological reason by a later Church as a hypothesis for contextualizing the theory of man's salvation. Christ should, inferentially, have actually risen because that is how he is preached. Moreover if we do not accept that he actually rose, what happens to our salvation? Jesus became Christ retrospectively with an imaginative construction of the events in his life. All events in the life of Jesus become objective and historical realities because of them being preached as such by a later apostolic tradition. History, for a monotheist, is the reification of his theology that actualizes itself retrospectively. The historical Jesus was just a Jew with Essene affiliations. Jesus was chosen as a symbol of salvation by a later post-Easter Christian Church by reinterpreting and exploiting the Biblical concept of man's original sin to insert Jesus' death as a neutralization of that sin. Jesus' habit of addressing god as 'abba', or father—a practice found in many religious traditions along with the Jewish—was used to declare that Jesus was god's biological son. Biblical scholars have proved that Jesus did not address god by the more common appellation of 'King' or 'Lord' but with the more honorific title of father or 'abba'. This was a traditionally dignified way of addressing elders in the Judaic society. Prof. James Barr has examined this practice and conclusively shown that in the case of Jesus: "Abba is not 'Daddy' ".[29] Traditional Jewish society believed Jesus to be a miracle worker of Galilee. The Jerusalem followers took him as a teacher but the Gospels and later apostles made him the 'Son of God' who suffered death, but was resurrected to become the redeemer of mankind. The physicality of Jesus' sonship, however, was not under doubt in the preaching of the creed. He was god's son as any son would be of his biological father.

The death and resurrection of Jesus are the two central and objective bases of the Christian religion. It would be legitimate to expect that on matters having a serious implication for the faith, the sources would show a fair degree of certainty and uniformity. Not at all; the gospels vary in their account of Jesus' life, death and resurrection to such an extent that credulity can be extended to them only on the basis of a strong disposition to believe. It was in the Epistles of Paul that the dogma of resurrection was given an eschatological meaning. Many scholars have tried to justify and explain the manifest contradictions in the scriptures in a variety of ways. It is not possible or necessary to mention all of them. We may allude to a few of them to understand the general slant of their argument. Wittgenstein explains the contradiction in these four gospels as deliberately intended towards a special effect: "So that the *letter* should not be believed more strongly than is proper & the *spirit* should receive its due...Queer as it sounds: the historical accounts of the Gospels might, in the historical sense, be demonstrably false, & yet belief would lose nothing through it..."[30]. This admission comes as a shock. The pagan and the polytheist has always been told and continues to be told even today that the superiority of monotheistic religions is based on their historically and objectively active god, the historically verifiable prophet / messiah and the accurate words of god enshrined in a body of Holy Scripture, as compared to the fantastic fables and genuflecting gods of the polytheistic systems. The emphasis, historically, has always been on the veracity of the *letter*. Prophetic monotheism is claimed to be a true living religion of a true living god because its god is objectively and historically true and each and every word of its scripture is infallible and historically correct.

It causes much astonishment if the great minds of the Christian faith offer such closet-explanations for the god of their faith when scholarship has conclusively proved the unhistorical nature of its chief protagonist and their scriptures. The surprise of the fallen pagan knows no bound when he is told that the truth of a monotheistic faith is less a matter of objective certainty than a faithful's hopeful belief. We may listen to Wittgenstein again: "This message (the Gospel) is seized on by a human being believingly (i.e. lovingly): *That is* the certainty of this 'taking—for—true', nothing else... And faith is faith in what my *heart*, my *soul*, needs not my speculative intellect."[31]

Research has now confirmed that the Gospels of the Christian faith were written and collated much after the life and ministry of Jesus came to an end. Most of the authors of these Gospels are not eye-witness to the incidents they are reporting. It was eventually by the fourth century that the works of the New Testament were finalized by the Church. These text were written and edited with the advantage of hindsight and the Church authorities interpreted the Jesus-phenomena in light of the needs of the Church and the nascent community. The New Testament is not the concurrent record of a one-time historical revelation but the result of nearly two to three centuries of scholarly editing, collating and critical selection. Inconvenient facts were omitted, oral stories were recorded, and apocryphal anecdotes were canonised by ascribing them to a revered name: "The boundaries of scripture are not something eternally and unchangeably established by god; what scripture included at one time and place was not identical with what it included at another; the study of scripture and the study of church history are not separable."[32] It is now accepted that: "Because of the theological motifs and presuppositions in the faith of the early Church in respect of Jesus it is difficult to write with certainty an authentic life of Jesus."[33] Writing about the Gospels, the Encyclopaedia Brittanica says,... "it has to be considered that their tradition was formed and collected from the point of view of the faith of the post-Easter Church, under the influence of its ideas and ways of thought and in close connection with its vital interests and the ways in which its life found expression..."[34] The Jesus of history therefore can only be abstracted from the motivated narratives of the later Gospel writers. And in that history it is difficult to find a stable character of Jesus, the man who was Christ. Beyond the words of the scripture there is little independent evidence of the Christ phenomena.

The very simple matter of relationship between the 'Father' and the 'Son', the generative paradigm of Christianity, was not resolved till the fourth century and it evolved in radically different trends in the theorizing of many authors and scholars. In the Gospel according to Luke, the Holy Ghost descended in the bodily shape of a dove on Jesus after his baptism and the voice of God said,... "thou art my beloved Son, in thee I am well pleased."[35] A fairly legitimate commendation for a son from a father. It also fits with the attitude of dependence of Jesus on God the Father: "The Son can do nothing of himself, but what he seeth the Father do..."[36] This subordinationist view is further confirmed in John 8:28 when Jesus says: ... "I do nothing of myself, but as my father hath taught me, I speak these things". We do not know whether Jesus actually said these words, but assuming he uttered and believed in them, the Jewish community must have been hurt and surprised by these assertions but not unduly alarmed. Then came the *coup de grace* and Jesus uttered the most portentous words: "I and my Father are one".[37] The Jews came to an end of their indulgent tether and lost their customary grace and patience at such blasphemy: "Then the Jews took up stones again to stone him."[38]

Regardless of Jewish sentiments, Jesus the Son was now proclaimed to be also the Father. But the confusion was not to end here and in John 14:28, Jesus tells his disciples that ,.. "Father is greater than I." To hold that Jesus the man was Son of God but he and god were the same and to still believe that god was greater than the son was an amazing religious dogma. But the dogma does not rest here and a new category of the 'Holy Ghost' is brought in. The Gospel writer postulated the existence of the 'Holy Spirit' as god's operating principle in the world. This Spirit was said to proceed from the Father on the instructions sent by the Son. But this Holy spirit is also a person who is present with the disciples when Christ spoke to them.[39] The Spirit in turn is also one with the Father and the Son. The 'Spirit' was postulated as a *deus ex machina* necessary to guide and justify the acts of generations of Fathers, Popes and subsequent Churches in their actions by providing direct divine sanction to their activities. If these precepts and inter-relationships appear very complex and untenable to us we can only have the satisfaction of knowing that not even a single Christian has been able to unravel and understand them. They have all accepted them on faith as the unfathomable mystery of Christ. Some of them agreed that it was absurd but then their faith always entailed risk: "credo quia absurdum." The inter-relationship of the three divine personages has never been happily worked out inspite of the declaration of Nicaea where the Bishops resolved: "We believe in one god the Father Almighty, Maker of all things... and in one Lord Jesus Christ, the only begotten of the Father, that is, of the substance of the father..." The God of Bible has changed unrecognizably inspite of his very late assurance to Malachi: "I am God. I change not,"[40]; and his exhortation to the believers to follow his revealed laws!

As long as the historicity and veracity of the original Christian dogma was inviolate the problem of proving Jesus as the son of god and the Son of God being of the same substance of the Father could be managed. The esoterical doctrines of god's unity within the ritual multiplicity and the problems regarding his omnipotence, omniscience, etc, were theological issues with which common believer was not concerned. The denial of the veracity of the original claim, however, would have been disastrous. Modern Biblical scholarship has now shown that the historical element in the story of Jesus' apostleship, death and resurrection is very tenuous, if any. Many people who heard and met Jesus, left no record of him and in most cases they were hostile to him. The events of the virgin birth, transfiguration and resurrection are not true antecedently. Keith Ward writes: "The original witnesses are all propagandists on behalf of the Christian faith, and there is no extant impartial account of Jesus' life and death."[41] Keith Ward clarified the situation further: "In sum, if the Bible is taken as a source of evidence for the existence and activity of a supernatural person, it fails miserably to live up to any of the usual norms of inductive evidence."[42] Scholars like Albert Schweitzer,

Julius Wellhausen, etc, have presented the view that Jesus Christ of the Gospel is not the Jesus of history. The Jesus Christ of faith is a theological construct of the Church much after the original event.

Albert Schweitzer tried to find a historical Jesus in the Gospel stories but did not succeed; he believed Jesus's personality was fictitious. Paul had personally never known Jesus and the Jesus of Paul's narratives is "not historical" but a product of Paul's own turgid imagination.[43] Julius Wellhausen shared the view of the unhistoricity of the Christ event but went a step ahead and proposed that even doctrinally, "Jesus was a Jew and not a Christian."[44] Ludwig Wittgenstein was correct in a sense when he said that while in the Gospels one finds simple theories, huts, so to say, they become,... "with Paul a Church." [45] But he never discounted the value of faith in the face of new data and believed,... "historical proof (the historical proof-game) is irrelevant to belief.."[46] Reverend Marcus Braybrooke believed Christ story to be more mythical than historical and wrote in the 'Guardian' of 1987 that: "Anyone who starts with the historical human being, Jesus of Nazreth, and seeks to understand him in the Jewish milieu of his time, will recognize later Christological development as mythological"[47]. What the later Christian stories do is to make Jesus, instead of God, the object of worship. The a-historicity of the Jesus story and later Christology is not disputed by any serious student of religion. Wittgenstein knew this fact and in his musings provides an alternative perspective for the defense of faith which became very popular in the twentieth century. Wittgenstein wrote: "Christianity is not based on a historical truth, but presents us with a (historical) narrative & says: now believe!... believe through thick & thin & you can do this only as the outcome of a life."[48] The new *mantra* was that historical facts were not necessary for Christianity to survive as a religion. The prominent theologian Paul Tillich would say: "A god disappears; divinity remains. Faith risks the vanishing of the concrete god in whom it believes... The certitude of faith is 'existential'."[49] Modern European philosophy and theology would gradually abandon dependence on historical data in Christianity and develop existential theories of perspectival rationality of religion and god, in which religious assertions and propositions about god were to be understood with reference to the belief-system specific to an individual or a community of believers, and not applicable generally and objectively.

There is no historical and verifiable content in the monotheistic idea of *god qua god,* less in the idea of Jesus Christ as god. The theory of a unitary Judaic god was the result of two parallel processes: one, a deity, a name, was picked up from the menu of deities available in a particular cultural tradition and it was extolled to divine supremacy at the cost of all other names and deities; second, the attributes and characteristics of all other deities—'gods'—were appropriated and pasted on the chosen deity or the 'one God' in a long process of syncretism and fusion. There can be no dispute on the metaphysical doctrine of a divine existence or a unifying truth which is unitary and the source of all that we see—the ontological 'One'. Monotheism makes the idea problematic by declaring the self-existent 'One' to be the *'Yahweh'*, or the *'Christ', or 'Allāh',* and after making such declaration propounds elaborate theological, and religious doctrines to prop-up its thesis of monodeitism which does not flow from the singularity of Truth either empirically or logically. Most certainly not ontologically. But monotheism lands itself in a devotional bind. If 'god' is, for example, only *'Allāh'* and the only way to know him is through his revelation in the Holy Quran and the *sunnā* of the Prophet, then one has to provide for some sort of philosophical *force majeure* for the logical and objective unverifiability of this claim. Monotheistic religions have an elaborate theory to explain the metaphysical leap from 'one-god' to god-as-Jesus and god-as-*Allāh*, and it is called the theory of 'faith' and 'revelation'. The two concepts serve to harmonise the privately dispositional and the projectively empirical components of the cognitive data involved in a religious experience.

Karen Armstrong should not have expressed surprise at the fact that in the Christian Churches it was, ... "Jesus Christ about whom we talked far more than about 'God'..."[50] Similar is the case with *Allāh*. Take the case, for example of the Urdu broadcast on any channel of Pakistan television wherein the salutation offered by the news reader or the anchor, is *Allāh hāfiz* in place of the more popular

Khudā hāfiz. This is happening also in India and in many of the radio programmes hosted by Muslim anchors we hear them pronouncing *'Allāh hāfiz'* instead of *Khudā hāfiz* as a preliminary or concluding salutation offered to the audience. Nothing wrong, perhaps, but it points to an attitude born from a very deep seated anxiety present in most of the monotheistic religions. *Elohim, elāhi, Khudā,* etc, are cult-neutral common names applied to the idea of the supreme divinity in many cultures. Apart from the Muslims, the *Parsis* also use the word '*khudai'* when they address their god. The use of the word *khudā, elāhi,* etc, would of course mean 'god' but it would mean god 'generally', uncoloured and undetermined by the tenets of any particular religion, and therefore fit for use in any religious discourse. An example is the use of the word *Rab* to denote god by the Sikhs and the Muslims alike. But a 'general god' that can be used by all men is not acceptable to monotheism. God becomes god only in a theology. *Khudā* means nothing: *Allāh* is god. Monotheism has a congenital dislike for generalization through universal application of the idea of god. A monotheist does not believe in god as such—a *khudā*—he believes only in the *khudā* who is to be known as *Allāh. Allāh hāfiz* is, therefore, the theologically correct way to invoke divine benediction. God at a non-denominational level, without reference to a particular theology, turns out to be a fairly acceptable persona when he is conceived as the Supreme Being, who alone exists by himself; who is behind the phenomena of the world; and who is infinite in perfection, power and knowledge. If these concepts are treated to be descriptive of god's nature then we may all without hesitation accept them as reflective of our own god and all religious disputes should rest. But no monotheist would accept this premise *per se*, although it emerges out of his own theory of god.

God as the Supreme Being, the one and the only defining truth of the whole cosmos has not been disputed as an abstract principle by any theologian. The disputation that monotheistic faiths raise relate to the concrete description of god and the annunciation of his will in relation to men. The early Biblical god was very reluctant to describe himself to his devotees. Abraham believed his *El Shaddai* to be a personal friend who promised him fertility and progeny. Jacob would wrestle with his god for a whole night without getting any nearer to seeing or knowing what that god really was. God was primarily realized as a source of rich mystery that was revealed to each man in accordance with his own capacity for perception, and in relation to his existential situation. God in his monotheistic avatar as *Yahweh* remembered this undefinable mystery of his earlier epiphanies and he warned Moses not to ask unnecessary and limiting questions: *ehyeh asher ehyeh*—I am that I am. It was under severe pressure of prophetic monotheism that god was to abandon his joyful expansive mystery and finally lodge himself in the stern concepts of a *Yahweh*, the Father and *Allāh*. The divine *mysterium* was subordinated to the *magisterium* of a theology.

The theological and ecclesiastical disputations in monotheistic faiths are conducted at two distinct levels. In the works of a philosopher, or the department of divinity in a university great scholarship is spent on the discussions regarding god's nature. At this intellectual level the examination of the general concept of godhead is conducted with a fair degree of impartiality and intellectual honesty. Scholars, philosophers and even theologians would discuss the nature of god in a variety of imaginative interpretations. The non-denominational and unencumbered god gave men opportunities to let their intellectual acumen take diverse and high flights. God seemed to be breathing rather freely in philosophy. At the intellectual level of discourse every commentator accepted that god essentially is a mystery and cannot be fully known by man. Philo of Alexandria (30-45 BC) believed that god's essence is fundamentally incomprehensible and we can only perceive him in his manifestations in the world through his *activities* and *powers*. The Gnostics of the first two Christian centuries believed that godhead was an utterly incomprehensible reality and was higher than all prevailing conventional concepts of god. Some scholars like Marcion proposed the existence, besides the harsh Biblical *Yahweh*, of a second loving god in order to explain the *agape* as manifested in Jesus. Origen believed that god was deeply mysterious and could not be expressed in human terms. As late as the thirteenth century the greatest theoretician of Christianity, Thomas Aquinas, was declaring that ...

"Quid deus sit, nescimus"—what god be we do not know, god simply was: 'He who Is'—"Qui est" [51]. Al-Ashari (878-941 AD) felt that god was beyond our understanding. According to Ibn al-Arabi (1165-1240), god is not an objective truth that could be summed up in one human experience, he is vastly mysterious.

The New Testament is aware of the incomprehensibility of the mystery of god. According to St. John, the universe still remains a mystery when some light has shone out into the darkness: "And the light Shineth in darkness; and the darkness comprehended it not."[52] St. Paul never doubted the ultimately unfathomable and mysterious nature of Reality and believed that man could only perceive it dimly: "For we know in part, and we prophesy in part.... For now we see through a glass, darkly; but then face to face: now I knew in part; but then shall I know even as also I am known."[53] Clement of Alexandria believed that the ultimate nature of god is inscrutable and he is characterized by 'apathia', or a changeless, impassable insouisance towards the world. At the level of his most fundamental ontology god was believed to be completely undefinable in a deity or through any set of ritual or cultic prescriptions.

Two inescapable philosophical corollaries of the idea of a completely unfathomable god are the impossibility of proclaiming one vision as complete and final and the undeniability of many possible modes of representing him. The possibility of many viewpoints for understanding the reality and mystery of god was recognized by many philosophers. Paul recognizes the existence of gods of the pagans and also their specific ways of apprehending god,... "For though there be that are called gods, whether in heaven or in earth (as there be gods many, and lords many)...But to us there is but one god... and one Lord Jesus Christ..."[54] Valentinus (200 AD) advises the abandonment of an external dogmatic search for god and exhorts men to begin the search from within themselves, because that is where god would ultimately be found. Origen believed that men can know god through personal efforts by the use of *theoria* or contemplation and become divine after achieving this knowledge. Origen was convinced that belief in Jesus was an intermediate and passing phase to be transcended when men became capable of apprehending the reality of god. Jesus was a temporary symbolic aid to the apperception of the divine. This philosophical attitude is present in the early Islamic tradition of the *falsayuf.* Al-Kindi (870 AD) taught that truth was ultimately one and can be apprehended from a variety of perspectives; a fact which was reflected in various religious traditions of man. Ar-Razi (930 AD) did not accept the final validity of any revealed religious doctrine and firmly held that man has a right to think about, explore and find the divine for himself.

The tolerance and eclecticism coming out from these early Christian and Islamic philosophers is jarringly liberal and almost pagan in its universalism. These views are completely opposed to the official and orthodox characterisation of divine truth by the monotheistic religions. This attitude does not gel with the innate exclusivism of Christianity and Islam. There was a reason for this early burst of liberalism to have taken place in these religions. The official dogma of Christianity regarding god and Jesus was not formalized till the fourth century. Besides, the Christian Church did not have the necessary political and administrative authority along with the required infrastructure to enforce its orthodoxy. The liberalism flourished in early Christianity under the pagan influence of Greece owing to the Hellenic background of most of the prominent early converts. In Islam the tradition of liberalism was encouraged by the early *mutazilis* under the influence of al-Mamun (813-832 AD) and other *falsayufs*. However, this liberalism was diffident and always remained afraid and respectful of the official orthodoxy which advocated belief in the God of Quran without any doubt or questioning—*bilā kaif.* Philosophical liberalism was an early intellectual quest that was later to be restrained within the perimeter of the creed by both Islam and Christianity, and man's reason was to be made the hand maiden of official theology. Al-Hallaj was killed because he dared to identify himself with the essence of god. Yahya Suhrawardi (1191 AD) was put to death in Alleppo on account of his belief that truth could be found in all religions because there could be as many paths to god as there are men. Eclecticism in monotheism has been a short lived and perilous intellectual enterprise.

The proclamations of the early Christian Church were considered to be fairly antedeluvian and contra-intuitive by many of the contemporary pagan thinkers. The Roman, Gaius Svetonius (70-160 AD) described the Christian religious theory as '*superstitio nova et prava*'—a new and depraved superstition. Karen Armstrong records that many in the Greco—Roman world found the Biblical god a ferocious deity unworthy of worship. Pagan philosopher Celsus (170 AD) found the Christian view of god highly parochial, and was appalled that Christians preached a revelation in which god gave special attention only to the Christians. Plotinus (205-270 AD) could never understand the Christian claim and found it a "thoroughly objectionable creed."[55] Symmachus was also surprised at the Christian claim and opined that,..."The heart of so great a mystery cannot ever be reached by following one road only."[56] This critical trend seems to have started at an early date, and it was perhaps to this general reaction of the educated *oeikumein* that Paul was referring when he described Christianity being treated as 'foolishness' by the Greeks and a 'stumbling block' by the Jews. He and other apostles, however, took note of this reaction for later handling and when the Church became powerful under royal patronage she brook no dissent—Christian or pagan—and intellectual discourse was discouraged and, when required ruthlessly curbed. Every human endeavour was henceforth to be some sort of an apologetic for the dogmas of religion. Arnold Toynbee has described this attitude of the monotheistic religions with a sense of melancholia: "For Pharisaism has been the besetting sin of the religions of the Judaic family, and this sin has brought retribution on itself in a tragic series of atrocities and catastrophes."[57]

But curb it as you may, human reason and intelligence have the prospensity to break all unreasonable restraints of tradition and dogma. Monotheistic religions gradually came to accept this characteristic of the human nature. Orthodoxy sought to provide some sort of a forum for intellectual debate within the broad rules of religious doctrine. The exoteric kerygma, proclaimed in the creed of the church and preached by priests for the understanding and observance of all believers was inviolate and beyond question. The esoteric field of philosophic analysis and mysticism was the area left for intellectual discussion and exploration of man. It is in this area that one finds great theoretical discussions taking place on diverse subjects like the nature of god's omnipotence, nature of sin, existence of angles, and man's relation with god, etc. Abstracted from the kerygmatic context of the faith god could have been discussed without any threat to the basic creed of religion. As long as the fundamental tenets of religion were not questioned, faith was ready to countenance some youthful exuberance of intellect.

It is the kerygmatic content of religion that is offered as an advanced alternative to polytheism of the pagan people; the abstruse dogmatic doctrines do not have value for ecumenical purposes. The world of the academia had its use for the kerygma of religion: it gave respectability to the credal content by providing rational apologetics in the intellectual idiom of that age. Philosophical erudition helped in proving to the laity that the religion of the Church was also the theme taught by the noble philosophers. Natural or philosophical theology became a 'defensive manoeuver' in which symbolic and equivocal concepts were propagated as univocal truths: "It is the product of a distinctive historic situation...The difference arises over the theologians' determined attempt to make univocal translations of essentially ambiguous propositions."[58] Walter Kaufmann has alluded to the hypocrisy of religious preachers reflected in their use of words and phrases—'throne of god', 'right hand of god', 'bodily ascent to heaven', 'Jesus as begotten Son of God', etc,—in their common meaning while preaching to the lay public from the pulpit, but modifying them to mean metaphorical concepts "under questioning" or attack by intelligent and impartial opinion.[59]

Every theologian and theoretician was, however, aware that the results of his intellectual labour should lead to hypotheses confirmatory of the articles of faith. Intellectual exploration was not an open-ended expedition where a scholar followed the way of truth wherever it led. In theology the countenance of truth should bear the mark of the Lord as preached *ex cathedra*. Reason is required to demonstrate what is already believed on faith. Those who undertook to prove the existence of god, etc were firm believers already.

St. Anselm gave this exercise the backing of a firm ideology when he said in the '*Proslogium*': "For I do not seek to understand that I may believe, but I believe in order to understand." Before him St. Augustine was also preaching the doctrine of '*credo ut intelligam*'. He believed that, "understanding is the reward of faith. Therefore do not seek to understand in order to believe, but believe that thou mayest understand".[60] These scholars believed that *fiducia* and assent to the creed were the beginning of reason and intellect. Right from its beginning as a religion the ecclesiastical doctors of Christianity have been aware of the dangers posed by reason and rationality and have been averse to the idea of theology ever becoming philosophical. We have the authority of St. Paul, the founder of Christianity as a religion, on these matters and we can refer to him to understand this distrust of intellectual investigation and philosophy. St. Paul says in his epistle to the Corinthians: "For the Jews require a sign, and the Greek seek after wisdom: But we preach Christ crucified, unto the Jews a stumblic block, and unto the Greeks foolishness;...Because the foolishness of god is wiser than men; and the weakness of God is stronger than men."[61]

Christianity was congenitally suspicious of philosophy. Since Christians believed they "had a supernatural knowledge revealed by god," faith as a dispositional category predominated at the cost of reason from St. Paul to Kierkegaard. Some modern philosophers have tried to redefine the word 'reason' to include revelatory faith, but that's besides the point. St. Paul had no doubt regarding the attitude of the new Christian community that he was establishing should have: "Beware lest any man spoil you through philosophy and vain deceit, after the tradition of men, after the rudiments of the world, and not after Christ."[62] The great Tertullian of Antioch (160-230 AD) is said to have recognized the inherent illogicality of the Christian creed, but after his conversion not only started believing in it on faith but proceeded to vindicate it and denounce "philosophy as the demon inspired mother of heresies."[63] In his views Tertullian was simply following St. Paul's advise regarding the dangers of philosophy recorded in II Corinthians 11:14: "And no marvel; for Satan himself is transformed into an angel of Light."[64] If pagan sciences, especially

Greek thought and philosophy, with which early Christians were familiar, were studied and some merit was grudgingly accorded to them, the reason was that such thoughts were seen to be compatible with Christian doctrine and helpful in preparing a pagan to accept Christianity: philosophy was good it if was *preparatio evangelica.*

Europe of St. Thomas Aquinas' time was agog with the philosophy of Aristotle which had reached her shores via the Arabs. Aristotlean intellectual rigour was exciting intelligent men all across Europe. Theologians and Church authorities, however, were not impressed by Europe's growing love for the Greek method. Thomas Aquinas believed that intellectual skills should not be cultivated for their own sake; they must be used only to justify Christian faith and revelation. Aquinas wanted to counter Aristotle's influence in Europe and, if possible, to tame it. Walter Kaufmann describes the Thomist methodology very picturesquely: "St. Thomas went forth, but did not slay the dragon. He pulled its fangs and made it subservient to the Church...He attempted nothing less than to pull the fangs of reason and to make it subservient to the Church".[65] Things which could be known by reason should also preferably be known by faith, because knowledge achieved by faith is readymade and full of certitude. In a sceptical age the 'Aristotelian' justification of faith offered by Thomas Aquinas came as a great moral prop for the beleaguered Church and the latter undertook the curbing of heresy with a fresh ardour of proven self-righteousness. The saintly Thomas Aquinas proclaimed that all doubters and heretics should be shut off from the world by death, and his theories provided a much-needed justification for the institution of the 'inquisition', which St. Thomas whole-heartedly supported.

Martin Luther was on the side of Aquinas in his emphasis on faith, his fight with Catholicism notwithstanding. As a matter of fact Protestantism has been more fanatical in its insistence on the reception of scripture in a strict, literalist sense. Luther advised the faithful to blind their reason and follow faith regardless of consequences: "The devil's bride, *ratio*, the beautiful whore, comes in and thinks she is clever".[66] Calvin, too, never trusted reason or gave any quarter to it in his philosophical system. He believed that the original sin of man corrupted his intellect forever and no truth, much less divine truth, could be discerned by human intellect alone. Martin Luther clinched the argument for faith when he said: "It is Satan's wisdom to tell what God is, and by doing so he will draw you into the abyss. Therefore keep to revelation, and do not try to understand."[67] Some of the gravest saints and theologians of Europe continued to hate free enquiry and human reason. Many of them presided solemnly over the death of innumerable human beings at the inquisition simply because some men wanted to assert the simple human right of free thought and sought the Protagorean facility for measurement of any claim of truth by the use of human effort. If some European scholars still declare that the civilization and culture of Europe has Greece as its spiritual source they perhaps do so *sola fide*, just on faith.

The obsession with 'faith' and the lingering suspicion of reason, intellect and philosophy is an attitudinal precondition for the acceptance of a religious dogma. There was no reasonable way to convince a person that God of the Old Testament was also the god of the New and he had begotten Jesus as his Son and raised him after death to be man's only saviour, and that the Son and Father were still the same persons. Every apostle of Christianity has been aware of the strangeness and uniqueness of the Christian claim. St. Paul conceded this logical flaw in the Christian doctrine when he advocated the theory of 'justification by faith'. It is argued that the logical, linguistic and empirical impossibility of the Christian claim could become clear and explainable only by taking, what Soren Kierkegaard called, the "leap of faith". Kierkegaard has beautifully explained this primary Christian experience in these words: "Becoming a Christian involves an either/or decision, rationally groundless but existentially necessary."[68] Soren Kierkegaard never doubted that Christianity was a 'paradox to reason' and therefore an alternative to despair and madness: ... "when the dread of sin and a heavy conscience torture a man into crossing the narrow line between despair bordering upon madness—and Christianity."[69] Truthfulness of a proposition has nothing to do with its rationality or verifiability or even inferential logicality; a proposition was true because leaders of the faith said so and it was found profitable by the faithful to believe in it: *"The true is the name of whatever proves itself to be good in the way of belief, and good, too, for definite, assignable reasons."*[70] Truth has nothing to do with faith; and faith does not dally with truth.

Now, let us revert to the problem emerging out of the ahistoricity of the Jesus of Gospel and the Christ event. Faced with irrefutable evidence regarding the implausibility of any objective basis of the Christ event, Biblical scholars and modern theologians proferred a theory that a historical person or an objective god was not necessary for their faith. This theory propounded by some of the great Christian minds regarding the nature of the Christian faith and its god is a complete reversal of the age old principle assertion of Christianity regarding the proven one-and-only true god who is offered as a concrete divine alternative to the infidel worshippers of false and non-existent gods. The Bible could never convincingly establish the worship of a 'one-and-only-god' on Israel. People continued to worship many deities and regarded the fanatical one-godism of the prophets as an example of their extreme monolatry. Micah tells us: "For all the peoples walk each in the name of its god, but we walk in the name YHWH our God for ever and ever".[71] Zachariah hopes that *Yahweh* of Israel would some day become poweful enough to overthrow other gods and become supreme: "And YHWH will become king over all the earth; on that day YHWH will be one and his name one".[72] God would become 'one-god' when the world would be conquered by the faithful in his name. One can be forgiven for seeing in these utterances the Millenarian visions of a traumatised and oppressed nation offering collective consolation to itself in the sovereign future of their chosen deity. But as of now, the cruel fact stared Israel in face that Yahweh was not one and his name was also not one. But Zachariah is ready to wait, and he assures the faithful that *Yahweh* would become one and 'his name will be one' in future when Israel under the leadership of its god would unite all nations and rule over them. People may worship many gods, but they do not worship the true 'one-god' unless they worship him as *Yahweh*.

The god of the prophets of the Old Testament was accepted by the Christians to be the god of their new religion; although many scholars believe that the god of Pauline Christianity is not the god of Bible. The New Testament god is completely different from the old *Yahweh*—morphologically, ideologically and functionally. Apart from a shared theological motive, there is no commonality between *Yahweh* and the god of Christianity. The latter was the product of nearly four hundred years of ecclesiastical and academic effort of the religious leadership of Christianity. Christians took the Jewish prototype of the divine, incorporated some Essenic ideas into it, adopted the Hellenic gloss of neo-Platonism as its ontology, and finally dipped the persona into the Greek mystery religions to create a wholly new Christian god. Keith Ward has this to say: "In thus incorporating other faiths, the god of Abraham and Moses became the one God"...[73] He further clarified that this one god was only a logical ruse, or a "central concept" used to unify the myriad ideas of revelation around it: "This revelation of the gods becomes monotheistic when one sees God as the source of all revelatory beings. That is, one sees them as having one unitary source..."[74] God is unitary or one because a believer sees him to be such; *Yahweh* is one, Father is one, *Allāh* is one because a believer 'sees' them as a unifying principle, a central concept or a rallying focus for all revelatory experiences. God as a person has imperceptibly become god as a theoretical source for a religious assertion and a concept to define religious ideas.

Prof. Keith Ward further elaborates his point on the theme of 'one-god' and says: "Monotheism is then basically the denial that the world has many unrelated grounds, the assertion that there is unity of values known under many different aspects."[75] One god is therefore the assertion of certain convictions regarding the gradually evolving subjective apprehension of something that is emperically undefinable, because... "The notion of a holy, good and perfect God develops by reflection upon disclosure of transcendence in moral and artistic experience; and it functions to specify appropriate attitudes in the believer towards this experience."[76] Men postulate god as some principle or power that explains the coherent and intelligent patterns of the world. God is not a case out there to be uniformly perceived by all persons in the same manner, he is a result of cognitive processes that Wittgenstein described as 'seeing as', and John Hick termed as 'experiencing-as' when he said... "all human experience is 'experiencing—as'."[77] God, like many things in life, is a subject of hermeneutics and a matter of cognitive choices. Wittgenstein, while defining the nature of religious language, said: "Don't think, but look." What we see in him is important for the character of God. Perhaps this cognitive preference or 'seeing-as' would explain why the three monotheistic Judaic religions, while claiming to share the same god, do not agree on what it means to be monotheistic.

The emphasis of the last one hundred years of European philosophy, theology and anthropology has shifted decisively towards a subjective interpretation of religion and god. European philosophy, anthropology and theology have generally worked in concert and on the question of defending and explaining Christian faith the three disciplines have regularly exchanged notes. While..."some schools of European anthropology did betray theological intent...",[78] Western philosophy and religion came so close to one another that philosophy became an elaborate apologetic of Christianity and ... "an ultimate separation of the two—at least as far as the mainstream European philosophy is concerned is impossible."[79] We know that the great Hegel believed that philosophy at its best should culminate in an apologetic for Christian theism. We should not be surprised to see modern philosophy and theology explaining god in psychological and linguistic terms. La Barre underscores the multiplicity of explanations of god and ascribes them to, what he calls, the peculiarity of the "grammatical behaviour" of god about whose locus men know nothing but base their religious doctrine on what ultimately are hypotheses: ""When we try to define God there is very little consensus on the proper connotations and denotations of the word".[80] To say that all religions have the same message and that 'god' means the same irrespective of whosoever utters the word is to concede that one has forsaken intellectual integrity in order to appear pleasant. To quote La Barre:... "Every face that looks into God's sees nothing but its own truth."[81]

A distinct change in the tone of Christian theology and European philosophy occurred around the late nineteenth century. This change was occasioned by two historical factors: growth of the physical sciences and Europe's encounter with various non-European and non-Christian cultures through the expansion of European colonial interest. Copernicus, Kepler, Galileo, Newton and Descartes gave birth to new physics and practically debunked most Biblical theories of cosmogony and cosmology. Many theories, earlier predicated on a god, were found to be self-existent and regulated by an impersonal physical law. The whole cosmos was a gigantic machine that moved under its own laws, and did not need a meddlesome personal god to direct its course. Darwin gave a body blow to the Biblical notion of man's creation and pushed the temporal frontier of creation to a much older antiquity than about 6000 years postulated by the Bible. Scriptural assertions looked complete hocus-pocus in light of man's intellectual discovery and most of the commands of god seemed highly jejune and nonsensical. The creator, regulator and a lordly god was facing serious threat from his own creation. Europe's colonial expansion brought her into the proximity of many new races and cultures. The sciences of sociology, anthropology, religious and linguistic studies were born. The opening up of the world also provided access to new schools of thought and philosophy.

The interpretive attitude of European scholarship was guided by their concern to fit the facts of other cultures in accordance with the tenets of Christian theology. It was accepted that man has apprehended the divine in an immense variety of ways. The philosophical underpinnings of religious belief have also varied from age to age and from culture to culture. It was soon discerned that in their special ways different human cultures have evolved satisfactory and workable theories of divinity that answer to their own specific socio-economic situation, and were perfect for their respective cultural milieux. Rather than accepting this natural diversity of human culture as a fact, European scholars started weaving theories to explain pagan cultures in terms suitable to the tenets of Christianity. It was a perspective in which man's religious outlook was shown as proceeding or 'evolving' from primitive stages of totemism, animism, manaism and polytheism towards an apotheosis finally achieved by monotheistic idea of a Christian god: "The whole edifice was crowned at the top with the figure of the monotheistic god".[82]

European Christianity took up the challenge of the post-reformation modern world in right earnest. One god as an objective outer reality that occasionally revealed itself in special situation was becoming untenable in view of the mounting evidence of many revelatory situations of god in various stages of human history. There was no way the uniqueness of god in its Christological manifestation could be proved and enforced in a world where the authority of the church did not extend to all corners; and when it had no power to enforce its theology on a vast portion of the globe. The merit of the religious perspectives of faiths other than the Judaic could not be ignored any more. As long as Christ's historical figure could be saved there was the hope of making a comeback. But when scholarship proved that the facts regarding Jesus Christ of the Gospel and the Church were historically not verifiable, there was panic all round. The monotheistic god was already sufficiently battered by becoming a concept, a unifying focus, or a subjective experience; losing the *fact* of Jesus Christ would have been a mortal blow to the whole edifice of Christianity. Late nineteenth and twentieth century philosophy and theology busied itself to defend from the danger of double—jeopardy to their faith. In the process a great theological circuit was completed: the tribal god of Abraham that was universalized as the one great monotheistic god of all history and all people again became tribalized as a deity understandable only in a particular 'religious tradition' or in a particular 'universe of discourse'. The edifice of the one and only god, besides whom none exist, sundered and god became the subject of revelatory discourse in a specific community of believers.

The principal proposition that emerged from modern scholarship suggested that it was impossible to find something like an objective 'one-god'. A student of religion meets different gods in the scriptures, in the creeds, and in the dogmas of the theologian. "To judge whether a proposition about God is true or false, we must know to what universe of discourse it belongs…"[83] because it is said that a bishop can only move diagonally. It was grudgingly accepted that scriptures of various religious denominations preached very different ideas of god which were completely independent of the question whether a general god existed or not. To ask happily whether god exists requires the reframing of the question by asking whether he exists according the Bible or the Quran. Depending on the perspective one is attached to, the answer could be: *Allāh* does exist but *Nārāyaṇ* does not. The second important principle related to the clarification that religious, language is a special kind of language and therefore religious propositions are valid only in a specific 'language game'. To the revered dogma that god was a singular person who objectively existed was given a completely new meaning through the explanation that he existed in a unique way. Paul Tillich wrote that... "It is atheistic to affirm the existence of God as it is to deny it," because the terms applied to God have a unique meaning depending on the rules of the language in which they occur—"God", therefore, "is not a univocal term"[84] So god is not only not a unitary person but not even a univocal word!

A small conservative and literalist resistance was mounted at the beginning of the twentieth century by people like Karl Baarth and Emil Brunner who were completely given to the eschatology of the Christian revelation and opposed all kinds of natural theology. This fideist scholarship was more popular among orthodox religious opinion, especially the organized Churches. Emil Brunner (1889-1966) believed that revelation is a proof of the living history of god and reached its unrepeated absoluteness in the personality of Jesus of Nazreth who was the Christ. Karl Baarth put no store on man's intelligence and believed that god could only be known through total surrender to Jesus Christ. There was neither subjective nor objective reality in god. When we speak of god we do not refer to anything given in history or human existence, because god was what Baarth calls truth in reality but still somehow fully revealed in Christ. The predominant trend of the modern age had, however, become non-literalist. Rudolf Otto believed that both rational and non-rational elements can be found in the tenets of religion and the real feeling of god emerges when intellectual concepts fail and man confronts a numinous feeling of the '*mysterium tremendum*'. Otto was aware of the tendency of certain religions to undertake a lopsided view of divine propositions and to believe that... "the essence of deity, and therefore the essence of religion, can be given completely in the rational attributions essential to the theistic conception of god and especially that of Christianity."[85] There was no way god could be made explicable in terms of the 'deity' of one religion and its credal principles.

Gradually the realisation sank that for theological scholarship ... "it is impossible to define its unique object: god."[86] Wilber Marshall Urban believes that in the god idea there is a great variety of divergent opinions. Prof. Anthur O. Lovejoy believes that the word 'God' is in the last degree ambiguous. The characterisation of god as being a 'person' has been seriously questioned by many scholars and Dean W.R Inge believed that ... "personality when attributed to god, is a symbol, and a very inadequate one."[87] Every symbol of God can only capture some aspects of the fullness of God's mystery, therefore any partisan soteriology was *ab initio* defunct: "It is a fundamental tenet of philosophical theology that god cannot be known by man in His inmost essence in all the fullness of His being."[88] These theories lead us to the standpoint which the pagans have always adopted vis-a-vis god, namely, that religious truth can be approached from many standpoints and that every religious doctrine is only inwardly justified. Schleiermacher generally endorsed the view that a religious conviction caould not be understood from the external justificatory viewpoint of other religions but from the internal perspective of that particular religion itself. Scheiermacher thought that Christianity was not a unique religion but only one particular historical type whose god was the Christian experience of god, and not some universally valid perception of god's station. The monotheistic certainty of an objective god nearly wilted.

The Christian religion has always boasted of its truthfulness and historicity as an evidence to the superior reality and veracity of its message. Modern theological scholarship came to the conclusion that insistence on historicity had become a serious handicap for it and without dissociating Christian religion from history one could not understand and save its principal message. Paul Tillich led this mood: "The identification of this myth with history was fatal, it is only by being completely severed from history that it now becomes capable of conveying its full freight of metaphysical truth."[89] By the twentieth century nearly every scholar believed that, "Christian history is irreparably ruined," so the only possible escape was to flatly deny the hoary history of Christianity as *ab initio* unimportant. Even Karl Baarth understood the problem and suggested study of Christianity without reference to history: "It is sentimental liberal self-deception to suppose that there is any direct way leading from Nature and History, from Art from Morals and from Science, from Religion itself, to God's impossible possibility".[90]

The problem caused by the rejection of religious history and therefore of the foundational elements of Christianity also engaged the attention of European philosophy. When modern scholarship discovered Christ event to be historically unverifiable—a conclusion that made Christianity untenable—scholars like Rudolf Bultmann suggested divesting Christianity of its defining mythology in order to concentrate only on its message—the *kerygma*. God as revealed in the words of the scripture, the faithful were told, was enough for faith and salvation, even if Jesus on the Mount was lost. The words enshrined in the scripture are enough to save a sinner. Rudolf Bultmann stressed the primacy of *kerygma* to break through and deal with the historical criticism of the Bible which had effectively destroyed its empirical basis. Not only Bultmann and Tillich, but most modern theologians concede that the quest for a historical Jesus has failed and it is not possible to verify the Christ event as a historical fact.[91] The only way out of this religious morass was to declare that Jesus Christ as a historical person was not necessary for Christianity! This theological stance was earlier propagated by Martin Heidegger who argued that the occurrence of a revelation in space and time was not necessary for faith; the important thing was the meaning it had for men. Heideggar emphasized a point that could have been an anathema only a few centuries ago: that the historical status of the resurrection was unimportant and the faithful should understand the urgent necessity of making a difference between Jesus of history and the Christ of faith.

There is a pervading sense of poignant sadness in the attitude and utterance of the modern theologian. They deny every fact on the basis of which their religion began and on which it was predicated for the last two thousand years, and still stress with conviction the final uniqueness and existential significance of the Christian message, as found in the preaching of the *kerygma*. Walter Kaufmann has picturesquely described this theological manoeuvre by saying that Paul Tillich wanted to have his Neitzsche and eat his bread at the communion too. Modern theology is of the view that the Christ of history and the attendant myths of Christianity are unnecessary for faith. Martin Heidegaar is said to have remarked that he was a theologian and not an archaeologist when someone asked him whether he believed in Christ. Once god as a 'person' was lost and Jesus Christ as a historical 'person' could not be located unerringly, Christian theology had a serious problem at hand. The only way to salvage some meaning, sense and stability from the wreckage caused by science and history to the edifice of the Christian religion was to fall back on the 'words' of the religious text. The burden of Rudolf Bultmann's theology lay in emphasising the primacy and importance of the words of the scripture when he said: "In the word of preaching and there alone we meet the risen lord."[92] The distinguished hermeneutician Paul Ricoeur proposed an interpretative method in line with Bultmann's suggestion when he talked about 'textuality' or the 'mode of being' of texts. Hermeneuticians led by Ricoeur proposed the theory that Jesus as Christ is not resurrected physically in history but in the *Kerygma* of Christianity which becomes the materiality of his living person, and the words of the scripture thereby become the body of Christ. It was suggested that a text becomes independent of an author's intention, and its meaning can speak anonymously. Therefore, the preachings of Christianity and the message of its scriptures are valid even if there is no evidence of Christ in history or a divinely revealed scripture because ... "the voice of a particular text need not be identical with the biographical person who is the author of the text."[93]

This was smart hermeneutical proposition and its implications were devastatingly clear: one could have a Christian religion without a personal god, an historical Jesus, the Cross, or even the resurrection, as long as one had the text of the scripture and a church to propagate it. Jesus can be resurrected in the *kerygma*; and the *kerygma,* in turn, as reflected in the words of scripture becomes the embodiment of Christ. All important phenomenologists and hermeneuticians—Heidegaar, Ricoeur, Gadamer, etc, have dwelt on the theme of historicity and contextuality with a distinct theological motive. God and Christ have left the world as objective sources of religious experience, therefore the words of the scripture and its preaching by the Church is the only basis of faith. Having come to this sobering conclusion they take a courageous leap and declare that Christ somehow lives in the words of the text. These theories were not offered as methodological palliative to the faithful; their claims were as eschatological as the previous dogmas. Not only does a text acquire a life and a tangible corporeality but it should be read and understood by according an antecedent credence to its myths. One was instructed to understand the text from the standpoint of a presupposition of faith, an euphemism used to introduce through the hermeneutical backdoor a dogma that was thrown out by historical and linguistic research. If Hans-Georg Gadamer advocates the importance of prejudices and biases as a person's openness to the world he is only according intellectual sanctity to religious and convictional prejudices. When Jacques Derrida talks of the need for a 'continuing conversation', he means the continued conversation regarding Christ through the words of the scriptural text. The withdrawal of Jesus Christ from history is not seen as a deterrent.

These are surprising assertions from the adherents of a faith that believed in a 'god—in—history' as the beginning and ever defining principle of their religion. Truthfulness, history, objectivity have all become unimportant but Christianity is still said to survive, even theologically. The faithful have nothing tangible left but even on such tenuous grounds Wittgenstein exhorts men to follow the Christian dogma; "Go on, believe! It does not harm." [94] Philosophers could take such a radical stand because they were reconciling themselves to a theoretical position that it was possible to look at reality only from a certain culturally given perspective. Perspectives generate separate systems of concepts, languages, beliefs and practices. Ingolf U. Dalferth explains this concept to underline the important idea that religious propositions can have any meaning only in the world of discourse in which they are uttered; no two perspectives can be juxtaposed in evaluative proximity as there does not exist a 'master-perspective' to begin with: "Accordingly religious perspectives and the whole way of life and network of beliefs which go with them cannot be justified by external criteria."[95]

It is now generally agreed that religious propositions or convictions can have any meaning only in the language which people use in a particular context to express their convictions. These convictions cannot have any universal appeal and are completely specific to the group or community that uses them. James Wm. McClendon Jr.et al. describe this phenomenon in the following words: "Religious convictions, like others, are expressed fully only in the full range of actions of the person or community that is convinced by them."[96] All religious propositions regarding god and cultic practices, therefore, can have meaning and validity only in the idiom of a particular community and does not have any universal meaning. To say something about god is to use language in a particular way, satisfying a very specific need of a convictional community. Religious propositions do not talk about an objective god; the propositions about god can have meaning only in a specific context. R.B. Braithwaite believed that a typical religious utterance does not make claims about or describe the world independent of the utterer. Their meaning does not depend on verifying claims or descriptions. Braithwaite has suggested that in order to understand a proposition we must look at the intention and lifestyle of the person who uses that proposition. A particular religious claim cannot be asserted by anyone as true or false, because religious claims cannot be used in an indicative way. Willem F. Zuurdeeg thought that the use of convictional or religious language in an indicative way is incorrect. To understand a religious utterance we must learn what the utterance means to the community that uses it by seeking a clarification from that community. God is language and community specific. "The concept of god," wrote John Macquarrie, "is an interpretive concept, meant to give us a way of understanding and relating to reality as a whole."[97]

Religious beliefs and propositions are rational or irrational, true or false depending on the actual internal religious practices of the community; there is no objective norm to judge them as true or false. "Religious believers," said D.Z. Phillips, "when asked why they believe in god, may reply in a variety of ways...The answers come from within religion, they presuppose the framework of Faith, and therefore cannot be treated as evidence for religious belief."[98] A religious proposition, otherwise than in a ritual situation, is neither true nor false, it is just meaningless. Rudolf Carnap held the view that, "The definitions that are given for god on closer inspection reveal themselves to be pseudo-definitions; they lead either to logically impermissible word–combinations...or to other metaphysical words—e.g., *Ungrund*, the Absolute, the Unconditional, the Autonomous, the independent, etc."[99] A similar view was also held by Wittgenstein who believed that religious propositions were not false but only nonsensical, and proposed that... "What one cannot speak about, one must pass over in silence."[100]

Religious views, then, are some sort of an interpretive outlook that men place upon facts. Religious language is limited to its perspectival use and primarily tells us what kind of a conception of god and truth we are committed to. But the use of religious language does not and should not tell us that a proposition becomes universally applicable because a believer backs it with his personal conviction. Richard M. Hare described adherence to religious propositions and beliefs as holding of *'bliks'*—convictions people live with but which are not necessarily based on any empirical or verifiable facts. They can be based on certain assumed principles which govern the attitude of the believer towards an idea or a fact of life. Rudolf Carnap was of the view that many religious words do not mean anything except showing the psychological connection a speaker makes between certain images and feelings with those words. He lists some words that are used for religious discourse but do not have empirical indicators and survive only on psychological associations. As example of such non-indicative religious words, he cites words such as, the Absolute, Idea, Infinite and of course, GOD—and calls them as '*babigs*' or '*google*'. Previous philosophers denied god an ontology but in the hands of a logical positivist we have a god who does not even have the sanctity of etymology. Theological utterances die in a process of falsification through a multiplicity of subsequent qualifications so much so that statements about god become non-verifiable, vacuous, hedged and hemmed. When it is said that only "one god exists" someone is uttering a statement which is, "literally without meaning, literally nonsensical, it holds no more cognitive significance than 'Creech creech'."[101] That's a very long way the monotheistic 'one-and-only-god' has travelled in its European journey: from 'I am the only god' to 'Creech creech'!

Nothing expresses the main drift of this chapter more eloquently than an incident reported by Russel Nieli in his book on Wittgenstein regarding the comment a friend of Martin Bauber made to the latter regarding god, and I propose to narrate it in full. This is how it goes: "How can you bring yourself to say 'god' time after time? How can you expect that your reader will take the word in the sense in which you wish it to be taken? What you mean by the name of god is something above all human grasp and comprehension, but in speaking about it you have lowered it to human conceptualization. What word of human speech is so misused, so defiled, so desecrated as this! All this innocent blood that has been shed for it has robbed it of its radiance. All the injustice that it has been used to cover has effaced its features. When I hear the highest called 'God', it sometimes almost seems blasphemous."[102]

To You Your God—To Me Mine

The statement to the effect that 'there is no god but Jesus Christ or Allah' and he is the one and the only god that man should worship, can have meaning and relevance only for the adherents of those Judaic religions that hold such beliefs. To claim that this 'one-god' should also become the god of all humanity is to elevate linguistic meaninglessness to metaphysical necessity. God is not 'one' in the Judeo-Christo-Islamic sense and he is also not the 'only one'. The theological hollowness of this claim is apparent from the perusal of the career of the same 'one-god' who appears on the pages of the Bible, the New Testament and the Quran. He is neither the same god genetically nor performatively. He grows in different communities at different places under very different childhood names in the company of other divine siblings till a prophet comes along and declares him to be the one-and-only-god. Look at the origins and history of *El, Yahweh,* and *Hubal* they all originate in very different circumstances and follow radically different biographical paths, but at some point in their career they are proclaimed to be the one and only god in an ever emerging definition of oneness. But for every succeeding view of the 'one—and—only—god' the previous avatar of the same god was false and blasphemous. The devotees of the one-god-as-Christ have always roundly desecrated everything that the one-god-as-*Yahweh* has stood for, and they in turn have been vehmently denounced as hypocrites in the words of the one-god-as-*Allāh.* It is a very complex system and most of it has to be accepted on faith without recourse to the office of reason.

A normal student of religion should be forgiven if he is baffled by the character of the 'one-god' of monotheism in his manifestation in the three faiths of Judaism, Christianity and Islam. It has been the considered view of the chronologically later religions that the message of the 'one-god' has been falsified and perverted by the prophets of the earlier religions. Prophets of monotheism accuse one another of falsifying the message of the 'one-god'; and if one goes by the words of these venerable prophets nothing would be left of god's revelation because each version cancels out the other two. In view of the theological recrimination it is impossible to tell which of the three messages is the true version of god's will, unless one is ready to lay one's blind and faithful wager on one tradition and hope for the best. Faith is the only way one can believe in the one-god. Truth of the monotheistic god actualizes when a person accepts a particular version on faith. In a monotheistic discourse god is said to become 'one' because god can be known only by one name in one particular way. He is said to be unitary because in him are unified all aspects of reality and he is seen as terminally encompassing all spiritual experience of a group of believers .

A focal point as god is selected and then every idea about man and this world, about morality and ethics and about secular life are projected *post facto* on that focal point; interpretable also as emerging from the same focal point. Monotheism recounts the presence and historical activities of god in personal terms. The world of scholarship now tells us that materially and factually the god of the monotheists is no more a personal or tangible existence than the gods of a polytheist. He is not to be found in any spatio-temporal grid but in the perceptions of men as the source of their supreme moral life; he is just an idea that men create to provide sacred meaning to unexplainable historical events and to posit an extra-human sanction for their ethical behaviour. Sacredness is not *a priori* inherent in an object of contemplation; sacredness is conferred on an object or a person by a group of believers. The prototype object used by them may or may not be historically verifiable, and we had the occasion to see that facts of history in their normal sense have nothing to do with the god of monotheism. For monotheism, history begins when they declare an event to be paradigmatic and ends when that event reaches its soteriological finale. Time begins at the moment of creation by their god and continues linearly. History constitutes only of the peoples and those events that occur within the creative 'future-cone', to borrow a phrase from Stephen Hawking, of god's will. Every event, every activity and all men outside that cone do not exist as subjects of history.

The past is not unique or holy in itself but is made so through a systematic reflection on certain events by a group of people who convince themselves and others that a particular event happened because god wanted it to happen. Historical veracity of a data is not necessary to prove any religious claim and Rudolf Bultmann was right in his assertion that inspite of the absence of corroborative historical facts about Jesus' life and personality, Jesus is The God because the Christian Church conceived him to be likewise. Jesus as a historical person, according to Bultmann, belonged to the history of Judaism; Christianity begins by treating the event of Jesus' death—the 'Christ event'—as paradigmatic of divine will. Christian sources very rarely show any interest in Jesus' life and personality. Jesus as a person and his original teachings had value insofar as they provided some basis for the subsequent assertions of the *kerygma* of the nascent church. Schuyler Brown explains the question of religious historicity in a novel manner: "Christianity is a 'historical' religion, that is, a faith whose fundamental credal affirmations are expressed in the past tense".[1] History stands defined as a function of grammatical construction in which physical occurrence of events are irrelevant for faith and salvation because faith is not contingent on any outside support. Brown believes that, for many Christians, the historical significance of any assertion or statement does not rest in an actual event but in the presupposition placed on that supposed event by a later theological doctrine. We are told that Christianity consists of some 'historical affirmations', some 'faith affirmations' and some that occupy an intermediate position.

It would be worth our while to pursue the argument of Schuyler Brown regarding historicity, objectivity and assertions of faith. He says: "The statement that Jesus' death brought about a change in the relationship between humankind and god, consisting in god's forgiveness of our sins, is clearly a faith statement not susceptible to objective verification...Since the passive construction, 'Christ has been raised', implies god as the agent, this is clearly a faith statement. There is no passage in the New Testament which names any witness to the actual resurrection of Jesus...The fact that all these witnesses were Christians, who came to believe in Jesus' messiahship precisely through his appearance to them, makes the content of this affirmation a faith experience, about which the historian can only speculate... A judgement on this matter is likely to depend more on the historians philosophical and religious convictions than on his competence as a historian...Faith affirmations and historical affirmations also differ in their degree of certitude. Given the nature of his evidence, there is little that the historian of Christian origins can affirm with anything more than some degree of probability. The numinous certainty of faith must come from some other source."[2] History has never been important for the establishment of the monotheistic truth: it becomes universal only on the basis of the presuppositions of a powerful church, enforced through subservient secular authorities.

Christian scholars emphasise the concerns of the Christian community and not the veracity of a particular event or occurrence in the life of Jesus as the determinative factor. Jesus became Christ because Stephen, Peter, Paul and Timothy characterised him as such and not because there were any extraordinary and historically verifiable data available for such attestation. It is not Jesus who is important as a person but the traditions of the Christian communities. Resurrection of Jesus is not a data which can be examined by any person; it is available only to persons who already believe on faith that Jesus was Christ because he was raised from the death by god. An event becomes history because a small group of people *ex post facto* decide to put a particular meaning on that event on the basis primarily of equivocal faith statements. Monotheism strives to live dangerously on the boundary of history and myth, while pretending in its public domain to be the inheritors of indisputable historical truth about god, even in face of overwhelming evidence to the contrary. Joseph M. Kitagawa says: "However, one must remember the admonition of Tor Andrae that the origin of religion is not a historical question; ultimately it is a metaphysical one."[3] Kitagawa supports the thesis of Sir Hamilton A. R. Gibb that any religion "is an autonomous expression of religious thought and experience, which must be viewed in and through itself and its own principles and standards."[4]

An important way of looking at religion, according to the current theories, would be to study it as a metaphysical hermeneutics applied on less than indisputable historical occurrences. Religion can also be studied after being severed from its historical limitations as a postulate in itself. Religion can be understood only within the life of the religious community when its assertions are evaluated in the light of the 'internal consistency' of the community of faithfuls. This fact has also been asserted by Wilfred Cantwell Smith who wrote: "For I would proffer this as my second proposition: That no statement about a religion is valid unless it can be acknowledged by that religion's believers."[5] It would not be a correct method of studying religions if one proceeded from the motive of confirming the validity of one's own faith in all other systems of spirituality. It would be equally improper to judge the merits of an alien religious system from the standpoint of the religious postulates of one's own faith. Unfortunately, monotheistic religions have not abandoned the claims of exclusiveness and singular validity of their divine message and they tend to see all other spiritual experience of man as base and inchoate. In view of the modern philosophical opinion, according primacy to one divine revelation is not possible and modern theoreticians propose to look at various insights into the reality of god as complementary to each other. Friederich Schleiermacher was among the few Christian scholars who were honest enough to concede that all religious experiences were aspects of one single reality: "The deeper one progresses in religion, the more the whole religious world appears as an indivisible whole".[6]

Inspite of the stern exclusiveness of the official creed of various monotheistic religions, there have emerged voices within their bosom that realized the untenability of the claims of finality or infallibility of the official dogma. Justin, Origen, Nicolas of Cusa in the Christian tradition; Al-Hallaj and Ibn-Arabi in the Islamic tradition have been among the important voices that solicited respect for all songs sung by man's soul in its moments of epiphany. That they were given harsh raps on their knuckles by the orthodox religious establishment makes their effort all the more poignant. Religious pluralism was strongly curbed in the monotheistic religions and the initial flush of eclecticism remained subdued for many centuries. In Christianity, however, these voices have witnessed a recrudescence in the nineteenth century as a result of the pressing evidence coming from those religions and philosophical systems with which Europe came into contact. It became increasingly difficult for a serious, non-partisan philosopher or historian to avoid the insight provided by various polytheistic and pagan religions. The handling of data was different according to the predilection of the analyst, but the realization that the citadel of monotheism has been breached was unmistakable. "The great majority of arguments with which Christian apologetics thought to substantiate the falsity and inferiority of Eastern religions have been rendered untenable by scientific inquiry into the direct sources of these religions."[7]

Scholarly opinion all over the world has now accepted the position that chasing a well defined and universally acceptable notion of god is a will-o'-the-wisp. Validity of a religious proposition is limited to the group which shares the same theological tradition as the utterers and assents, *a priori*, to the fundamental premises of such propositions. W.M. Urban has rightly said: "It is impossible to evaluate religion without understanding it and it is impossible to understand it without participating, in some form and in some degree, in the life of religion."[8] All religious propositions about god are based on the specific experiential background of the utterer and does not have any meaning outside that experiential background. The assertion that God led Israel out of Egypt would mean nothing outside the group of Judaic faiths, especially Judaism. A Hindu would not find this assertion of any lasting importance. He would be bemused if told that this statement is the proof of god's selection of Israel as his chosen people. What is said about god in monotheistic religions is principally the articulation of an inherited cultic pedagogy which derives its strength and justification from the faithful adherence to the letters of a revelation. All such utterances become meaningful and valid at the precise moment at which a person agrees to believe in them. God acts and acquires reality in the belief of a believer: he is what the follower says he is. Jesus is Christ because Christian Community says it is so; there was nothing in Jesus' life and message to confirm this. The 'one-god' does not exist outside the credal proclamations and the ambit of the scriptures of a monotheistic religion.

In the same religious tradition, the god of the philosopher was conceived differently from the god experienced by the orthodox theologian and preached from the pulpit. Some of the greatest Christian theologians like Augustine and Tertullian were against the idea of theology becoming philosophical. They believed that explanation of god in terms of the 'cosmic order' or 'the ultimate principal' would militate against the Christian idea of god. The tension between philosophical rationality and dogmatic belief has been a constant theme of the monotheistic religions, and an objectively valid basis of religious belief about god has never been accepted by them, even in principle. What is left after these erosions is only the god of faith, and such a god cannot claim any universal suzerainty in a world which has become skeptical of dogmas of all kind. Ingolf U.Dalferth maintains that Christian claims about god were, even in best of times, never received without offence by philosophical minds: "In short, Christian theology was not a philosophical theology and never managed to become philosophically a fully respectable discipline."[9] The chief reason for this problem related to the 'Christological' orientation of Christian theology. Dalferth believes that the problems of Christianity has emerged from the primacy accorded to revelation and faith in comparison to direct religious experience and metaphysics.

Modern man seems ready to accept the universal appeal of an idea but not its absolutist claim. It is possible to have many universal perspectives about god and still not accord privileged status to any one of them. In the current era, it is impossible to intellectually defend the idea of an exclusive revelation. Christianity and Islam are treated by philosophers as one among many religions of the world. Schleiermacher, whose intellectual honesty transcended the boundaries of Christian dogma, was an important protagonist of the idea that accorded sanctity and respect to the piety found in other spiritual traditions: "If you want to compare religion with religion as the eternally progressing work of the world spirit, you must give up the vain and futile wish that there ought to be only one; your antipathy against the variety of religions must be laid aside, and with as much impartiality as possible you must join all those which have developed from the eternally abundant bosom of the Universe through the changing forms and progressive traditions of man."[10] Schleiermacher was raising a new and novel theological voice in a world of discourse that was very wary of religious pluralism. Friedrich Heiler records the fact that most Christian theologians have always been fearful of 'relativism', and then proceeds to answer their fear by saying, "I have a way of answering such theologians that the greatest of all relativists is God himself, the Absolute, for he is fulness in itself and his fulness is revealed in the immeasurable diversity of nature and spiritual life."[11] *Christ* would, then, only be the Christian experience of god as *Allah* would be of Islam. And all would be well with the world—perhaps.

Modern philosophers and historians of religion now agree that since there are no *a priori* criteria to judge the merit of an idea, an evaluator must be careful to distinguish between facts and the hermeneutical interpretations put by a tradition on those facts. R. Rorty believes that interpretation of a fact or an idea can have any truth value only as a matter of convenience, taste or convention. The truth value of a fact would depend on the convention that a philosophical or theological system constructs and such construction of convention may differ from culture to culture. These conventions would depend on the importance a particular culture assigns to certain metaphysical premises. Valuation would also be determinable by the moral importance societies accord to certain spiritual truths.

The belief of a particular culture cannot be judged from the hermeneutical perspective of a different culture. In order to understand an assertion about god one would require acquaintance with the interpretative principles used in a particular religious tradition. R.G Collingwood has suggested that all our knowledge is relative to the questions we ask and we cannot ask cultural—neutral questions and cannot give neutral and 'universal' answers. Every question asked and every answer given proceed from many assuptions which are presupposed to be true. Collingwood believed, therefore, that the task of metaphysics is to study these presuppositions. To answer the question, 'what is meant by one god' would require the knowledge of who is asking the question; otherwise our answer would not be intelligible. God serves as an interpretative category used to explain our view of reality. This category is invariably culture—specific and exists not a *priori*, but only in its role as explanatory of certain special feelings of joy, awe, terror, holiness, etc.

Keith Ward is in agreement with the approach that relates the description of god to its cultural environment: "But it is nevertheless a highly important fact that talk about God does not usually take place in a cultural vacuum. It is bound up with the cultic practices of a particular religious community, and it finds there a constant reference point."[12] Understanding a community's belief in god will depend also on understanding the rites and traditions of the community. Various doctrinal and credal assertions of a religion emerge as a construct of specific socio-pyschological preferences. To offer a new and alien idea of god as an advanced divine alternative to the existing god of a person is therefore theologically meaningless. A person would not know the meaning and value of that god unless he first becomes a member of the brotherhood. The eschatology in the system of a religious belief has no value for a person who does not subscribe to it. A person becomes a sinner in need of redemption the moment he accepts becoming a part of the Christian community; as a pagan he is a proud and inseparable unit of this divine world and notions of the Biblical fall and Christian redemption do not bother and affect him. The danger of adopting a monotheistic theology lies in the fact that a man becomes heir to a sinful history retrospectively and therefore requires the justification of an ersatz saviour. As an unconverted pagan man is not a congenital sinner, he has not been thrown out of Eden by a jealous and malevolent god and therefore does not require redemption of the monotheistic kind. Man does err but his errors are all of his own making and he is required to face them as a *man* and work to free himself from their effects. A man becomes a *homo justificandus* only after he places himself *corum deo* of a saviour god of some monotheistic faith.[13] In other words: "At any rate it was necessary, if you were to become a Christian, to accept the Jewish theology of history, and every Christian must become a kind of spiritual Jew before he could grasp the place of Christ in God's unfolding plan for mankind... To appreciate the finality of the New Dispensation you must first accept, and see yourself as having in some way been involved in the Old."[14] If you don't fall in his divine trap the monotheistic god is non-existent and powerless; bow before him and he will trample you.

The concrete 'personality' of which god was proud, slowly became a liability for him and his followers, so much so that scholarly attempts were undertaken to deny that god could be a personal god. Keith Ward has suggested that the Judaic god is not a person but an all inclusive intentional object that serves as a "focal or controlling image" to unify the idea of transcendence as an absolute moral demand. This line of argument originated principally in Kant and was later used in varying degrees by most theologians. It is for such reasons that theological exegetists call their religions 'ethical monotheism' or 'moral monotheism'. But we hit a serious contradiction in the concept of god wherein he is just a unifying or 'focal image' of transcendence but nonetheless, declared as the source of absolute moral command. An idea, or an image, or an interpretative category cannot become the source of a moral command whether absolute or contingent. Moreover, man's sense of moral duty does not necessarily derive from commands of a god, and many cultures have developed ethical systems without recourse to a theological prop. Adherence to a life of non-violence does not become lesser in moral value because a man adopts it as an attitude inherited from his cultural tradition, and not as a command issued from some god. Philosophers have opined that men generally use theological 'ought sentences' for others when they themselves are not in a position to issue orders. Morality, said to derive from a divine source, is mostly the collective wish of an individual or a society mythologized as the will of god. P.H. Nowell-Smith strikes a note of caution: "It is for this reason also that it is a mistake to try to define moral 'ought' in terms of god's command or 'god's will'."[15] On the other hand it can also be argued that a command issued by an authority, even god, is no reason to obey it. Nowell-Smith has tried to probe why some religious traditions locate the source of ethics in their god, and his study suggests that this attitude is the product of a practice that projects on god those acts that such traditions in any case already want to do: "But this is because they have a general pro-attitude to doing whatever God commands."[16]

Peter Geach has made a similar assessment of the monotheistic thesis of absolute morality and he believes that the concept of absolute morality is just a ruse to secure blind obedience to various irrational demands. G. Van der Leeuw also comes to roughly the same conclusion and says: "Nevertheless *tabu* and categorical imperative have in common the character of complete irrationality as well as absoluteness. "Thou shalt"—what one should do is a secondary issue; why one should do it is not a question at all."[17] It is perhaps in view of the irrationality of such extra-human moral demands that Peter Geach believes that the much vaunted moral motivations of religious men are only the fear of the consequences of disobedience. Walter Kaufmann has characterised prudence as an important Christian virtue in view of the fact that Christian morality is primarily prudential and other worldly—'*Lohnmoral*'—so much so that the sermon on the Mount is seen by him as constructed around the theme of "enlightened selfishness."[18] This may perhaps be the reason why monotheistic religions not only locate the source of morality in the commands of god but also establish harsh secular institutions to punish the disobedience of those commands. Strangely enough, god cannot enforce commands that he so frequently keeps issuing and needs the help of the arms of faithful kings, the courts of inquisition and pious clergymen to get his will implemented. Mankind has been observed to disregard god's unreasonable commandments if not constantly forced to obey: "And if this were not so, the mere fact that god commands something is no more a reason for doing it than the fact that a cricket coach tell you to do something... the fact that you ought to do it cannot be identified with nor is it entailed by the fact that god has commanded it." [19] Scholars have pointed out that G.E. Moore in his 'Principia Ethica' believed that when Emmanuel Kant said something ought to be done he made it sound as if that was commanded.

The insistence of Judaic religions on moral demands of god should be seen in the light of the nature of their god. Had god been a person enjoying some lawful authority the question of obedience or disobedience may have had some ethical implication. Nothing could still have had prevented a person from not obeying an offensive command. But when 'god' himself becomes just a cultural idea, a linguistic convention, an 'underlying unity', an interpretative focus used to bind various aspects of moral behaviour in a coherent whole, the authority for such moral demands becomes even more questionable. To assert, as Keith Ward suggests monotheistic religions do, that ... "an unlimited and unitary moral demand upon individuals ...originating in one tradition of encounter with god, becomes universally incumbent upon all humanity..."[20] is to autocratically claim unlawful extension of ecumenical jurisdiction over men who are not concerned with how a monotheistic faith encounters its god, and may be having extremely different ideas of ethics and morality. That Judaic religions still, albeit hesitatingly, claim some sort of a universal application for their objective morality, makes such posturing highly unethical and it would be prudent to keep the inherent danger in mind: "It is no accident that religious persecutions are the monopoly of objective theorists."[21] Universalist theories of objective morality have stopped attracting subscribers from the field of serious philosophy and philosophers like R.M. Hare consider it nearly impossible to have any universal moral command: "It is, in fact, almost impossible to frame a proper universal in the imperative mood...," because... "imperatives do not state anything, they only express wishes."[22]

But wishes can only be subjective and situational; and religious wishes *a fortiori* cannot have any meaning beyond the convictional consensus of a particular person or a group. If god is a product of the spiritual proclivities of a community of believers, without any objective and historical validity, and his moral commands are the phatic manifestation of the wishes of that community, then any effort at the universalisation of such commands can be seen as a counterpart theory for the secular ambitions of that community. In view of the fact that for a religious man, "'God' is a key word, an irreducible posit, an ultimate of explanation expressive of the kind of commitment he professes...",[23] every action of a believer taken in the name of his god would only be a product of his own volition for which he uses god as an explanation. In the light of the modern critical research and philosophical opinion, the god we encounter in the Judaic faiths does not posses any historical, objective, or personal characteristics and comes to life only in the faithful utterances of a believer. But religious utterances are not empirical assertions or logically verifiable statements; they derive their meaning only from the manner of their use as expressive of the intention of the asserter. It follows from this premise that the justification of a religious utterance is in the belief of the utterer, and the contentment of the user serves as an indicator of the usefulness of an utterance. Whether, a religious assertion like, 'god exists' or 'Jesus is god's son' has any meaning will depend upon the attitude of the person who made these assertions. A.J. Ayer maintains that such religious statements are 'cognitively empty' because there is no way of verifying them. A statement can have literal meaning only if it is analytically or empirically verifiable. God is neither true nor false: he just *is*. The assertions of 'one-god', then, would appear to be a chimera split into three hostile and contradictory linguistic conventions which their followers try to concretise through a belaboured theology.

But let us assume the 'one-god' to be an objectively verifiable and empirically demonstrable person. In that case he must have a recognizable character and a consistency of behaviour that can be categorised as his personality. For a person who acts in history and directs every activity of human beings, behavioural consistency is a *sine qua non* given the fact that on his commands men undertake errands some of which involves material and physical degradation of other societies. The god that we encounter in the Judaic religions seems to score poorly on account of psychological and volitional consistency. He does not generally initiate a process and we see his words and deeds appropriating every event to his divine will after the event comes to pass. Most of the time he is seen to provide retrospective sanction to the moral choice of his communicants or forecasting as preordained what the devotee has already decided to do. If there is any existential necessity in his character it is marginal and his contingency is determined not by his own free will but by the existential choices of the community he has chosen as his own. In choosing a people for fulfilment of his will he forfeits his own freedom and becomes an accomplice to group atavism. If we trust his words and believe his actions to be purely his own then we cannot escape noticing a deep ethical malady that afflicts his character. God has not spoken in one voice in his encounter with man. If a degenerate pagan considers joining the monotheistic god's religion he has a serious problem at hand; the pagan has to choose between the three religions that, severally, are said to embody the exclusive and unrepeatably unique revelation of god. Where does he go? How does he choose between three unique revelations of the only 'one—god'? Apparently, the pagan's choice would depend on the market presence of the theology that happens to be strong in his territory and the pursuasive skills of its executives. But the fact remains that the pagan would get only a specific brand and not some original generic formulation. If Judaism, Christianity and Islam are the three words of the one-and-only god then, theoretically, a believer in god should believe in all three monotheistic versions with impartial devotion; but the moment a believer takes this most logical stand he degenerates into polytheism. Tertullian was right: you can believe in the exclusive idea of 'one-god' only if you can resolve and sublimate theological absurdities.

The implication of god's will point to the fact that although he himself is one, he has at least three authentic and authorised versions of himself. This is a complex theological burden that Judaic religions carry congenitally with them within their shared religious space. Over the centuries they have discharged this burden with bitterness and acrimony. 'One-god' is the cultural obsession of the Judaic religions and can be understood only within the limited convictional world mapped by them; beyond its cognitive boundaries he does not make any sense unless accompanied by peremptory non-theological compulsions. But once the possibility of god revealing himself in manifold ways in diverse historical situations is accepted—an easy conclusion drawn from the three revelations of the 'one-god'—it is impossible to assign theological primacy, much less finality, to a particular manifestation and say that the revelatory capacity of god reaches its acme and stops at that particular revelation. If god has revealed himself in such diverse ways to the Jews and the Arabs, he had most certainly revealed himself in other pagan and polytheistic cultures; and he would continue his revelation as long as a human being chooses to lift his mind and open his heart to him.

The possibility of multiple manifestation, based on the differences in the revelatory experience of men and also on their capacity of apprehension, rules out the assignation of pre-eminence to a particular manifestation of god. If god's character is conditioned retrospectively by the choices of a community of believers then the reality of god can only be specific to the observational standpoint of all such convictional communities. There cannot be a privileged or *a priori* standpoint. If there is only one god in the world, then, whether he is called *Rāma* or Christ or *Allāh* would depend on the spiritual perception and linguistic practices of a culture. Various names can just be various modes of apprehension rather than enumerations of god. The validity of a particular representational symbol cannot be judged by a pre-set theological standard. If the tribal God of Abraham can become, in the hands of Moses, the jealous national god of Israel and—via Second Isiah—the god of Egypt and Assyria, and god of all humanity according to St. Paul and Prophet Mohammad, then logically this god of all humanity stands proclaimed as *Rāma, Kṛṣṇa* and *Śiva*. Prophet Muhammad had declared that god had revealed himself to humanity through very many prophets in all cultural groups and nations prior to his own time. The Veda, Purāṇa, Upniṣadas and the vision of some of the great saints of India would then undoubtedly and undeniably be the inspired glimpse of the nature of divine reality. The claim of abrogation of the past theophanies are not attested by the internal evidence of the sacred books of the non-Semitic civilizations. We do not find in them god declaring this or that vision as abrogated or superseded till we reach the relatively localised, and, by volume smaller, epiphanies of the Judaic faiths. The insistence of Judaic religions on god's claim of finality for a chronologically later revelation at the cost of all previous revelations does not synchronise with god's nature as revealed during the millenia that man has known him. The supreme god has manifested himself as *Śri Rāma* or *Śri Kṛṣṇa*. To deny such revelations is to deny god's own nature on the one hand and to claim on the other that a particular man in history has finally understood the unfathomable mind and method of god.

All names of god are either an epithet for his power and function or names of popular deities elevated to the status of divine authority subsequently by a community of believers under the pressure of certain historical circumstances. Names are used to denote the presence of god in a particular experience. These names are symbols, spun out of the cultural life of a people based on their own very real encounter with god. God is concretised in the world of worship through the assignation of a name and a character. 'God' when measured in a vision and concretised for worship by the use of a name and form becomes a deity or a *devatā*. A moral life should endow virtuosity on all human beings. Whether they worship one particular deity or another should be immaterial. A pious Hindu whose life has been spent in complete truthfulness and love of his fellow beings should be worthy of the veneration of a Christian and a Muslim as much as the saint belonging to their own faiths. But this is not what happens in reality. The life even of the noblest Hindu is considered worthless, and he is believed to be destined to burn eternally in hell fire because of his refusal to utter a sentence to the effect, more or less, that there is no god but one of the Judaic gods. This utterance is a monotheistic substitute for all human virtue and morality. A less than honourable faithful is much better than a saintly pagan or *mushrik*.

Certain assertions of monotheism can have the effect of freeing man from the compulsions of leading a universally valid moral life, as long as he confesses to believe in one of the many versions of popular monotheism. A believer may consider himself freed of all obligations towards non-believing humanity except perhaps the obligation to coerce and convert it. Humanity does not remain one: it is split, most unnaturally, into two antagonistic and irreconcilable factions and the faithful are taught to practice discriminatory ethic. A believer thinks he should be afraid only of wrong theology and not immoral deeds. Sahih Muslim records a *hadis* (171) by Abu Zarr in which Prophet Mohammad is said to have clarified that any person who dies as a member of his community—*ummā*—without associating anything with *Allah* will go to paradise—"Yes, even if he committed adultery and theft"—but a virtuous polytheist has no escape from hell and torment, his moral life notwithstanding. It has been confirmed in another *hadis* (220) of Sahih Muslim that all misdeeds of a person howsoever grave are expunged the moment he utters the *kalimah* that there is no god but Allah and Muhammad is his prophet: "Are you not aware of the fact that Islam wipes out all the previous misdeeds?" Muslims are enjoined to treat one another with respect and brotherliness, but a non-Muslim is to be treated with the worst possible contempt. God reveals in the holy Quran: "Mohammad is Allah's apostle. Those who follow him are ruthless to the unbelievers but merciful to one another."[24]

We also have Jesus' authority on the matter of different ethics for the faithful and the infidels: "I pray not for the world, but for them which thou hast given me"[25] Humanity was never to be a single cohesive family henceforth, unless one or other of the monotheistic faiths triumphed in bringing the world under its exclusive jurisdiction. Till such time, the world that man inhabits will be a world of incessant strife between the faithful and the unbeliever. Ethics is determinable by its conformity with the commands of a prophet or a messiah and morality is prudential because god the source of such morality, is the prudential product of a particular culture. If god is the ultimate sacred power behind all reality then it is only he who is revealed in the ritual settings of diverse religions rather than... "that a new power is created every time."[26] It is not possible to describe god's nature finally, the very nature of god precludes this possibility; all religious insights perceive only a small portion of god's infinite existence and the final frontier of divine knowledge is not known. This thought has been succinctly summed up in this Urdu couplet:

"khudā jāne had e-manzil-e-irfan kahañ tak hai
patā har śakhs detā hai pahuñch jiski jahāñ tak hai"

In the face of the charges of inconsistency in god's character and the untenability of his personality, monotheistic theologians sometimes argue that god's character needs to be understood analogically and direct correspondence should not be read between a predicate applied to god and to men. Personality, of a man and 'personality' as found in god's character are said to be completely different. When god is said to be 'one' he is said to be one only as a focus of a person's devotional attitude. If god has predicates analogically then all conceptions of his power and will should also be interpreted and determined analogically. But the same theologian believes that the commands of god are not to be interpreted analogically and their implementation generally follows a literal interpretation. If god commands that a *kāfir* is to be punished he is to be punished not analogically but literally. At least that is how monotheistic religions have interpreted their god and followed his dictates in practice: the person of the god is only analogically a person, but his commands are commands literally. This brings us to the crucial contradiction in the theology of the revealed religions. God's will is determined by the interest of the community as reflected in the directives of his prophet; therefore its temporal concreteness is inescapable and it is to be enforced literally. The reality of god, however, can live with the holy vagueness of his analogical personality and super-eminent existence.

Monotheism has always maintained this impossible balance between the hortatory proclivity of its god and his morphology. Inspite of the complete transience and non-physicality of god as a phenomenon his commands have been given a legality that generally accrues to the commands of a recognizable sovereign. St. Thomas Aquinas believed that god is the reality that informs the visible order of things as wisdom and power, and following him philosophers have described the inherent postulated reality in nature as god. Keith Ward believes that to say that god is wise…"serves primarily to locate the use of the term God in contexts of causality, order and purpose, as the reality which is postulated or disclosed in such contexts".[27] This theory makes god a pseudonym for the wise order of nature. But, Keith Ward also believes that the neutral account of causal order does not directly lead to inference of an objective rational ground of universe. Neutral account of moral experience is no basis to infer existence of a moral demand. So we are back to where we began. If we do not have an objective god we cannot have him as the source of moral commands. The difficulty in providing an explanation for the monotheistic god has been increasingly felt by modern philosophers of religion who tend to believe, that god, in the end, is something completely incomprehensible. In the Judaic religions the incomprehensibility of god is not used to urge the faithful to strive harder to unravel his deep mystery; it is used to preclude rational questions about god and terminate every enquiry on the bulwark of faith owing to the belief that..."explanation is therefore not necessary to faith".[28] It is believed that to understand and explain is to diminish the contingency of god.

Since belief in a personal god as the focus of the wise order in the universe does not derive from empirical evidence, every descriptive epithet can be made to fit god by a particular religious discourse. If an explanation of god is to come from its emotive interpretation in a religious community, then the views of that community become sufficient justification. Belief in a god is then the product of a commitment to a religious tradition and to the moral ordering of one's experience in the light of that tradition. All attempts at a rational explanation of god has been given up by monotheistic theology and new hermeneutic paradigms like 'creative mystery', 'mysterious spontaneity', 'unfathomable creator', etc, are increasingly used as categories of explanation. To accept this sort of explanation, one has to "take the decisive step of faith", and this faith... "derives from a religious commitment...in a particular religious tradition."[29] God, we are told, can at best be understood as a ... "rational purposive and intrinsically valuable context", where even this context is a function of faith because to believe..."that there is such a purpose, is a matter of religious apprehension and faith."[30] The personal god acting in history is in fact just a 'valuable context', and a frame of reference, for ordering a man's own moral experience!

In the background of the aforementioned facts the definition of monotheism and polytheism offered by Prof. Keith Ward makes interesting reading. He narrates how the Biblical god has grown out of the syncretistic tradition of many elements of the Canaanite religion: "In thus incorporating other faiths, the god of Abraham and Moses became the one God....This revelation of the gods becomes monotheistic when one sees God as the source of all revelatory beings. That is, one sees them as having one unitary source...Monotheism is then basically the denial that the world has many unrelated grounds, the assertion that there is a unity of values known under many different aspects."[31] All very fine, except, this unity of values or unitary source of revelation is explored not through contemplation of the world as it is but determined through the *diktat* of a personal will. To assume a divine explanation as the source of the finality of a man's dogmatic assertion is to turn epistemic causality on its dumb head. The same school also assumes that many gods of polytheism ... "must split up various revelations amongst themselves..." and posit... "indefinite number of distinct absolute values."[32] But they forget that gods of polytheism are not always sources of supernatural revelation; and they do not promulgate doctrinal compulsoriness for man's redemption.

The theological and philosophical explanations of the existence of god in the Judaic religious tradition, however, postulate god only as an abstract and necessary theoretical construct to justify a sectarian philosophy. For a normal person the very fact that god exists and cares for the world would have been sufficient explanation to assuage his existential anxiety. The modes in which a man relates to god are a matter of ritual detail that depend on his understanding of the encounter with god and his psychological and intellectual predilection and capacity. Cultic and ritual practices, including the invocation of a deity, would then just be a product of cultural experience. If a person turns his heart, mind and soul towards god and utters an invocation it would only reach the '*god-which-is*' irrespective of the tonal and linguistic peculiarity of the invocation. Let us agree, for argument sake, that the existence of god has been proven following the thesis of either St. Thomas or Ibn-Rushd. It should be a grand and happy theological ending to a highly contentious and problematic issue. With the unanimity regarding the existence of a supreme and divine being, all religious disputations should end. More so, in view of the implicit premise of the aforementioned agreement that there is only 'one-god' who is all powerful and omniscient, and can therefore understand all languages and decipher the correct addressee behind the various names to which man's piety is addressed.

Monotheistic religions do not seek to prove god's existence in the form of a divine reality freely available to men. His existence is proven for a theological reason. The inference of Jesus as god—"I am He'—from the premise of the basic existence of god is *non-sequitur*. This ratiocinative illogicality is further compounded when it is realized that god not only is Jesus or *Allāh,* but also 'only Jesus' and 'only *Allāh*' in the different revelatory situations ascribed to him by Christianity and Islam. Metaphysical apophacy wedded to sectarian theological hypostatization produces the monotheistic god. Christianity and Islam believe that man's intelligence and intuition have been irreparably violated as a consequence of his original sin and fall; whereupon man with his tainted intelligence cannot understand the essence of god. As late as the year 1968, we find Pope Paul VI cautioning the faithful of the pitfalls lying in the road of enquiry and research: "But at the same time the greatest care must be taken that the important duty of research does not involve the undermining of the truths of Christian doctrine...If this happens, and we have unfortunately seen it happen in these days—the result is perplexity and confusion in the minds of the faithful..."[33] This is a complete inversion of the epistemological order of knowledge. Normally, we use our senses, our reason and our ordering intelligence to grasp a certain information and then build a system of belief based on that information. Prophetic monotheism insists that a certain postulate is required to be first accepted as true on faith, and then a faithful man should spend rest of his intelligent life in finding necessary reasons to support that postulate which he has already testified on faith to be true. Man's intelligence, man's science, his research, his enquiry is to be guided by one primary concern of finding support for his faith. The Vatican has clarified this point very lucidly: "This certainly does not prevent the Church, in her awareness of the progress of human thought, from considering it her duty to have these mysteries continually examined by contemplation of the faith and theological examination, and to have them fully expounded in up to date terminology. But while the necessary duty of investigation is being pursued, diligent care must be taken that these profound mysteries are not interpreted in a sense other than that in which the Church has understood and understands them..."[34]

Not only are the mysteries of religion to be examined by 'contemplation of the faith and theological examination' alone—not by any meticulous scholarship—but even this limited scrutiny is expected to expound the mystery only in the old sense in which the Church understands them but in 'uptodate terminology'. That in essence sums up the burden of man's intelligence and reason in the world of prophetic monotheism. Prophetic monotheism regards the belief in the god as revealed in its tradition, as the life line of its religious superstructure. Belief in a Supreme Being *tout court* and following a righteous and virtuous human life *tout court* is not enough to make a person good and spiritual; he has to accept god as Christ or *Allāh* to be seen as really believing in god. A god as a god is a demon. To say 'Almighty god lead me to light' is nonsensical voodoo; to say 'Christ lead me to light' is piety *par excellence*. After all it is a question of protecting and preserving the divine brand name irrespective of the essential unity of the product that is sought to be purveyed under those names: "By itself, acceptance of God the creator is worthless for salvation; it is a living faith only as an integral part of our acceptance of God the redeemer. Only then does man regain his status as an image of God and thereby acquire the light both to see and to follow God the creator."[35] To survive under such theological compulsions monotheistic god must surrender all self-respect. Professor James Collins has mentioned, in the context of examining the theory of partial providence, "William James' picture of a limited, struggling deity who needs our manly help to make the good principle prevail."[36]

Faith, revelation, and god are inter-related categories that exist in a circular symbiosis with one another. For a Christian, god's nature, will and person can be seen only in the life, death and resurrection of Christ. The tenets of Christian theology can very well be called, and many scholars have called it, as 'Christology' because the '*theos*' has been conceived only as the '*Christos*' in Christianity. That Jesus is Christ and as such is of the same essence as god has to be accepted on faith. There was nothing in Jesus' life to make him a 'revelatory event' and we have earlier seen that historicity of the events of Jesus' life as being eschatologically unique has been disproved by research. Jesus' life became revelatory of god's self-disclosure in him because a group of people decided to interpret Jesus' life to be so *post facto*. Faith is not engendered by a uniquely revelatory event; an event of everyday occurrence becomes revelatory in view of its contemplation in faith. It is the predisposition to believe in something—our faith—that makes a person divine and an incident revelatory. For all monotheistic religions the basic burden is the disposition to believe what is offered as divine clue—the event or the person on whom the clue is based is unimportant. Christian dogmas continue to be asserted as the only truth even if the veracity of Jesus' life, his death and resurrection, or even the validity of his message have now been found to be suspect and unreliable. Questions of ethics, metaphysics and spiritual experience are marginal compared to the belief in the basic revelatory event on the basis of faith. Ingolf U. Dalferth characterizes this tendency of Christianity as "concentration on the universal relevance of a singular eschatological event",[37] where revelation is the final court of appeal to judge the significance of an idea or a statement. The revelatoriness of an event is only a matter of faith and not the intrinsic virtue of the event. An event becomes revelatory if accepted by men on faith, because revelation is… "correlative with faith"[38] and "there is no faith without revelation…no revelation without faith".[39] Revelation and faith are 'co-dependents' and not causally hierarchical, and the only evidence for god's self-revelation in Christ is "faith and the testimony of the spirit."[40]

To consider an event revelatory merely on the basis of faith is to hold an opinion like the venerable Professor in R.M. Hare's parable who believed without any basis that all other professors on the campus were after his life—it is to believe in a *'blik'*. Subsequent ages are given the tedious task of finding smart and sinuous explanations to justify and explain the *'blik'* of the original propounder. The *blik* that Jesus is Christ and the final revelation of god is first proclaimed and accepted on faith, and then begins the great enterprise in which religious philosophy and theology embark on a…"permanent process of 'faith seeking understanding' of itself, and everything else, in the light of faith."[41] The impossibility of the thesis that there is a god who reveals himself only to special persons in a special manner has been realized by theologians, and this thesis never received any intellectual respectability outside of the tradition of religious apologetics. John Hick has proposed to look at this problem differently when he suggested that all religions are either erroneously projecting different illusions upon the universe or… "they are each responding to an infinite divine reality which exceeds our human conceptualities and which is capable of being humanly thought and experienced in these fascinatingly divergent ways."[42] Lately a new standpoint has emerged which can be summarized in the words of Dalferth as: "Accordingly religious perspectives and the whole way of life and network of beliefs which go with them cannot be justified by external but only by internal criteria".[43] This should be a fair enough premise provided this principle is not confined only to the justification of Christianity, but extends to all other traditions of worship revered by men. Logically, then, it cannot be denied that the justification of a tradition of worship should primarily be found from within that tradition and not in an external prototypical perspective of a different tradition. Then no religion can be characterised as false, primitive and decadent in comparison to some that are allegedly true.

If all religions accept the internal truthfulness and validity of each other's message, theological strife may soon end because the need to force a particularistic theology on other faiths will become redundant and men can then really understand the true meaning of, "*Lukum deen-e-kum waliye deen*—to you be your way and to me mine!" Implicit in this theory should also be the recognition that the way of the other is not only accepted as true but also respected. Only then can this Quranic assertion mellow the dogma of treating one religion as better than others and lead to some sort of a tolerance of other religions and ways of worship. Unfortunately, monotheistic faiths do not carry the argument of internal perspective to its logical conclusion and therefore are not ready to yield an inch from their assertion that theirs is the only way to god. Islam is justified internally because of its special revelation, but the teachings of Bhagawān Buddha are not—neither internally nor externally; they are a bundle of gross heresies which need to be supplanted by the teachings of the Quran. Christianity, too, wants to be judged by its own internal perspective of faith and at the same time wishes to apply Christian presuppositions to judge the faith of others. Christianity is sacrosanct, but all other religious insights are to be tested for their coherence with the truth of the Christian religion, and merited on the basis of its *pro-rata* compatibility with Christianity—"Every truth contributes in a perhaps imperfect and preliminary way to the absolute truth revealed in Christ."[44]

It is impossible to ever understand the truth of the propositions regarding god uttered in the Hindu tradition if the premises of judgement and evaluation are chosen from the Judaic religious traditions. Judaic religions believe everything on 'faith'. Their world of discourse is totally different. For a Hindu it is very easy, almost natural, to pray with piety at a *mazar* of a venerable Muslim Saint or even before Christ in a Church, if he happens to enter one. It is common sight to find as many Hindus praying at a popular Muslim shrine as Muslim devotees. It would, however, be a prime time media event to find Christians or Muslims praying to a Hindu deity, or in a temple, whatever be the eminence of the deity or the shrine. The reason is theological. To a Christian or a Muslim his own religious vision is the only reality that counts; other visions do not matter and, in fact, need to be obliterated if possible. In the world view of the monotheistic faiths there is no quarter for the other deities. This behaviour is the eschatological outcome of the monotheistic assertion that 'there is no god but god'. A monotheist cannot accept a world-view different from his, a way of life not in conformity with his dogma, a way of worship not in accordance with his own standards and men that are not moulded after the monotheistic cognitive map. The eschatology of uniqueness and exclusivity of revelation, the assurance of being a chosen people and the uncompromisable faith in having received a final revelation from god combine to make monotheism an ideology that tends to brook neither dissent nor diversity.

For a community of monotheists the world exists in the manner of their collective solipsism, and it is metaphysically difficult for them to accept, much less respect, the plurality of cultures and civilizations. The test would lie in asking a monotheist to consent to a very simple proposition held devoutly by most Hindus; an idea that Gandhiji used to recite with joyful eclecticism: *'Allāh Iśwar tero nām'*. He should be asked whether he agrees that *Rāma* and *Allāh* are the equipollent and true modes of apprehension of the same reality. He should be asked whether he agrees that *Kṛṣṇa* is as important and true a self-revelation of god as Jesus. If he consents one can perhaps talk about pluralism and respect for others. If he does not, then, he is hiding an exclusivist agenda behind a theological facade, waiting for an opportune moment to strike and therefore he should be told that he is doing so. No *Sanātan dharmi* would have any hesitation in conceding that Jesus for a Christian can be the most noble revelation of god and for a Muslim, *Allāh* is the most respectful mode of apprehension of the divine reality, and these faiths are entitled to their respective spirituality without, however, seeking to undermine the god and, spirituality of others. That is pluralism, anything less than that would be a ruse; hiding an inflexible and insular agenda behind the fig leaf of a religion and claiming immunity because of that.

Peter B. Clarke and Peter Byrne in their book have defined pluralism as: "Pluralism is the negation of the thought that any one religion is unique in truth, in salvific effectiveness, or in relation to the meaning of history."[45] The fact that truth is granted to all religious traditions, and religions are only human means of grasping the one underlying reality behind the multiplicity of phenomena, is now conceded by most philosophers and non-partisan historians of religion. John Hick, for one, challenges the Christian claim of uniqueness and exclusivity. Clarke, et al, describe Hick's attitude in the following manner: "John Hick's theory of religion stems from the thesis that all religions worship the same transcendentally real focus, albeit under the guise of different culturally conditioned *personae and impersonae*".[46] To this characterisation the authors add their own pregnant conclusion: "However, there is a strong case for saying that the actual course of historiography of religions shows no clear case for regarding one religion as distinct in its relation to human history when compared with others... The character of the world yields, neither by observation nor proven inference, any religious truths."[47] Scholars have warned of dangers of religious intolerance if one religion is claimed to be superior to all other religions. Friedrich Heiler has quoted Rabindranath Tagore in support of the idea that every faith must guard against their... "antipathy towards the diversity of religions and the will of one religion to dominate". Tagore says: "The attempt to make their own religion the ruling one everywhere and for all time is natural to men who incline toward sectarianism. Therefore they do not want to hear that God is magnanimous in the dispensing of His love, or that His dealings with men are not limited to one blind alley which comes to a sudden halt at one point in history. If ever such a catastrophe should break in upon mankind that one religion should swamp everything, then God would have to provide a second Noah's ark to save his creatures from spiritual destruction."[48]

Every religious claim to oneness or universal uniqueness has become suspect in the eyes of historians and philosophers of religion. The idea and the nature of the Supreme Being has been expressed in different forms during man's long history. Various forms of the Supreme Being are the products of different cultural realities in which it found an expression. Words like 'one-god' or 'many gods' are not empirical or ontological statements but expressions of cultural and individual preferences of an asserter, and they represent the recitation of a culturally determined and inherited theological response. Van der Leeuw has quoted Wundt with approbation that: "Even for 'developed' religion, concepts like 'Monotheism' and 'Polytheism' are empty numerical schemes, by which the value of a religion can be measured just as little as can the worth of a marriage by the number of children sprung from it' ".[49] He further adds that: "'God is One'... therefore is to be regarded not as an assertion or conviction, but simply as an expression of faith in the sense of the classical exclamation... 'God is One'."[50] All determinative epithets and characteristics predicated on god are the products of a human mind operating in a cultural matrix. Prof. Henry Dumery believed that the only epithet which can perhaps be applied with some confidence to god is that he is 'one'; other appellations are just modalities, and Jean Danielou while commenting on this thesis elaborates it and adds: "Indeed, insofar as they are determinations, these modalities do not come from God. He is beyond all determinations. They come, then, from the activity of the mind...In other words, determination, which of course is foreign to God in himself, is equally foreign to God in man and in the world, that is to say, it has its sole origin in the very mind or spirit of man."[51] To speak about god in terms of certainty and everlasting finality is to destroy the meaning and majesty of god. Don Cupitt believes that the right way to understand various conceptions of god in the monotheistic tradition is to speak of him not as a general god but as 'the-god-who-is-the-Father-of-Jesus-Christ' or 'the-god-whose-prophet-is-Muhammad'—because "'God' exists, not as a universal essence, but only in his various particular specifications, whether religious or metaphysical."[52] Cupitt has no doubt in his mind that the god of Moses, the god of Jesus and the god of Muhammad are "three different specifications of god".[53]

Let us look at the problem from a different angle. The three religions of the Judaic family consider themselves the recipients of the grace of a single god. It was most natural that the three religions should have witnessed god and his will in a similar manner. There is no reason why the people of a single god would have such divergent views of this single divinity and his single message. The very fact that the Semitic 'one-god' has spawned three religions destroys the case of god's singleness and the uniqueness of his message. We have, instead, the paradox of 'one-god' and three competing versions among three 'chosen-people' The fact that Christianity, Judaism and Islam are three separate religions swearing by a single god is an eloquent testimony to the fact that the 'one-god' has been received in three different traditions in three completely different spiritual paradigms. In view of this reality it is logically impossible to disclaim the possibility of equally valid, albeit different, receptions of 'one-god' in various other religious traditions. It can be argued that the finality of god's revelation in the Judaic religions is not a matter of rational analysis but a factor of god's mysterious ways. But we know that the mystery of a final revelation has been breached thrice in the three Judaic religions and we may impugn this thesis by proposing to extend the very same mystery of god to all other spiritual visions. To say that god's mystery stops at a particular religion and does not extend to this whole wide world is to merely use god as a facade for personal illusion. No religion should become an insurmountable dyke against the free and ever lasting flow of divine grace and mercy. A straitjacketing of the infinite presence of god by a group of people can only result in untold misery for them and for other people in an unending cycle of repression, atrocity and pain. Uttering god's name for fulfilment of patently sectarian and political ambitions is blasphemy. God intends to plant the fragrant flowers of love, friendship, brotherhood and respect in man's soul and not the denominational cross of sectarian theology.

The visions and messages of god preserved in various scriptural and devotional traditions of mankind are the revered and common heritage of all humanity. They show us the grandeur of man in his flight towards the final truth and also his very noble frailty in not being always able to fully reach the truth. This existential dynamics of success and failure constitutes man's essential humanity. In our failure we are reminded of our limiting humanness. In our complete success lies the secret of the severance of all restrictive bonds when man ascends above the bondage of phenomenal existence to a realm where the distinctions of human and divine do not matter. But as long as we do not reach that height we must not stop the search at a particular point. A Vyāsa, a Buddha, an Abraham, a Zarathrustra and a Mohammad are spiritual pioneers who have tried to show to man various possible pathways to spiritual fulfilment. For their respective disciples they may be the most satisfying perceptors and all spiritual groups are entitled to pursue without any hindrance from one another their own path in an amicable and respectful fellowship. They should not refrain from exchanging notes and maps *en route.* The goal is same; we are heading towards it from different directions using different perceptual vehicles. We must learn from one another because it will hold us in good stead during our long and arduous journey. We shall do well to heed fruitfully to the humbling thoughts of William Shakespeare:

> "There are more things between heaven and earth, Horatio, than are dreamt of in your philosophy."

God is in the Mirror of My Heart

Before an exploration of the *Sanātan Dharma* is undertaken, a conscious severance with the ideological world of other religions should take place as a preparation for an encounter with a completely new environment of beliefs and practices. It is a world where the ideas of man and god and their inter-relationships originate and develop from a metaphysical standpoint that is wholly dissimilar to that of the Judaic religions. Words and concepts like god, man, worship, creation, deity, etc, do not have the same significance as these words have in the Judaic religions. Unless the mind is desensitized of the conceptual paradigms of the Judaic religions it would not be able to grasp the import of the spiritual discourse of the *Sanātan Dharma*. Man's relation to god forms an important component of his *dhārmic* life but this relationship does not exhaust his *dhārmic* responsibilities. *Dharma* in its totality has a meaning that goes far beyond standardized practices of prayer and worship. It is possible for men to be *dhārmic* without explicitly invoking a god in their lives and Bhagawān Buddha and Bhagāwan Mahāvīr are shining examples of this approach. When men belonging to the *Sanātan Dharma* invoke a god they do so in a profoundly different manner because they believe in different theories of creation and god's place in the phenomenal world. *Sanātan Dharma* does not take a dogmatic view of man's encounter with the divine but treats every encounter as the unfolding of the mystery of the world.

To understand the *Sanātan* view of god it is necessary to approach the idea from the standpoint of the concepts that are operative within the world view of the *Sanātan Dharma.* Unless we apply the internal criteria of evaluation the ensuing cognitive results shall always be wrong. If all religious seeing is 'seeing –as' in the convictional world of a worshipper, then the best way to understand the *Sanātan* idea is to follow the lead of the texts, the teachers, and the behaviour of the common practitioner to get the true meaning of a concept or an utterance that finds mention in the spiritual world of *Sanātan Dharma.* Since the world of the *Sanātan Dharma* is free of structured dogma, it appears chaotic to a new explorer who tends to assign its fluid creativity to the lack of spiritual coherence when he juxtaposes it against the sterilized regimentation of a monotheistic religion. The difference has less to do with the nature of the divine persona than with the formal structures that monotheism puts to delimit that persona. The history of the monotheistic religions itself is a testimony to the fact that man has never found himself comfortable in the religious groove of a single theology. Judaism had established a religion based on stern monotheism and one would have expected subsequent generations of monotheists to follow it. But comes a Jesus from within the Jewish community itself and he breaks the mould of Jewish monotheistic tradition to create a completely different religion. Only six centuries later Prophet Mohammad created a new religion by using the same god and the same prophets. Never has man remained satisfied with a singularly limiting explanation of the divine mystery, and his enterprise has forced him to chart ever new spiritual courses. The fact that a shared god has been worshipped differently in the three distinct religions of the Judaic group lends support to the *Sanātan* thesis of one god and many paths. The only difference is that Judaic religions deny the reality of other religions whereas *Sanātan Dharma* revels in the fecund manifestation of man's creativity.

Respect for the spiritual and *dhārmic* conviction of various social and racial groups of humanity is a by-product of India's unique civilizational experience. Within her vast geographical limits, stretching from Afghanistan to Burma, lived and flourished from time immemorial vast multitude of human societies that differed from one another in matters of language, dress, social mores and religious practices. Nearly all human racial types, ranging from the Mongoloid to the Australoid, are found within her boundaries. Many non-indigenous elements like the Śaka, the Huṇa and the Mongol poured in within her borders from outside and merged amicably as a cohesive unit of its eclectic culture. The cultural and linguistic variety that India had to cope with during her recent history of nearly six thousand years is stupendous, and it posed challenges before her leaders that few civilizations had to ever face. The task not only involved the unification of various socio-cultural traditions but also finding an acceptable *modus vivendi* to satisfy the aspirations of such economically divergent groups as the relatively primitive *bhil* and *kirat* to the urban traders of her prosperous cities. It was the challenge akin to what an artist would face in harmonizing multifarious moods and colours in one rhythmic collage in a manner that the constituents do not appear dissonant. The civilizational challenges of India needed a higher order resolution and her intellectual leaders gave her a highly creative worldview to achieve that end.

The geographical specificities of India's location was never in doubt. None disputed that the inhabitants of the land *Bhāratvarṣa* constituted a single specific group of people that can be characterized as a nation on the basis of a shared history and a common framework of socio-cultural norms. The unity of Indian nationhood was based on a shared civilizational worldview that ensured a meaningful commonality to remain unimpaired within the wide local cultural and religious variations. The principle idioms of cultural discourse were common and every region by and large shared the same spiritual sources as the fountainhead of their cultural and devotional practices. It was for this reason that sage Agastya from the north was completely intelligible in the extreme south and Ādi Śaṁkarācārya found himself at home in the northern extremities of the country. When a Manḍan Miśra of Mithila discoursed with Śaṁkara from Kerala they were not only satisfying their intellectual curiosities but were in many ways proclaiming the civilizational unity of India. It was for this reason that Ādi Śamkarācārya established four *peethas* or spiritual centres in four corners of the country and put a seal of cultural unity over the geographical boundaries of India. This was as bold and eloquent an assertion of composite nationhood as one would ever require.

The acceptance of a shared nationhood is reflected in the careers of some of the greatest savants of India. Gautam Buddha and Mahāvīr travelled to many parts of the country preaching their message of *dharma*. Śaṁkarācārya left Kaladi in Kerala and wandered throughout India propagating the message of the *Sanātan Dharma*. Guru Nānak moved out of his native Punjab and travelled to all corners of this country with a view to not only transmit his experience but also to reinforce his own belongingness to the common spiritual tradition available in various parts of the country to which he considered himself a full heir. As late as the twentieth century we see Mahatma Gandhi embarking on a journey across the country before launching a meaningful movement of independence. Social, political and spiritual leaders have always had a pan-Indian vision. Some of the greatest minds have picked up intellectual stimulus from various cultural traditions of this country to formulate their cohesive and all embracing vision. The presence of this syncretic vision in their teachings gives them a national appeal uncircumscribed by the factors of geography. These interactions helped India develop a core of cultural and civilizational attitudes that was shared by her people across the limitations of religion and language. It is a pleasant quirk of history that all important proponents of *Vaiṣṇavism* that later became so popular in contemporary north India—Rāmānuj, Nimbārka, Madhva, Vallabha—were all *Dākṣinātya* or teachers hailing from southern part of the country. India was civilizationally and culturally always one nation which lived under different political dispensations. One would do well not to judge Indian nationhood only in terms of modern political theories.

The biggest challenge before the leadership of India has been the management of her fecund diversity. The problem that agitated them related principally to the evolving of a system of shared cultural principles within which human socieities are allowed full freedom to develop in a decentralized and plural manner. Problem of pluralism is not a modern phenomenon; Indians have lived with it for many millenia. One of the cardinal principles evolved in India to manage the problem of diversity was the full acceptance of the fact of diversity in its apparent phenomenal manifestation. An ideology has never received India's favour if it tried to develop an esoteric or insular standpoint; and her leaders strove incessantly to purge society of such aberrations whenever such a tendency arose. Acceptance and respect for diversity to be fully effective would necessarily require the acceptance of a multipolar social and religious world. It would not do that few groups believe in the right of others to exist while the others do not. This would cause strife. True pluralism has to rest on the equal respect of the cultural and spiritual tradition of other people as one would respect one's own. Respect for democracy and freedom of ideas did not stop the free world of the modern era from fighting the totalitarian ideologies of Fascisim and Nazism because the latter were considered serious threats to the very idea of democracy and pluralism. The greatest threat to a plural society comes from those ideologies that do not brook any difference of culture and religion and want to impose their own vision on all other people. If pluralism has to survive, totalitarian and intolerant ideas would require to be countered at all levels. Pluralism cannot survive in a society if one section of that society believes in and respects the inherent diversities of cultures and religions while others want a uniform world in which only their truth pervails.

India has accepted the plurality of man's belief systems and the diversity in the structures of cultural apparatus, of geography, social factors and ethnicity that provide different perspectives from which men view reality. The pictures they conjure are happily synchronous with their own intellectual and emotional requirements. As a man is respectfully attached to his own way of life, he accepts that others have a right to be equally attached to their own respective traditions. Rare would be an Indian who claims exclusive privileges for his own viewpoint and negates the view points of others. India has always accepted that the diversity of human life is a natural outcome of the world of material phenomena and in order to weave an identifiable civilization from the multiple threads of its ethnic and social communities, she relied more on preserving the natural texture and design of each participating unit. Diversity needs to be accepted not only in social and ethnic sense but also in the sphere of religious and cultural beliefs. Indians went a step ahead: they not only recognized the plurality of human society but accorded to every system other than theirs, respect equal to that accorded to their own system. Differences of opinion did exist, but they were resolved through dialogue and not with the use of force or an overbearing theological argument. If plurality of human life and the polymorphism of its social institutions are recognized as a civilizational reality, acceptance of polytheism is the inescapable spiritual corollary of this worldview.

Full acceptance of a man and his social mores would involve accepting the god that he worships and the systems of prayer that he constructs around that god. But such acceptance does not extend to irrational and inhuman practices that illegitimately pose as religious doctrine. Impurities are required to be carefully separated and purified and Indians have been continuously doing it, whenever an occasion arose, through dialogue, discourse and intellectual persuasion. Man's spiritual insight was, however, respected and his right to hold a view point was inviolable. As humanity was one but flourished in different cultural communities, likewise truth was one but reflected in some measure in diverse spiritual traditions. Primacy was not attached to any specific perspective. It was believed that all temporal perspectives were transient and in the ultimate perspective these differences cease to matter. In the ultimate analysis there is just one undifferentiated and non-dual reality. S. Radhakrishnan underscored the *Sanātan* viewpoint that every conception that man has of divinity is venerable when he said: "To despise other people's gods is to despise them, for they and their gods are adopted to each other. The Hindu took up the gods of even the savage and the uncivilized and set them on equal thrones to his own."[1]

If diversity was accepted without hesitation the underpinning for this conviction was provided by the unshakable belief that the diverse epiphanies of god are permeated by only one supreme truth. Each human society in its own peculiar way strives to attain a system that ensures a fruitful and happy life for its constituents. But the happiness of one group is not contingent on the trauma of others. The reservoir of cosmic happiness—*ānand*—is rich enough to provide for all humanity. In our own ways we draw sustenance from the same source and share the same cosmic unitariness. The differences are apparent and at the most fundamental level each of us accost a single divine reality. Truth in its essence is one although it manifests itself in different forms. Humanity is one although it exists in various cultural and racial diversifications. Diversity as phenomenal existence is only an obverse apprehension of the unity of essence in a historical time-frame where the 'one' allows itself to be perceived in multifarious modes. Diversity within the bosom of an all pervading unity was the core existential question with which India grappled.

Indians produced a body of doctrines that translated the vision of unitariness of reality and its multiple apprehension into ethical, moral and spiritual precepts that became the benchmark for evaluating all social and devotional theories. It was for this reason that, inspite of their differences, various communities of the *Sanātan Dharma* constituted a unified cultural and civilizational unit sharing a common history and ideological viewpoint. At the centre of the spiritual belief of *Sanātan Dharma* is the human being in its profound uniqueness as an individual amidst the vast multitude of the phenomenal and the noumenal whole. Every doctrine is a creation of man's personal vision and it is he who recreates his immediate reality on the basis of his own experience. Each individual is entitled to his own personal insight into the nature of reality and create a life for himself based on that reality. It was possible for the insight and experience of one individual to become grand enough to be accepted by others as emulatory, but a 'second-hand' religiosity was never considered a noble vocation in India. Man stood resplendent at the centre of creation, and all manifested phenomena and even the 'gods' hinged on the creativity of man. Each individual has the capacity to recreate the whole for himself because in its essence each indivudual is also the whole—*Aham Brahmāsmi... sarvaṁ brahmaṁ idaṁ jagat.* S. Radhakrishnan believes: "If God is the Creator of the world, we participate to some extent in His nature. We are co-creators with the Divine."[2]

Sanātan Dharma develops its world view on the basis of the dialectical relationship of the 'one' with the many. The reality of man is viewed from the perspective in which the world of phenomena is seen as emanating from a unitary source. Supervening the apparent multiplicity of names and forms is a single supreme and non-dual essence. Since man is a part and parcel of the phenomenal world he exists in manifold physical formats but retains the primal unitariness that is common to all humanity. In the small microcosm of his personality the essence of the macrocosmic reality exists as the deep-seated but active and defining principle of his existence. This whole world is the manifestation of one single primal essence—*ekoham bahusyām*. At the basal level there are no differences at all. If it was possible to reverse the flow of time as we know it, the multitudinous names and forms would be seen as merging into one another in an undifferentiated realm of many virtual possibilities. This being so, there also arises the question of man's relationship with the physical world that exist outside of him. India's answer to the question of the relationship between man's psychology and the ontology of external phenomena came in the form of "the correlativity between the senses and the objects, based on their being due to the division of the principle into the subjective and objective poles of man's experience"[3] The subjective and objective aspects of reality resolve into the personality of man. The objects of senses—the light of the sun; the air; and things of the world—exist as much outside as inside man's own existence. The outward fire is also the speech-function of man, the external sun has entered man's eye as his sight and the wind has entered him as his own breath of life. The primal essence, the *Ātman*, becomes witness to manifest creation only in the form of man: "Thus the senses and the mind of man and their corresponding objects became the realms (bases, *ayatans)* of the gods of the world. And all the gods were subordinated to the *Ātman*. Man thus became the meeting point of the gods of the universe or its controlling forces."[4] If man looks out he sees the variegated world; if he looks inside he sees only an all pervading singularity that is not amenable to any indicative description.

Description of a phenomenon can take place only when a phenomenon is segregated as a distinct and separated entity from all other possible phenomena that exist in the realm of unitary reality. In order to describe an object it is necessary to antecedentally determine and locate an object for description, and this determination is not just the picking up of a given objective reality but a fresh creation of reality by the factors of our conscious choice. Modern physics is currently occupied with finding the clue to the dilemma of apparent but objectively observable reality in the thesis of 'observer-created reality'. The general scientific consensus is echoed by John Gribbin who believes that, "Nothing is real unless it is observed."[5] Gribbin suggests, on the basis of the proposition of John Wheeler's 'delayed-choice' experiment, that we may "consider the possibility that, because of the infinite regression of cause and effect, the whole universe may only owe its 'real' existence to the fact that it is observed by intelligent beings."[6] John Wheeler has proposed the thesis of the "participatory universe" in which everything that is real is only a result of "the statistics of billions upon billions of such acts of observer-participation"[7] It is the act of participatory observation that gives reality to the whole universe not only now but back also to the beginning.

Vedāntic viewpoint regards *māyā* as the inherent power of the *Brahman;* as the factor responsible for the superimposition of the apparent multiplicity of names and form on the non-dual singularity of the *Brahman*. *Māyā* allows the supreme consciousness, the *Brahman*, to be measured in order to create appearance of temporal reality through the agency of many sentient observers. All duality or multiplicity is apparently actualized within the framework of the non-dual and undifferentiated supreme reality. It is through *māyā* that the non-dual, 'non-material' reality attains the characteristics of duality and consequent materialization of what we call 'objective' reality: *māyayābhiddyate hyetannānyathajaṁ kathaṁcan*.[8] Reality, otherwise, is without any limitation, without measure, and without a fixed name or form—*amātro' nantamātrāsca*[9]. It is *māyā* that measures and imposes duality upon the non-dual reality, and thereby puts a sense of limitation on that which is intrinsically limitless and indescribable. J. Gonda believes that *mātrā* or the factor of measurement are the boundaries of objectification; they are the structures by which the *amātrā*—the immeasurable—becomes apportionable, *advait* becomes dual *dvait,* the limitless reality or the *Brahman* appear limited.[10] *Māyā* serves to superimpose categories of quantification such as space and time on the immeasurable.[11]

But the imposition of name and form on reality is not a real occurrence; it is believed to be apparent or definitional. Such superimposition of form cannot be a permanent feature of reality in as much as it only entails the projection of the categories of quality and quantity that is non-real on the real—*adhyāsonam atasminstad buddhiḥ*[12]. As long as nescient observation is devoted to Reality it materializes in certain set forms. Withdraw the observer, and reality vanishes into its inertial state of uncertainty and multiple possibilities. An act of temporal observation through the categories of mind that causes pure Reality to present itself in various forms is an act of nescience—*avidyā. Māyā* is the cognitive correlate of *avidyā* and it veils Reality through the superimposition of causal categories on it. The world is both a product of *māyā* and *māyā* itself—*viswa hi māyās.* Rāmānuj believed that *māyā* caused the obscuring of the godhead and engendered an intellect directed towards creation of images fit for temporal consumption and utility. It creates concepts which distort the essential purity of Reality: *bhagawat swarupatirodhānaṁ svasvarūp bhogyatva buddhiśca*[13]. It is *māyā* that holds together the manifest world of phenomena in a framework of incessant coming and going that appears real above its intrinsic non-truthful nature:

> *ahonukhalu citreyam māyā saṁsārbandhani*
> *asatyaivāti satyaiva svajñānamvihitam taya.*[14]

Śaṁkarācārya believed that *māyā* limits reality in the same manner as our ignorant minds project whiteness, darkness or blueness on the ontologically non-apparent and colourless sky: *apratyakṣepihyakāśe vālāstalamalinatādyadhyasyanti.*[15] Stephen

Kaplan believes that, "Maya is the traversing of the non-objectifiable with structures and limits which appear to make it into objects—which allows being to appear as becoming, as the world of objects, as maya".[16] But these appearances are illusory because nothing new is created since what does not exist at the beginning and at the end also does not exist at the present—*ādāvante ca yannāsti vartamāne" pi tattatha*.[17] Stephen Kaplan has argued that in the act of projecting identifiable contours on any external object 'out there' it is our mind which gets located 'out there'. In other words the theory of projection means that mind which gets projected 'out there' is not confined to the brain. Kaplan suggests that *māyā* should be seen as "a phenomenology of experience and not an ontology of experience."[18] Viewed in this manner *māyā* can be seen as embodied in the very act of perception: "The mind that is projected out there is *maya*."[19] *Māyā*, therefore, becomes the movement of the mind—*cittaspandita*—that creates the world of objectively perceived phenomena from within the non-dual and undifferentiated realm of immense possibilities. Ultimate reality or the *Brahman* remains indescribably one; myriad forms are only a product of our categorizing mind projected from a specific point of view. We can borrow a phrase from Alfred Karzybki and say that "the map is not the territory". Indian sages have recognized long back that to escape the illusory world of phenomena and exist in the domain of all pervasive unitary Reality, the movement of mind needs to be checked by the discipline of *yoga—yogaścitta vṛtti nirodha.*

Modern neuropsychology has proffered a 'holographic theory of brain'. Scientists like Dr. Karl Pribram, Wilder Penfield, Eccles, etc, have rejected the materialistic—reductionist view of man and posed instead that intentionality of a perceptor plays a part in determining the nature of reality within his perceptual milieu.[20] A perceptor's choice results into a quantum leap in which a single actuality emerges from "multifaceted potentiality."[21] It is only when an observer looks at reality in order to measure and describe it that one among many possibilities actualizes. If there is no perceptor there aren't any phenomena: "Without perception the universe continues, via the Schrodinger equation, to generate an endless profusion of possibilities."[22] A measuring and cognizing consciousness is necessary to create tangible reality. Gary Zukav takes up a pertinent question: "How is the Universe being actualized ?" And his clear answer is: "We are actualizing the Universe... Since we are part of the Universe that makes the Universe (and us) self actualizing."[23] The great physicist Werner Heisenberg has questioned the possibility of any fixed and objective meaning that can be assigned to the Universe: "What we observe is not nature itself, but nature exposed to our method of questioning."[24] Science seems to be redirecting our attention to ourselves away from the illusoriness of the world owing to which we cannot see it as it really is—*swapnamāyā swarūpeti*.[25]

Quantum physics has proposed that all so called material particles 'exist' only when we set up an experiment to measure them. Beyond the ambit of an experiment it is impossible to predict where a particle is and what it does. As a cognitive correlate to the quantum domain of physical reality it is held that, "consciousness, at the most fundamental levels, is a quantum process."[26] It is consciousness, then, that is interpreting and systematizing the quantum chaos of the Universe. Left to itself "the whole universe is a quantum mirage, winking in and out of existence millions of times per second. At the quantum level the whole cosmos is like a blinking light."[27] At that level linear temporality ceases to operate and past, present and future exist co-terminally. Time and causality give way to the sempiternal presence of all actuality and non-actualized possibility simultaneously. Scientists like Stephen Hawking are looking beyond the point of the 'singularity' before the big bang that marked the beginning of the universe. It has been suggested by them that reality before the beginning of the universe was a quantum object. There were many possible baby universes superimposed upon one another in potentia. Our particular universe materialized because the conscious desire of a sentient being chose to observe it. The universe does not begin at any particular time, it always *was* waiting for consciousness to actualize it. *Māyā* imposes the limits of form on the otherwise quantum world of virtual and undifferentiated reality, through the working of mind.

Indian thought, unlike the belief of the Judaic religions, does not consider the world as a singular event created from a mythical nothingness by a worldsmith god. But unlike other craftsmen, the worldsmithy of the Judaic god does not use any raw material to transform it into an artefact of his liking. He acts more as a conjurer who brings rabbits out of an empty and non-existing hat. Only god was existent prior to creation; therefore creation added an ontologically new category to the sum total of existence. The universe begins at a point and is led by an external controller god towards some pre-determined end in often most capricious manner, depending on the contingency of his ever changing plan for his creation. The split between the realm of the divine or the spirit, and the realm of ordinary manifest life, was formalized in Western science. Indian philosophy, on the contrary, stresses the basic unity of the universe in which all things exist in close inter-relationships. Once individuality is transcended man can meet the ultimate reality which is very much like his own self. This world is not ruled by an outside ruler but impelled by an inner and innate power that permeates all manifested phenomena as *antaryāmi parmeṣṭhin*. Man knows this reality not on hearsay but through his very own experience—*anubhava*—in which he feels the touch or *saṁsparśa* of reality through the exercise of his whole person. Indian experience of truth is empirical. And in that experience god does not exist in separation from man.

Once a man reaches the truth of the transcendent unity of creation it becomes difficult for him to remain satisfied with limited perspectives. Man wishes to break free of the limitations of ego, the 'I', and reach all 'others' as the only way to live with truth. With this realization the movement away from the individual ego—*ahaṁkāra*—and towards the collective and fundamental truth of the *Oṁkār* begins. Diverse people and diverse cultures, all move in their own way towards the unity of the fundamental reality like diverse streams moving towards and merging in the sea. The differences are illusory and men should not quarrel over such illusory and transient details but strive to look at the bigger and more real picture. This consuming desire to grasp the real picture gave courage to teachers and saints to transcend their own ego in a courageous effort of self-effacement. Lifting oneself above the pull of egotistical impulses involved the sacrifice of the self for the sake of attainment of the truthful cohesion of reality. It was not the denial of the self and the world of phenomena but a stepping away from an imperfect perspective and moving ahead on the scale of cognition of reality. Once a premise has been examined and found to be only partially explanatory of truth it was transcended to reach to a more advanced premise. The whole universe was permeated by only one reality—the *Brahman*. Chāndogya Upaniṣad says that this whole world is the *Brahman—sarvam khalvidaṁ brahma*. Śvetāśvatara Upaniṣad suggests that the whole cosmos is pervaded by the Supreme *Brahman: yenāvṛttaṁ nityaṁ idaṁ hi sarvaṁ*. But this standpoint can be accepted only by those who free themselves of all doubts, attachments, anger, fear and hatred and view their own selves as reflected in all other creatures:

> *yastu sarvāṇi bhūtānyātmanyevānupaś' yati*
> *sarvabhūteṣu cātmānam tato na vicikitsati.*[28]

Every individual derives meaning only in his sympathetic relationship with the rest of the world. Fritjof Capra says that, "The most important characteristics of the Eastern worldview—one would almost say the essence of it—is the awareness of the unity and mutual interrelation of all things and events, the experience of all phenomena in the world as manifestations of a basic oneness. All things are seen as interdependent and inseparable parts of this cosmic whole; as different manifestations of the same ultimate reality."[29] Material existence is just an abstraction unless it interacts with various other systems. In the language of quantum physics one can say that individual phenomena is not only a separate entity but also a relationship: " The world thus appears as a complicated issue of events, in which connections of different kinds alternate or overlap or combine and thereby determine the texture of the whole."[30] However, the multitudinous manifestation of the same ultimate reality is not an one-off productive affair but a continuously evolving and growing dynamic cosmos impelled by its own inherent force. Reality is pregnant with creative possibilities and it continues to alter, modify and create phenomena in the manner of the patterns created by new elementary particles that emerge and vanish incessantly in the bubble chamber of a particle accelerator. Reality appears to continuously change, but at the same time it also remains steadfast in its 'suchness' or, as the Vijñānvādins would say: its pristine *tathatā*. The dynamics of ceaseless change within the framework of the universal equilibrium of the *Brahman* is the reality of the Universe as captured in the image of the dancing *Śiva*. Marret has rightly suggested that many primitive religions were not as much 'though out' as 'danced out'. We may disagree with his use of the world 'primitive', but his prognosis was faultless. This universe is a ceaseless dance of the ultimate Reality—the *Brahman*.

Within this flux of events everything is a *saṁsāra*, i.e., a continuos process of appearance and disappearance in which man comes and goes in a series of many existences. The world of phenomena materializes within the infinite scope of the cosmic consciousness of the *Brahman*. The individual subject is just a finite cognizing unit in which the pure consciousness is restricted because of its association with *ahaṁkāra*. The process of existence begins not in an unitary manner but self-refrentially in association with many other phenomena. Buddhist philosophers describe this process as the law of Dependent Origination or *paticcasammupāda*. The world of names and forms come into existence in co-referentiality with one another, and if one thing arises it leads to the possibility of the existence of many others. Supreme *Brahman* chooses to create the world when it desires to sacrifice its unitariness to become many through focussed contemplation on its own existence. In its undisturbed state Reality is only existence, only consciousness and only bliss—*sat cit ānanda*. In its undisturbed and essential purity nothing exists but the Supreme *Brahman* in its self-subsisting infinite wisdom.

Śivasṁhitā records that the one reality is beginningless and endless, eternal consciousness. Nothing really exists except the eternal *jñān* and the differences are only appearances resulting from the extension of the singular reality through the discriminative attributes of various sensory functions:

ekaṁ jñānaṁ nityamādyantaśunyaṁ
nānyatkiṁcid vartate vastusatyam
yadbhedo' asminnindriyopādhinā vai
jñānasya bhāsate nānyathaiva.[31]

What exists is one single primal Being which tradition has called as *Brahman* or *Ātman*. Multiplicity arises when the *Brahman* is reflected variously in the limiting minds of *jīva* as the rays of the sun appear in different forms in the waters of different pots—*ekasya bhātyasaṁkhyatvam tadvadbhedo'atra dṛśyati.*[32] *Brahman* is the absolutely real but the multiplicitous and *saprapañca* world is only empirically real. Nevertheless it is the same unitary reality that is the material and efficient cause of phenomena; it is the *abhinna nimittopādāna kāraṇa* of the world and men. There may exist many pots but there exists only on real clay holding their differing forms onto it.

The knowledge of reality is not given in revelation. Man has to personally strive to seek the meaning of reality. The first step to start his search is from the contemplation of the structure of the universe of which he himself is an inseparable organic part. If man's congnizing functions determine the reality of the universe the best way to begin the search for the universal reality is to examine the structure of his own self. Indian philosophy emphasized the need to know our own selves when it proclaimed the doctrine of *ātmānam viddhi*: know yourself. Various schools of Indian epistemology have been generally inclined to inter-connect with psychology. Man is an organism endowed with the faculty for understanding and he is encouraged to use his discriminating intellect to dwell upon the nature of its inner self as well as the cosmic self. Śatapatha Brāhmaṇ describes man as possessing the necessary intellectual capacity to undertake this exercise: *atha khalu kratumāyo 'yam puruṣaḥ*. When man delves deep within himself he is able to see reality for himself. Aitareya Āraṇyaka regards all reality as dependent on a knowing self whose existence is said to be contingent only in the act of knowing:

tat prajñā netraṁ prajñāne pratiṣṭhitam. If the world exists as a function of consciousness, an examination of the reality of man's sentient faculty may give us a clue to the reality of the world itself. Examination of our forms of knowledge can reveal the nature of the phenomenal as well as the meta-phenomenal reality. The primal reality itself is knowledge—*prajñānam brahma.* It is in our experiential self that the whole world emerges, exists and finally perishes:

ātmanya eva jagat sarvaṁ dṛṣtimātraṁ satattvakaṁ,
udbhūya sthitiṁ āsthāya vinaśyati muhur muhuḥ.[33]

The Vijñānvāda School of Buddhism maintains that the world is inherently established in the creative activity of the self and an enquiry into the world should begin from the perspective of an individual's knowing self: *cittamātraṁ yadā lokaṁ prapaśyanti jinātmajāḥ.*[34]

The supreme consciousness limits itself into a creative mind when it desires to actualize the universe. The desire to observe splits reality simultaneously into an objective pole of observable phenomena and the subjective pole of a perceiving person. The subject-object polarity is created by the selective or measuring propensities of consciousness. The primal seed of phenomenal creation was sown in the essence of *Brahman* when it desired to see something other than its unique and blissful purity of existence. With this desire is born the primal mind that acts as the cosmic principle of which desire becomes the creative energy:

kāmas tadagre samvartatādhi
mahso retaḥ prathaman yad āsit.[35]

If the theory of dependent origination is followed then the first act of manifestation by the supreme person would begin an interminable cycle of emergence of many self-referential individual selves. All subsequent originations would however be mutually contingent upon one another and the supreme first person. If supreme *Brahman* chooses to materalize, for example, my individual self, my person only reflects his nature within myself. We all exist in reference to one another; remove the passions of the individuated mind and the great chain of cosmic causation is broken. The moment the 'I' vanishes the whole world resolves into its primal undisturbed blissful unitariness. The intent to be an individuated egotistical self is one of the important *vṛtti* of our consciousness and therefore Buddha was correct in advising us to transcend the constraints of desire. The desire 'to be' is one of the strongest of them. In the blissful nature of things perceivability ceases and we reach a state of a *darṣṭavyopasamam.*

Various means have been accepted by different schools of philosophy as contributing to the growth of knowledge. Taittirīya Āraṇyaka lists *smṛti* (scriptural testimony), *pratyakṣaḥ* (direct observation), *aitihya* (tradition) and *anumān* (inference) as various means of knowledge. It was believed by the proponents of Nyāya Sūtra that the means of knowledge and the objects of knowledge both go together in the sense that a lamp also illuminates itself. For this reason primacy was accorded to the direct experience of reality by an experiencer. Scriptural testimony was accepted as valid because they were the records of the personal experiences of reliable *mahātmās* who were qualified to record these judgements. However, every scripture was not regarded uncritically as valid means of knowledge, and tradition was always seen with a certain amount of scepticism. Kumārila Bhatta believed that tradition consists of much that is untrue and therefore it cannot be regarded as a reliable source of knowledge. Sāṁkhya Karikā describes knowledge of truth perceived by others as infused with impurity and subject to decay; tradition was a highly spurious source of knowledge: *dṛṣṭavadānusnavikāḥ sa hy aviśuddhikṣayatiśayayuktaḥ.* Rāmānujācārya was of the view that scriptural testimony is not always trustworthy and one's own direct knowledge of reality should take precedence over second hand revelation received from other men or some body of canonical doctrines.

The teachers of *Sanātan Dharma* believe that every idea, every concept should be subjected to the searing scrutiny of man's intellect and no doctrine was too sacrosanct to escape man's discerning intelligence. The job of philosophy is *tattva darśan* or seeing of truth personally. If *Brahman* is the truth then the way to know it is to enquire into that truth—*athātu brahmajijñāsa*. Śaṁkarācārya has categorically stated that no fact should be accepted by man without a proper enquiry. He advises that the knowledge of an object is only gained by perception, by investigation and not by blindly following the devotional theories or ritual practices of cultic life: *arthasya niścayo dṛṣto vicāreṇa hitoktitaḥ na snānena na dānena praṇāyāmśatena va.*[36] Truth is self-justificatory and it cannot be overridden by the authority of a revelation as fire cannot be said to be cold even if hundreds of assertions are quoted to say so from scripture.

Sanātan Dharma has steadfastly held the premise that an assertion does not become truthful simply on account of its being proferred by a holy man or by being written in a holy book. A propostiion is true only if can stand the test of experience and reason. Truth should be capable of being verifiable by all men. Śaṁkarācārya has clearly emphasised this point in his *bhāsya* on the Bṛhdāranyaka Upaniṣad: *na vākyasya vastvanvākhyānaṁ kriyānvākyānaṁ vā prāmānyāprāmāṇyakāraṇam kimtarhi? Niscitphalavat vijñanotpādakatvam. Tat yatra asti, tat pramāṇam vākyaṁ; yatra nāsti, tat apramāṇam*. The test of the validity of a sentence is not in the content of statement about a thing or about an act. Its validity lies in its capacity to generate certain and fruitful knowledge. A sentence that has this is valid; while one that lacks it is invalid.[37] Truth therefore is different from the sectarian and cloistered dogmas of a sect because the latter are never "subjected to the rigorous scrutiny of reason and being thrown open to universal verification."[38] Romain Rolland's comment on the Vedantic viewpoint can be said to be the characteristic feature of all schools of Indian philosophy: "It possess absolute liberty and unrivalled courage among religions with regard to the facts to be observed and the diverse hypotheses it has laid down for their coordination. Never having been hampered by a priestly order, each man has been entirely free to search wherever he pleased for the spiritual explanation of the spectacle of the universe."[39]

S. Radhakrishnan has cited various authorities to suggest that the spiritual leaders of India have always taken a "rational approach to the investigation of problems. This rational approach to the investigation of problems has been with us for a long time — *Buddhau śaraṇam anviccha"*.[40] Radhakrishnan states that Indians always had an empirical approach to reality and they claimed to attain some idea of truth only as the result of actual investigation. He says: "Śāstra-yonitvāt, *Śastras* merely register experiences. If these *śāstras* conflict with one another, *samanvāya eva sādhuḥ*, reconciliation is called for. Do not quarrel about other people's religion."[41] The *samanvaya or* reconciliation is a factor not of any dogmatic shoehorning but the application of discerning intellect. *Bhagawān Kṛṣṇa* advises Arjun in Gītā to know truth through humility and an enquiring disposition—*tadvidhi praṇipātena paripraśnena.* An instance of the intellectual, spiritual and existential freedom accorded to man in the *Sanātan Dharma* is available in Gītā. *Bhagawān Kṛṣṇa*, god himself, narrates to Arjun the truth of life and spirituality. At the conclusion of his discourse *Kṛṣṇa* does not force his will on his pupil. God does not command Arjun to accept on faith what has been told to him; Arjun is encouraged to deliberate on the matter intelligently and then follow a course which he thinks is truthful, just and best for himself:

> *"iti te jñānmakhyātaṁ guhyādguhyataraṁ mayā*
> *vimṛśyaitdaśeṣeṇa yathecchasi tathā kurū."*[42]

Even god's words are not to be forced violently on man. The ultimate validity of all wisdom is man's verificatory personal experience. No revelation, no prophetic vision is to be accepted without subjecting their propositions to detailed scrutiny. Teachers of *Sanātan Dharma* have repeatedly emphasized the values of *tapas* or deep spiritual enquiry and *manan* or reflection on the nature of a proposition. Truth cannot be asserted in the form of a dogma by an authority. Gautam Buddha cautioned his audiences against accepting his teachings and propositions on blind faith on account of the reverence in which they held him. Buddha exhorted his disciples to test his assertions personally before accepting and acting on them: *parīkṣya bhikṣavo grāhyaṁ mad vaco nātha gauravāt.*[43]

Buddha's exhortation resulted from his awareness of the fact that final truth cannot be captured by simply repeating the words of a teacher and the scriptures. Radhakrishnan provides an explanation: "So said the Buddha: *anakṣarasya dharmasya śrutih kā deśana kā* ; where is the scripture, where is the teaching for that which is inexpressible by letters ? For the truth which is inexpressible by the letters, there is no scripture, there is no teaching. Every man has to find it himself. It is the lonely seeker."[44] The desire to embark on a 'fearless quest' for truth has also been noted by many non-Indian scholars. Robert Ernest Hume, in his book 'The Thirteen Principal Upanisads', says: "In them we are always in the company of earnest students and teachers who discuss the central problems of all philosophy and religion with a sincerity and thoroughness, objectivity and detachment, rare in the history of philosophic thought."[45]

In a world view permeated by the dictates of experience and reason there was no place for rigidity and intolerance to emerge, as hatred for the views of others is a product of dogmatic and unscrutinized acceptance of an insular ideology. In a worldview based on detached and spiritual contemplation of the world the only acceptable dogma is the insistence on truth, and truth alone. Radhakrishnan has said in his 'Eastern Religions and Western thought': "Toleration is the homage which the finite mind pays to the inexhaustability of the Infinite." Obversely, insistence on the exclusivity of an idea and the intolerance of other viewpoints is the homage paid by the finite mind in its illusion of omniscience to its own megalomania. When this whole universe is considered to be emanating from a single source as an organically inter-dependent unity, all viewpoints that do not pay obeisance to this fundamental unity of reality cannot be said to lead us towards realization of the final and most fundamental truth. In their quest of truth Indian sages have brought to the altar of enquiry every idea, every experience and every tenet they happened to encounter. The differences in the spiritual vision of god is due to the differing circumstances and nature of men. Swami Vivekanand has said: "To the Hindu, then, the whole world of religions is only a travelling, a coming up, of different men and women, through various conditions and circumstances, to the same goal. Every religion is only evolving a God out of the material man, and the same God is the inspirer of all of them."[46] The manifest world of multiplicity is a product of the *māyopādhic* discernment of the *Ātman* in its abode of the *jīva.* Perceived by the mind in different attitudes the one appears as many; but at the fundamental level one and the many are the aspects of the same reality. Denying the right of his individual perspectival stance is to deny a man his ontology. The whole edifice of India's spiritual philosophy is based on the bedrock of tolerance, reason and a ceaseless process of quest. The outcomes of an enquiry were never pre-determined and teachers had the courage to accept the fact that their precepts can be debated, discussed and even proven inadequate. Swami Vivekanand was underlying this Indian attitude when he wrote: "We should, therefore, follow reason and also sympathize with those who do not come to any sort of belief, following reason. For it is better that mankind should become atheist by following reason than blindly believe on the authority of anybody."[47]

The spirituality of the *Sanātan Dharma* does not originate in the blind reception of a dogma on faith. Doctrines regarding the nature and worship of god, which in the Judaic tradition is called religion, emerge from within the soul of man as a process of his inner transformation. In this process man casts away every falsehood with the use of his discriminating wisdom. The path leading to god cannot be traversed by recitation of a few credal proclamations and the observation of prescribed rituals. It is not a path on which a herd can travel in the hypnotic fervour of an auto-suggested doctrine accepted on faith. The path leading to god is extremely thin and precarious; it is a pathway like the razor's edge—*kṣurasya dhārā*—which connect a man and his god face to face and one to one without the mediation of a third person or a doctrine. It is a path not demarcated with dogma but a path which, as Carlos Castaneda has put it, has a throbbing and loving heart. The most sacrosanct doctrine urges man to find truth and touch god in his own personal way. 'Religions' born in India within the framework of the *Sanātan Dharma* treat spirituality as an internal revolution in the existence of man. It is a revolution that does not destroy but transcends, under the light of the arisen discretion, the adjuncts of personal ego, the 'I-ness" of man, and brings his soul in intimate awareness of the all-pervasive reality of god. This spiritual revolution breaks free of every ritual and cultic practice. It is a search for the cosmic oneness within oneself by removing the *māyā* of multiplicity born out of our own ignorance. When the veil of *māyā* is lifted we see god; and when we see god we also *become* god:

tejo yatte rupaṁ kalyāṇataṁ tatte paśyāmi
yo asāvasau puruṣaḥ so ahamasmi.[48]

True spirituality does not lead man to the vision of a deity. In fact true spirituality begins when man starts transcending the specifications of various deities and focusses his attention on the fundamental truth behind them. Spiritual seekers are able to perceive the same truth behind all manifested and concretised deities. They are not perturbed by the apparent difference of human groups and their cultures. They know that on the other side of the prism of ignorance the patricoloured spectrum resolves in just one coruscating brilliance of divine light. But this quest is not possible for the meek of spirit and the fearful of disposition. This journey can be undertaken only by those seekers of immortality and truth who have a brave heart: *tamasomā jyotirgamaya, asatomā sadgamaya, mṛtyormā amṛtaṁgaṁaya.* Once the divine light dawns on man, the fear of death vanishes and he looks at the world with an eye that sees the same *parmātman* in all deities and the same *ātman* in all men. With the dawning of this realisation differences of caste, colour, religion and status vanish and all men become one fraternity of blessed humanity:

ajyeṣṭhaso akaniṣṭhās ete sam bhrātaro vāvṛdhuḥ
saubhagāya.[49]

What the Ṛg Vedic seeker saw through his *tapas* is now confirmed by the explorations of scientists. Gary Zukav while summarizing the standpoint of modern quantum and sub-atomic physics says: "There is only *one* reality, and it is whole and unified. It is one ... Everything is a manifesation of that which is. That which is, is."[50] When an Indian sage asserts reality to be one within the multiplicity of its manifestation he implicity accepts the possibility of finding that reality, whom he calls the *Brahman*, in every spiritual quest of man even if some pictures have dim and blurred contours. He does not follow the logic of those religions that believe, "God may be omnipresent, but his voice is in Jerusalem."[51] A Hindu on the contrary believes that god's voice is heard in every heart that sings of him with love:

nāham vāsāmi vaikunṭhe, yoginām hṛdaye na ca
madbhaktā yatra gāyanti, tatra tisṭhāmi narad.[52]

The fear of death and mortality derives its power from the belief that human beings are one-time gratuitous creation of god who would one day irrevocably destroy them and judge their souls on the basis of their adherence to a dogma. Mortality ceases to haunt the moment it is realized that every individual is a manifestation of the divine in a limited spatio-temporal cognitive environment. Once a person jumps out of this limiting environment he sees himself as the only eternal existence. The jumping-out from the perspective of individuation is accomplished by knowledge, *vidyā* or *jñān*. The Śvetāśavatara Upaniṣad tells us that to know this reality is to attain immorality—*tvaṁ jñātvā amṛtā bhavanti*. The same Upaniṣad informs us that the acknowledgement of man as the manifestation of the supreme *Brahman* confers immortality on the knowledgeable souls: *hṛda hṛdistham manasā ya yenamevaṁ viduramṛtāste bhavanti*. With the attainment of wisdom the differences of 'I' and 'thou' disappear and each enlightened soul is conscious only of an ineffable unity—*jñāte dvait na vidyate*.[53] The *prapañca* of names and forms, the *saṁsāra* of ceaseless coming and going dissolve in the blinding light of wisdom. What exists then is the Self in its all-pervading glory—*ātmalābhāt na paraṁ vidyate*.[54] Paradoxicadly, when all selves are transgressed only the Self remains. Till such time as this wisdom is reached man must not fall in the despair of egotism and he should respect every other human being because, even in their *māyic* manifestation, every individual is a temple of the divine and eternal *Śiva*: *deho devālayaḥ proktaḥ yo jīvaḥ sa sadāśivaḥ*.

Although the aim of all schools of philosophy and traditions of spirituality was to apprehend the full and final truth of the supreme *Brahman* or the *Param Puruṣa,* they never belittled the devotional beliefs and practices of the common worshipper. In the *vyāvahārik* or phenomenal perspective the world is real and meaningful, and in this world the *Brahman,* in association with its creative *māyā,* transforms itself as the divine creator and controller *Iśvara.* So long as man remains in the *vyāvahārik* world his view of god will be limited by the constraints of that perspective in which only one aspect of reality can be viewed by him depending on the perceptual techniques that he adopts. A scientific analogy can be found in the 'double-slit experiment' in which an electron can be either viewed as a particle or as a wave-pattern depending upon the observational tool that an experimenter sets up. The observed phenomena responds to the mode of observation. Beyond the ambit of the exercise of observation it is impossible to tell what the nature of the observed sub-atomic phenomena is. Reality as reflected in the process of cognition depends on the nature of questions man asks of it. Essentially, Reality is just the ground of all empirical phenomena that actualize in the experience of a sentient observer.

Every image of god that man creates for the purposes of devotion and worship constitutes the actualization of the one-and-only-god in that specific act of worship. The wide diversity in the manner of the apprehension of god, and the multiplicity of names and forms in which god is worshiped, is due to the wide diversity in the intellectual and attitudinal disposition that various men bring to bear on the existence of god. God actualizes itself in the devotional experiment that is set up for him as the specific deity or *devatā* of that particular act of worshipful apprehension. It is possible to have as many visions of god as there are men. Indians believe that every man can have his very own *iṣṭa devatā,* a god that he fervently wishes to have as his own. The meaning of the word *iṣṭa* corresponds to 'that which is wished for' or 'the occurrence of that which is desired'. In this sense *iṣṭa devata* is that aspect of god which reveals itself to man in a specific act of apperception. God does not split into many or *polytheize* into the distinct entities of manifold *devatās* any more than the reality of the quantum domain can be said to simultaneously split into different and distinct empirical entities. It is the same *Iśvara*, the same *devatattva* that manifests into and pervades the many names and forms of god: *mahaddevānāmsuratvamekaṁ*.[55] The Ṛg Veda tells that as the one fire burns in many hearts, one sun illuminates the whole world, one dawn variously removes darkness, so does the one divinity manifest itself in many forms:

ek evāgnirbahudhā samiddha
ekaḥ suryo viśwamanu prabhutaḥ
ekaivoṣā sarvamidaṁ vibhāti
ekaṁ vāidaṁ vi babhuva sarvam.[56]

The existence of many *devatas* is the spiritual correlate of the existence of the variegated world of phenomena. Just as the world is an undifferentiated non-dual reality in the transcendent or *paramārthik* perspective so are all *devatās* always reconciled and subsumed in the singularity of the supreme god, the *Parameśwar* or the *Parabrahman*. The *Parambrahman* limits itself in order that the world of phenomena may appear in a concrete and realizable form in the realm of physical existence. Likewise the *Parabrahman* submits itself to the categories of divine attributes and powers and becomes a *devatā* in the psychic realm of spiritual cognition. The Upaniṣads have proclaimed the correlation between the world of the soma and the world of the psyche: the illuminating power of the outward sun is only a physical correlate of the power of the eye. The sun, the seeing and the sight are fundamentally one. Therefore, if man desires to know god it is because the god within him wants to self-realize itself. It is possible to invoke god in the form of various *devatās* because all *devatās* are the essence of *Iśvara* perceived differently and they are collectively situated in every individual—*ātma ātmaiva devataḥ sarvaḥ sarva hyātmanyavasthitam*. As long as different people inhabit the earth there are bound to be different views of god. India has accepted and resovled her diversity through a unique stratagem that is rooted in her spiritual vision. The reality of difference is an essential part of the existence of our universe; the universe exists only because the one appears differentiated into many, and as long as we remain at the lower level of worldly perspective, differences would continue to define our world: *etā eva śrutayo bhedapratipatte saṁsārgāmanam darśayanti.*[57] The world of phenomena exists precisely because it is diverse and differentiated. But this apparent diversity is only a nescient state of cognizance. Fundamentally all differences resolve into an unity. In the understanding of this basic unity lies the secret of building a tolerant and fraternal civilization on the one hand and the attainment of spiritual salvation on the other: *abheda pratipattesca mokṣam darśayanti.*[58]

Sanātan Dharma encourages all men to follow a path of devotion and spirituality that is best suited to their individual disposition and state of enlightenment till full wisdom is attained. Indian traditions believe that man can attain union with god through the ways of righteous deed *(karma)*, devotion *(bhakti)* and knowledge *(jñān)*. All paths, if diligently pursued, lead to god. The aim of Indian devotion is not to secure a luxurious and opulent heaven but to grasp god with man's whole being. Everyman has to make the beginning at the foot of the hill of reality but with his slow ascent to the top the disturbances of vegetation and habitat are left behind and every step brings him that much closer to the undisturbed vision of the summit. Teachers of India have never denigrated any act of worship even though they may have found it inefficacious. They may at best point out the lower metaphysical merit of a particular practice, and encourage men to move towards a higher levels of spirituality. Three modes of spiritual practice have been recognized by various schools of religious philosophy. At the primary level men are required to adopt the means of *śravan*, or listening to the words of a doctrine or the spiritual perceptor with an open and respectful disposition. The act of reading and listening is not preceded by an attitude of compulsory faith. Every doctrine must be subjected to the process of *manan*; a process in which man applies his logical and rational intellect to the purport of a teaching because true knowledge can be attained only by the application of thought: *notpadyate vina jñānan vicāreṇānyasādhanai.* However the final means of attaining truth is the detached contemplation of truth itself—*nididhyāsan.* With the ripening of wisdom man leaves behind every doctrine in the manner of the removal of lower scaffoldings when a higher stage of a building is reached. In their own manner various texts guide man towards the finality of god's realm, and in a state of developed spirituality man is expected to transcend the limits even of the holy scriptures: *vihāya sarvaśastrāṇi yat satyaṁ tadupāsyatam.*[59]

Since men exist at various stages of intellectual development their devotional practices formalize in a wide variety of techniques. Various techniques of ritual, devotion, idolization, yoga, *dhyān, etc,* are specific means which are employed severally or together to focus the mind on god who is the integrating point of all human action. John M. Koller believes that, "The range of deities recognized and celebrated by the seers reveals the range of auspicious powers they felt and recognized"[60]. Various entities of the world—fire, water, food, air—were treated as the manifestation of some aspect of god and it was recognized that they are endowed with powers to control the workings of some part of man's composite existence. Every image that man made was the image of god even if only an approximation. The devotee was constantly reminded by learned teachers that all ideas and images can only be a dim approximation of the infinite existence of god. True devotion lies in moving beyond the world of a deity or a cult to the pure apprehension of fundamental nature of reality. An idea has a validity only because it serves as the starting point of a journey that would ultimately take the devotee to the truth beyond that idea. A deity can symbolize for a devotee in an ultimate manner the nature of god as he sees it, but the possibility of the apprehension of a richer mystery is always alive. A deity is ultimate in a *vyāvahārika* sense but not in the *paramārthik* sense: "To the extent that the symbol participates in the reality that it symbolizes, *Vishnu* (or god) is the ultimate. But to the extent that the reality symbolized goes beyond the symbol, Vishnu (or god) is less than ultimate[61]." All deities are only the symbols of the ultimate reality which itself has no name or form. Every deity is just a finger that points beyond its own self.

Therefore, in every symbolic representation of god, the emphasis has always been put on the content of reality which the symbol seeks to represent rather on the contours and forms of the symbol. A symbolic or deity-based representation of god only denotes and suggests a particular mode of apprehension of god. Deity is the projection of a name and form on god's unique reality that cannot be fully grasped by a human mind mired in the causal network of phenomena. The human mind is destined to see things through a complex of space-time and causality. The formless *Brahman* takes on name and form—*chadvarān āviveśa*—in order to create; and in the world of man it is possible to know only that aspect of the *Brahman* which intrinsically he is not: *anyad yuṣmāka—mantarṁ babhuva.*[62] In the *Brahma Sūtra*, Bādarāyaṇ Vyāsa has designated *Sūrya, Gāyatri,* etc, as the symbols of *Brahman*. A devotee was advised to see the vision of *Brahman* in the image or deity that he chose to contemplate. Meditation on the form of the symbol without a firm realization of the content of the symbol was considered futile. Men were encouraged not to meditate *on* the symbol but *through* the symbol.

Every symbol used to represent the reality of god is produced within the specific milieu of a culture. Symbols have a unique cultural validity and lose their meaning outside the culture that creates and uses them. Various cultures may use different symbols to symbolize universal realities like, beauty, goodness and god, but the difference in the form of the symbol does not negate the commonality of the reality being symbolized. It is therefore possible to break the façade of a symbol if the quest is directed towards the universal reality captured within the world of the symbols. Once the universal truths are known the modes of their representation become non-essential. Indian spiritual traditions have been aware of the transient necessity as well as the ultimate redundancy of a particular symbol and never quarrelled among themselves on account of a deity or an image because they knew that symbols are used: "not to designate, but cloak and conceal the imageless one, which stands behind them and towards which they strive."[63] In stark contrast to the viewpoint of Indian spirituality, Judaic religions propagate the complete and ultimate validity of their respective symbols. The symbol of the deity in a particular religion was considered to be the only reality that was worth contemplating. There may exist a reality beyond the confines of the specific symbol but it is considered unimportant and the faithful of the monotheistic religions is enjoined to limit himself to the particular deity of the faith. This symbol-related exclusivism is the root cause of the intolerance, heresy-hunting and insularity of monotheistic religions. Ernst Cassirer strongly advocates the inseparableness of the spiritual reality and the symbols of its representation in a religious tradition. He believes that India's attempt to use symbols as a *pro tem* measure in order to finally transcend them is a fruitless exercise because the essence of spiritual truth is available only in the symbol. There is no truth beyond the truth of the symbol and "taking the road back" from the symbol would be destructive of that truth because "the negation of the symbolic forms would not help us to apprehend the essence of life; it would rather destroy the spiritual form with which for us this essence proves to be bound up."[64]

Sanātan Dharma has never belittled any mode of worship. Worship of god in the form a deity in various devotional practices was, however, declared valid only in the world of common perceptions. The Supreme Reality, the *Brahman*, is indescribable, nameless and without a form. It is impossible to encapsulate his glory in any image that human mind can conjure. The Yajur Veda proclaims that the *Brahman* cannot be fully expressed in any form or image that is said to represent him—*na tasya pratimā asti yasya nām mahad yaśaḥ*. However, all forces of nature and all *devatās* are settled in the being of *Brahman* in the manner of the branches of the tree being eternally settled in the tiny seed: *tasminchhruyanne u ke deva vṛkṣya skandhaḥ parit iva śākhā*. Śaṁkara explains the apparent duality in the formless and attributive natures of *Brahman* on the basis of the perspective adopted to approach it. If the *Brahman* is approached for the purpose of knowing it, it is without any attributes. Attributes are projected on it for the purpose of devotion and worship—*upāsanārtham*. Depending on the way we relate to it, *Brahman* acquires form or remains without any attribute: *dve vāv brahmaṇo rupe murtam caivāmurtam martyaṁ camṛtāñca.*[65] In its essence *Brahman* is the ineffable supreme experience of existence, bliss and consciousness. The superpersonal aspect of *Brahman* can only be meditated and known; the personal aspect can be worshipped; and that is what the various traditions of devotion advise.

Radhakrishnan has said: "Our thought of the Supreme is, however, by means of images or pictures. Few there are who believe profoundly in god, and do not seek a symbol for their faith. Popular symbols have to be employed for the many who are not mentally fit to receive the true wisdom. We must not offend the little ones that believe, those of narrower intellectual horizon, who have also their rights."[66] Every form in which a seeker worships god gets suffused by the light and the spirit of the same eternal divinity. In accordance with the spiritual disposition of man the divine person assumes a form best suited to that particular disposition:

> *cinmayasyāprameyasya nirguṇasya' śarīriṇaḥ sādhakānāṁ hitārthāya brahmaṇo rupakalpaṇā.*

The nature of divine reality defies categories of measurement and description. Reality perceived by man is based on his personal spiritual experiences, and in every description of divine reality man exemplifies the essence of his own life. If god creates man in his own image the process is reciprocated by man in creating god on the basis of his own inner values. Deepak Chopra has rightly suggested that we select a deity based on our interpretation of reality, because in the absence of an act of choosing there would not be any defined outcomes. He goes on to add that, "In the same way god seems to grow directly out of our deepest inner values... I believe that God has to be known by looking into the mirror."[67] Every image that a worshipper creates of god is also his way of showing the mirror of his own being to the vast luminosity of god's reality. Since there are many experiential mirrors in which god's reality is reflected it is impossible to choose a single representative image: "No one can shoehorn god into a single base. We must have a range of vision as vast as human experience itself."[68]

Sanātan Dharma indulgently accepts the wide variety of modes in which god can be known and worshipped. All modes of worship are truthful, even though in a limited manner: "Even if they are shadows, they are cast by the light of lights... Unless there is a correspondence between our deepest spirit and the religious representation, we shall not be impressed by it."[69] It is the same eternal and formless, *nirupādhik, Brahman* that is given the attributes of names and forms in every act of worship. Although *Brahman* and its nature are indistinguishably synthesised, it is possible for spiritual seekers to describe it by the use of various concrete epithets: *bhedābhāve'pi bhedavyavahārnirvāhakā anantā ek viśeṣaḥ*.[70] The transcendent *Brahman* is also immanent in the world, and it is its immanence that all religious exercises try to comprehend. It was, however, never forgotten by a *Sanātan* worshipper that in whatever form he was worshipping god the worship was in the ultimate analysis directed to the one and only lord, the Supreme *Brahman*:

namaste gaṇapataye tvam eva kevalaṁ kartāsi
tvameva kevalaṁ hartāsi tvameva kevalaṁ khalvidaṁ
brahmāsi.[71]

Man cannot pray to many 'god'; he can only pray to god in many different manners. All men live within the reality of the *Brahman-Paramātman* and the *Paramātman* constitutes the core of every man's existence. Therefore, the same *Paramātman* is invoked in every image of divinity cherished by man. Those who realize this truth cast away the bonds of anger and hatred of others:

yastu sarvāṇi bhūtānyātmanyevānupaśyati
sarvabhuteṣū cātman tato na vijuguptasate.[72]

Sanātan Dharma has taught the world that it is possible. The incredible Hindu tolerance emanates for the civilizational belief that the dieties of every culture are but a symbol of the one single divine reality.

Ekoham Bahusyam

I am one but I become many

One of the serious problems that impede the understanding of god in various traditions of *Sanātan* spirituality arises from the dubious equivalence assumed between the notions of *Iśvara* or *Bhagawān* and *deva* or *devatā*. Many commentators on Indian religions have fortuitously used the words *devatā* and *Iśvara* as interchangeable. The perception of many common Hindus follows the lead of scholarship and confuses the two terms as expressive of the same idea. This line of thinking generates highly dubious theories of 'many–godism' which is popularly known as polytheism. In the Indian context it is explained as *bahudevavāda* or *anekeśvarvāda*. The metaphysics of the S*anātan* tradition uses the concept of various *deva* or *devatā* for a very specific purpose. The divine unitariness and spiritual elevation expressed by the words *Iśvara, Bhagawān* and *Parameśwar* are completely different from the concept of *devatā*. Since there are many *devatās* the not so subtle equivalence between *devatā* and *Iśvara* creates the egregious theory of the belief in the existence and worship of many 'gods' by Hindus. If the confusion between the two terms are not resolved the understanding of Indian idea of god would always remain inadequate.

The confusion worsens when the concepts of *devatā* and *Iśvara* are equated with the notion of the Judaic god. The Judaic notion of god is highly personalized and theistic. Theism of the Judaic variety is not considered necessary for the notion of god in the *Sanātan* tradition. In fact, theistic understanding of god is only one of the many ways in which S*anātan Dharma* interprets the idea of god. It is important to remember that the Judaic and Indian views of theism differ greatly from one another. In order to clearly understand the notion of god in the *Sanātan* context its correlation with the notion of the Judeo-Christian god must be severed. Unless the paradigmatic boundary between the two notions are clearly demarcated and understood the danger of illicit metaphysical trespass cannot be obviated. The Judaic god is not the *Iśvara* of S*anātan Dharma*. *Iśvara* creates differently, it manifests itself differently and its relationship with man and the world are of a very different order. At a fundamental level an Indian seeker looks at a reality that is even greater than the theistic notion of *Iśvara*. Saints and sages have impelled men to push beyond the limits of a particular manifestation and apprehend the one great truth that exists `everywhere and in everything. Godliness or *Iśvaratā* is only an expression of the Supreme Being who is the ultimate reality and the ultimate truth.

The mixing of the divine metaphors was caused, to a large measure, by the efforts of some modern exegetists whose desire to find a forced commonality between the gods of various traditions uncritically followed the lead of some of the Western scholars of Indology. Special respect was accorded to those scholars who were associated with the ruling establishment and the academia of Britain. It was their views that acquired a normative value in the eyes of many important modern Indian scholars. In spite of the considerable scholarship brought to bear upon Indian texts and traditions, a majority of the British indologists of the late eighteenth and nineteenth centuries either missed, or misinterpreted, the core issues of the texts under examination. They did not try to understand the message from the standpoint of the original source but heard only its distorted echo in their minds full of pre-conceived prejudices. To begin with, they benchmarked their own European and Christian ideas of divinity as the standard for the evaluation and understanding of the Indian spiritual tradition. Parameters of exegesis were not derived from the tradition that was the subject of analysis but from a religious tradition that subscribed to a totally different metaphysics. References to various *devatās* were forcibly interpreted in reference to the gods of the Greek and the Roman pantheon. As a result the scriptural idea of *devatā* was completely distorted and trivialized. The distortion proceeded to such an extent where *Śri Rāma* was identified with Dionysus and the Vedic *Uṣās* with Eos.

Many European indologists tended to emphasize the ritualistic and cultic interpretation of the Vedic *mantra*. Scholars like William Jones, Max Muller and A.A. Macdonell chose to borrow mainly from the Vedic commentaries of Sāyan (born1315 AD) and Mahidhar. In their desire to find a theological and ritual motive behind the Vedic Samhitā, many important translators found in the commentaries of Sāyan a strong indigenous support. There were, however, many other scholars who found in Sāyan's interpretation of the Vedas an attempt to transpose the contemporary meaning of classical Sanskrit and the ritual practices onto the totally different worldview of the Vedic hymns. Professor Roth has questioned the tendency to treat Sāyan and Mahidhara as the indisputable authorities for the interpretation of the Vedic hymns. He said: "As the so called classical Sanskrit was perfectly familiar to them they sought its ordinary idiom in the Vedic hymns also. Since any difference in the ritual appeared to them inconceivable and the present forms were believed to have existed from the beginning of the world, they fancied that the patriarchs of the Indian religion must have sacrificed in the same manner.... It has never occurred to any one to make our understanding of the Hebrew books of Old Testament depend on the Talmud and the Rabbins, who hold it as the duty of a conscientious interpreter of the Veda to translate in conformity with Sayan, Mahidhara, etc."[1]

Scholars associated especially with the Boden professorship—H.H. Wilson, Max Muller, etc—continued to stress the superiority of Sāyan's interpretation over other commentators like Yāska. They based their translations not on the sense in which the Vedic seers visualized them but in a manner that rendered the divine poetry and spiritual symbolism of the Veda as an accompaniment to liturgical exercises. The relegation of ancient etymologists like Yāska was encouraged by Max Muller who found the learned lexicographer an impediment to his own hermeneutical design: "As the author of the Brahmans were blinded by theology, the authors of the still later Niruktas were deceived by etymological fiction, and both conspired to misled by their authority later and more sensible commentators, such as Sayan."[2] Majority of the Western scholars implicitly believed that the ancient corpus of the Vedas must be the product of a primitive and barbarian civilization because in their worldview any spiritual tradition chronologically prior to the evolution of Christian theology must necessarily be bereft of a higher vision. Comparative mythologists, philologists and anthropologists supplied the necessary theoretical framework for comparison of religions that was indiscriminately applied by scholars to all cultures. The argument ran that if a primitive and less evolved society of Australia, Africa or Polynesia formulated mythologies and systems of worship in a particular ritualistic way there was no reason why the ancient seers of the Vedas would be any different from them. Historical antiquity was enough ground for the assumption of the lower spirituality of a culture and on this ground the Vedic seer was obviously an incorrigibly superstitious ignoramus. The message of the Veda was interpreted with a viewpoint to portray its affinity with the ritualistic practices of other primitive societies. The Vedic *mantra* was seen as an Indian equivalent of the voodoo performance of savage society.

Comparative mythologists sought to link Indian spiritual thought to a wide range of primitive liturgical practices obtaining in diverse and unrelated cultural settings. The logic was simple: since the Vedas are old they are *ipso facto* primitive, and therefore they must elicit a close affinity with the ideas found in the rituals of other primitive societies. These rituals were believed to have preserved the hoary and common original vision of man as a frozen embryo in the formaldehyde of their isolated geographical enclaves. Sir William Jones was of the firm faith that, "Gods of all shapes and dimensions may be framed by the boundless powers of imagination, or by the frauds and follies of men, in countries never connected." Jones believed that *Ādiśakti Śri Lakṣmi* was only the Indian version of

Ceres; Manu was the corruption of the Biblical Noah; and the stories of *mahāpralay* are borrowed from the deluge myth found in the Hebrew tradition. Apart from interpreting Indian tradition in the light of the mythological data from certain primitive societies, Western exegesis propagated the notion that the similarities between the idolatrous practices of India, Greece, etc, were a result of these nations migrating and branching out from a common homeland. Once the association with primitive religious practices was premised it became possible to traduce the Indian idea of god and *devatā* as fanciful divinization of natural phenomena and material objects.

Sir William Jones is on record as saying, "...the whole crowd of gods and goddesses in ancient *Rome* and modern *Varanes* mean only the powers of nature, expressed in a variety of ways and by a multitude of fanciful names...Be all this as it may, I am persuaded, that a connexion subsisted between the old idolatrous nations of Egypt, India, Greece and Italy, long before they migrated to their several settlements." H.H. Wilson believed that teachers and saints, like Jaideva and Anandgiri, were scheming crooks and compulsive liars. In his translation of the Viṣṇu Purāṇa, Wilson tried to prove that some of the Purāṇa were the product of a very recent period while others were just counterfeit renditions held by tradition to be sacred. Max Muller never gave up his principal belief that the Vedic corpus was the product of an uncivilized race of heathens and savages whose labours were as valuable as the rantings of fools. Max Muller said, "The general character of these works is marked by shallow and insipid grandeloquence, by priestly conceit, and antiquarian pedantry..."[3] He believed that these works deserve to be studied for the same purpose that the physician studies the twaddles of idiots, and the ravings of madmen. According to Max Muller, various *deva* were the bright natural objects who were gradually sacralized to become heavenly gods. In spite of this naturalistic interpretation of the *deva*, Max Muller always translated the term to mean god.

These European scholars developed and propagated the theory that Vedic hymns were a largely barbaric representation of primitive religious conceptions. Sāyan's admission of recognizable historical elements in the Veda encouraged these scholars to find clues in the words of the Veda to the history of a 'primitive' Vedic society and its propitiatory sacrifices. The deficiencies of the methodology of comparative mythology has been pointed out by many later day Indian scholars who believed that: "It has founded its interpretation on a theory which saw nothing between the early savage and Plato or the *Upanisads*."[4] Śri Aurobindo has recorded with satisfaction the positive spin-off of the modern foreign scholarship which "broke after many centuries the seal of final authoritativeness which Sayan had fixed on the ritualistic interpretation of the Veda." Śri Aurobindo was aware of the limitations of foreign scholarship in dealing with the Vedic material and his views on this matter are very pertinent to the issue which is under current investigation. He writes: "The ancient scripture was delivered over to a scholarship—laborious, bold in speculation, ingenious in its flight of fancy, conscientious according to its own lights, but ill-fitted to understand the method of the old mystic poets; for it is void of any sympathy with that ancient temperament, unprovided with any clue in its own intellectual or spiritual environment to the ideas hidden in the Vedic figures and parables. The result has been of a double character, on the one side the beginning of a more minute, thorough and careful as well as a freer handing of the problems of Vedic interpretation, on the other hand, a final exaggeration of its apparent material sense and the complete obscuration of its true and inner secret."[5]

The ritualistic interpretation of the Western interpreters branded a conjectural meaning on the Vedic texts. A corpus that was universally recognized as the source of some of the finest philosophies, metaphysics and religions was interpreted in the manner that befits the interpretation of bedtime stories. Śri Aurobindo has regarded the Western interpretation of the Vedic tradition as totally off the mark. He said: "Both of them present one characteristic in common, the extraordinary incoherence and poverty of sense, which their results stamp upon the ancient hymns."[6] Vedas have been commented upon by many Indian scholars through the many millenia they have been in existence. In some sense most of Indian philosophy and the schools of metaphysics have been an attempt to understand the deep Vedic message from a specific perspective. The unfolding of the Indian civilization itself is a living exegesis on the Vedas. And the process has not stopped. The subtle attempt to split the essential spiritual vision of the Vedic corpus between the *Saṁhitā* and the Upaniṣadic parts is a contrived attempt to separate the message of the cryptic formulas of the *mantra* and its philosophical elaboration in the Āranyakas and the Upaniṣads. Swami Dayananda in his commentary on the Veda has also decried the practice of simplistic reading of the texts as if they were a historical record. He believed that the Vedas were the source of much of Indian spiritual wisdom and their message can be garnered only by a careful analysis of their symbolism. An interpretation that tries to crack the symbolism of the Vedic literature with the help of clues derived from ritualistic practices and comparative mythology rather than the internal suggestiveness of the texts would miss their complex and rather fluid import. Śri Aurobindo was aware of the danger and believed that, "It is only by a violent struggle with the text that we can force on it a less complex aspect."[7]

The aim of intellectual exercise should be to understand the correct meaning of a concept by disengaging from the unnatural and violent struggle of forcing an alien meaning on it, and by listening to what the original users have to say about those concepts. A beginning can be made by not treating the concepts of *devatā* and *Iśvara* as homologous. The idea of *devatā* or *deva* is used in the Indian religious literature in a complex variety of ways. In certain contexts the word *devatā* may connote a meaning close to that of god or *Iśvara,* but this is a very special use of the word and even in such usage it was never intended to become a complete substitute for the idea of 'god'. *Iśvara,* of course, can be known as a *devatā* but he is also much more than that. The word *devatā* was originally used in the *mantras* of the various Vedic Saṁhitās. In the Veda the word is used for a very specific purpose that is closely related to their design and structure. It is said that no Vedic *mantra* can be properly understood unless the seer and the particular *devatā* of that *mantra* are identified, and the intention of the seer of that *mantra* is kept in mind. The subject matter of the *mantra* and the intention of the seer are closely related. In fact, what the seer intends to express through a *mantra* determines what the *devatā* of that particular *mantra* would be. A particular vision of the seer relates to the invocation of that vision of reality in the form of a specific *devatā*. Stylistically, *devatā* can be seen as a part of the structural design of the text that helps in understanding its intention and meaning. Another important characteristics of *devatā* is its religious import wherein the word becomes a limited but powerful apprehension of a much higher reality. The Bṛhaddevatā says that one should know the divinity or the *devatā* of a *mantra* with precision in order to understand the object of the *mantra*:

> *veditavyaṁ daivataṁ hi mantre mantre prayatnataḥ*
> *daivatajño hi mantrāṇāṁ tadarthamavagacchati.*[8]

At the primary level, therefore, the word *devatā* means the subject matter or the theme of the Vedic verse. But the seers of the hymns do not treat their *devatā* in an isomorphic manner. The subject matter or the *devatā* of a hymn is determined by the intention of the seer and the sphere of the cosmos which the seer in a particular instance is concentrating his focus on. The eulogies addressed to the *devatā* directly and indirectly are the most numerous in the Veda. Yāska says: *Tastṛvidhā ṛcaḥ. Parokṣakṛtāḥ pratyakṣakṛtāḥ ādhyātmikyaśca.*[9] A *mantra* or hymn is mostly addressed to a *devatā* because the Vedic seer prefers to express himself in relation to a particular aspect of reality that engages his reflective attention at a particular moment. When a particularly powerful vision presents itself before the *ṛṣi* he correlates in that vision the cosmic, social and personal similarities with reference to the *devatā* that serves to epitomize the essence of that vision. The *mantra* is a verbal representation of the intention, desire, thought and reflective disposition of the seer:

> *yatkāma ṛṣiryasyaṁ devatāyām ārthapatyamicchan*
> *stutin prayuñkte taddaivataḥ sa mantro bhavati.*[10]

There are certain *sūktas* in the Veda where the seer does not specifically mention a *devatā*. For such cases two alternative courses are proposed by the ritualistic interpreters and the etymologists respectively. According to the interpretation of the ritualists (*yajñika*) the *devatā* of such *sūkta* is *Prajāpati*, whereas according to the etymologists *(nairuktāḥ)* the *devatā* is *Narāśaṁs*. In some of the *mantra* we come across reference to certain persons, objects and natural entities that are mentioned in the place of the more familiar Vedic deities. Yāska believes that for the purpose of that particular *mantra* all the aforementioned objects should be regarded as the *devatā* of the *mantra*. Human beings, animals, even plants and inanimate objects are indicated by the seers as *devatā* of a hymn because they are believed to shine by the glory of the one Supreme Self that pervades everything:

> *Prāyodevatā vā. Asti hyācāro vahulaṁ loke devadevatyamatithi devatyam pitṛdevatvam ... yajñadaivato mantra ityapi hyadevatā devatāvat stuyante yathaśvaprabhṛtinyoṣadhiparyantānyathāpyṣtau dvandvāni.*[11]

The Vedic seers conceptualize the *devatās* of various *mantra* by assigning those *devatās* to the different spheres of the universe. The three spheres in relation to the earth are, earth *(prithivi)*, space *(antarikṣa)* and the trans-space region *(dyāu)* or the heavens. Depending on the sphere of the universe which is the perspectival determinant of the seer's contemplative vision, the nature and name of the *devatā* evolve in the invocation of a *mantra*. The invocation represents the spatial and the cognitive framework within which a particular aspect of reality is contemplated. *Devatā* of a mantra is not only indicative of the mood of the seer but also exemplifies his perception of a phenomena within some manageable category of, otherwise, infinite and complex space. The forces of the universe appear differently modified in the various realms of space and time and their interactions among themselves and with men is regulated by the characteristics they acquire within that particular realm. Seen from a cosmic perspective, the world appears split between the realms of the earth, the space and the heavens, and, therefore, accordingly the underlying force behind the whole created cosmos also appears modified in relation to these three spheres. When the seer looks at the universe he does not see a creation that has only a material nature; he recognizes a deeper divine meaning underlying the materiality of the world of phenomena. The sun, the stars, the moon, etc, do not remain mere material objects but acquire a deeper significance that transforms them as spiritual entities embued with the power to affect everything that enters in a relationship with them. Space is not only a disembodied *antarikṣa* but a realm of infinite evolutions and dissolutions taking place incessantly within its body.

In its characteristic flourish, Indian tradition attests to the existence of three hundred and thirty million *devatās*. That apparently is the largest number mentioned by any text regarding the existence of *devatās*. The Ṛg Veda mentions three thousand three hundred and thirty nine *devatās* whereas the Aitareya Brāhmaṇ speaks of the existence of thirty-three. The larger number appears only to be a stylized way of enumeration drawing from a ritual tradition in which the number thirty-three, and its variations, are considered to have special efficacy—*trayas trimśad devaḥ*. Although different numbers have been mentioned in various texts, Vedic literature and the scriptural treatises generally talk of the presence of thirty-three *devatās*. The *devatās* in thirty-three forms can be indentified as belonging to the three principle groups of the *Vasus*, the *Rudras* and the *Āditya*. The Aitareya Brāhmaṇ says: t*rayastriṁsādvai deva aṣṭau vasu ekadaśrudra dvādaśāditya prajāpatiśca vaṣatkāraśca*.

The division of all the *devatā* references into three functional and spatial categories is comparable to the division of the created world into the three categories of the terrestrial, mid-region and celestial realms. Each group of *devatās* is, therefore, assigned its abode in one of the three realms. Although we find references to many *devatās* in the Vedic literature, these are only an imaginative expansion of the three basic *devatās*. These three basic *devatās*, according to the Nirukta of Yāska, are *Agni* in the terrestrial region or the earth, *Vāyu* or *Indra* in the mid-region and *Sūrya* in the celestial realm: *tisṛ eva devatā iti nairuktāḥ. Agni pṛthvisthāno vāyurvendro va'antarikṣaṣthānḥ Sūryo dyuhsthānaḥ*. All *devatās* resolve into the three primary images of *Agni*, *Sūrya* and *Vāyu* who dwell in their respective cosmic realms as its controlling and defining power.

Bṛhadāraṇyaka Upaniṣad narrates an interesting exchange between the sages Vidagdha Śākalya and Yājñavalkya regarding the nature and number of *devatās*. When asked to indicate the number of *devatās* that exist, Yājñavalkya reads the popular *Vaiśvadeva* protocol to Śākalya in which a total of 3,306 *devatās* are mentioned. This answer did not satisfy Śakalya and he continued with his probing in a rather rude manner. After every response he would repeat his original question—how many *devas* are there? Yājñavalkya enumerates the traditionally accepted numbers mentioned in various texts but finally adds his own firm view that in reality there is only one *devatā*; the multiple *devatās* that found mention in the texts are the diverse apprehension of one single primal *devatā*. Yājñavalkya accepts the suggestion of thirty-three *devatās* relatable to the three cosmic realms not as separate entities but only as the glory or *mahima* of one *devatā*: *mahimān evaiṣāmete trayastṛṁśatteva deva iti*.[12] The Upaniṣadic thought conforms to the Vedic design of treating the three *devatās—Agni, Vāyu, Āditya*—as the most fundamental among all the powers that are manifest in the world. Other *devatās* are regarded as the functional modifications and elaborations of the three principal ones. Yājñavalkya has categorized the three cosmic realms as being *devatās* in their own rights and hinted at their possible identity with the *devatā* that manifest in those realms: *ime eva trayo loka eṣu hīme sarve deva iti*.[13]

The thirty-three principal *devatās* are divided by some texts into Soma-drinking or the *somapā* and the non-Soma-drinking or the *asomapā* groups. The *devatās* of the *somapā* group are sub-classified as *Vasus, Rudras* and *Ādityas* while the *asomapā* group is sub-classified as *Prayāja, Anuyāja and Upayāja*, having eleven *devatās* in each group. A small reminder, however, would be in order here that the differences in names of the *devatās* in the same group should not be construed to signify different *devatās*. That is not how the Vedic tradition views and describes reality. It is not rare to find one *devatā* being addressed by various names, and sometimes two *devatās* being equated functionally across the notional distinctions imposed on them by their respective realms. The Ṛg Veda informs us that *Indra* can be seen by the seers in various forms which the former assumes because of his extraordinary power—*rūpam rūpam maghvā bobhaviti māyāḥ kṛṇvanastanvaṁ pariswam*.[14] It is the *māyā* of the great *Indra* that transform him in many forms in the vision of the *ṛṣi*. The meaning of a Vedic *mantra* is dependent on the interrelationship of the seer, the metrical form in which the *mantra* is expressed (*chanda*), and the *devatā* which is the principle focus of the *mantra*. When a *mantra* is used for the performance of a ritual, the purpose (*viniyoga)* of the ritual is an additional aspect of the meaning of the *mantra*. Without the knowledge of the seer, the meter, the purpose and the *devatā* of the *mantra,* its application and recitation would not serve any purpose:

ṛṣi cchando daivatāni brāhmaṇārthasvarādapi
aviditva prayuñjano mantrakantaka ucyate.

This complex structure is inevitable because a *mantra* is not intended to convey ordinary descriptive meaning but the deep spiritual secrets of the world. Therefore, they necessarily carry an aroma of teasing mystery about them. A *mantra* seeks to convey, in human language, a truth that is hidden at the core of reality, and defies a straight forward translation according to the normal rules of discourse—*yad guhā tad addhātaya id viduh*.[15] The Vedic seer saw a deep reality within every manifested and unmanifested phenomena of the world. It is a reality that precedes everything that has ever existed and also remains ever present in everything that exists and will exist. It is this ineffable, indescribable and non-formal heart of reality that is sought by the *rsi* in his deep and austere contemplation. The *ṛṣi* does not create or author a *mantra* because the *mantra* has always existed; the *ṛṣi* only sees and comprehends the *mantra* that otherwise remains outside the limitations of time and space. A *mantra* is an image of reality which is reflected deép in the heart of the *rsi-hṛdā sutaśtam mantram.*

The *ṛṣi* wants to observe and convey a principle that is the pure and supereminent source of all reality. It is impossible for any contemplative effort to grasp that principle in totality. Whenever a glance is cast towards that principle it only reveals an infinitesimally small aspect of reality. In order to make some sense of this infinite incomprehension, the *ṝṣis'* spiritual vision ascribes some form on the object of vision in order to make his vision communicable. His ultimate goal is a vast ocean of consciousness that manifests itself in various forms and varying degrees of potency in many aspects of nature. It is possible for certain objects to possess great potency and spiritual power because their powers are embedded in their nature owing to their organic relation with the common source that is the fountainhead of all power in the world. A human being can become aware of this power if he is able to connect to his own true nature and redirect the inexhaustible flow of energies inside his own heart. It is possible for a truly awakened soul to visualize various aspects of reality. Reality materializes in the spiritual experiment of the seer in which he becomes the observer, his intention serves the purpose of his experimental setup and the *devatā* emerges as the result of his observation. *Devatās* symbolize an aspect of reality that has materialized in the seer's vision and become symbolically shareable with other human beings through the medium of the *mantra*. But it is not a static and immutable aspect of reality that seeks to perpetuate the name and form originally assumed by it; it is the ever emerging dialectical flux in which names and forms are fleeting occurrences that emerge, blur and re-emerge in an eternal process of becoming. What the *ṛṣi* sees is just one nugget of the infinite possibility that sleeps in the bosom of the eternal being. The fact that millions of *devatās* are said to exist, only serves to underline metaphorically the utter non-finality and transience of every vision, with the suggestion that it is possible to see a totally new vision of reality that conforms to a shift in the angle of vision. It is the finality of the substrate on which images of reality superimpose that is true; the superimposed images are temporary appurtenances that human mind uses to make some sense of the deep underlying mystery.

A *mantra* translates the seer's vision of the cosmic order with the interplay of natural and moral laws enacted in the world, and also within himself. He does not draw a conclusion based on hearsay or second-hand information but sees things for himself as they actually happen at the highest levels of existence. The importance of the personal vision of the *ṛṣi* is stressed by Yāska when he refers to them as ṛ*ṣirdarśanāt*. The Taittiriya Āraṇyaka derives the word *ṛṣi* from the root '*ṛṣ*' which mean to go upward, to appear. The *ṛṣi* is a visionary whose vision takes a man from baser to higher levels of reality, till the highest level of the *Brahman* is realized: *ajān ha vai pṛśniñstapasya mānan brahm svayambhavabhyanaṣat tad ṛṣyo' abhavan.*[16] It is said that a *mantra* could be seen by a *ṛṣi* after a life of strict and strenuous discipline in which the outward vision is also authenticated by their own inner experience. Visions of truth do not come by factors of accident or a sudden and immediate but unsolicited input from an alien source. Truth is sought by a *ṛṣi* through great penance, learning and laborious spiritual effort: *yamṛṣayo mantrakṛto manīṣiṇaḥ anvaichan devaḥ tapsa śramen.*[17] The secret of the core of truth is, however, finally illumined by the light that burns in the pure heart of the *ṛṣi.* The heart of the *rsi* becomes the place where god descends to meet man and unravel those secrets that otherwise remain hidden from the normal gaze.

An event is bound to have its locus in one of the three realms of the universe. Human experience of these events would always arise with reference to one or other of these spatial specificities. At a higher level the three realms are just the statements or the experiential modifications of a single act of creation; for practical purposes the three-fold division serves to causally arrange in a temporal hierarchy the components of a world that fundamentally has its past and future simultaneously present in an eternal now. It is a limitation of the normal human mind to see reality in terms of the categories of time and space, existence and non-existence, and subject and object. The desire to identify a thing and describe it in human terms would impose an *a priori* necessity of separating it from other things and assigning to it an identifiable locus in space and time. But reality at the most fundamental level does not exist with such discreet categories in attendance. At that level, time, space and matter do not exist in the way they are understood in the phenomenal world and everything stays resolved in an undifferentiated unison. The Atharva Veda informs that the only existing reality is the one pervading being as *Viṣṇu* in whom all measuring categories are innately established. It is said that existent is established in the non-existent; in the existent the past and present are established; the past and the present are established in the future; the future is established in the past and the present; and all in turn are established in the one great *Brahman* who causes and pervades them as *Viṣṇu*: *asati satpratiṣṭhitaṁ sati bhūtaṁ pratiṣṭhitam bhūtaṁ ha bhavya āhitaṁ bhavyaṁ bhūte prastisthitaṁ tavedviṣṇo bahudhā vīryāṇi.*[18] But when *Viṣṇu* manifests in and pervades the world of phenomena he assumes the power of measuring his own reality by becoming the *trivikram:* that which measures and thereby causes the emergence of the world of three realms by taking three giant steps as it were. That may be the reason why sages call this world the product of a measuring *māyā.*

Different names and forms of *devatās* are the identifying categories of the power and force of the one supereme being of *Viṣṇu—tavedviṣṇo bahudhā vīryāṇi*—who is apprehended in many spheres and objects of the world. The seers repeatedly point out that invocation of many names does not imply the invocation of parts of god that can be said to have been caused by the splitting of his nature into many centres of lesser potencies. These invocations are not addressed to the material object that happens to be symbolized by a name. The invocations address the underlying majesty of the one supreme power which is the ground of all reality, although its glory and power is manifested in many forms. In the cosmic sense the glory of the Supreme Lord is reflected variously in the three realms of earth, mid-region and space as *Agni, Indra* and *Sūrya* respectively. Acosmically these three *devatās* converge into only one *devatā.* Yāska holds the view that the three principle forms of *devatās* are rooted in the nature of a single reality—*ekasyātmano'anye devāḥ pratyañgāni bhavanti.* The essential power, the *Ātman,* is one *devatā* of all *devatās,* while various *devatās* represent merely multiple aspects thereof: *ātmā sarvaṁ devasya.* Although the seers use many names and forms in the *mantra* to describe and eulogize various activities of the Lord, their heart is steadfastly fixed on its unitary essence: *māhābhāgyādekaikasyā api bahūni nāmdheyāni bhavantyāpi va karmapṛthaktvāt.*[19] The one *Ātman* possesses great powers—*mahābhāga*—but due to its manifestations in many forms the seer invokes him in many different ways.

The Bṛhaddevatā of Śaunaka is a very important compendium on the nature, origin and function of various Vedic *devatās*. Its methodology for the examination of the *devatās* of the *mantra* follows the system of the Vedic triad. Various *devatās* of the Veda are said to belong to three principle groups of which *Agni, Sūrya* and *Indra* are the representative *devatās.* Numerous *devatās* of a group do not exist as different individuated entities but as of the same nature of the principle *devatā* of their group:

p*rathamo bhajate tvāsāṁ vargo'gnimih daivatam*
dvitiyo vayumindraṁ va tritiyaḥ sūryameva ca.[20]

Śaunaka maintains that the multiplicity of names and forms applied to denote each of the three principal *devatās* is a recognition of their power and majesty that is encountered in various realms of the cosmos in multiple forms:

etāsāmeva mahātmyān nāmānyatvaṁ vidhīyate
tattatsthānvibhāgen tatra tatreh dṛśyate.[21]

Śaunaka's interpretation finds support in Yāska's Nirukta where it is maintained that the power of the one Supreme Reality apprehended by the *ṛṣi* in many forms gives the one its many names and causes the one *devatā* to appear praised in manifold ways: *tāsāṁ mahābhāgyād ekaikasyā api bahūni nāmadheyani bhavanti.*[22] Although *Agni* is the *devatā* of the terrestrial realm, it has been shown to have its counterparts in other realms as well. The Vedic seer uses such names to address it as depends on the power which is meant to be described, or the activity of *Agni* which is to elaborated. The seer ostensibly appears to invoke *devatās* like *Vaiśvānara* and *Jātavedas* as belonging to the group of *Agni*, but the invocation is not addressed to a *devatā* different from *Agni*. All *devatās* originate and subsist in one another. Śaunaka says that *Agni* is contained in *Vaiśvānara,* Vaiśvānar is contained in *Agni; Jātvedas* is contained in these two, and these two are but the forms of *Jātvedas*:

v*aiśvānaraṁ ṣṛtohyagnir agniṁ vaiśvānaraḥ ṣṛtaḥ*
anayorjātvedāstu tathaiti jātvedasī.[23]

One *Agni* becomes many when its activities in the *yajña* in the household hearth, and in the human body, are teated as distinctive spheres of its power. Fundamentally, all *devatā* of the group of the terrestrial *Agni* are only different names of *Agni* based on the different spheres of its activity. In reality, *Jātavedas, Vaiśvānara, Draviṇodas* and *Tanunapāt* are all contained in and are the manifestations of Agni: *draviṇodāstathedhmaśca ṣṛtaścagni tanunapāt.*[24]

Śaunaka thus provides a clue to the schema of the Vedic poetry wherein all *devatā* are believed to have mutual origin, while their various names serve only to characterize the manifestation of their power:

tāsāmiyaṁ vibhūtirhi nāmāni yadanekaśaḥ
āhustāsāṁ tu mantreṣu kavayo' anyonyayonitām.[25]

Terrestrial forms of *Agni* are identical in abode, origin and nature but they are praised separately as different *devatā* owing to their different functions. Since all *devatās* that belong to the realm of *Agni* are praised with the attributes of *Agni,* they should all be considered to be taken over in *Agni*. Similarly all *devatās* having the attributes of *Indra* should be treated as summed up in *Indra,* and those attached to *Sūrya,* in *Sūrya*:

agnibhaktistutānsarvān agnāveva samāpayet
yadindrabhakti taccendre sūrye sūryānugaṁ ca yat.[26]

An analogous idea lies behind the characterisation of *Indra*, the *devatā* of the middle sphere, in whom are contained *Pārjanya, Rudra, Vāyu, Bṛhaspati, Varuṇa, Kā, Mṛtyu and Brahmanaspati*, along with many other *devatā* of that sphere:

indrāṣrayastu pārjanyo rudro vāyurbṛhaspatiḥ
varuṇaḥ kaśca mṛtyuśca devaśca brahmaṇaspatiḥ.[27]

Indra is also praised in combination with many other *devatās* of his sphere including *Viṣṇu*: *sanstutascaiva puṣnā ca viṣṇunā varuṇena ca.*[28]

It is interesting to note that both *Rudra* and *Viṣṇu* are shown as identical with and included into *Indra*, the presiding *devatā* of the middlesphere. A similar trend can be witnessed in the celestial realm of the *Sūrya devatā*, where many *devatās* are shown as connected with and contained in *Surya.* Some of the important *devatās* of the realm belonging to *Sūrya* are *Aśvins, Uṣās, Pūṣān, Yama, Viṣṇu, Savitr, Manu* and *Viśvedeva.*

All the *devatās* that are encountered in the realm assigned to a presiding *devatā* are only functional diversifications of that *devatā.* Varied manifestations do have individual efficacy but they do not cause any ontological schism in the nature of the presiding *devatā.* Another interesting point worthy of note is the description of the *devatā* of one sphere in assocation with, and contained in, the *devatās* of two different spheres. For example, *Viṣṇu* is found simultaneously in the realms of *Agni, Sūrya* and *Indra* as a *devatā* that is intrinsically connected with them and shares their praise and their sovereignty. The obvious inference is that the seer is using various appellations to draw his mind towards a reality that is so complex and vast that individual and fixed attributes fail to do justice to its ineffably mysterious nature. But the unification of all the *devatās* in one single defining *devatā* of a realm does not conclude the process of descriptive implosion. The process of unification proceeds further and many texts offer explicit clarification that the three principle *devatās—Agni, Indra/Vāyu, and Sūrya*—are but the functional emanations of a single *devatā.* Even the greatest of the seers and the finest exegetists have found it nearly impossible to fully explain the nature and station of various *devatās* or their power, sphere and mode of origin; they feel comfortable only with the perception that the whole world seems to be pervaded by them:

> *na caivaiṣaṅ prasutirvā vibhutisthānajanma va*
> *nirvaktuṁ śakyametairhi kṛtsaṅ vyāptmidaṁjagat.*[29]

It should, therefore, not be a matter of surprise when the seers are seen describing the night, dawn, vanaspati, steed, birds, frogs, rivers, waters, plants, śraddhā, iḷā, prithivi, in fact everything that exists in the world, as contained within the *devatā Agni.* It is a fascinating example of the creative polytheism of India that many phenomenal entities of this world are not only seen as *devatās;* but they are also seen as part and parcel of the divine *Agni*: In fact they are viewed as the manifestations of *Agni*. But the seer is not satisfied with the sectoral unitariness of the *devatās* of the terrestrial sphere with *Agni*, of the middle sphere with *Indra* and of the celestial sphere with *Sūrya*. His vision takes him to the truth beyond the distinctions of the three spheres, and at that higher level of perception he sees the three principle *devatās* as being the manifestations of a single supereminent *devatā*: *Agni, Sūrya* and *Indra* are recognised as the names of that one absolute divine entity. The seer unequivocally avers that the mode of perception of an individual makes the one *devatā* appear as three, whereas in effect they are identical in their ontological essence:

anena tu pravādena dṛṣtā mūrdhanvatā stutiḥ
sūryevaiśvanarāgninām ekatmyamih dṛśyate.[30]

The seer of the Ṛg Veda states that *Agni* is also known by the names of *Indra, Vāyu, Brahmā, Viṣṇu and Brahmaṇaspati*:

tvamagn indro vṛśabhaḥ satāmasi tvaṁ viṣṇu rurugayo namasyaḥ
tvaṁ brahmā rayividbrahmanaspate tvaṁ vidhartaḥ sacase purandhyā.[31]

The Ṛg Veda further states that both *Varuna* and *Mitra* are only different functional manifestations of the divine *Agni*:

tvamagne rājā varuṇo dhṛtavṛatastvaṁ mitro bhavasi dasm īḍayaḥ.[32]

Agni is also *Rudra* along with *devatā Viṣṇu and Marut: tvamagne rudro asuro maho divastvaṁ śardho mārutaṁ prikṣa īśiṣe*.[33]

Thus all *devatās* of a particular realm get established in the one presiding *devatā* of that realm, and the three principle *devatās* of these three realms are then said to be identical with one another and their various manifestations. All *devatās* resolve in one and, conversely, the one is always manifesting itself as many. The question, however, remains to be answered as to wherein are all the *devatās* contained and whereof are they the myriad manifestations.

The seers say that all *devatās* and divinities are so many sacred forms of that entity which is collectively known as *Prajāpati*. The same *Prajāpati* in its *devatā* form is individually addressed as *Agni, Indra/ Vayu and Sūrya* respectively:

vyāhṛtīnāṁ samastānāṁ daivataṁ tu prajāpatiḥ
vyastānāmyamagniśca vāyuḥ sūryaśca devatāḥ.[34]

With this assertion one meets the core spiritual vision of the S*anātan Dharma* that permeates all nuances of its spiritual life. This vision states that in the ultimate analysis the only truth that exists is *Prajāpati*. *Prajāpati*, a source of both what is existent and what is non-existent, is at once eternal and imperishable but becomes an object of speech on account of its perception by the seer who translates his vision of it in a *mantra*. This *Prajāpati* is then identified as the eternal *Brahman*:

asataśca sataścaiva yonireṣā prajāpatiḥ
yadakṣaraṁ ca vācyaṁ ca yathaitadbrahm śāśvatam.[35]

It is the one and only *Brahman—tad ekam*—'that one', that is known by the seers also as the divine *Sūrya* which pervades and abides in the three realms of the cosmos and causes all the *devatās* to emerge from and rest in its own refulgant glory:

kṛtvaiṣhi tṛdhātmānam eṣu lokeṣu tiṣṭhati
devānyathāyathaṁ sarvānniveśya sveṣu raśmiṣu.[36]

It is the one *Brahman* whom the seers adore in their songs as manifested under three names; perhaps thirty-three names or even three hundred and thirty million names. They believe that it is the fundamental reality of the *Brahman* that becomes all that was, is, and will be—forever: *ṛṣyo gīrbhircanti vyañjitaṁ nāmabhistṛbhiḥ.*[37]

The reality whose nature is eternal truth, eternal existence and eternal bliss is also the eternal god as well as the one and the only supreme *Puruṣa*, *Prajāpati* or the *Brahman*. It is to this unitary and absolute truth that the sages offer their adoration in many forms and through many names:

indraṁ mitraṁ varuṇamagnimāhuratho divyaḥ sa suparṇo garutmān
ekaṁ sadviprā bahudhā vadantyāgniṁ yaṁ mātariṣvānmāhuḥ.[38]

By whatever name one invokes, it is ultimately the *Brahman* who is the subject of such invocation, and in the loving apprehension of one *devatā* all *devatās* stand simultaneously, and collectively, adored and invoked.

But the ultimate unitariness of the divine truth does not render the presence and reality of many *devatās* a chimeral product of a seer's imagination. All the *devatās* are specific powers that regulate certain aspects of existence. These *devatās* are variously experienced and named on the basis of the functions they perform, and the powers that they possess. These powers perform certain important cosmic functions and help maintain the orderly structure of the manifested universe and the human existence. Their presence can be encountered everywhere if the working of the cosmic system, or the internal reality of man, is closely observed. The name assigned to a *devatā* depends on the function performed by it: *tat khalvāhu katibhyastu karmabhyo nām jāyate.*[39] A *devatā* is known as *Agni* because it was born, as it were, during the process of Creation, at the beginning of all beings *(agre)* and because it is invoked as a leader of the sacrifice *(agraṇi)*. There are other powers that regulate the orderly functioning of the cosmic family. These powers control the rhythm of the seasons, the coming and going of things, the orderly changes in the universe and the psychosomatic complex of the living beings, including humans. *Prajāpati,* owing to his pre-eminent and primary manifestation, is also known as the *Agni. Indra* is the supreme power of the mid-region of the universe, but when he abides as the most subtle form that pervades the whole world in the form of air the seers refer to him as *Vāyu:*

aṇiṣṭha esa yattu tṝn vyāpaiko vyomni tiṣṭhati
tenainamṛṣyo'arcantaḥ karamaṇā vāyumbruvan.[40]

When the same power of the universe covers with concrete moisture the three realms it is spoken of as *Varuṇa*:

tṛīnīmānyāvṛnotyeko mūrtena tu rasen yat
tayaiṁ varuṇaṁ śaktyā stutiṣvāhuḥ kṛpaṇyavaḥ.[41]

The seers praise the power of *Rudra* when they see a force roaring in the air and giving rain with lightening:

āroditantarikṣe yad vidydvṛṣtiṁ dadannṛṇām
caturbhirṛṣibhisten rudra ityabhisaṅstutaḥ.[42]

It is not the rain, or the air *per se,* that is eulogized as the *devatā* by the seer; it is the spirit and the power behind, and within these events, that is considered worthy of contemplation.

It is important to bear in mind that the name assigned to a *devatā* by the seer is not necessarily equivalent to the object which is normally indicated by the use of that name. When a *devatā* is mentioned as *Sūrya, Vāyu and Uṣās*—it is not only the physical presence of an object that is under consideration but primarily the manifestation of certain special powers of which the physical object becomes a point of focus. We have evidence of many *devatās* in the Vedic lore that do not have any similarity with objects that can be perceived by senses. *Devatās* like *Rudra, Pūṣan* and *Pārjanya* come in this category. Further, difficulty is encountered when the identity of a *devatā,* which has no form or an objective—correlate, with a *devatā* having an apparent indicative form is established by the seer. The suggestion that *devatās* are personifications of natural objects as anthropomorphic entities misses the very critical distinction between an object being treated as a *devatā* and an object being seen as the locus of divine forces. If the spiritual vision of the sage considers everything in the world as the manifestation of the *Brahman*, no object can be said to be without an element of the divine presence in it. There is, however, the possibility of some persons, objects or forces possessing the power of a very high order due to the extent that the divine energy proceeds towards and reveals in their case. Practitioners of *Sanātan Dharma* do not create gods out of natural objects. Their method follows a different course. They accept the possibility of god descending into and manifesting in a person or a natural phenomenon and imbuing that person and the phenomenon with a higher degree of meaning than it objectively possess. It is possible to encounter in a man the full realization and awakening of the god that abides in all men as their inner essence or *antaryāmi*. And when this happens we see and touch god in our own lives.

The seers do not make an object into 'god' or 'gods' by giving it a personality, nor do they give god anthropomorphic features. This is a very simplistic way of looking at the *Sanātan* method and this viewpoint suffers from the danger of evaluating the *Sanātan* tradition from the reference point of animistic practices in the framework of 'mythology'. The descriptive analysis of myth is based on certain presupposition. The presuppositions are regarded as necessary to characterize a way of expression as mythological. Conversely, if a way of expression is branded *a priori* as mytholigcal, disadvantages of the presuppositions are most naturally imposed on it as its characteristic feature. If the idea of *devatā* is treated as a myth then the conclusion is inescaple that... "they represent in fact the conjectural science of a primitive mental condition."[43] When a tradition is evaluated with *a priori* prejudices, fantastic conclusions like "the personality of the deity is thoroughly interpreted by the physical element",[44] become the hallmark products of scholarly labour. How far this diagnosis is from the reality of the Vedic system can be gauged by juxtaposing it with the analysis of the Vedic *devatās* attempted in the previous paragraphs. The picture will be clearer if the shape, form and the alleged anthropomorphism of the Vedic *devatās* are put under closer scrutiny. The use of shapes and forms to designate various *devatās* is a symbolical and poetic way of expressing an idea that defies categories of common speech. The *devatās* do not come out as having a clear identifiable personality; their features exhibit a formal 'spread' which extends in a sharable mode to the personalities of one another.

The charge of deification and personification of natural objects as divine personages can be countered with conviction if the logical structure of relevant texts is properly understood. It is important to understand the conditions under which the description of *devatās* takes shape in the Vedic literature. The fundamental unity of all phenomena in the nature of the *Brahman* or *Ātman* is the cornerstone of nearly all expressions of the nature of the *devatās*. The multiplicitous *devatās* are treated as the integral aspects of the one *Atman*: *ekasyātmano'anye devāḥ pratyañgāni bhavanti.*[45] Not only are the *devatās* aspects of one *Ātman,* but the characteristic accompaniments of many *devatās* are also a manifestation of the same *Ātman*. In the Vedic corpus *Indra* is associated with his *vajra*, *Sūrya* is shown as riding a chariot, and the other *devatās* are depicted in the manner that metaphorically emphasises their activities in various spheres of creation. The chariots, the arrows and the bolt need not be seen as confirmatory arguments in support of the thesis of personification and anthropomorphism. The implausibility of various *devatās* as stand-alone entities have been discussed in the earlier portion of this study; the implements by which they are shown as performing their assigned functions are a part and parcel of the nature of the *devatās* and not a separate material acquisition by them. They all originate reciprocally from one another as if each one of them is both the cause and the effect of the other. Yāska has beautifully described this idea in the following words: *itaretar janmāno bhavantītaretarprakṛtayaḥ karma janmānaḥ ātmajanmānaḥ.*[46] The things associated with the *devatās* are not different from the *Atman* in the same way as the *devatās* themselves are not different from it. The chariots, the horses, the arms, the arrows; they are all nothing else but the *Ātman* itself: *ātmaivaiṣaṅ ratho bhavati, ātmā aśvaḥ, ātmā' āyudham, ātmeṣavaḥ, ātmā sarvaṁdevasya.*[47]

The *Ātman* or the *Brahman* is the natural undisturbed state of which everything else is a modification or perturbation. All modifications of the world take place in the *ātman-prakṛyate'asyaṅ sarve vikārāh.* When a seer describes a horse, or a chariot, or a pressing stone, he is only reinforcing the presence of the one truth within all manifest modifications of the revealed world. By celebrating the diversity of the world he focuses on its primal unity. The Vedic method would appear less complicated if it is understood that in the world of the Veda normal concepts of cause and effect do not apply in a hierarchical manner. Cause and effect are variously shown as indistinguishable and without any concern for primacy or antecedence of the one over the other. What appears as the cause of a thing can be the effect of the same thing simultaneously: *pari prajātaḥ kratvā babhūtha devānāṁ pitā putraḥ san.*[48] Two *devatās* can be father and son of one another at the same time, and it is not infrequent to find references in which a *devatā* is shown as emerging from another and giving birth to its progenitor in turn. *Aditi* is born of *Dakṣa* and *Dakṣa* is born from *Aditi*: *aditerdakṣo ajāyataḥ, dakṣadvaditiḥ pari*. The name and form of a *devatā* is extremely ephemeral and contingent on the timeframe in which its vision materializes. *Varuṇa* is seen as *Agni* in the evening, and *Mitra* in the morning: *sa varuṇaḥ sāyamagnirbhavati, sa mitro bhavati prātrudyan.*[49] The world of the Vedic *devatās* does not follow the rules of personality and anthropology as understood by the modern post-Freudian mind, or the traditional Judeo-Christian obsession with revelatory literalism.

It is nonetheless important to bear in mind that the Vedic seers have formulated their *mantras* in such a manner that they can serve the twin purposes of performative action and contemplative spirituality. The two perspectives, as understood for the purposes of the *Yajña* and the spiritual purpose of *ādhyātmika* introspection, has, however, given birth to two viewpoints. The ritualistic or *adhiyājñic* viewpoint emphasises the necessity of acknowledging some form for the *devatās* if oblations and sacrificial incantations are to have any attitudinal meaning in the body of the *mantra*. According to this viewpoint, the *devatās* come alive in the words and imports of the *mantra* for its application in the performance of a *Yajña*. If a form is not kept in the mind while performing an action the focus of that particular action would be blurred. So the action bound performer —*yajmān*—creates the image of the *devatā* in an identifiable object through the use of attributes normally associated with mankind—*puruṣvidha*. This is done in order to make a particular activity correspond to the intention that is in his mind. All activities in the phenomenal world relate to certain recgonizable outcomes, and the outcomes take concrete form because of the function of the consciousness when it gets attached to the motive and the result of a performance. When a particular power of the devatā is invoked in the *mantra* for performance of an act, the *devatā* is said to assume a human-like form to acknowledge and accept the performance of that action. According to Yāska, the human-like form of the *devatā* is an aspect of the *yājñic* life of a performer at the non-absolute or the *apara* level of comprehension: *purusvidhāh syuḥ ityekam, cetanāvadvadhi stutayobhavanti. Tatha'abhidhānāni. Athāpi pauruṣavidhi kairaṅgeḥ sanstūyante.*[50] The *Yājñic* idea corresponds to the notion of the *saguṇ brahman* apprehend by a seeker in the phenomenal world of names and forms, and it was given a certain amount of credence by the proponents of the *Mīmāṁsa* school of thought.

However, many commentators do not accept the description of *devatās* in a manner that is suggestive of human similarities. They reject the notion that allusions to human-like attributes of a *devatā* in a *mantra* should be seen as indicative of human-like qualities in a literal manner. Those descriptions should be understood as analogical tools intended to fulfil the requirements of the structure of communication. The theories of anthropomorphism and theriomorphism lose their relevance and theoretical force when it is discerned that in many *mantras,* objects like mortar, pestle, crushing stone, fire-sticks, etc, are also described and invoked with reverence. Obviously, the seer of the *mantra* was not suggesting godhood to the *soma*-crushing stone any more than he was ascribing to it the power of crying with its green-hued mouth; although one comes across such references in the Ṛg Veda—*abhikrandanti haritebhirāsabhiḥ.* Similarly, the Ṛg Veda refers to rivers, plants and herbs as *devatās* and ascribes virtual human motives and actions to them. The river *Sindhu* is shown as having yoked its horses to a fine chariot while traversing its earthly course. Such *mantras* use metaphorical language to make a certain idea comprehensible and these references should not be taken as veridical accounts of literal human action. Yāska has correctly written that, *apuruṣavidhāḥ syurityaparam, apitu yaddṛśyate apuruṣvidhaṁ tadyathāgnirvāyurādityaḥ pṛthivīcandramā iti.*[51] The fire or the sun in their visible form and shape are gross and insentient objects having no resemblance to any human form. A human being gets its name not only by virtue of its gross human body but as a complex of a material body and a supervening consciousness. When a seer invokes a *devatā,* which apparently has a visible form, he is not concerned simply with that form, but with the factor of consciousness that abides and inheres in it as its controlling force. Gross fire in association with divine consciousness becomes *agni devatā*. It is the inherent conscious form—*adhiśṭhātr devatā*—that is referred to as *devatā* in the Vedic *mantra*.

Yāska believes that the bodily organs employed by a performer in the performance of an action is superimposed by them onto the *devatā* to whom that particular action is addressed: *api vobhayvidhāḥ syuḥ. Api vā puruṣavidhānā meva satāṁ karmātmān ete syuḥ yathā yajño yajmānasya eṣa cākhyānasamayaḥ.*[52] The forms of the *devatās* are reflective of the actions they are associated with. Although it is the priest who performs a *yajña* on behalf of the person who organises it, it is the latter who by virtue of being the controller and superintendent of the *yajña* becomes the actual performer and possessor of that *yajña*. Likewise, the invoked *devatā* acquires the shape in accordance with the intention and resolve of the seer. An impression of personality on the impersonal nature of reality is projected to relate it to the explanation and purpose of a particular activity or spheres of activity. The same priest of the *yajña* can become *adhvaryu, hotra or udgātā* depending on the role he performs in the actualization of the *yajña*. *Agni, Vāyu,* etc. are non-human in the context of direct perception but become owners of human similitude through the testimony of speech. From a *yājnic* viewpoint allegorical references to the *devatās* as having human features are deemed necessary for the successful performance of the *yajña*. If an action is to be successfully performed the destination of that action would require to be visualized as a concrete possibility. That the attributes of the *devatās* representing objects and features of nature are not humanized is accepted by many Western commentators who believe that in the *Vedic Saṁhitās*,... "the anthropomorphism is only incipient...Personification has, however, nowhere in the Vedic mythology attained to the individual anthropomorphism characteristic of the Hellenic Gods."[53]

There are many passages in the Veda wherein *devatās* are eulogized in a combination of two or more *devatās*. In many other *mantras* an individual *devatā* is not praised by the seer, but all *devatās* are invoked together by the use of the appellation, *viśvedevatā*. If the combinations of *devatās* are closely observed it would soon be apparent that the *devatās* combine with one another rather randomly and show scant regard to the fixity of 'character' or the sphere of activity of a particular *devatā*. A characteristic assigned to a particular *devatā* in one *mantra* can be assigned to another *devatā* in a second *mantra*. A close examination reveals that the Vedic *devatās* have but very few distinguishing features and many of them share many attributes and powers among themselves. It seems as if a single *devatā* is encountered under many names in the deep spiritual vision of the seer and also in the day to day *kārmic* life of the people. A.A. Macdonell has pointed out that in the Atharva Veda *devatās* appear to be some sort of a deification of abstractions in which the essential nature of the individual *devatā* is hardly touched upon. Macdonnel is right in suggesting the implausibility of *devatās* becoming so many different discreet entities but wrong in asserting that the *devatās* are deification of 'abstractions'. The lack of discreetness cannot be a reason to assume deification of abstract thought. It can be a proof of the recognition by the seer of the near impossibility of describing the nature of certain forms of reality. And as such, no fix or immutable form can be fixed on that supreme truth which is not subject to the constraints of any particular name and form. The untenability of describing the nature of reality in terms of fixed forms and attributes was fully understood by the Vedic seer. It is no surprise that the *mantras* of the Yajur Veda are not addressed directly to any *devatā,* and in the sacrificial descriptions of the *Śatapatha* and *Aitareya Brāhmaṇs* the individual traits of *devatās* have become very indistinct. If *devatās* reveal some distinguishing traits it is due to the reason that the nature of truth can only be perceived in a discreet form in man's observation and his description of it.

Whatever distinct characteristics the Vedic *devatās* possess are few and far between and allegorical in nature. Most of them share the few specific traits that they have with other *devatās* of the same sphere. Several *devatās* are said to have grown from different aspects of the same phenomena. Macdonell has shown that the character of each Vedic *devatā* is made of only a few essential traits combined with a number of other features such as brilliance, power, beneficience, wisdom, etc, which are common to all the known *devatās*. In many instances two or more *devatās* are shown to share the attributes commonly associated with some other *devatā*. *Agni* is called 'soma-drinker' or 'Vṛtra-slayer' in many mantras, whereas these epithets are most commonly used with the activities of *Indra*. In his own manner Macdonell was able to underline the problem which faces a theoretician if he attempts to derive the pleasure of 'polytheism' from the existence of numerous *devatās* in the Vedas. The problem relates to the absence of clear, and identifiable personalities of the *devatās* and the ease with which two *devatās* seem to exchange places, roles and functions between themselves. Macdonell wrote: "Indefiniteness of outline and lack of individuality characterize the Vedic conceptions of gods... The indefiniteness of outline caused by the possession of so many common attributes, coupled with the tendency to wipe out the few distinctive ones by assigning nearly every power to every god, renders identification of one god with another easy."[54] The fact is that identification of one 'god' with another was easy because of the belief that all *devatās* were just so many aspects of the same ultimately truthful reality. Macdonnel did sometimes tend to get the idea right when he saw the concept of *devatās* in its true light and said that,... "the various deities are but different form of a single divine being."[55] The vision of the Veda leaves no doubt that it is the same reality which appears differently to the seer in different experiential situations:

> *tvamagne varuṇo jāyase yattvaṁ mitro bhavasi*
> *yatsamiddhaḥ*
> *tve viśve sahasasputra devāstvamindro dāṣuśe martyāya.*[56]

The very same reality that is *Agni* is known as *Varuṇa* at its birth but becomes *Mitra* when fully kindled. All *devatās* are centred in that *Agni* which becomes the adorable *Indra* for the purposes of a worshipper.

Aditi is identified with all the *devatās*, all men, all that has been and shall be born, with air, heaven and the cosmos:

aditirdyauraditirantarikṣamaditirmātā, sapitā saputraḥ viśvedevā aditiḥ pañca janā aditirjātamaditirjanitavam.[57]

Every *devatā* is invested with the highest divinity when it becomes the sole focus of a seer's spiritual attention. No other distraction compromises his deep contemplation because in his mind nothing else exists but the truth which is the subject of his contemplation. Max Muller's thesis of henotheism assumes the existence of many different *devatās* as several supreme godheads from which the worshipper chooses a particular *devatā* at a time to the exclusion of other members of the pantheon. The evidence of the texts do not support his hypothesis. Whatever form a seer chooses for his contemplation contains the full and meaningful picture of reality that ever can be for him. The act of choosing to apprehend the supreme reality in the name of a particular *devatā* does not exclude other *devatās* in the manner of preferential subordination, because that would presume the existence of other realities besides the one being contemplated. When a seer devotes himself to a *devatā,* the truth fully and finally materializes as the *devatā* of his contemplation, and thereupon all alternative or subsidiary possibilities cease to exist for him. Devotion to a *devatā* at a particular point does not exclude other *devatās,* but includes their full essence in the one image that is the subject of devotion. Since every *devatā* possesses the characteristics of all other *devatās,* and all *devatās* are but aspects of the same reality, the contemplation of a particular *devatā* causes the concentric merger of all *devatās* onto one point and nothing else exists that can be said to have been excluded. Macdonell has rightly observed that, "A classification according to gradations of rank would therefore not afford a satisfactory basis for an account of the Vedic Gods."[58]

When Yājñavalkya initially said there were thirty-three *devatās* he was only reiterating the popular perception in this regard. However, he gradually took his audience up the numerical scale of manifested reality and proclaimed the unity and oneness of the *devatās* in the truth of the *prāṇa* (life) which is the same as the *Brahman* in the acosmic sense. All *devatās* take their various lives from, and then reabsorb and converge in, the nature of 'that one' which is the only true existence. Accordingly, to the Yajur Veda everything in this world and all the *devatās* find their abode in 'that one'—*yatra viśvaṁ bhavati eka nīḍaṁ*. The seer has no doubt in his mind that his invocations ultimately address the reality of 'that one'. Śaunaka in his Bṛhaddevatā has explained the question of unity and multiplicity of *devatās* by saying that when a *mantra* mentions two *devatās* in a similar context they must be regarded as constituting a single *devatā*:

asaṁstutaṁ saṁstutavat pradiṣṭaṁ daivatam kvacit
yatra dvidaivate mantra ekavaddevatocyate.[59]

It is also clarified that if many devatās are mentioned in a *mantra* but not eulogized together, the many *devatās* should be understood to constitue a single *devatā* in that context:

vibhaktastuti tadvidyād bahuṣvabahuvacca yat.[60]

Śaunaka believes that the effort to ascertain a particular *devatā* on the basis of its characteristic marks or *linga* is a futile exercise that would, if undertaken, yield unsatisfactory results. The only way to know the real nature of the *devatā* is through the injunctions of the *mantra*:

ādeśāddaivataṁ jñyeyam ṛṅgmantrāṇām, na liṅgataḥ
na śakyaṁ liṅgato hyāsāṁ jñatuṁ tattven daivatam.[61]

It is nearly impossible to identify a particular Vedic *devatā* on the basis of those characteristic marks that can be assigned specifically to it. There aren't a set of marks that can be said to belong specifically to one *devatā* and not to the others. Some specificity can be ascribed to a *devatā* only on the basis of its special activity but not on the basis of bodily forms. Macdonell has suggested that the anthropomorphism of a *devatā* like *Varuṇa* is developed more on the moral than the physical side because the Vedic narrative stresses more on the moral activity of *Varuṇa*. What does one make of the personality of the *devatā Varuṇa* whose countenance is as radiant as *Agni* and whose eyes are *Sūrya* itself?

citraṁ devānāmudgādnīkaṁ cakṣurmitrasya varuṇasyāgne.[62]

Another case in point is the character of *Savitra* who is said to be a *devatā* with a golden hue. That epithet is also applied to the sun in view of its being the arouser and stimulator of life. *Savitra* is called the *sarvasva prasavitā* because it stimulates everything. The Ṛg Veda describes *Savitra* also as *Prajāpati* of the world: *divo dhartā bhuvanasya prajāpatiḥ pisaṅgaṁ drāpiṁ prati muñcate kawiḥ.*[63]

The one distinct mark which can be discerned from the description of the *devatā, Pūṣan* relates to its activity as the guardian of people and the remover of worldly dangers, otherwise the information about its personality is very scanty. It is, however, addressed as *Narāśamsa* in some of the *mantra* which identify it with *Agni* and *Sūrya.* Very few personal details are available about *Indra* in the Veda; most of the information deals with the mighty deeds that it performs and the *devatās* with which it is associated. This *Indra* is identified with *Sūrya* and also addressed as *Savitra*:

aham manurabhavaṁ suryaścāhaṁ kakṣivāñ ṛṣirasmi vipraḥ.[64]
ṛtaṁdevāya kṛṇvate savitra indrāyāhighne na ramanta āpaḥ.[65]

The *devatā Mātariśvan* is usually identified with *Agni* and on many occasions the same name is employed as an alternative appellation for *Agni.* Macdonell says that, "As heavely germ, he is called *Tanunapāt*; becomes *Narāśamsa* when he is born; when as *Mātarisvan* he was fashioned in his mother (*amimita mātari*), he becomes the swift flight of wind."[66] The Ṛg Veda points out that:

tanunapāducyate garbha āsuro narāśaṅso bhavati yedvijāyate
mātariśvā yadmimīta mātari vatasya sargo abhavatsarīmaṇi.[67]

Mātariśvan is also one of the forms of *Bṛhaspati. Agni,* a very prominent *devatā* mentioned in the Veda, has a very protean and quicksilver personality. All that can most certainly be said about it is that its bodily characteristics resemble the terrestrial fire in its sacrificial aspect, otherwise the *mantras* enumerate no distinctive features of its personality apart from certain highly poetical and symbolic allusions. *Agni* is described as the progenitor of all the *devatās* and yet it is known as their son because it was discovered by the latter:

> *pari prajātaḥ kṛtvā babhutha bhuvo devānāṁ pitā putraḥ san* .[68]

Agni is identified with *Sūrya*, *Indra* and many other *devatās*. It would be fruitful to note the epithets that are used by the seers to address and describe various *devatās* because they provide a key to the unlocking of the mystery of their true nature. *Agni* is addressed as a guest *(atithi)*, having two births *(dvijanman)*, priest *(purohita)*, lord of the house *(gṛhapati)* and *purandara*. In a literal manner most of the epithets do not provide specific clues about the nature of a fixed *devatā* like *Agni*, and it is possible to apply these marks to many other *devatās* with equal happiness. It is interesting to note some of the words assgined to a *devatā* while eulogizing and describing it. *Apām Napāt* is called 'Son of Waters'; *Agni* is called 'butter-faced', 'twany-haired' and 'twany-beard'. *Agni* is also called a 'bull' and an 'eagle' in the sky simultaneoulsy. The *Aśvins* are called the 'wondrous' *(dasra)* and the 'not-untrue' *(nāsatya)*. Most of the marks alluded to here can be used to describe practically any other *devatā*. With the assistance of such descriptive clues there is no way that a thesis of anthropomorphism, or deification and personification of natural phenomena, can be honestly put forward, much less defended. It is not a natural phenomenon that is made into a god but the sages recognize the possibility of god being seen in many natural phenomena.

The etymological meaning of the word *devatā* or *deva* can be traced to the Sanskrit root 'diva' which means illumination *(dīpana)*, brilliance*(dyotanā)* and bestower of virtues *(dāna)*. This view has been supported by Yāska in his analysis of *'deva'* in the following words:

devo dānād vā dīpanād vā dyotanād vā dyusthāno bhavatīti vā. yo devaḥ sa devatā.[69]

Devatās are the possessors of great brilliance, illumination and virtuosity and they have the capacity to bestow virtuosity on those who contemplate their effulgence and seek to imitate their righteous ways. Radiance and brilliance are the common characteristics of all *devātās*: *yamapyetarhi devānām paśyanti jyotirivādṛśmetyevahuḥ.*[70] In a different sense the root *'diva'* also signifies the divine and celestial regions and the forces that inhabit those regions. These forces are *divya* because they inhabit the regions that are beyond the immediate region of the terrestrial world. Śatapath Brāhmaṇ stresses the celestial and non-material nature of the *devatās: tad devānāṁ devatvaṁ yad divamabhidyāsṛjyanta.*[71] If the analysis of Nirukta is followed then all forces and entities that bestow wisdom, light, peace, and bliss can be called *devatās*. It is for this reason that Veda and other scriptures use the word *deva* to address the wise and righteous teachers who transmit knowledge and illuminate the true nature of things. The Śatapatha Brāhmaṇ says that men of wisdom are as venerable as devas—v*edvaṅso hi devaḥ*. The Aitareya Brāhmaṇ regards the righteous among mankind as the true *devas—satyasaṁhita vai devaḥ*. As wise guide, righteous teachers and providers for their children, even parents, are regarded with reverence as *devas—matṛ devo bhavaḥ, pitṛ devobhavaḥ*. The predicate *deva* is used to identify and address a person, a power or an aspect of the almighty god in recognition of the virtues they possess and not for the purpose of treating them as separate 'gods'.

In the spheres of divine activity the word *devatā* has a rather special connotation. In the Vedic *mantra*, *devatās* are the particularized perceptions of the seer that are generated on the basis of the seer's intention to describe a desired phenomenon or a thing that presents itself in his vision as possessed of a larger and richer meaning. Yaska says: *yatkām ṛṣiryasyāṅ devatāyāmārthapatyamichanstutiṁ prayuñkte taddevat.*[72] The literal meaning of *devatā* would, therefore, be a thing that is endowed with light; and in a secondary sense it can be used for anything that has divine qualities. The word *devatā* should be understood not as expressive of a quantifiable entity but as a qualitative indicator. The word *devatā* has also been used to mean *Iśvara* or god because the latter is regarded as the source of all life and wisdom in the world and the illuminator of the sentient minds. But this correspondence can not to be inferred in every context, and generally the term *devatā* is used to refer to things that possess the desired qualities of wisdom light, munificence, righteousness, and power. When one looks at the character and actions of the *devatās,* this aspect of their meaning emerges in fairly bold relief. *Devatās* are said to be engaged in the observance of truth in accordance with the cosmic and moral laws, and thereby they act as the leaders and deliverers of men:

te hi satyā ṛtaspṛśa ṛtāvāno jane jane
sunithāsaḥ sudānavoṅhościdrucakrayah.[73]

The *devatās* are free from physical and moral decay. They are full of cognitional activities and bereft of any sense of malice: *viśve devāso asridha ehimāyāso adruhaḥ.*[74] All men are, therefore, exhorted to follow the path of the *devatās* in order to fully live a life divine and accomplish all that they are capable of:

ā devānāmapi panthāmaganma yacchakanvām tadanu pravoḷhum.[75]

The seers make a significant and solemn promise to the *devatās* and to themselves that they shall remain united with true knowledge and shall never be at variance with the divine guidance provided by the Vedas: *saṁ śruten gamemahi mā śruten vi rādhiṣi.*[76] The path shown by the Vedic seers is the path of truth and noble action: *tadetatsatyaṁ mantreṣu karmāṇi kavayo yānyapaśyaṅstāni...*[77]

The spiritual path shown by the Vedas, Upaniṣad, Gītā and Purāṇa admit of only one supreme existence and truth, which all *devatās* are but an integral and cohesive aspects of. The one *Parmātman,* the *devatā* of all *devatās,* is the location and support of all the *devatās* who are subsumed in it as its organs or powers:

yasya trayastrinśaddevā aṅge sarve samāhitāḥ,
skambhaṁ te bruhi katāmaḥ svideva saḥ.[78]

The only *devatā* that matters is the Supreme *Brahman* that is located at the centre of the phenomenal existence but pervades it fully as its controlling warmth and energy. It spreads as the material and psychic manifestation of the world on the surface of the river of infinite potentiality. All the *devatās* find shelter and support in it like the branches of the tree around the trunk:

mahadyakṣaṁ bhuvanasya madhye tapasi krāntaṁ salilasya pṛṣṭhe
tasmiñchrayante ya u ke ca devā vṛkṣasya skandhaḥ parit iva śākhā.[79]

That alone is the creator, upholder and sustainer of the universe. It knows the whole universe, and although invoked by the names of various divinites, remains forever its own unique self because all *devatās* are super-eminently based and contained in it:

yo naḥ pitā janitā yo vidhātā dhāmāni veda bhuvanāni viśvā,
yo devānāṁ nāmadhā eka eva taṁ saṁpraṣnaṁ bhuvanā yantyanyā...[80]

It is the *Brahaman-Parameśwar* who bears all the names of all the *devatās* that are invoked. The names of *devatās* belong primarily to *Parameśwar,* and only secondarily to other powers and forces. 'That one' is known as *Agni* because it is endowed with wisdom; as *Āditya* because it is imperishable; as *Vāyu* because it sets everything in motion; as *Candramā* because it gives pleasure; as *Śukra* because it is pure; as *Brahman* because it is greater than all; as *Āpah* because it is omnipresent; and as *Prajāpati* because it sustains and nurtures all created existence:

tadevagnistadādityastād vāyustadu candramāḥ
tadeva śukram tadbrahma tā āpaḥ sa prajāpatiḥ.[81]

It is the *Parabrahma Parmeśwar* who is the Ordainer, the Venerable, the Judge and the Great Lord. It is 'That One' which exists as the divine fire, the resplendent sun and the supreme controller; all *devatās* are but only its very own nature:

so'aryamā sa varuṇaḥ sa rudraḥ sa mahādevaḥ..[82]
so agniḥ sa u sūryaḥ sa u eva mahāyamaḥ.

A similar thought can be encountered in many Upaniṣads where the *devatās* are mentioned as the symbols for various attributes of the *Paramātamā* when they are employed for the purposes of contemplation, *yajna*, or worship: *sa brahma sa viṣṇuḥ sa rudraḥ sa śivaḥ sa akṣaraḥ sa paramaḥ swarat. sa indraḥ sa kālāgniḥ sa candramāḥ.*[83]

Durgācārya in his commentary on Yāska's *Nirukta* states that although various *devatās* appear to be differently projected, in reality they are all one inasmuch as they are the aspects of the one *Brahman*, and therefore cannot overreach their true abode. In this one reality of the *Brahman* are rooted all the diversities of names and forms, men and beasts, objects and implements. A seer sees no harm in invoking plants, rivers and even inanimate objects as subjects of worship because he sees them as *devatās* that carry the divine stamp of the one *Ātman*. Kātyāyan in his Sarvānukramaṇi agrees with the fundamental *ādhyātmik* interpretation of the *devatās* and asserts that it is only the great *Ātman* that is worthy of being known as the one and only. *devatā—ekaiva va mahānātma devatā.* That *Atman* alone is one, the only one, the one alone: into him all the *devatās* subsist in organic wholeness by accepting its fundamental oneness: *sa eṣa eka ekavṛdeka eva, ete asmindevā ekvṛto bhavanti.*[84]

It is this eternal *Brahman*, the Supreme *Puruṣa,* that one should strive to know through the devotion of one's heart and soul and mind. Manu says that it is this *Parameśwar* that is adored, prayed and eulogized as *Agni,* as *Prajāpati,* as *Indra*, as *Prāṇa* and as the eternal *Brahman*:

etameke vadantyagniṁ manumanye prajāpatiṁ
indrameke' apare prāṇampare brahm śāśvatam.[85]

The apperception of various *devatās*, however, does not detract from the majesty of the *Paramātman*, and its laws remain uninfringed and inviolate by the activity of a particular *devatā: indrasya karma sukṛtā puruṇi vratani devā na minanti viśve.*[86]

Everything that is and is not, follow the immutable righteous laws of the Lord: *yasya vrataṁ paśavoyanti sarve yasya vrata upatisṭhanta āpah.*[87]

All *devatās* abide within the Lord in respectful and uninimical coexistence. There is no question of two deities having ill will towards one another:

asya vrate sajoṣaso viśve devāso adruhaḥ.[88]

The import of a *mantra* depends on the purpose for which the *mantra* is employed. In the *adhiyajña* perspective, the *devatās* are said to materialize individually to accept the oblations offered in the ceremony and to grant the intended merit of the *yajna* to the performer. The interpretation corresponds to the injunctions regarding performance of various duties by men in their social life. It draws the map for their *karma-mārg* and the *devatās* become their beacon lights on that path. The Vedic *mantras* and the *devatās* serve as the role models for the conduct of various human activities that comprise man's *dharma: codanaiva dharme pramāṇam.* From the *adhiyajña* perspective, the *devatās* are important as the impellers of action modelled on the cosmic laws which find their manifestation in their activities. The invocation of a *devatā* in a *yajña* is also a commitment to perform an action that reflects the truthful laws of that realm in which the *devatā* is seen to operate. The performer, by his commitment to observe the truth *(satya)* and the operating systems or laws *(ṛta)* that find its phenomenal manifestation in a *devatā*, aspires to become a *devatā* himself. It is perhaps for this reason that many glossators have used the word *devatā* for the *ṛtvij, stotā, adhvaryu and yajmān* of a *yajna*. The performer of an action, the *yajmān,* can become a *devatā* if his actions follow the path of truth and righteousness. Even Sāyan believed that the true knowledge and observance of *dharma* produces the knowledge of *Brahman.* The *devatās* are the upholders of truth and their nature is a concrete representation of the eternal laws of life: *tehi satyā ṛtaspṛśa ṛtāvāno jane jane.*[89] A *devatā* would grace a *yajña* only if all actions are performed with complete care to the truthfulness and the merit of those actions. A *yajña* is not successful if the performer is less than truthful and it would not be possible to please the *devatā* with such imperfect *yajña*. The scriptural emphasis on right action—*samyak karma*—can be understood properly when seen in the light of the theoretical premise that man's action in this world should always follow the action that is being performed in this whole cosmos by the *devatās*—*ādevānāmapi panthāmaganma*. Man's whole life is a pious *yajña* whose diligent performance can force the *devatās* to come down and hold his hand in divine partnership.

The *ādhidaivata* perspective emphasies the importance of true knowledge of the nature, station and meaning of the *devatās*. It is important to clearly visualize the nature, function and powers of *devatās* before they are invoked and a sacrificial offering is made in the performance of a *yajña*. Yāska has stṛessed the importance of careful meditation over the performance of a *yājñic* action in the employment of a *mantra*. The principle purpose of a *mantra* is to lead towards contemplation—*mantra manānat*. An action can be frutifully performed if the correct meaning behind the action is properly understood. An action performed with correct understanding has greater puissance and efficacy than an action performed in a state of ignorance: *yadeva vidyayā karoti ṣraddhayopaniṣadā tadeva vīryavattaraṁ bhavati*.[90] Correct understanding of the meaning of a *devatā* is necessary to penetrate the veil of apparent reality and ascertain the true meaning of truth that lies behind. *Devatā* can be visualized only in a state of complete psychic concentration in which the mind transcends the limits of time and space and opens up to the presence of the divine. Wide and extensive learning *(bahuśruta)* that allows no quarter to prejudice and cultic presuppositions is a condition precedent for the understanding of god's nature. Śaunaka in Bṛhaddevatā lists yoga or mental concentration, assiduity, self-discipline, deep learning, austerity and the Vedic injunctions as the principle desiderata for the knowledge and apprehension of a *devatā*:

yogena dākśyeṇa damena budhya bāhuśrutyena tapasā niyogaih.
... ha yo veda so veda devāna.[91]

A *mantra* is the intuitive vision of the seer and only through the application of focussed intuition that the meaning of the *mantra* can be ascertained. The *devatās* reveal the deep mysteries of the Supreme Self which is both transcendent and immanent. It is possible to know the meaning revealed by the *devatās* through the application of a wise and discerning inner light that dwells in all human soul. The Supreme Self reveals itself in a *devatā* form before the contemplative disposition of the seer. When the true knowledge of the *devatā* is obtained, the distinction between the perceiver and the perceived is obliterated and in this state of wisdom the seer himself is raised to the level of the *devatā*. The *devatā* signifies the evolutionary becoming *(bhāvavṛttāni)* of the great Self whom the seer mirrors in the inner recess of his own soul. When their identification is achieved the seer himself becomes the *devatā*: *ya ṛṣiḥ saiva devatā.*[92] Knowledge of the *devatā, (samjñān),* is essential because knowledge as the *devatā Bṛhaspati* was the first born among all the *devatās*: *bṛhaspatiḥ prathamaṁ jāyamāno maho jyotiṣaḥ parame vyoman.*[93]

True knowledge of the nature of the *devatās* leads the seer to a higher degree of understanding where his attention is drawn to the abstract reality behind the nuances that are represented in diverse forms. In the *adhyātmik* mode of higher knowledge all multiplicities gradually begin to fade away. Individual *devatās* point to a reality that transcends them by unifying them in one matrix of pre-eminent existence where their individualities only serve to highlight the unity of the truth. When the unity of the *daivat* level is understood it becomes easy to realize that the same unity of purpose also permeates the world of human beings. All *devatās* are merely expressions or emanations of one reality that constitutes the self of all the *devatās*. The *devatās* represent so many powers of their primal self, projected in multiple forms at the cosmic level yet they remain abiding necessarily and intrinsically in that one primary principle. Differing perceptions of this reality give rise to divergent forms and many names within that, which is ontologically one:

suparṇa viprāḥ kavayo vacobhirekaṁ
santaṁ bahudhā kalpayanti.[94]

The seer knows that the nature of all *devatās* is constituted of a single reality and their individual characters are rooted in the vast expanse of the one *devatā* whom the sages also call as *Brahman: Brahma va idamagra āsit...* Sri Aurobindo has very lucidly put the *devatā* discourse in its correct perspective in the Hymns to the Mystic Fire: "The Vedic deities are names, powers, personalities of the Universal Godhead and they represent each some essential puissance of the Divine Being. They manifest the cosmos and are manifest in it ... the gods, the powers of light and Truth are powers and names of the one, each god is himself all the gods or carries them in him..."

The Cosmic Emanation

In the final analysis all the *devatās* eulogized in the Vedic corpus are the manifestations of the one *devatā*. It is a singular reality that forms the integrative web in which various *devatās* are woven. They are apprehended in the three cosmic realms in accordance with the powers that they possess and the functions that they perform. Their activities intra-sphere and inter-sphere, nevertheless, are not predicated on a principle of exclusion but on a deeper motive of complementarity. The *devatās* share their activities among themselves and also lend their names and functions to one another. They do not follow an evolutionary linearity that would assign hierarchical pre-eminence to one over the other, rather they co-emerge from one another across their vocational and spatial particularities. Each individual *devatā* has an individuality in the sphere it occupies or the functions it performs and, according to the view of the *Mīmāṁsaks,* they are available individually to a devotee for the purposes of performance of a *Yajña* and as the object of devotion. But the individuality of a *devatā* is contingent on a much higher power in which they are rooted and from which they emerge in their individual manifestations, not as component parts but as its creative modification. In their essential nature all *devatās* subsist in functional and spatial unitariness where various modes comingle in an undifferentiated whole: *tatra sasthānaikatvaṁ, sambhogaikatvaṁ copekṣitavyam.*[1] That one reality precedes, transcendentally not historically, all phenomenal modifications in its nature wherein the question of individual form or subsisting cohesive pervasiveness ceases to remain valid as cognitive categories. Every wave is simultaneously a wave and the ocean itself,without cancelling the phenomenal contextuality of one another. Fundamentally, the *devatās* are rooted in the self; they are the self whom teachers have called *Ātman* or *Brahman.* At the most fundamental level the seers visualize a single, unitary but all pervasive reality.

The existential unitariness does not only encompass the sphere of various *devatās* but embraces within its fold the entire manifested universe along with its sentient *(cit)* beings and insentient *(acit)* matter. The reality of the phenomenal world is not separate or juxtaposed in contradistinction to the reality of the spiritual truth; the former is merely a grosser and perceptible format of the latter. The world of *devatās*, cosmic entities, men and other living things are all different perceptual categories of a single reality. In various spiritual discourses the same fundamental reality has been expressed as *Brahman, Ātman, Puruṣa* or *Iśvara* depending upon the perspective from which the reality has been visualized by various seers. That the unity of the existential drama is assured within the all important and fundamental truth of the *Paramātman*, is a standpoint which is repeatedly stressed by the Vedas and other books. Differences in the description of the nature of reality occur due to a preceptor's view point or the idea which determines a particular direction of his vision. This whole universe is contained within the nature of the Supreme Existence and whatever is encountered phenomenally is only the illumination of an aspect of that existence:

eka evāgnir bahudhā samiddha ekaḥ sūryo viśvamanu prabhutaḥ
ekaivoṣāḥ sarvamidaṁ vibhātyekaṁ vā idaṁ vi babhūva sarvam.[2]

It is that one supreme existence that has become the world of phenomenal reality.

It is the nature and manifestation of the fundamental 'That *One*' which is explained and expounded in the Vedic corpus, the Bhagavad Gītā, the schools of philosophy and the Pūraṇas in their own peculiar ways. Traditions have never found it easy to put a clear distinguishing mark on the *One* which is believed to be beyond the ambit of any qualification. However, various designations have been used by various commentators and teachers to indicate that universal reality for the purposes of discourse. The use of the epithets *Brahman, Ātman, Puruṣa, Paramātman , Iśvara*, etc, serves only as dialogical tools to refer to the one truth—*ekam sat*—in a specific context to determine the flow of a particular spiritual enquiry. The fundamental unitariness of truth is never doubted, and the unhindered belief in the reality of the one supreme *deva* runs like an ideological thread through the entire scriptural corpus. It is 'That One'—*tad ekam*—alone which forges the heaven and earth from its own nature and creates their necessary operative order by personally inhabiting the creation in a manner of possessing it as its mouth, feet, eyes and arms:

> *viśvataścakṣuruta viśvatomuko viśvatobāhuruta viśvataspāt.*
> *saṁ bāhubhyāṁ dhamati saṁ patatrairdyāva bhūmī*
> *janayandeva ekaḥ.*[3]

The multiplicitous world is true only temporally but not absolutely. The seer ceaselessly tries to break free of the phenomenal reality and reach the inherent truth that constitutes the foundation of the whole creation. It is this indescribable truth which holds the three realms of the cosmos firmly in its grasp and provides the inexhaustible creative impulse for the heaven and earth to be carved out of. It is this truth that an enquirer is expected to contemplate:

> *kim svidvanaṁ ka u sa vṛkṣa āsa yato dyavāprithivi niṣṭatakṣuḥ*
> *manīṣino manasā pṛchatedu yadyadadhyatiṣṭhadbhuvanāni dhārayan.*[4]

The principle that is elaborated as an object of enquiry in the aforesaid Ṛg Veda *mantra* assumed far greater clarity in the *Brahman* literature wherein the seers seem to have cast the traces of hesitation from their minds and intuitively understood that it is the *Brahman* which has provided the creative impulse or the 'wood' for the creation of the heaven and earth—*brahma vanaṁ brahma sa vṛkṣa āsit yato prithivī niṣṭatakṣu.*[5]

The whole cosmos is not only the expression of the *Brahman* in accordance with its intrinsic nature to manifest, but it is also inundated fully by the divine force and prowess of the *Brahman.* It is the *Brahman* alone that constitutes the inner essence of all the creatures by entering into them. All the enlightened forms and all the *devatās* that the human mind is capable of perceiving coalesce and coverge into the nature of *Brahman.* This *One* only is the acceptable and really existing primary truth; it is the one alone that determines the core of reality regardless of whatever names are assigned to it:

> *sa prajābhyo vipaśyati yacca prānāti yacca na tamidam nigatam*
> *sahaḥ sa eṣa eka ekavṛdeka eva ete asmindevā ekavṛto bhavanti.*[6]

Therefore, a permanant and non-ephemeral realization would lie in the attainment of the knowledge of this One reality that surpasses all other realizations of a transient nature. Every glory and fame, all attributes and powers, and all worldly categories that are perceived as cosmically assigned to various forces and *devatās* are principally of the nature of the *Brahman* in their transcendental reality. 'That One' alone exists rooted in its supreme nature, consciousness and bliss, and it does not accept or allow any multiplicity to detract from, and diminish, its unitary majesty. There is no second, third, fourth or fifth, and so on: there is only one Lord in which everything and all *devatās* find a home and rest:

> *na dvitiyo na trtiyascaturtho nāpyucyate, ya etaṁ devamekavṛtaṁ veda, na pañcamo no ṣaṣṭhaḥ saptamo nāpyucyate, ya etaṁ devamekavṛtaṁ veda.*[7]

In that one reality all realities rest infinitely. No name can do justice to its nature because all names are only a cognitive superimposition on it. On the converse, any name can be used to refer to *it,* albeit in a limited manner. *It* is neither feminine nor masculine because these phenomenally distinctive attributes exist in *it* in an equal and supereminent mode. *It* is the abode of all characteristics, virtues and distinctive norms and therefore cannot be indicated by the use of any single attribute or a group of attributes and characteristics. The *Supreme Brahman* is not *Indra*, not *Agni*, not *soul*, not body, not the world, not the sky separately: it is all of these collectively although it can be seen as infusing those entities with its reality in their individual manifestations. When the seer says that the truth is 'not this'—*neti, neti*—he is not denying the truthfulness of the description presented to him as an exemplar, but only reminding himself that reality does not exhaust itself in the instance of any single exemplar. Reality is not only the '*this*' accepted as the final vision by a person, it is '*this*' and also many more that human beings are not aware of. Reality is the infinitely rich source and base of every physical and psychic phenomena encountered in mundane and spiritual life. It is for this reason that the Vedic seer generally uses the neuter prepositions '*tat*'—that—to address the Supreme Truth and not the masculine or feminine form. It is possible for the *Paramātman* to manifest itself in both masculine and feminine forms, but fundamentally these notions of gender do not characterize its real nature wherein both male and female aspects as also other polarities, coexist in eternal creative partnership. The seers call that Supreme Truth by the name of *tajjalān*; that from which all things emerge; that in which they subsist and perpetuate; and that in which they are finally withdrawn. It is that truth which is the common regulator and denominator of death and birth, coming and going and all other modes and scales of existence.

Vedas characterize the Supreme Reality as the subject and possessor of sacred knowledge and fervour; glory and fame; water and rain; intellectual brilliance and all material objects:

brahma ca tapaśca kīrtiśca yaśascambhaṣca nabhaśca
brāhmanvarcasaṁ cānnaṁ cānnadyaṁ ca.[8]

P*aramātman* is the cause and reason of past, present and future; beauty and faith; and the sustaining principles of the universe: *bhūtaṁ ca bhavyaṁ ca śraddha ruciśca svargaśca svadhā ca.*[9]

Paramātman itself is death, immortality, fear and succour: *sa eva mṛtyuḥ so'amṛtaṁ so'abhvaṁ sa rakṣaḥ.*[10]

Paramātman is the constituent principle of everything, and everything in turn is derived from it. The bountiful Lord is self-effulgent in its own grandeur and everything is only a manifestation of its glory, giving the impression as if manifold forms are tied to it and it exists in a hundred million manifestations:

tāvāste maghavanmahimopo te tanva'aḥ śatam
upo te badhve baddhani yadi vāsi nya' arbudam.[11]

The Veda categorically proclaim that the Lord of the cosmos is one but it can be visualized in varying manifestations and known by various names: *bhuvanasya yaspatireka eva. Paramātman* has the capacity to reveal itself in many forms that severally possess its full potency without in any manner compromising its cohesiveness and its transcendent unitariness. It is the one Lord who existed in the beginning and in whose womb everything finds its ultimate rest. It is the *Paramātman* that has many times revealed itself in the world and shall continue to reveal itself in the future through the aegis of many *devatās* and many *avatārs*, while itself remaining steadfast in its nature that encompasses creation from all angles and presents itself wherever one looks for it:

eso ha devaḥ pradiśo'anu sarvāḥ pūrvo ha jātaḥ sa u garbhe antaḥ
sa eva jātaḥ sa janiṣyamānāḥ pratyaṅga janāstiṣṭhati sarvatomukhaḥ.[12]

When the seer tries to see reality he strives towards a wholistic vision and not a fragmentary run-away analysis of a certain aspect of that reality. God, men, and the world do not form distinct and separable entities but aspects of a single impartible unity, so much so that a discussion of one would have no meaning without a concomitant discussion of the other. In its essence every phenomena is assimilated antecedently in the existence of the *Brahman* and when it is not a subject of analysis with reference to a sentient seeker, the Lord continues to exist in its own undefined and ineffable glory. Seen from the perspective of a sentient *jīva* it appears to sprout into a whole spectrum of the objective manifold. Reality, comprises of the complete and seamless interrelationship between man, the *Brahman* and the world of phenomena. In the nature of the Supreme Truth the factors of unity and manifoldedness exist in a dialectical relationship of harmony where the manifestation of one aspect does not negate the simultaneous hiddennes of the other. Seeming contrariness of oneness and multiplicity subsist in the *Paramātman* as its own *prakṛti* which does not really admit of multiple categories ontologically. The Vedic seer invokes that resplendent Lord in his prayers who is the only one truthful, all-knowing and invincible *Paramātman* that can be worshipped by humanity:

ya eka iddhavyascarṣaṇīnāmindraṁ taṁ gīrbhirabhyarca ābhiḥ
yaḥ patyate vṛṣbho vṛṣṇyāvāntsatyaḥ satvā purumāyaḥ sahasvān.[13]

The idea that humanity can worship 'two' or 'many' gods is preposterous *ab initio* and it is the product of an illusory metaphysics that assigns exclusive pre-eminence of glory and merit to a particular idea of the divine and, as a necessary correlate, treats other ideas of divine reality as multiplicitious and therefore false. Such metaphysics is the result of a nescience that treats the earthly shadow cast by man's own ego as the substance of divine reality. A wise sage believes that the divine is not the prisoner of any formal finality. *Sanātan Dharma* looks beyond the formal and phenomenal catgories and ceaselessly seeks the divine essence. The Ṛg Veda urges humanity to worship none but that one *Parameśvar* who discloses itself to man in the process of gradual self-realization:

ma cidanyādva śansat sakhāyo mā ripaṇyate
indramitstotā vṛṣaṇaṁ sacā sute muhurukthā ca śansata.[14]

The earnest seeker does not rest his spiritual efforts unless he reaches the heart of reality. The Atharva Veda proclaims the *Brahman* to be the source of the well-spread and delightful warp and woof of existence and its controlling cosmic laws. It supports the realization in that this world all the enlightened ones and the immortal *devatās*, spread out from and then ascend to the common abode of the *Brahmātmā*:

pari viśva bhuvanānyāyamṛtasya tantuṁ vitataṁ dṛśe kam
yatra devā amṛtmānśānah samāne yonāvadhyairayant.[15]

That *Brahmātmā* alone is the creator and sustainer of the whole universe and to that alone are all homage and prayers rightfully due—*divyo gandharvo bhuvanasya yaspatireka eva namasyo vikṣaviḍayah.*[16] Every homage is automatically owned by the one sustainer of the earth, who is the Lord of universe, the only one who deserves worship: *mṛḍādgandharvo bhuvanasya yaspatireka eva namasyaḥ suśevaḥ.*[17] But this one *Brahmātma* is also possessed by the quality of *māyā* that enables it to become many in the world of phenomenal existence, and in that *māyopādhic* context the learned seers describe it in various forms: *suparṇa viprā kavayo vacobhiḥ ekaṁ santaṁ bahudhā kalpayanti.*[18] The Vedic seers do not disregard the presence of many *devatās* but redefine them into a harmony that points ultimately to the one source of grace, bliss and divine power. The Aitareya Brāhmaṇ unhesitatingly proclaims that *Agni* is all the *devatās* and *Viṣṇu* is all the *devatās*: *agnirvai sarvā devatā viṣṇuḥ sarvā devatā.*[19] The Āraṇyaka portions of the Veda corroborate this theme and many reference to similar sentiments are found in them where it is said that all *devatās* are inherently established in every *devatā* who is invoked by men. If *Rudra* is invoked then all other *devatās* are seen as subsumed into the image of *Rudra* and subsidiary divine multipolarity is ruled out: *sarvo vai rudraḥ.*[20] But the inferences do not stop at this level and the argument is carried to its logical conclusion where every *devatā*, all worlds, all lives and all elements are dedicated to the Supreme *Ātman* which is seen as the root of the inverted tree of creation:

asmin sarve prāṇaḥ sarve lokāḥ sarve devāḥ
sarvāṇi bhūtāni sarve ete ātmānaḥ samarpitāḥ.[21]

If such be the case then the concept of the Supreme Truth in the phenomenal perspective gets inextricably linked with the nature of man and the world. Man's analysis of reality is clouded by the pressing presence of the world of objective phenomena and, from the viewpoint of a man immersed in this world, reality appears modified and circumscribed. But an enlightened soul refuses to accept the limitations of the objective world and believes that there exists a reality that is trans-sensual in nature. The idea of the Creator and the mode of creation critically determine the nature of god and the world in a metaphysical tradition. On the primary data of how the world comes into existence is based the clue to unlock the mystery that shrouds the nature of man and his god, and also the relationship of an individual to other aspects of the manifested creation. If the world is believed to have been conjured from nothingness by a 'wholly other' creator as a one-time historical artefact, then the materiality of that world will be its defining characteristics. Such a creation will perpetually remain under the thraldom of its creator. A sentient being living under the impulse of such metaphysics would have grave and fearful visitations of disaster that can be unleashed by the imperial creator at his will. The existence of man and the world is precariously poised on tip-toe, mortally afraid of the god who would not suffer a pang of remorse in destroying what he has contingently created. If the creator is an outside and alien agency then its interest in creation is limited to the extent of ensuring that it behaves in the manner suited to the purpose for which it was brought into existence.

An almighty, but unrelated and ontologically detached, god would necessarily be a fearful controller of the world and men. Humanity living in a 'created' universe would never be allowed a moment without the acute awareness of its dusty beginning and equally dusty and grimy end. A figure fashioned out of a clod of mud would be as safe as a lump of soil covered under a thin leaf amidst torrential rain. Such ideology believes that the material foundation of man is his primary reality; his sensate faculties and his consciousness are epi-phenomenally endowed to him as an act of divine charity. As a result the complete fusion of the two never takes place and human consciousness is continually mortified of the brittle foundation on which it rests. The fact that he is a one-time stand alone creation, with a clearly fore-ordained finality of destruction, lends to man's personality a neurotic craving to do whatever he believes is the bidding of the creator god. More often than not men create their own notion of what they hope the master would commend as proper behaviour. Humanity suffers a frightful brittleness of existence where a limited life waits expectantly for a rather longish death when the soul of mankind shall be under the complete control of the master. The creator god has starkly shown on many occasions that he is not loath to demonstrate his power by causing untold misery and destruction in the world just to prove the point of his overlordship. These grim demonstrations of capricious and uncontrolled power serve adequately to keep that part of creation, which believes in such theology, on tenterhooks and a state of anguished paranoia. In the world of an outside creative agency humanity is always in danger of losing its moral freedom and equanimity by sacrificing its innate truthfulness and grandeur in the mad race of appeasement to its god. The fate of the earth does not affect god otherwise than in relation to the promulgation and proclamation of his glory. Man tosses helplessly between the curse of eternal sinfulness and the contingent promise of redemption by acknowledging god's majesty and power. It is a world in which the creator's own passion is the prime and only determinant; human beings are incidental props in a game of high-stake divine solitaire.

A grafted and historical humanity, indeed, would be mortally afraid of the end of history. Till such end draws nigh it shall be furiously engaged in making itself worthy by deferring to every command that it thinks the creator god has issued. It is the necessary fate of a one-time created universe that it would have a fragile and volatile existence characterized by excited activity that frequently results in make-believe theological bravado to disguise the nagging sense of dependence and helplessness. Existential fragility takes the shape of anger in which one man strives to prove his superiority by the harassment he can cause to others. The metaphysical dislocation of the world from its creative source has the potential of making the former a dangerous place to live in. It is a world haunted by the murky phantoms of suspicion and jealousy based on the notions of superiority of one man's creed over other. Man tries to appropriate god's overpowering authority to subjugate and control other men in a dangerous stimulation of what he thinks to be the divine pattern of desirable behaviour. The two most important characteristics of an externally situated creator or god are his ever present awareness of his own power, and the propensity to use that power over its captive creation in order to assert its authority at will. It would necessarily manifest a sense of self-importance in those who hold this god to be their ideal and would find its outlet in acts of self-righteous imposition on the world-view of others. But, of course, there is no intrinsic reason to subscribe to such notions of creation and divine providence and a *Vedāntin* would calmly ascribe these thoughts to the workings of ignorance or *avidyā* that hides the real nature of reality.

In the S*anātan* tradition simplistic and mechanical explanations of the man, the world and the creative principle have never satisfied an earnest seeker. Reality entails in itself the necessity of creation and dissolution in a never-ending cycle of self-manifestation and self-withdrawal. The seers and the sages realized the real nature of truth through generations of austere and disciplined exploration of the features of the world and man before they proclaimed an integral basis of the whole creation. The principle of creation held by the Indian tradition operates on the basis of complete harmony and existential synchronicity of the created universe and the creative agent. It has no notion of a creator external to the universe because it believes that... "the material stuff and the intelligence of the universe are eternally contained with it... At the deepest level, intelligence and the material stuff of the universe are not separate or distinct but, rather constitute the unified primordial ground of all existence"[22]. The manifest universe does not share a different ground of existence from that which could have caused its manifestation. The Vedic tradition does not permit of an outside 'god' who, at a designated point of time, fashioned a complex world of sentient and insentient beings out of sheer nothingness.

In the spiritual vision of the Vedic seers, the world of phenomena emerges out of a primordially self-existing creative basis which itself gets involved and enmeshed in whatever emerges in the world of objective reality. Creation and destruction are rather inadequate expressions of the interplay of existent and non-existent categories that actualize and deactualize themselves, depending on the choices that the supervening consciousness as the substratum of all reality makes in a given cosmic framework. The existent and the non-existent are equally real ontologically because they together originate from the nature of reality itself. The categories of existent *(sat)* and non-existent *(asat)* have relevance only from the viewpoint of a human observer, whose sensory capacities to perceive put such lables on the phenomena that it observes. What a human agent is able to perceive is existent for him, and what he is not able to perceive he believes to be non-existent. But in a reality divested of a human context for reference, existence and non-existence have no fixed relevance and they remain co-present in the nature of the Supreme Person whom the *Sanatan* traditional variously describes as the *Brahman, Ātman, Puruṣa, Paramātman or Parameśvara.* These epithets collectively denote a single unique being, although individually they may refer to particular dimensions in which each epithet assigns a rather refined and determinate meaning to that unique being which nevertheless exists in its own undifferentiated and ineffable (*anirvacanīya)* existence. The multiple denotations are not intrinsic of the Supreme Being but the products of the compulsions and limitations of the human world of discourse and its linguistic forms.

The foremost enquiry into the act of creative manifestation is to be found in the *Nāsadīya Sūkta* (10.129) of the Ṛg Veda. It is interesting to note that the seer of the *Sūkta* is *Prajāpati* and the *devatā* is mentioned as *Bhāvavṛtta.* It may be recalled that *Prajāpati* has been mentioned in the Vedic corpus as a *devatā* who is the lord of all created beings, and who should be regarded as the *devatā* of all hymns where no specific *devatā* has been clearly indicated. In the *Nāsadīya Sūkta, Prājapati* itself is placed in the role of a seer and what is seen as the *devatā* or the defining power of its vision is *Bhāvavṛtta,* a term which would etymologically mean the occurrence or performance of the act of 'becoming'. Clearly the *Sūkta* is describing an act of evolution based on the intent of the primordial creative consciousness to self-reflect and self-create. It is later clarified in the Upaniṣadic and the Purāṇic texts that *Prajāpati* is the first existent entity that emerges from the creative stirring of the primal spirit. According to the Bṛhaddevatā, the seer himself is said to be recognized as the *devatā* in those *sūktas* which are described as '*bhāvavṛtta*'. There are two possible interpretation of this rather unique method of presentation. In one sense, the first stirrings of the creative impulse can be equated with the modifications and expansion of the seer's own consciousness striving to make some objective sense from the undifferentiated but living reality of pure existence. In another sense, the first manifestation of the conscious will can be seen as self-reflecting on a state of reality that permitted no distinction of existence and non-existence until a desire arose in the all embracing consciousness to manifest, through a process of self-actualization, so that it transformed as *Prājapati.* Seen from both perspectives the real import of the *Nāsadiya Sūkta* is to point out towards the related possibilities of the primal spirit striving to become and, the simultaneous action of the consciousness of an actualized potency striving to transcend its becoming-ness, to retain its sense of unity with the primal spirit. Creation is the *bhāvavṛtta,* the beginning of a great chain of emanations from the primal consciousness as a result of the first act of its desire.

Before the initiation of creative manifestation there was neither the non-existent nor the existent. There were no realms of the air or space. Everything that would come into existence later was wrapped and sheltered in the unfathomable depth of a profound and self-sustaining existence:

nā sadāsinno sadāsīttadanīṁ nāsīdrajo no vyoma paro yat kimāvarīvah kuh kasya śarmannambhaḥ kiṁāsid gahanaṁ gabhīram.[23]

Death was not then, nor was then immortality. There were no signs of day and night. The breathless 'One' breathed upon its own self-sustaining power. Apart from the one nothing whatsoever was there:

na mṛtyurāsīdamṛtaṁ na tarhi na rātryā ahna āsītpra ketaḥ ānīdvātam svadhayā tadekaṁ tasmāddhānyanna paraḥ kim canāṣ.[24]

Life and death are temporal occurrences of the phenomenal world but from the *ādhyātmik* viewpoint they do not allude to separate incidents of 'creation' or 'destruction'. The idea of death, *mṛtyu,* has a very different meaning in the *Sanātan* tradition than the normal import of the word. *Mṛtyu* is not the destruction in a final and irrevocable manner of something that was once 'created' by someone. The birth of the world of phenomena, including human beings, is not an act of one-time unprecedented creation in which a totally new entity gets fashioned out from nothingness. A theological system that treats creation as a one-time phenomena, carries with itself the congenital promise of a highly transient and, therefore, unsure and vulnerable existence because of the grim reminder of imminent and complete destruction. What is created shall be destroyed. The terror of death assumes heightened intensity once its non-repeatable finality is metaphysically assured. Man is then seen as coming out of a chimera and also vanishing into the chimera of either an unsure heaven or, more likely, torment of eternal hell-fire. It is apt that the cultures that believe in creationism address man as mortal.

In the *Sanātan* tradition the phenomenal world is believed to be an emanation from '*that One*' which existed in its infinite majesty, consciousness and bliss. This world was not created by '*that One*', rather this world drew its form from that which itself was formless but eternally existent. It is only possible for an entity that has no fixed shape and size to provide form for all manifested phenomena and also the basis for all forms to actualize. Fixity of form would limit the creative flexibility of the *Paramātman* who constitutes the heart and soul of every feature of the objective manifold. What is manifested is just the transient cosmic existence in a particular spatio-temporal form, and death is the dissolution of that particular form without affecting in any manner the spirit or *Ātman* that constitutes the controlling essence in temporary possession of that form. Nothing of the sort that 'X died' ever happens: what transpires in actuality is that 'the form' that X was possessing has dissolved. 'He' or 'I' never cease to be because the constitutive principle of the 'He' and 'I' is immutable and eternal, oscillating between phenomenal manifestation *(sṛṣti)* and dissolution *(pralaya)* in an eternal spiral of coming and going of inexhaustive names and forms in the 'bubble chamber' of divine nature.

The world of material phenomena *(prakṛti, virāj)* co-exists eternally in the nature of the Lord. Only the nature of manifestation changes because of the superimposition of names and forms on the eternally pre-existing spirit of the *Brahman*. Man is not a mortal and sinful lump of brittle earth; he is the progeny of immortality—*amṛtasya putrāḥ*. Death and immortality are the twins born out of the same womb of creative nature and need not be treated as comparative entities on the scale of metaphysical relevance and importance. What is death in one perspective is birth and immortality in another. The Ṛg Veda regards death and immortality as of the same nature—*amartyo martyenā sayoniḥ*. The immortal *Ātman* passes from one form to another endowed with the power of the life-breath. It leaves possession of one body and moves on from one life to another, from one form to another:

> *anachaye turgātu jīvamejaddhruvaṁ madhya ā pastyānām*
> *jīva mṛtasya carati svadhābhiramartyo martyena sayoniḥ.*[25]

That One which existed in the beginning was neither of the nature of matter nor of the nature of energy; he was the cause and basis of both.[26] It pervaded the whole of space and lived by its own self-sustaining power as life eternal. It existed since eternity and shall continue to exist eternally, breathing without air, as it were, in the bliss of the pulsations taking place in its own nature. It was/is an eternal existence of consciousness, energy, bliss and life. It manifests and creates as *Brahma*, preserves by assuming the form of *Viṣṇu* and dissolves everything into raw essence for new manifestation to take place by assuming the nature and form of *Śiva*. In the mode of the unattached, undisturbed state antecedent to the acts of manifestation, preservation and destruction, it transcends its natural and inherent *Brahmatva* and *Śivatva* and remains in the peaceful *(śānta)* state of his *Praṇava or Oṁkār* nature. In that state it is of the nature of pure and undifferentiated existence, conciousness and bliss as *saccidānandasvarupa*. In its elemental *saccidānand* nature it transcends being a *devatā*, god or *Iśvara*. In its primal nature it does not appear as an *Iśvara* because at that stage nothing, apart from its own divine reality, exists in reference to which a functional and contextual predicate can be given to it. '*That one*' absolute reality cannot become an *Iśvara* or *devatā* for its own sake. It can only become an *Iśvara* in the process of its desire to manifest and create. Godhood is a synchronous function that it assumes with reference to a manifested world of phenomena of which it has to act as the preserver and controller by providing and propagating the necessary cosmic and moral laws. With the unfolding of creation it unfolds itself as *Iśvara*, and manifests in potencies of various *devatās* in the myriad realms and aspects of its creation. The *paramātma-tattava* becomes *Iśvara* in a world of phenomena that is subject to a ceaseless process of coming and going. *Iśvara* is the active state of the Supreme Being in reference to a *saṁsāra* of human beings. In the event when the *saṁsāra* ceases to be, the Supreme Being remains just what it is essentially—its infinitely peaceful pure existence, consciousness and bliss.

The *saccidānanda svarupa* Supreme Being entered into a state of austere and concentrated resolve, and from this resolve was born *tapah* or an empty space united under a causal covering: *tuchyenābhvapihitaṁ yadāsītta pasastanmohīnā jāyataikam.*[27] The advent of space or the void throbbing with the subtle and pervasive mind force as the base of all unmanifested energy, provides the basis for the emergence of *ṛta, satya, rātri and samudro arṇavaḥ:*

ṛtañca satyaṁ cābhīddhāttapaso' adhyajāyat
tato rātrayajāyat tataḥ samudro arṇavaḥ.[28]

According to this *mantra,* the Supreme Being seems to be setting the rules and defining the limits within which a particular cycle of creative manifestation would take place and whose boundaries would limit the dimensions of material reality of that cycle. The delimitation of existential boundaries is necessary because "Existence refers to what is structured, determined and moving. By contrast the non-existence is the unstructured the undetermined and the unmoving..."[29] The limitations, however, are only perceptional superimpositions of certain dimensions on that which is without any limitations. they do not in any way affect the inherent nature of the absolute reality: they only serve to provide a relative focus to it. The defining principles that emanate from the *tapas* or the mind-force of the Supreme Being are described by the seers as *ṛta, sūrya, rātri and light*. The world *ṛta* denotes motion and movement that constitute the fundamental principles behind the physical and moral laws that sustain and preserve the cosmos. *Satya* is the quality of existence and stability, whereas *Rātri* along with its plural *ratrani,* indicates the property of mass and inertia that are essential for the generation of grosser particles that would go into the formation of all physical evolutes.[30] But enclosing all this in its embrace was the primary emergence of light—*Sūrya, Agni*—as the foremost principle and the leader of the unfolding of cosmic phenomena. Light was to provide the limits of the universe. It is said about the Special Theory of Relativity that, "The theory sets out to define the outer limits of the three-dimensional world in which we live, and hints at an illusive reality beyond it. In the speed of light it sees the boundaries of the material reality in which we live..."[31] But beyond the boundaries set by the motion or the laws of the cosmos in association with light, there can exist "a dimension in which energy and mass are infinite, invisible and immortal."[32] This dimension can be comprehended only beyond the boundaries set by light. One of the drawbacks of the phenomenal world is that it circumscribes ordinary vision to a very small sphere of reality.

With the emanation of the principles of motion, creative stability and inertia, the stage was set for the emergence of an undifferentiated watery mass of rich but still unmanifest energy—*samudro arṇava*—as the field of all future creation. One of the meanings of *arṇava* symbolizes *Viṣṇu* who is universally known as the impeller of motion and, thereby, the preserver of the reality of this world. It is *Viṣṇu,* who pervades the whole cosmos with his power by taking three grant strides and, in this symbolic act of movement, initiates the process of continuous cosmic motion. The motion impelled by *Viṣṇu* ensures the massive stability of this universe and his presence into it provides the guarantee that the universe would not be governed by the force of random movement but an intelligently directed motion. It is now widely believed by scientists that material realities are principally the functions of motion. The Indian seers, as well as many other teachers of ancient civilizations, have accepted the centrality of intelligent and orderly motion as the basis of cosmic life: "The acceptance of an intelligent form of motion in all activity whether this be within the confines of matter, the human will, or in the movement of extraterrestrial bodies, appears to have been part of all ancient beliefs."[33] The Ṛg Veda describes in a graphic manner the essentiality of movement or momentum for the purposes of creation, preservation and destruction, where the whole cosmos is seen in continous motion around the eye of the sun:

> *sanemi cakramajaraṁ vivāvṛtta uttānāyāṁ daśa yuktā vahanti*
> *suryasya cakṣu rajasaityāvṛttaṁ tasminnārpitā bhuvanāni viśva.*[34]

With the emergence of *Ṛta* and *Satya* and the impetus of motion, the huge waters of the unmanifest and plasmic subtle stuff gave birth to the parameters of time, light, nights and days, and also to the particles of grosser matter.[35] The process remains under the control of the Supreme Being who supervises the blinking and the vibration of the ocean of subtle energy:

> *samudrādarṇavādadhi samvatsaro ajāyat*
> *ahorātraṇi vidaddhaviśvasya miṣato vaśi.*[36]

The primal reason for the beginning of creation, however, has been described as the divine desire of the Supreme Being. It was the first seed in the cosmic mind. The seers recognize the desire of the Lord as the bond that operates between the existent or manifested reality and the non-existent or unmanifested base of all existence. Manifestation is a function of the desire of the Lord to self-actualize itself and observe in the process how it could cause the becoming of many—*ekoham bahusyam.* Desire, concentrated austerities and motion in a regulated manner are the major principles behind the stability of creation:

kāmastadgre samvartatādhi manaso retaḥ prathamaṁyadāsit
sato bandhumsati niravindahṛdi pratīṣyā kavayo manīṣā.[37]

The Nṛsimhapūrvatāpani Upaniṣad echoes a similar sentiment in its description of the state of reality before creation and the emergence of the Lord on the 'waters' of the subtle conscious force. With a pious desire, it proceeded to create the world and transformed itself as the creator and preserver *Iśvara*, or the Lord of all created beings: *āpo va idamāsan salilmeva sa prajāpatirekaḥ puṣkarparṇe sambhavat, tasyantar manasi kāmaḥ samvartat idam sṛjeyam iti.*[38]

The Supreme Being, the formless and the attributeless *Brahman*, coevally begins the dual process of creation and its personal actualization as an *Iśvara* or God. As the subtle void is ready to burst forth through assumption of form so does the creator *Iśvara* in step by step consonance with every aspect of its creation. The spirit descends into matter in the world, and the *Brahman* assumes its divine role as the *Prajāpati*; the bountiful protector of all creation. The emergence of *Prajāpati* on the unmanifested void impregnates the void with immense possibilities and turns it into the fecund womb, designated as *hiraṇyagarbha* by the seers, for the phenomenal world to deliver from it. The desire of the Supreme Being ties it inextricably with its creation and serves as the conjunctive principle between the existent and the non-existent. The *saccidānanda* Being offers itself in oblation by sacrificing its unbounded, unmanifest and pure spiritual nature to become the substratum for the projection and establishment of the whole cosmos on it. Supreme Being is ready to assume the role of *Prajāpati* or *Puruṣa* at the moment of the emergence of desire in its nature; and it understands that the consequence of its desire would lead to its deep involvement and attachment with every moment in the life of the fruit of its desire.

The epithet *Puruṣa* has been assigned etymological meaning signifying, variously, 'that which moves ahead of everything'; 'that which fills everything with force'; 'that which pervades embodied phenomena'; and also 'that which pervades and protects'. All embodied entities are called *'pura'* and the creator and pervader that constitutes the soul of these embodied beings is recognized as *Puruṣa*:

purāṇyanena sṛṣtāni nṛ-teryagṛṣi devatāḥ
śete jīvena rūpeṇa pureṣu hyasau.[39]

This *Puruṣa* that resides as the inner essence in the bodies known as *pura* is also identified as *Viṣṇu—purusanjñye śarīreasmin sayanātpuruṣo hariḥ*. The *Puruṣa*, however, transcends all materiality and objectiveness of embodied phenomena and does not have any fixed identifiable form or characteristics in the phenomenal sense. It remains just the fullness of the Supreme Being in whose existence desire has arisen to create. *Puruṣa* is the all pervading and unmanifest self whose nature only he himself is aware of: *avyakttāthu paraḥ puruṣaḥ vyāpako'aling eva ca.*[40] In the Bṛhadāraṇyaka Upaniṣad a very significant insight is given into the nature of *Puruṣa* in the act of creation. The Upaniṣad undoubtedly believes *Puruṣa* to be the *Brahman* in a significant mode as the indwelling spirit of all created beings, but it characterizes the activity of the *Puruṣa* in its creative endeavour in a manner that involves the miracle of the *Puruṣa* becoming the whole universe. By a divine alchemy the *Puruṣa* becomes the whole world: *purusa evedam viśvam.*[41] The Bṛhadāraṇyaka Upaniṣad describes the nature of *Puruṣa* entailing within itself the two concepts of *pura* or the antecedent unconditioned principle, and *auṣat* as the 'burnt up' state where the obstructions in the process of creation are transmigrated and consciously effaced by the sacrifice of the *Puruṣa.* This act require a critical modification in the nature of the Supreme Being. In association with the identifiable creative desire, it provides the seer with some cognitive hold for his baffled imagination and appears somewhat recognizable or *puruṣavidha*.

This *Puruṣa* is designated as *Prajāpati* by the seers in the Śatpatha Brāhmaṇ and the Taittirīya Āraṇyaka. This *Puruṣa* is the first principle of creation from whose desire all forms emanate. The Taittīriya

Āranyaka identifies *Puruṣa or Prajāpati* as the first born of the universal order of *ṛta* but still unaffected by the distinctions of space and time. As the first born it provides the base for the emanation of all the worlds and all the beings contained within it. Every aspect of creation is eternally pervaded by the spirit of the *Puruṣa*: *iti sarvamevedamāptvā sarvamavarudhya tadevānupraviśati ya evam veda.*[42] *Puruṣa* has also been designated by the terms *Nārāyaṇa* in the Śatapatha Brāhmaṇa: *puruṣo ha nārāyaṇo*. The Supreme Being is characterized in various texts as *Puruṣa* and *Prajāpati* when it is seen as animated by the desire to create. To become the creator of the world *purusa* was required to sacrifice its original unconditioned nature in a manner that seers describe as the performance of *puruṣamedha*. "What was required to be sacrificed (viz. given up for a purpose), in this case was the own nature of purity, formlessness and transcendence of *Puruṣa*. *Prajāpati* could become the creator *(srashta)* and the lord of the created universe only as a result of *Purusha's* sacrifice. And the offsprings of *Prajapati*, viz, the devas, also sacrificed *Purusha* in their turn."[43] The *Supreme Puruṣa* sacrificed its innate pure, undisturbed, blissful and unmanifest nature to create and, therefore, become the Universe in the dimension of space and time. By sacrificing its pure Being the *Supreme Puruṣa* becomes *Puruṣa* as a subject that has resolved to give up its original form for the sake of creation.

The Ṛg Veda describes this cosmic sacrifice by the *Param Puruṣa* in the ninetieth *Sūkta* of the tenth Mandal. The *Puruṣa* of the *Puruṣa Sūkta* should not be mistaken as a person. All the attributes used to describe it should be understood as poetical metaphors of its immensity and vastness. Tradition regards *Puruṣa Sūkta* as the eulogy of Lord *Viṣṇu* who traverses and permeates the whole cosmos and causes the three spatial realms along with their *devatās Agni, Sūrya and Indra* to emerge. The Ṛg Veda says:

> *puruṣa evedaṁ sarvaṁ yadbhutaṁ yacca bhavyaṁ*
> *utamṛtatvasyeśāno yadannenātirohati.*[44]

The world of phenomena is the nature of the *Puruṣa* alone. This *Puruṣa* is the lord of immortality but seems to grow up and manfiest by the use of material elements. While assuming material form it may appear to sacrifice its original nature; its transcendental spirituality and non-phenomenal immortality, however, are never fully obscured. It is further added by the seer that whatever exists in the phenomenal world is just the reflection of *Puruṣa's* majesty. All that exists can be said to consist of only a fraction of its nature, one quarter as it were, while its remaining quarters are hidden beyond the ken of this world, unaffected by change, decay or dissolution. In its fundamental nature the *Puruṣa* is much greater than the world of phenomena:

etāvānasya mahimāto jyāyānsca puruṣaḥ
pādoasya viśvā bhūtāni tripādasyāmṛtaṁ divi.[45]

What the *mantra* purports to say is that ... "the Purusha is all this which is within the framework of space and time, and also all that is outside this framework, and that he is the lord of '*amrtatva*' as well as the phenomenal world which grows by all that the living beings incline towards."[46] The unmanifest (*avyakt)* source of creation (*mahat*) is only an aspect of the *Puruṣa* . "The Purusha includes this avyakt but is not confined to it".[47] The *Puruṣa* is the highest:

mahatah paramvyaktaṁ avyaktāt puruṣaḥ paraḥ
puruṣānna param kiṅcitsa kaṣṭha sā parā gateḥ.[48]

Puruṣa is absolutely devoid of form and beyond all manifest and unmanifest condition. "He abides in the interior of all things and beings of the manifest world, and also outside them. He is therefore the reality that is transcendental, while being at the same time immanent in creation."[49] From this primeval *Puruṣa* emerge *Virāj* as the basic building block of material reality. The *Puruṣa* is also said to enter the *Virāj* and create the phenomenal man in whom the cosmic forces find an exact correspondence: The sun in the cosmos becomes his eyes, the air his breath, the fire his speech, and all the *devatās* settle in his person as his manifold sensory capacities. But in order that the material existence attain certain recognizable stability and reality the unmanifest *Puruṣa* would be required to offer himself as the divine oblation in the grand ceremony of the cosmic creative sacrifice. In this *yajña, Puruṣa* is the sacred offering of which the spring season is the clarified butter, summer season the dry fuel and autumn the oblation. The divine *devatās* perform the sacrifice of the nature of *Puruṣa* inasmuch as they emerge as a product of that sacrifice. *Puruṣa* offers to concretize and immanentize its otherwise undisturbed and formless state whereby many powers of the world arise from within its inexhaustible nature; the spring blooms and the summer sizzles in the process of that sacrifice wherefrom time was born. "The devas were created in the image of the Purusha (or Prajapati); this creation itself is called the sacrifice, for the Purusha gave himself up to the *devas*... This was because the Purusha himself was of the nature of yajna."[50]

In this spiritual *yajña* and mental resolve—*mānasād yajñāt*—the *Puruṣa* performs the divine act of creative *karma* and offers itself to become the entire creation. It was an act of reciprocal giving in which everything tied together collectively in a deep spiral of continuous sacrifice in order to maintain the realizability of the phenomenal world—*tasmāt yajñāt sarvahutaḥ*. *Puruṣa* became all the *devatās* and all *devatās* became *it*; *it* became all men and all men transcendentally resolve into *it*. The sacrifice of the *Puruṣa* is an uninterrupted meta-temporal creative activity in which the *saccidānand Paramātman* appears modified and 'sacrificed' for the perpetuation of the phenomenal creation. The *avyakt,* the unmanifest, becomes the world upon the nature of the *Puruṣa*. The *Parabrahma* sacrifices its eternal formless equanimity to become the active, creative, and co-present *Iśvara*. The sacrifice of the *Puruṣa* is not ontological but only relational and contextual; it appears, in a creative mode from the viewpoint of a world that emerges as a result of its psychic penance. In its own self *Puruṣa* is still the same profound existence in which urges of any kind do not cause an existential ripple. It just is: Fully conscious, fully existent and fully blissful; one without any other. Urges and intentionalities are the functions germane to the realm of manifestation.

The Supreme *Brahman* is omnipresent in its original state. In the process of phenomenal manifestation, the world of reality which presently constitutes the observable and humanly measurable phenomena, may just be one small part of its creative product. There may exist many other dimensions of reality of which man is not currently aware of. The possibility of many more probable universes out of which this particular universe gets chosen by a specific act of conscious awareness of its inhabitants cannot be ruled out. If the Lord is omnipresent and omnipotent, creation would necessarily be cyclical and recurrent; a spiral movement creating rosette patterns of coming and going in the blink of the creator's eye. Atharva Veda mentions that this universe is dependent on the power of *uchiṣta*, a term which can be translated to mean, figuratively, the 'left over': *uchiṣte nāmrupaṁ cochiṣte loka āhitaḥ.*[51] Human imagination can only grope in conjecture about the immense possibilities residing in the body of the main. But all acts of creative manifestation do not in any manner diminish or reduce the Being of the *Brahman*. It remains the full and complete *Brahman* even after the full emanation of the creative reality. It transcends any sense of aggregation and subtraction, and what seems to be a 'coming-out' from it, does not imperil its fullness even infinitesimally:

purṇamidaṁ purṇamidaḥ purṇāt purnamudacyate
purṇasya purṇamādāya purṇamevāvaśiṣyate.[52]

The *Parabrahman* is the supreme Truth. Truth is believed to be that which never modifies or digresses from its essential nature and remains unsublated at every point of time and space. Śaṁkarācārya states this aspect of the nature of truth by saying, *yadrupeṇa yanniścitaṁ tadrupaṁ na vyabhicarati tat satyaṁ.*[53] What appears as the modified world of phenomena is the effect of the *māyā* of the *Brahman* and not the *Brahman* itself. *Brahman* is unqualified truth: *sanmātram hi brahma.* The word *Brahman* is etymologically derived from the root *'bṛh'* which connotes the attributes of pervasive growth, greatness and outward expression. Śaṁkara regards the etymological meaning of *'bṛh'* to signify the sense of profundity, eternity, purity and growth: *brahma śabdasya hi vyutpādyamānasya nityaśuddhatvavāda ya' arthāḥpratīyante bṛhaterdhatorarthānugmat.*[54]

Brahman is the primal force behind the reality of the evolved nature and it has been addressed by seers by the use of many adjectivals. Some call it the *Paramapada,* while other call it *Prajāpati* or *Puruṣa.* Upaniṣadic sages usually refer to it as the *Brahman* and the *Ātman.* The Upaniṣads serve as the most elaborate exegesis of the principal spiritual theme adumbrated aphoristically in the Veda. Taking the cue from the Veda they undertake a deep investigation of the nature of the manifested reality and proceed gradually to understand its relationship with their primal and unitary source. It is noteworthy that one of the earliest Upanisads, the Bṛhadaranyaka, begins with a discussion of sacrifice and death as the first apprehendable happening prior to the emergence of the present cosmic epoch. According to this Upaniṣad, nothing existed in the beginning but 'death' which seemed to provide a cover in the nature of void or phenomenal nothingness: *naiveha kiṅcāgra āsīnmṛtyu naivedamāvṛtamāsitt.*[55] 'Death', however, can never be the reality of any creative beginning, unless the notion of some antecedent life that could have already been is necessarily read into it by implication. The sage is perhaps hinting at the limitless and infinite cycles of emanation and withdrawal of phenomenal existence of which the beginning of a particular epoch is the subject matter of his study. If *mṛtyu* or 'death' is read in the sense of non-existence then the description would appear to closely echo the sentiment expressed in the first *mantra* of the *Nāsadīya Sūkta.* According to the Bṛhadāraṇyaka, the *Brahman* which was in the nature of *mṛtyu* or the phenomenally unmanifest existence became the three realms and the three *devatās* presiding over them. After the material manifestation occurred in the *Brahman* it desired to energize it and therefore yoked mind and speech to the material base:

> s*oakāmayat dvitiyo ma ātmā jāyateti sa manasā vācaṁ mithunāna sambhavat.*[56]

All operative powers of the manifested creation, the *devatās,* actualize from within the infinite nature of the *Brahman* or the Supreme *Puruṣa* and establish themselves in various aspects of the world by not only completely pervading them but also focussing the disposition of their activities. They use the world like a horse which they ride with full realization of its ultimate futility, when it would have to be abandoned in its phase of dissolution. At the time of dissolution of the world the *devatās* too return to unite indistinguishably in the Supreme Being of the *Brahman: hayo bhūtvā devān…so punarekaiva devatā.*[57] The *devatās* apprehended in the macrocosmic perspective are the pure and sinless forces that remain beyond the contingency of death in a realm that is not subject to the ravages of time: *devatānāṁ pāpmānaṁ mṛtyumapahatyāthaina mṛtyumatyavahat.*[58]

The cosmic *Agni* resides as speech in the body of a human being: *tadyeam vāk so ay'amagni.*[59] The faculty of seeing, the eye of the human being, is the cosmic *Surya* that enters their bodies and supervises the capacity to see: *yadidaṁ cakṣuḥa so'asāvādityaha.*[60] Air, or *Vāyu* of the external universe, is also the life-breath of the human selves: *tadyo'ayam prāṇaḥ sa vāyuḥ.*[61] The *devatās,* as aspects and powers of the *Brahman,* become both the cosmic sun and the human eye simultaneously. All *devatās* of the cosmic universe have their functional seat in the existence of the human body and the universal cosmos gets miniaturized and conscientized as an observer—participator in the form of a human being.

Human senses are the *devatās* of the human bodies in association with the compulsion of temporal decay. The *devatās* of the cosmic sphere are immortal and pure because of their wisdom and righteous nature. When the soul takes hold of human speech and transports it, as it were, beyond sinfulness and nescience and therefore death and decay, speech becomes *Agni*:

> *atha cakṣuratyavahattadyadā mṛtyumatyamucyat sa ādityoabhabha*
> *vatso'asāvādityaḥ pareṇa mṛtyumatikrantastapati.*[62]

In a similar exercise of spiritual purification, human eye, ears and mind become the sun, all directions and the moon respectively:

> *sa vai vācameva prathamāmatyavahatsā yadā mṛtyumatmucyat*
> *so'agnirbhavatso' ayamagniḥ pareṇa mṛtyumatikranto dīpyate.*[63]

Realization of the divinity of human body and its various faculties dawn on the sentient soul when the senses transcend the impurities and limitations of egotism, sin, unrighteousness, untruth, vanity and selfishness which cloud the self in ignorance and render it subject to death and decay. When a false sense of egotistical I-ness possesses a human being, the fear of death arises in him. Death does not exist but in its phenomenal liaison with unrighteousness and ignorance. The *Ātmā* or *prāṇa* of the human being is its *āṅgiras*, or the essence and spirit of all the limbs and the senses that constitute the human body. In its essential nature *Ātmā* or *prāṇa* sublates and transcends the phenomenal limitation of the body with which it is temporarily enmeshed, and exists as the all-pervasive spirit of the whole cosmos: *ebhistribhirlokaih samo'anena sarveṇa tasmādveva samānuśte sāmnaḥ.*[64] *Atma* is the microcosmic but supra-phenomenal aspect of the macrocospic Supreme Self—the *Brahman.*

In the presence of King Janak of Mithila, his teacher and priest Aśvala raised the issue of the overpowering reality of death and the perpetual destruction of everything that comes to life in this world. Aśvala was unsure of any measure that can defeat death and lead to immortality, therefore he turned to Yājñavalkya for a clarification. Yājñavalkya's answer gives a clue to the Upaniṣadic themes of spiritual life, knowledge, and freedom from bondage, i.e., *mukti.* Yājñavalkya explains that during the performance of a *yajña*, the presiding priest gives to the speech of the performer the nature of *Agni*; to the eyes the nature of *Sūrya* or *Āditya*; to his mind the nature of *Candramā;* and so forth. Every element of the human existence is aligned with and turns into the *devatās* of the cosmos during the performance of a *yajña.* In fact every action of a human being becomes a pious *yajña* when the human senses operate with the spirit of the divine *devatās.* To know that one is an aggregate of many *devatās* is to emerge from the shadows of death. Deliverance from the bondage to death is achieved after the human individuality is aligned with the divine universality, and the body becomes a part and parcel of every other body in the cosmos. With the realization that every *devatā* resides in his own body, an individual can awaken these *devatās* and unite his own microcosmic phenomenal body with the macrocosmic trans-phenomenal reality of the supreme consciousness. Death can be conquered by the conciliation of the human self and the cosmic self under the benign guidance of the awakened consciousness. *Mukti* or liberation consists in the act of the bodily eye becoming the cosmic *Āditya*: This awareness is the proclamation of the end of death and the attainment of *param mokṣa.* Once the basic non-separateness and non-materiality of the phenomenal existence, which is not in contra-distinction with the eternal and unitary reality, is understood while an individual is living amidst the ceaseless flow of coming and going, death is overcome in the blazing light of *ati mukti.* What is death but the fear of losing a temporally contingent phenomenal and material form. Once it is understood that this form is but a spatio-temporally contextualized materialization of a cosmic and eternal life, death is feared no more. Break the mirror of phenomenally limited perspectives and humanity stands as one in its pristine and immortal glory. Yājñavalkya has hinted at this possibility many millenia before: *hotṛartvijāgninā vācā vāgvai yajñasya hotā taddyeyaṁ vāk so'ayamagniḥ sa hotā sa muktiḥ sa atimuktiḥ.*[65]

At the primary level just the one Lord constituting the basis of all phenomenal existence remains. '*That*' alone was there in whose being the feminine and the masculine principles and all other antinomies were so resolved as to appear tied in a deep and loving embrace: *sa haitāvānās yathā stripumañsau saṁpariṣvaktau.*[66] Reality is neither masculine nor feminine but a deep synthesis of the two like the two, parts of the grain of a chickpea seed: *tasmādidamarḍhabṛgalamiva sva it ha smāḥ.*[67] Human race is born of the creative intercourse of the masculine and the feminine energies that eternally abide in the person of the Supreme Being and contingentally emerge to procreate the world of living things: it is the spiritual intercourse of *Brahmā* with the self-actualized feminine principle of *Sarasvati* that leads to the one becoming the many by the impulsion of desire. The Aitareya Upaniṣad provides an insight into the true nature of the human beings. When various *devatās* as powers of the *Brahman* emerged in the process of creation, they wanted a form in which they would enter and obtain a medium of creative expression. When the form of man was created the Lord instructed the *devatās* to enter into it—*tābhyah puruṣamānayattā... ta abravidyathā—ayatanaṁ praviśateti.*[68] *Agni* entered the form as its speech; *Vayu* entered as life-breath; *Sun* as its eyes and other *devatās* in various other aspects of its constitution: *agnirvāgbhūtvā mukhaṁ praviśadvāyu prāṇo bhūtvā nāsike praviśadādityacakṣurbhūtvā' akṣini praviśa.*[69] *Devatās* emerge as aspects of the *Brahman* and settle in the person of a human being as aspects of its *Ātman*. Śvetaketu was rightly informed that he was essentially that: *tattvamasi Śvetaketu*.

The Munḍak Upaniṣad declares that the whole cosmos is but the *Brahman*: *brahmaivedaṁ viśvaṁ variṣṭhaṁ.*[70] It is the *Brahman* that is the only truth that ever was and forever will be: *sarvaṁ khalvidaṁ brahma.*[71] The seers exhort every human being to raise itself to the supreme height of spiritual realization and declare that they all are nothing but the *Brahman* itself—*aham brahmāsmi*. Man does not need a mediatory redemptive agency as an outside aid to elevate him spiritually; he is potentially divine and needs only to remove the false and manifold golden covering that has hidden the face of reality and confront the Lord directly in a very personal and meaningful revelation:

> *hiraṇmayena patreṇa satyasyāpihitaṁ mukhaṁ*
> *tattvaṁ puṣannpāvṛnu satyadharmaya dṛṣtaye.*[72]

The discourse on the dual aspect of the *Brahman* held between King Ajātaśatru and the sage Gārgya is very instructive. Ajātaśatru calrifies that the Supreme *Brahman* appears in the enquiry of men in two forms: incarnate and non-incarnate. He says: *dve vā ve brahmaṇo rūpe mūrtaṁ caivāmūrtaṁ ca martyaṁ cāmṛtam ca sthitam ca yacca sacca tyacca.*[73] *Brahman* as the infinite *Puruṣa* can be said to possess simultaneously the attributes of form and formlessness; changelessness and change; motionlessness and movement as reconciled and non-contradictory aspects of its nature. From the standpoint of the cosmos *Brahman* is the effulgent soul of the universe and from the standpoint of the individual it is the soul of the living body.

The non-relative and absolute *Brahman* freely reveals its *Iśvara* form. However, in its involvement with the manifested world *Iśvara* does not lose its originality. S. Radhakrishnan has rightly observed that the absolute *Brahman*, the creative *Iśvara*, and the *Iśvara* manifested in the world are not a part of historical and physical series; they have only a logical relationship between them. The formless and the incarnate *Brahman* are not separate realities but the aspects of a reality viewed from two completely different perspectives. Radhakrishnan quotes Jayateertha as saying—*brahmaṇo dvairupyasya apramānikatvat*. Form and formlessness are the two comingled possibilities of the same entity. A particular worshipper can choose one of the many aspect of the *Brahman* for the purpose of his spiritual fulfilment. The selection of one aspect does not, however, negate the reality of the other aspects. Upaniṣadic sages have recommended various ways and means for understanding the truth of the *Brahman*. Chāndogya Upaniṣad recommends both *ādhyātmika* and *ādhidaivat* forms of worship. When a person sees the *Brahman* located within his own heart as a non-dual principle he chooses the *ādhyātmika* form of worship, if he chooses *Brahman* in a divine form external to himself he follows the *ādhidaivika* path of worship:

> *mano brahmetyupāsīttetyadhyātmamathadhidaivat mākāśo–brahmetyubhayamādiṣtaṁ bhavatyadhyātṁ cādhidaivataṁ ca.*[74]

Both paths are recommended by the sages as fruitful and valid for different kinds of worshippers. *Brahman*, after all, has many bases—*tadetaccatuspad brahma*[75]—and the Lord as *Āditya* is just one, but real and certain, base of it: *ādityo brahma iti...*[76] In the phenomenal world the *Brahman* is a qualified *devatā*.. In relation to the the individual it is his own inner truth and in the respect its own nature *Brahman* is just one pure existence, consciousness and bliss possessing nothing that can be said to be its distinguishing mark, since it possesses all of them.

A worshipper, if possible, should strive to go beyond the presence of the symbol and the word that constitute the focus of his worship and attain a higher state of realization. The reading of all the Vedas as the words of *Brahman*, and the worship of *Ākaśa, Anna, Jal,* etc, as the forms of *Brahman,* are still only the acknowledgement of the 'names'. The worship of *Vācaṁ brahma, mano brahma, saṁkalpa brahma, bala brahma,* etc, are but only *Brahman* as name—*nāma brahma.*[77] The sage Sanatkumar does not censor or advise Nārad to jettison as false or worthless the knowledge of reality, which the latter has acquired through deep learning, wide reading and stern austerities; on the contrary, he enables Nārad to move step by step from one reality to a next deeper perception of reality till they both came to, what Sanatkumar terms, the extreme or the *ativādi* reality of the *Brahman.* Those who see reality in its undisturbed purity move ahead of the pack of spiritual seekers and realize matters that are beyond the reach of normal minds: *evaṁ paśyanneva manvān evaṁ vijānannativādi bhavati.*[78] But the notions of truth which were left behind in the spiritual quest of Nārad were not considered to be false or abrogated precepts but a less perfect knowledge of reality. *Brahman* as the *Puruṣa* in the sun—the *Āditya Puruṣa*—is true and fully valid but only phenomenally; at the final or extreme limits of knowledge, *Brahman* is seen just as itself—*tad ekam.* To reach this stage of knowledge is termed as a spiritual 'moving beyond', as *ativād* ; but normal minds are well within their rights to understand and worship the *Brahman* as it manifests itself in so many veridical forms within their specific levels of understanding.

True knowledge of reality is extremely difficult. The Upaniṣads refer to the truth as hidden deep beyond the ken of simple intellectual tools of understanding; it is *nihitam guhāyām* and its discernment has been considered a rather complex and painstaking exercise. A normal seeker was advised to understand the incarnate and manifest appearances of truth, *nāmabrahma,* as equally efficacious for spiritual experience provided the worshipper is able to see them as the embodiments of the same. Even simple *bhakti* and *saguṇa upāsanā* can take a person onwards on the path of truth. The nature of the Supreme would depend on the particular aspect of his nature as the subject of contemplation. "They are two ways of looking at the Eternal. The Supreme in its absolute self-existence is Brahman, the Absolute and as the Lord and Creator containing and controlling all, is Iśvara, the God. 'Whether the Supreme is regarded as undetermined or determined, this Śiva should be known as eternal; undetermined He is, when viewed as different from the creation and determined when He is everything."[79]

nirguṇas saguṇas ceti śivo jñeyaḥ sanātanaḥ
nirguṇaḥ prakṛter anyaḥ saguṇas sakal smṛtaḥ.

It is the one pure and non-dual reality that is variously known as *Brahman*, *Ātman* and god or *Bhagawān*:

vadanti tat tattvavidah tattvaṁ yaj jñānam advayam
brahmeti paramātmeti bhagavān iti śabdyate.[80]

It is true that the *Brahman* is the unqualified and eternal absolute towards whom all spiritual quest should ultimately move, but "apprehended *sub specie temporis'*[81], it is also the world. In the Brahmasūtra Bhāsya, Śaṁkara has argued that "Brahman is apprehended under two forms; in the first place, as qualified by limiting conditions owing to the multiformity of names and forms; in the second place, as being the opposite of this, i.e., free from all limiting conditions whatsoever."[82] To the unqualified and qualified aspects of *Brahman,* Śaṁkara assigns the epithets of *parā* and *aparā*, transcendent and phenomenal, depending on the perspective adopted for its contemplation. Since *Brahman* as the creative principle is both the efficient and the material cause of the world it can escape being attached to the phenomenal perspective of its creation. As a creator in the context of the world, the unqualified and formless *Brahman* appears qualified by names and forms. The world. is said to be the *taṭasthalakṣaṇa,* or accidental definition, of the *Brahman* whose essential definition or *svarūpalakṣaṇa* is his *saccidānanda* nature; the former definition serves to indicate the *Brahman* in association with the creative powers or *māyā* . In association with *māyā* the *Brahman* becomes the creator, sustainer and destroyer *Iśvara.* The difference between the qualified and unqualified *Brahman* is only a matter of disposition. It is the one non-dual Supreme Being, that creates and becomes the Lord, *Iśvara,* with reference to the creation: *eko hi rudro na dvitiyāya tasthurya immāṅlokāniśat īśanībhih.*[83] *Saguṇa* and *nirguṇa Brahman* are the results of the perception of reality from two different viewpoints; the qualified or *saguṇa Brahman* serves as the focus of worship: *nirguṇamapi sadbrahma nāmrūpagatairguṇaiḥ saguṇam upāsanārtham tatra tatropadiśyate.*[84]

In the commentary on the Brahmasūtra, Śaṁkara mentions the concept of '*upāsā traividhyāt*', the three-fold means of worship of the one Supreme Being. The three modes are: *jivopāsanam* as the attention to the inner self of the soul, *mukhya-prāṇopāsanam* or the devotion to the primal *prāṇa* as the divinity presiding over the individual's constitution, and finally *brahmopāsanam* as the comprehension of the "absolute and undifferentiated reality."[85] Another scheme prevalent among the *Viśiṣṭādvaitin* constituted of *prāṇa dharmeṇa, prajñā dharmeṇa* and *Brahman* in its own nature: *trividham iha brahmaṇaḥ upāsanam vivakṣitam.* "The three-fold distinction in devotion follows the eligibility and capability of the different devotees."[86] This idea is expressed as *tad tad upāsanā yogyataya ca puruṣānām.* Some worship *Brahman* as the all pervasive spiritual consciousness, some visualize it within their own hearts, while others worship the same *Brahman* in the form of an external image:

keṣāṅcitsarvagatatvena keṣāṅcid hrdaye hari
keṣāṅcit bahirevasau upasyaḥ puruṣottamaḥ.[87]

Śaṁkara endorses the importance of *adhikara* or qualification of a devotee as an important determinator of his mode of worship: *na hyavikare'anante brahmaṇi sarvaiḥ pumbhiḥ śakyā buddhiḥ sthapayitummandamadhyamottamabuddhitvāt pumsāṅ iti.*[88]

However, in every mode of worship the disposition and character of the devotee is required to be perfectly righteous if the mode and means of worship he has chosen was to result in any fruitful spiritual merit. Unless the worshipper inculcated the virtues of truth, non-violence, charity, and mercy while he dedicated himself to god, his worship was not expected to result in the pleasure of the Lord; the character and attitude of the worshipper is regarded as of primary importance, irrespective of the form of god he has chosen for worship:

ahiṁsa satyavacanaṁ dayā bhūtesvanugrahaḥ
yasyaitāni sadā rām tasya tuṣyati keśavaḥ.[89]

If the character and attitude of a devotee is pious and righteous, then whatever form of god he begins his prayer with, it ultimately leads him to the truth of the one and only Supreme *Brahman*: *yasmin sarvaṁ yataḥ sarvaṁ yaḥ sarva sarvataśca yaḥ.*[90] In his commentary on the *Brahmasūtra,* Śaṁkara (3.3.59) advocates the necessity of according complete freedom to every human being to choose a particular manifestation of god according to its own liking. It was, however, realized by the teachers of *Sanātan Dharma* that everyone cannot reach the understanding of the infinite Truth all at once and therefore the worship of qualified manifestations has been made possible by the grace of god as preparatory to a long and arduous spiritual journey:

nirviśesam param brahma sākṣātkartumanīśvaraḥ
ye mandaste anukampyante saviśeṣanirupanaiḥ.[91]

But the worshipper was always reminded that pervading the nature of a specific manifestation was the ever-present Truth of the Supreme Being—*naitavada eva paro anyad asti*—and *Brahmā, Viṣṇu* and *Śiva* are the incarnate articulations of the one *Parabrahman* in its phenomenal and creative mode:

sṛṣṭisthityantakaraṇim brahmaviṣṇuśivatmikāṁ
sa samjñā yāti bhagwāneka eva janārdanaḥ.

It redounds to the great wisdom, sagacity and genius of the ancient sages of India that they accepted such a wide variety of religious doctrines and integrated them into an overarching unitary vision of reality that encompassed all forms of worship and, concomitantly, all kinds of men without any force, coercion or compulsion. The socio-cultural and religious unity of India was predicated on this broad vision that had a place for every man and his god in its heart. This vision was not the product of any political strategy but a reflection of the nature of cosmic truth in which all diversities and contrariness are just a phenomenal but necessary product of the single source of inexhaustible creative energy. If all that is today was only the Supreme Being in the beginning, its subsequent manifestations should also adhere to the metaphysical imperative of the grand unity in diversity. With such unitary etiological beliefs regarding the world and human beings, *Sanātan Dharma* was bound to have a syncretic vision of life. Its tolerance was not a situational prop but a deep existential realization. The sages and the *rsis* determined the nature of reality based on their personal audiences with it, but collectively they sang in unison of the subterranean presence of the same divine truth in their respective visions. The assertion of Udayanācārya regarding the one god present in the eulogies of every group of worshippers could perhaps have been happily endorsed by each and every saint of the *Sanātan Dharma.* If someone really wants to have a glimpse of the heart of Indian spirituality he should try and understand the grandeur of this verse which declares that all men–Śaiva, Jaina, Baudha, Vedāntin, etc.—invoke and pray to the one and only god of the universe:

yaṁ śaivā samupāsate śiva iti brahmeti vedāntinaḥ
bauddhā buddha iti pramāṇapaṭavaḥ kartetinaiyāyikāḥ
arhannityatha jainaśāsanratāḥ karmeti mīṁāmsakāḥ
so'ayaṁ no viddhatu vāñcchitfalam trailokyanātho hariḥ.

Yo Vai Viṣṇuḥ Sa Vai Rudro

That which is Viṣṇu is also Śiva

Yes, many *devatās* do exist in the world of the *Sanātan Dharma* and they variously receive worship by diverse groups and sects in the manner of their liking. But when a devotee worships *Viṣṇu,* he regards him as one and the only supreme deity not by negating and rejecting *Rudra, Indra, Sūrya* and *Agni* as less powerful or false gods, but by including all of them in the body and person of *Viṣṇu.* When *Viṣṇu,* or for that matter *Śiva,* is worshipped, all devatās converge and subside in the person of *Viṣṇu* or *Śiva,* as the case may be. Every *devatā* is just a potent aspect of the Supreme Being, and once a particular form is apprehended the Supreme Being fully flows into that form as the only important reality *vis-a-vis* the devotee. In its own nature, the Supreme Being contains inexhaustible possibilities and potencies, but to a spiritual aspirant it reveals itself fully in the *devatā* that is engaging his attention. Every *devatā* is the manifestation of the Supreme Being in its fulness, therefore, when one *devatā* is worshipped all *devatās*—*Viśvedevah*— are automatically worshipped alongside. Nothing is excluded because there is no one to be excluded. This can be attested by the empirical evidence found in the scriptural texts and ritual details. A devotee of *Viṣṇu* would never be encountered belittling or criticising

Śiva; in fact, in the next breath he may eulogize *Śiva* in the same ecstatic manner in which moments ago he was eulogizing *Viṣṇu*. In his mind both *Śiva* and *Viṣṇu* are equally and fully the Supreme Truth. *Viṣṇu* and *Śiva* can be more than one only in the sense a person can be more than one as a father and a husband to his son and his wife respectively. Kabir was right in challenging the idea that there can be more than one god: *dui jagadisa kahāñ se āyā*.

The same *Iśvara* or *Bhagawān* performs various creative functions in the cosmos that has emerged out of the psychic energy of its primordial desire. The world is created not because *Iśvara* wants to prove a point or teach a lesson to humanity in accordance with a historical plan, but because it is its nature—*svabhāva*—to manifest in order to self-actualize. It is possible for every epoch to see *Iśvara* in a different light but the difference would only be contextual and not actual; fundamentally the one *deva* is sporting itself in so many modes: *eko devo nityalīlānuraktaḥ*.[1] That one *Janārdan* assumes the three roles of creator, maintainer and eventual destroyer and becomes *Brahmā, Viṣṇu and Śiva* when the inherent attributes of *rajas, sattva* and *tamas* activate and associate with its undisturbed and formless primordial nature:

rajoyukta namaste'astu brahmamurte Sanātan
tvayā sarvamidaṁ nāth jagatsṛṣtam carācaraṁ
sattvādhiṣṭhita lokeśa viṣṇumurte adhokṣaja
prajāpāl mahābāho janārdan namo'astu te.[2]

But if it is possible for the pure undifferentiated *saccidānanda Paramātman* to cause grosser nature to emerge within the reality of its consciousness - *samudre arṇava*—it is equally and concomitantly possible for it to descend into material form and manifest itself in the world. However, during its formal actualization the *Paramātman* transcendentally continues to abide in its unqualified nature. It is interesting to note the words that have been used to describe the presence of *Bhagawān* in the world. The scriptures generally use the word *avatāraṇa* and *sambhāvanā* to describe *Bhagawān's* manifestation in the world. The first term denotes descent into a grosser and compact form from within the body of something that is relatively vaster and rarified. It may also mean condensation and compaction within the non-material essence of a vast entity. The second term significantly has a meaning that appears to contextualize the descent by providing the phenomenal and generative explanation for its happening. *Sambhāvana* is the very clear expression of the possibility of formal immanentization of that which is impersonal and absolute in its nature. The Veda believe that *Iśvara* pervades every entity of the phenomenal world and the sages pay their obeisance to him in all phenomenal manifestations:

yo devo'gnau yo'psu yo viś'vam bhuvanam, āviveśa
yo oṣadhiṣu yo vanaspatiṣu tasmai devāya namonamaḥ.[3]

Rāmānuj believed the whole world, and not a denominational church, to be the body of god.

In the belief—system of the practitioners of *Sanātan Dharma* the distance between god and men is, ontologically speaking, very small and completely bridgeable. *Iśvara* is not the 'wholly other' *mysterium tremendum* but a presence that is within every human being as his inner self. Chāndogya Upaniṣad describes this process as the entering of the Supreme Spirit or the *Brahman* in every embodied manifestation of individual life—*anena jīvenātmanā anupraviśya.*[4] "That which underwent individuation and become *jiva,* the finite self, is of course none other than the Upanisadic spirit or god. Its assumption, through *maya,* of embodiment is referred to as *anupravisa* in the Upanisad. Thus *anupravisa* or entry means just the development of particular cognitions corresponding to the elements of the objective manifold—*labdhavise savijnanaī* Therefore the *anupravesa* is nothing more than a notional association of god with organisms that are structurally different from one another. In one and all of them alike, the identical Upanisadic spirit is timelessly present. That the Supreme reality is cognizable in the *antahkarana* of man is the truth conveyed by the Upanisadic notion of *anupravesa.* In other words, the individual *jiva* is in essence the supreme reality present in the psycho-physical complex that empirically undergoes temporal experiences."[5]

The world of phenomena and the reality of the individual *jīva* is a result of the entanglement of the Supreme Spirit with various *upādhis*, "which are nothing but human and explanatory postulations"[6] that create an objective illusion of multiplicity and gradation. Warrier has further pointed out that the reality of a *jīva* materializes when the Supreme Spirit is associated with inferior *upādhis* whereas, in conjunction with its own inherent *upādhis*, it is termed as God.[7] "Hence the conclusion follows that the philosophy of the Upanisads recognizes two kinds of perceptions; one contingent on the operation of *upadhis* like the sense-organs, and the other, immutable and eternal, the very essence of the SelfīThus the basis of empirical distinctions among the *jiva*, god and the Absolute is an unstable appearance or *maya;* with its abolition, these distinctions also will be abolished."[8] But within the objective existence of the world of phenomena it is possible for the *Paramātman* to fully reveal and enflesh itself in sentient forms.

The incarnation of the Supreme *Brahman* does not involve any change in its nature because the *avatār* is an event valid only in the perspective of the objective manifold in the phenomenal realm. Warrier quotes Śaṁkara's commentary on Gītā to suggest that the embodiment of god is "embodiment as it were" or "born as it were"—*dehavāniva, jāta iva ca.*[9] *Paramātman* is always present, even when no phenomena exists, as the eternal ground state of everything. The question of its being born does not arise phenomenally; it can only choose to concretise itself and reveal in a recognizable form in view of certain worldly and spiritual contingencies, by redirecting its own creative *māyā* internally. Corelatively it is also possible for a human being to recognize the truth of *aham brahmāsmi* and raise itself to the level where the dictum becomes existential reality. It is possible for a human being to know the unity of the *Ātman* and the *Brahman* and attain the *Brahman* as a result of such realization. This realization confers immense power on the person who attains a status akin to godhead and whose whole life becomes a model of mundane and spiritual ideals. The *avatār* is principally a leader and a teacher, spreading the message of *dharma, ṛta* and spiritual life to all humanity through the example of his own life and action. The *avatār* does not use a vicarious medium to interpret and codify its intentions for all times to come while itself remaining *in absentia*. An *avatār* happens directly whenever a situation arises and mankind is face-to-face with the words and deeds of the *Paramātman* who lives and works within their midst. There have been many incarnations, and there shall be many more in order to fulfil the promise that god makes in Gītā.

S. Radhakrishnan has tried to put the question of *avatār* in its cosmic and spiritual perspective in his Introductory Essay to 'The Bhagvadgita'. He says: "If the Infinite God is manifested in finite existence throughout time, then Its special manifestation at one given moment and through the assumption of one single human nature is but the free fulfilment of that same movement by which the Divine plentitude freely fulfils itself and inclines towards the finite... If a human organism can be made in the image of god, if new patterns can be woven into the stuff of repetitive energy, if eternity can be incorporated in these ways into succession, then the Divine Reality can express His absolute mode of being in and through a completely human organism ... In the great souls we call incarnations, God who is responsible for the being and dignity of man has more wonderfully renewed it. The penetration of successiveness by the Eternal which is present in every event of the cosmic is manifested in a deeper sense in the incarnations...Whenever by the abuse of freedom unrighteousness increases and the world gets stuck in a rut, He creates Himself to lift the world from out of its rut and set it on new tracks. Out of His love He is born again and again to renew the work of creation on a higher plane."[10]

From the spiritual or *ādhyatmika* perspective the idea of *avatār* also underlines the possibility of awakening the immanent aspect of the *Paramātman* present in every individual. When the veil of ignorance is lifted the divine presence in every human being is realized as if materially altering the physical aspect of that person. The *avatār* serves a dual role: on the one hand it represents a combined praxis of thoughts and deeds through the aegis of an individual and, on the other, alludes to the elevation of an individual's own self to a near divine height. S. Radhakrishnan's analysis is quite apt when he suggests that, "That *avatār* is the demonstration of man's spiritual resources and latent divinity."[11] But *avatār* is paramountly the temporal manifestation of the divine in a human or, at times, a non-human frame. In the Bhagavadgitā, *Bhagawān Śri Kṛṣṇa* personally explains this complex matter to Arjun in an exposition of the nature of god's self-revelation in an incarnate form. This explanation serves to contextualize his place in the perspective of the whole creation and redefine the relationship between the individuated *jīva* and the infinite divinity. *Kṛṣṇa* explains that though he is unborn, imperishable and the Lord of all creatures, yet he establishes himself in his own nature and comes into being by his own power (*ātmamāyā*):

ajo'pi sann avyayātmā bhūtānām iśvaro' pi san
prakṛtim svām adhiṣṭhāya saṁbhavāmy ātmamāyayā.[12]

Free from the impact of *karma,* god establishes himself in his own nature and becomes embodied in tangible form of his own free accord.

There is an important concern that impels the manifestation of the absolute in a finite form. This concern relates to the restoration of the balance of cosmic and moral righteousness. *Śri Kṛṣṇa* explains the point to Arjun by saying that whenever righteousness declines in the face of ascendant unrighteousness he self-creates himself in an incarnate form:

yadā yadā hi dharmasya glānirbhavati bhārata
abhyutthānaṁ adharmasya tadā'tmānaṁ sṛjāmyahaṁ.[13]

It is further asserted by *Śri Kṛṣṇa* that he comes into being in many ages in order to protect the noble, destroy the sinful and establish a realm of righteousness:

paritrānāya sādhunaṁ vināśāya ca duṣkṛtāṁ
dharmasaṁsthāpanārthāya sambhavāmi yuge yuge.[14]

The fact of incarnation is not limited to the welfare of a chosen section of people, and the promise of *Śri Kṛṣṇa* has no denominational undertones. His promise extends to all humanity without reservation and does not rest on a prudential quid pro quo. *Śri Kṛṣṇa* does not demand an *a priori* confession of loyalty to his person in return for the promise of mercy and benevolence. The activities of god in the world are not contingent on the confession of communicant loyalty. His mercy extends freely in the world only by the concerns of restoration of *dharma* and protection of the righteous and the noble.

In the Judaic religions god's benevolence is contingent upon a man's surrender to his wish as interpreted by his chosen prophet or messiah. Those who do not surrender themselves to god's one-off exclusive revelation do that at the risk of grave peril to themselves. The Judaic god rules out all forms of worship that do not conform to the particularistic devotion outlined in one of his revelations as proclaimed by his prophets. All other 'gods', their images, and various systems of worship were sought to be utterly destroyed. This has been a common feature of all revelations of god in the three Judaic religions. In the *Sanātan* tradition god strikes a radically different note in his revelation . God does not ask man to worship him exclusively in the form of a particular *avatār* in a particular manner. God exhorts men to choose any form of worship that helps his soul and leads him to a state of spiritual awakening. *Bhagawān Kṛṣṇa* assures humanity that he accepts human beings in his grace through all modes of worship, because all men through their respective modes of worship ultimately follow his own divine path:

> *ye yathā maṁ prapadyante taṁs tathai'va bhajāmyaham*
> *mam vartmā' nuvartante manuṣyāḥ pārtha sarvaśaḥ.*[15]

This promise of unconditional and universal benediction extended by god to all humanity, irrespective of the names and forms used by various groups of human beings to worship the divine, is the unique spiritual heritage of the *Sanātan Dharma.* Every song emerging from every human soul in a state of spiritual ecstasy is addressed to the one and only *Paramātman.* There is only one god who is the subject of every prayer and ritual established by man, therefore calumnizing a system or a notion of god as false and wrongful is a travesty of the majesty and glory of the most merciful god. Therefore why should man not believe god's words in the Gītā and only listen to his peroration in the Bible?

God's promise of grace to all modes of worship is not limited only to the message of the Gītā. In the Ramcaritmānas of Tulasidās one finds the personal devotional example of *Śri Rāma*—another incarnation of the Supreme *Viṣṇu*—who has shown how the eclectic principle of worship can be put in practice. He showed respect for all the deities that were worshiped by men in his time. In fact, *Śri Rāma* personally established the worship of *Śiva* as *Rāmeśvara* or the 'god of *Rāma*', and declared that a person cannot endear himself to *Viṣṇu* if he decried and belittled Lord *Śiva*:

śiva drohi mam bhakta kahāvā
so nar mohi sapanehu nahi bhāvā.

This declaration of the incarnate god provides an important insight into India's spiritual tradition. In India, god does not reveal himself to demand a formal adherence to him in the form of a particular deity. God's majesty is not contingent upon the destruction of every other deity apart from the one that is favoured by his self-proclaimed particular messiah. On the contrary, the manifested god exhorts men to be reverential towards all other manifestations of god that humanity has been vouchsafed at different times and in different epochs. *Sanātan Dharam* believes that every manifestation of the divine is a revelation of the same Supreme Being. A *mantra* in the Bṛhannāradīya firmly states that, "Viṣṇu is Śiva and Śiva is Viṣṇu and whoever thinks they are different goes to hell":[16]

harirupi mahādevo liṅgarupi janārdanaḥ
īśạd api avtaraṁ nāsti bhedakṛn narakaṁ vrajet.

This thought is an explication and extension of the core idea which the Veda and Upanisads have been consistently teaching: namely, that the divine light is one but is manifested in many forms—*ekaṁ jyoti bahudha vibhāti.*[17] All incarnations and revelatory manifestations held sacred by mankind are the embodied rays of the same divine light. The teachers of *Sanātan Dharma* do not ask their pupil to eschew the deities of his ancestors or destroy the altars of his community, and abandon the spiritual practices that are held sacred by his society, in order to attain the salvific grace of god through the office of a single deity and a single messiah. The burden of their spiritual message is to assure the pupil that his own mode of worship is wholly adequate and supremely salvific provided he engages in it with a pure heart and noble intentions. God declares in *Gita* that whatever form a devotee chooses for his worship, he accepts that form unreservedly and makes the devotee's faith steady in that form:

yo yo yām yām tanuṁ bhaktaḥ śraddhaya'rcitam icchati
tasya-tasya' calam śraddhām tām eva vidadhamyaham.[18]

In one sublime assurance god himself restores to honour every conception of the divine that humanity over the ages has cherished, and bars for all times to come the lurid discourses devoted to the denigration of the deities of other human societies. Indians were receptive to the hint given by their teachers and never ever entertained the thought of proselytization. They realized that every act of proselytization involves the necessary condemnation of the idea of god held as sacred by others. Denigration of the god of other people for ecumenical purposes is not only metaphysically bogus but carries with it the danger of denominational tension and ill-will. It is a path strewn with hatred and strife. Moreover, if all divine manifestations are the means to reach the same supreme reality then denigration of a particular manifestation would be the denigration of god himself.

The message of *Śri Kṛṣṇa* regarding the reasons for god's personal incarnation in the world provides a clue to the necessity that informs god's desire to sacrifice his infinite nature and incarnate himself in a finite form. *Gītā* cites the restoration of *dharma* and the preservation of the righteous as the reason behind the incarnation of god in the world. The concern for the preservation of *dharma* is an important idea that needs to be studied in some detail. The idea of *dharma* has been discussed in an earlier chapter of this book wherein its non-denominational, non-religious and non-cultic aspect has been brought into focus. It should also be kept in mind that *dharma* as the moral order that sustains human life is the earthly correlate of the universal cosmic order known as *rta*. *Ṛta* and *dharma* are the two poles of the phenomenal manifestations in a conjoint discipline of physical, moral and spiritual order. Seers of the *Sanātan* tradition have striven to enunciate the doctrines of *dharma* by drawing its fundamental ideas from the way the whole cosmic phenomena evolves and sustains itself in the process of its enfoldment and dissolution. Since the whole creation is believed to be the result of the desire of the Supreme Being to self-actualize itself by moving from a state of absolute to temporally defined existence, it is natural that the maintenance of the structure of this phenomenal manifestation would necessarily be a function of its divine nature. The cosmic order—*ṛta*—is the preservative aspect of the Supreme Being brought to bear on the phenomenal world.

Veda describe the *devatās* as the protectors and preservers of the *rta*. The Taittirīya Saṁhitā describes the interrelation of the *devas* and the human beings in terms of their two worlds being interwoven together: *anatarhito hi devaloko manuṣyalokāt*.[19] The powers of the Supreme Being are constantly acting in the phenomenal world and in the minds of all creatures. The Ṛg Veda attaches seminal importance to the preservation of *ṛta* in the cosmic sphere and *dharma* in the social and individual sphere. It is stated that the solar system maintains its course by *ṛta (ṛtenāditya)*, and it is *ṛta* that reigns supreme over the wide world, from the depths and expanse of the earth to the vastness of the heavens:

> *ṛtaṁ yemān ṛtamidvanotyaṛtasya śuṣmasturayā u gavyuḥ*
> *ṛtāya pṛthivi bahule gabhīre ṛtāya dhenu parameduhāte.*[20]

Ṛta holds sway over all the realms of earth, mid-region and the celestial spheres. The power regulating *ṛta* is denoted by the use of the word *gopā* in the Ṛg Vedic corpus. The word *gopā* means the protector and preserver of the whole universe—*sarvasya jagato rakṣakah*. In the Ṛg Veda the world *gopā* is usually employed in conjunction with the concept of *ṛta*. This conjunctions signifies the idea of protection of the cosmic order. We find the use of ideas like '*gopāh rakṣakam ṛtasya*', '*ṛtasya yā abhiraksanti gopāh*', '*mahā ṛtasya gopām*', '*ṛtasya gopā*', etc., to highlight the fact that divine providence is constantly active to maintain the moral and cosmic equilibrium of the universe and prevent it from scurrying towards a path of disharmony and destruction. The Supreme Lord is the protector and preserver of the rhythm and order of the world.

When the *Parbrahman* is seen as the protector, preserver, and regulator of the entire cosmic phenomena it is recognized and eulogized by the seers as *Viṣṇu*. Apart from the many general references to the idea of *gopā,* the Ṛg Veda has specifically identified *Viṣṇu* as the protector of the supreme, immortal and the righteous path of the whole universe: *viṣṇuorgopāḥ paraṁ pāti pāthaḥ priyā dhāmānyamṛtā dadhānaḥ*.[21] In another *mantra* it is said that the invincible and most powerful protector and upholder of the universal laws of natural order, *Viṣṇu* strode across the whole cosmos in three strides and in this process of stepping out manifested and established the unmanifest world: *tṛni padā vi cakrame Viṣṇurgopā adābhyaḥ ato dharmāṇi dhārayan.*[22] "If *rta* is the cosmic order prevalent in the aggregate, *dharma* is the individual version of the same order, consisting of the right conduct that facilitates the preservation of the cosmic order as well as the welfare and integrity of individual human beings":[23] *dharmān viśvasmin jagati dhārayitavyāni karmani, dhārayan san vicakrame iti sambandhaḥ*.

The Supreme Being, as *Viṣṇu*, creates, ordains and preserves all the aspects of *dharma* and *ṛta* that maintain the structure and the orderliness of the universe. It is for this reason that all the *avatāran* or incarnation of the Supreme Being is said to be the incarnation of its *Viṣṇu* nature—the great upholder and the protector of the whole creation. The concept of *Viṣṇu* encompasses into it the idea of the godliness of the supreme *Brahman* in the process of the manifestation and sustenance of the universe. The word *Viṣṇu* is derived from the root *Vislr* which means to permeate and pervade, "it indicates that Vishnu is the creator of the entire universe, and also the material out of which the universe is fashioned; in fact, therefore; he is everything and everywhere."[24] *Viṣṇu* is the name of the Supreme Reality in its functional aspect of manifesting and upholding the edifice of creation by pervading it so fully that all beings and all the worlds become only a temporal manifestation of him: *bhutani Viṣṇurbhuvanani Viṣṇuriti*. The Ṛg Vedic seer says that *Viṣṇu* bears and upholds the three realms of earth, sky and the heavenly space and all the worlds and all the creatures that inhabit those worlds: y*a u tridhātu prthivimuta dyāmeko dādhār bhuvanāni viśvā.*[25] "All the inhabitants of the three worlds, in their endless variety, are borne by Vishnu, who is not only the creator and supporter of the three worlds, but the sweet essence (madhu) and internal controller (antaryami) of each living being in each of the worlds. Living beings are countless, and their groups numerous; but the foundation of all of them is but one (viz., Vishnu). He is variously called Agni, Surya, and so on."[26]

The fundamental "import of the expression Viṣṇu is universal pervasion, omnipresence"[27], and this pervasion is graphically expressed in the Ṛg Vedic *mantras* by the employment of the idea of striding across the worlds *(vikramana)* by *Viṣṇu* in three giant strides *(tṛvikram)* and thereby generating the three cosmic realms and then fully entering into them. If the earlier discussion regarding *devatās* is recollected it would be possible to see the relationship between various *devatās* of the three realms and *Viṣṇu.* Given the premise of the pervasion of *Viṣṇu* in all the worlds, various *devatās* only become the manifestation of certain contextual potencies of the former. The combined essence of the *devatās* is contained and established in the nature of *Viṣṇu,* and wholly dependent on him. It is *Viṣṇu* who empowers various *devatās* to operate in their assigned realms as facets of his own power. The Taittirīya Saṁhita narrates this idea in the mantra, *viṣṇumukhā vai devāh*. The Aitareya Brahman corroborates the primacy of *Viṣṇu* and states that he is the guardian and protector of all the *devatās—devānam dvarapah*. In this sense *Viṣṇu* can be considered as the all-encompassing being that contains within itself all the realms and all the *devatās.* Afterall, it is the striding or stepping out of *Viṣṇu* that creates in its wake the variegated universe: v*iṣṇukramairvai prajāpatirim lokamāsṛjat.*[28] The Aitareya Brāhmaṇ says that *Agni* is considered as the first or foremost of the *devatās, and Viṣṇu* is the supreme or the most exhalted of them and, between the two of them, all other devatās find their place, power and expression:

agnirvai devanamavamo Viṣṇuh paramah
tadantarena sarva anyą devatāh.[29]

When it is realized that *Agni* is only another appellation of *Viṣṇu*, it becomes clear that these descriptions show all *devatās* as established in the nature and reality of *Viṣṇu.* It is said that *Agni* represents all the *devatās—agnir va sarva devatāh—*likewise *Viṣṇu* is also said to be the embodiment of all the *devatās—Viṣṇuh sarva devataḥ*. *Viṣṇu* as the creative and preservative form of the supreme *Brahman* is regarded as *Bhagawan* or *Iśvara.* Raghavendra Tirtha in his exegesis on Rg Veda *mantra* (1.22.17), says that, *Viṣṇuḥ bhagawān, idaṁ viśvaṁ;*[30] *Viṣṇu* is god; he is also the world. *Viṣṇu* is the most ancient principle. He was there prior to the commencement of the act of creation and remains ever present in it thereafter as its "source, support and sustenance"[31] The Ṛg Veda encourages men to concentrate their spiritual devotion towards that eternal and immutable reality which is the most 'ancient' as well as the ever young creator and sustainer of all things. Those who devote themselves to the eternal divine reality enter into the presence of that divine reality:

yah pūravyāya vedhase navīyase sumājjañaye viṣṇave dadāśati
yo jātamasya mahato mahi bravatsedu śravobhi ryujyaṁ cidabhyasat.[32]

It is possible for men to enter into the divine presence of god by realizing and then concentrating on his nature and reality. God is not a distant and fearful master but a friend. God enters human life in a spirit of intimate comraderie when men are ready to recognize and awaken his latent presence in their own souls. The seer *Dirghatama* beseeches god *Viṣṇu* to become a dear and helpful friend to all humanity: *bhavā mitro na śevyo ghṛtāsutirvibhūtadyumna evayā u sapratha.*[33] *Sanātan* tradition treats friendship and intimacy with god as an important idea in defining the relationship of man with the divine. God is a *mitra*, a *sakhā*, perhaps even a lover grasping the whole existence of man in a blissful embrace.

The doctrine of 'One Reality' but many names and forms, is reiterated in the *Viṣṇu Sūktāni* of the Ṛg Veda. "Whether it is Indra or Vayu, in the most fundamental import (paramamukhya-vrtti), the name refers only to Vishnu. The scriptures unequivocally declare that the supreme reality is one, and that all names indicate only Vishnu (the supreme reality)—Differences in names suggests only the special activities that are involved (Tura-Sruti)"[34]:

dvirupatvād bahutvam ca viśeṣādeva kevalam
ekasyaiva harernātra bhedaḥ śankyaḥ kathancam.

Pāṇini-Sruti supports the viewpoint that there is no reality apart from the one reality of *Viṣṇu* whose glory entails the existence of all *devatās* within itself. Nothing exists beyond the reality of the one supreme *Viṣṇu* who is the ultimate destiny of all human strivings:

svotkarṣe devadevasya viṣṇormahātatparyaṁ naiva cānyatra satyam
avāntaraṁ tatparatvaṁ tadanyat sarvāgamānāṁ puruṣārthastato'taḥ.[35]

The Viṣṇu Purāṇa states that the one supreme reality causes and then enters into the world of phenomena in association with his supreme *maya*, and this unitary reality is known by wise men as *Viṣṇu: yasmādviṣtamidam sarvam tasya saktya mahatmanah tasmādViṣṇuriti khyato viserdhatoh praviśanāt.*[36] *Sanātan Dharma* does not prescribe any hard and fast devotional rules for unexceptionable acceptance by all humanity on the pain of eternal damnation. The Ṛg Veda says:

tamu stotāraḥ pūravyaṁ vida ṛtasya garbhaṁ januṣā pipartan
āsya jānanto nāma cidvivaktan mahaste viṣṇo sumatim bhajamahe.[37]

The message of the *mantra* is that seekers should propitiate with their invocation and devotion the supreme reality of *Viṣṇu* alone "in accordance with their understanding of him (yatha vida) and in their own natural outpourings (janusha), unpressurized by anyone or by any circumstance."[38] He is the first principle of the Universe and the womb of the world order (*ṛtasya garbham)*. Man should partake in his noble path by following a life of *dharma*. *Viṣṇu* being the womb of the cosmic order would naturally manifest himself when that order is threatened by the accretion of unrighteousness. *Viṣṇu* as the creative manifestation of the supreme *Brahman* is without any name and form intrinsically but appears in individuated forms with a view to lead men towards the reality of the infinite truth.

The divine manifestations, therefore, are not instances of the presence of many 'gods' but the apprehension of a singular reality in the spiritual strivings of great variety of men and women. No single idea can be said to fully represent the nature of the Supreme Reality for all men and all times to come. The teachers of *Sanātan Dharma* have, therefore, accepted with utmost respect the sanctity and holiness of all modes of worship. It is said that a man can only please god if he listens to the spiritual messages of all religions and respects, as his own, all forms of god that are revered by mankind:

> *śrunute sarvadharmāṅsca sarvānn devannamasyayati*
> *anusuyurjit krodhastasya tuṣyati keśavaḥ.*[39]

The most noble spiritual seeker is a person who is the worshipper of *Śakti* from within; follower of *Śiva* in his ritual observance, and a *Vaiśṇava* in his outward dispositional attitude: *antaḥ śākto bahih saivo sabhāmadhye ca vaiṣṇavah.*[40] The supreme *Brahman* in association with its *māyā* becomes the creator, sustainer and the destroyer *Iśvara. Brahmā, Viṣṇu and Śiva* are not three separate entities but three appellations of the functional manifestations of the same supreme *Iśvara:*

> *sṛṣṭisthityantakaranīn brahmaviṣṇuŚivātmikam*
> *sa samjñā yāti bhagawaneka eva janārdanaḥ.*[41]

All *devatās* are the branches of the *mahāviṣṇu* who, in turn, is their ontological and existential ground: *viṣṇo sarvādevātmakasya asya devasya anye devā vayā śākhe iva bhavanti.* Lord *Śiva (rudra)* is the form of the *Paramātman* in its ascetic and destructive mode, whereas *Viṣṇu and Brahmā* denote its creative and beneficial aspects:

> yo *vai Viṣṇuḥ sa vai rudro yo rudraḥ sa pitāmahaḥ*
> *eka murtistrayo devā rudraviṣṇu pitamahah.*[42]

Viṣṇu and *Śiva* are the two forms of the one and only supreme *Brahman* whose godhood is principally known by the scriptures and sages as *Bhagwān Viṣṇu*. Therefore all the *avatāras* of *Viṣṇu* are essentially the descent of the *parabrahman* in the phenomenal world. All *avatārs* are the manifestations of *Viṣṇu*. *Vāsudeva Kṛṣṇa* is therefore the incarnation of the *Brahman:*

parabrahmane tasmata nityaneva namo namaḥ
yadrupaṁ vāsudevasya paramātmasvarūpiṇaḥ.[43]

The non-difference between the *Śiva* form and the *Viṣṇu* form, of the *Parabrahman*, as the two manifestations of the same supreme reality has been repeatedly stressed by various teachers and the scriptures of the *Sanātan* tradition. The Śvetāśvatara Upaniṣada regards *Śiva* as the *Parabrahman*, who alone exists in the world as its eternal creative principle: *eko hi rudro na dvitiyāya tasthurya. Imānllokān īśata īśānībhiḥ ... Hiraṇyagarbhe janayāmāspūrvam tataṁ paraṁ brahma paraṁ brhantam.*[44] This characterisation is reminiscent of the descriptions that has been assigned to the *Viṣṇu* form of the *Brahman*. The Maitrāyaṇi Upaniṣad identifies *Śiva, Prajāpati, Viṣṇu and Nārāyaṇa* as the manifestations of the one and only *Parabrahman—Sambhūrvo prajāptisatyam prāno haṁsaḥ viṣṇurnārāyaṇo'rkah*. The Baudhāyan Gṛhyasūtra (1.2.7.23) depicts *Śiva* as the all-pervading *Parabrahman* in a manner that is reminiscent of the nature of *Viṣṇu: rudro viś'vā bhuvanā viveśa tasmai rudrāya namo' stu iti*. The similarity between *Śiva* and *Viṣṇu* becomes clearer when references treating *Śiva* as the supreme and primal *Puruṣa* and the divine creator is encountered in various scriptural and liturgical texts: *tvamekāmadyam puruṣaṁ purātanam rudraṁ Śivam viṣvasṛjaṁ yajāmahe.*[45] The underlying principle is the same: every divine manifestation of the *Paramātman* is essentially so many different revelations of the one divine truth.

The *Rāmāyana* belongs to the *Vaiṣṇava* tradition, but it treats *Śiva* as the highest *Iśvara*: *evamuktastato devairdevadeveśvarah prabhuḥ.*[46] The author of Mahābhārat describes *Śiva* as the world-creator, infinite and indescribable *Brahman*; he is regarded as the source of all aspects of material existence while himself retaining his pure and undisturbed existence. In the Karṇa Parva of the Mahābhārata it is mentioned that the *Paramātman* as *Śiva* is one but is recognized in many forms by his devotees: *ekaśca bhagawānstatra nānā rūpānyakalpayan.*[47] *Viṣṇu* in his *Kṛṣṇa* manifestation devoutly eulogizes *Śiva* as the most exalted Lord:

tvam vai brahmā ca rudraśca varuṇo'gnirman urbhavah
dhata tvastā vidhātā ca tvam prabhuḥ sarvato mukhaḥ.[48]

There cannot be a turf war between *Śiva* and *Viṣṇu* for the souls of men because they are not two separate realities: *madādhināstrayo loka yathā viṣṇau tathā māyi.*[49]

The unity of divine nature and the ontological similarity behind the notion of *Brahmā, Viṣṇu and Śiva* is not only a part of intellectual debate but a shared spiritual belief among the common men of India. The spiritual idea behind such belief regards *Viṣṇu* and *Śiva* as the two names of the one *Parampuruṣa: puruṣo viṣṇurityuktaḥ sivo vā nāmataḥ śrutaḥ.*[50] Any multiplicity in the nature of god is *ab initio* ruled out and he is said to be known by various names only from the nescient perspective of the emerging and dissolving phenomenal world:

ekaḥ svayambhuvaḥ kālastribhistrīn karoti ya
sṛjate cānugrhṇāti prajāḥ saṁharate tatha.[51]

A majority of the important *Puranas*, whether belonging to the *Śaiva* school or the *Vaiśṇava* school, stress the doctrine of the unity of godhead beyond the apparent manifestations of *Brahmā, Viṣṇu and Śiva.* The Saura Purāṇa, which is a Purāṇa of the *Śaiva* school, regards *Śiva, Viṣṇu and Brahmā* as the modifications of the one Supreme God who appear different because of their playful grace, *līlā.* Reality is just pure *Śiva* but appears differentiated according to the functions it performs:

eko'pi bahudhā bhāti līlaya kevalaḥ Śivaḥ
brahmaviṣṇuvādirupeṇa devadevo maheśvaraḥ.

The Vāyu Purāṇa further elaborates this point by asserting that this whole cosmos is the product of the *māyā* of 'that one' which is conjointly known as *Śiva* and *Viṣṇu* apart from many other subsidiary names: *viśvarupamidaṁ sarvaṁ rudranāryāṇātmakaṁ.*[52] There is no confusion in the mind of a *Sanātan dharmi* that *Śiva and Viṣṇu* are the names of the same entity and he does not hesitate to address *Śiva* by the appellations which are normally reserved for *Viṣṇu*. *Śiva* is addressed as *Nārāyana and Laksmipati: namo'stu laksmipataye sṛmate hṛmate namaḥ.*[53] As a corollary, a specific appellation of *Śiva, pinakadhari,* is used by the devotee to address *Viṣṇu: namo namo viśesatvaṁ tvaṁ brahmā tvaṁ pinākdhṛka.*[54] It is the trickery of *avidyā* or ignorance of the higher spiritual reality that captivates men into treating the *Param Puruṣa* as a variegated entity: *avidyāmohitātmānaṁ puruṣa bhinnadarśinaḥ.*

Śri Bhagawān is himself simultaneously *Śaṁkara and Hari: yeyam murtirbhagawataḥ śaṁkar ās svayam hariḥ.*[55] The unity of essence does not confine only to the similitude of *Viṣṇu and Śiva* but extends to other deities also. According to the Gaṇeṣa Purāṇa, *Gaṇeṣa* is the creator, sustainer and destroyer of the world; he is also known as *Mahāviṣṇu, Śiva* and the *Parambrahman* itself:

ahameva jagad yasmāt sṛjāmi pālayāmica
ahameva mahaviṣṇurahmeva sadāśivaḥ
mohayatyakhilān māyā śresṭhān mam narānamūn.[56]

Polytheism, as generally understood, is a logical and metaphysical impossibility. *Sanātan Dharma* believes in the revelation of the Supreme Person in many potencies and many forms in every aspect of the manifested world and in the inner self of every human being. It is the light that reflects variously in the mirrors of receptive souls in a unique manner. It appears to create a spectrum of many colours at a lower level of perception; once a person transcends the limitations of ignorance, reality emerges as a singular phenomena. A spiritual seeker is constantly reminded to move ahead on the spiritual path and transcend the mechanical practice of outward observance of rituals devoted to particular deities. The noblest aim of man's spirituality should be to embrace the highest realization of the one Supreme Brahman: *uttamo brahmasadbhāvo.*

Hai Hari Bas Kuch Aisā: God is what it is

Beyond the texts of the scriptural treatises and the canons of the philosophical schools that discuss the matter relating to the nature of the world, human life and god in it, Indians revere a vast body of literature comprising of the works of various poets, saints and spiritual teachers that provide a popular perspective on those themes that have been the subject matter of philosophical discussions. Over the centuries the saints and savants of India have interpreted and disseminated the core message of *Sanātan* spirituality into an idiom that could be adopted for the purposes of the day-to-day life of the common man. The metaphysics of the Veda, Upaniṣads, Purāṇas, Gītā and other philosophical treatises was distilled into a body of spiritual practices and secular behaviour by demystifying the abstrue theoretical constructs of the texts in an easily comprehendable system of spiritual and religious praxis. In the process of interpreting the message of the scriptural and philosophical texts, various saints provided to the core themes of the texts a slant that was suited to their own world view as well as to the contingencies of the age in which they lived. In spite of their apparent stylistic differences most of them remain steadfastly true and loyal to the basic postulates of the core themes. Their interpretations of the idea of divinity, and the meaning of a life of spirituality, are in keeping with the fundamental premise of Indian spirituality that the ultimate reality is one but sages visualize it in their own specific ways. Therefore a life of *dharma,* righteousness and human brotherhood was the common concern of most saints and *dhārmic* teachers of India. No official theology or core dogma can be said to constitute the essence of *Sanātan* spirituality, therefore the theory of rebellion or revolt against a non-existent uniform orthodox position, as many scholars in modern India tend to characterize the labour of our revered saints, is a product more of their own intellectual disposition than the analysis of the true nature of the message of these saints.

As far as notions of divine life and man's place in the world are concerned, even the most venerable texts—the Veda and Upaniṣads—do not offer a unilinear, uniform and pre-determined course of action. They offer various insights into the nature of divine reality and its relationship with human beings, and exhort men to realize the fundamental rhythms of existence and model their lives on the basis of their own specific experiences of *dharma, ṛta* and god. Most scriptural texts encourage men to chart their specific spiritual path with complete trust in their own vision of the divine. *Sanātan* spirituality has consistently stressed the idea of the uncompromisable unitariness and singularity of the fundamental reality behind the whole creation, while at the same time it has also accepted the possibility of multiple apprehensions of that reality. A culture which adopts the concepts of '*ekam sad viprāḥ bahudhā vadanti', 'ek eva atma bahudha styuate' and 'santam bahudha kalpayanti'* as the defining premise of its spirituality, implicitly accepts only one dogma: the utter and absolute freedom for men to interpret, visualize and follow a divine vision that is in accord with their own station, intellectual growth and inner self. When the possibility of many spiritual paths is a shared cultural belief, whence come the talk of a rebellion, and against whom? As far as cultic and ritual practices are concerned *Sanātan Dharma* has never accorded any inviolable sacrosanctity to them and they have been subject to continuous internal modification over the ages.

Both, Gautam Buddha and Mahāvir, have stressed the performance of righteous deeds as superior to the vanity borne out of mere recitation of scriptural texts and mechanical performance of sacredotal routine. Their stress on *dharma,* or the principles of ideal life, highlight the importance they attached to noble deeds and righteous thoughts. But so did the Veda themselves. We had the occasion to examine the categorical assertion of the Veda regarding the *Brahman* and all the *devatās* being the guardians of righteousness and cosmic order: *ṛtasya gopāḥ*. The emphasis on moral and *dhārmic* life is one of the paramount concerns of the Veda. A *mantra* of the the Ṛg Veda, can be cited as an example of the seers' concern for the primacy of moral life and righteous conduct. It says that the divine reality has forged many fetters and barriers against unrighteousness, and a wicked mortal would find it impossible to escape them. The *devatās* should be invoked to assist men in leading their lives on the path of *ṛta* and *dharma* in accordance with universal moral principles. Only a life of righteous *dharma* would conduct men beyond despair as a sturdy boat sails over the turbulent waters of the river:

> *tā bhuripāśāvanṛtasya setu duratyetū ripave martyaya*
> *ṛtasya mitrā vāruṇā pathā vāmapo na nāvā duritā tarema.*[1]

Ṛg Veda says in no uncertain terms that mere knowledge and recitation of the *mantra* of the Vedas are of no avail unless a person follows a righteous life and understands the truth of the cohesive and corporate nature of human life and the world. Only those righteous persons can come close to the supreme person who know this spiritual reality:

> *ṛco akṣare parame vyomanyasmindevā adhi viśve diṣeduḥ*
> *yastanna veda kimṛca kariṣyati ya ittalvidusta ime samāste.*[2]

The basic import of the Vedic message revolves around the conduct of man in his life on earth. The ultimate goal of human life is to raise its mundane existence beyond the limitations of the earthly body and reach the levels of the *devatās* by following a life of supreme wisdom, spirituality and righteousness. The seer of the Ṛg

Veda desires to transcend his mortal existence and reach the immortal status of the *devatas: yadagne martyastvaṁ syamahaṁ mitromaho amartyaḥ sahasaḥ sunvahut.*[3] The gift of god can never be received without inculcating noble virtues in life. The devotee must understand the fact that though he belongs to the realm of the divine he can receive spiritual wisdom only if he engages himself lifelong in the performance of noble deeds:

> *tve idrāpyabhūma viprā dhiyaṁ vanema ṛtayā sapantaḥ*
> *avasyavo dhīmahi praśansti sadyaste rāyo dāvane syam.*[4]

The stress on *dharma* and a life dedicated to nobility and righteousness finds notable place in the Upaniṣads. The possibility of a human being becoming a *devatā* is recognized as the function of righteous *karma: devo bhūtvā devān āpyeti.*[5] Once a human being follows a *dhārmic* life of righteousness he can declare, in the manner of Vāmadeva, to have become one of the *devatās: aham manurbhavam suryaścāham.*[6]

Excessive reliance on the ritualistic interpretation of the Vedic message has overshadowed its spiritual and *dhārmic* concerns in favour of a viewpoint that treats the entire Vedic corpus as a manual for the performance of superstitious sacrifices. Such a lopsided interpretation distorts the fundamental nature of the Vedic *yajña*. *Yajña* concerned itself mostly with the performance of all human action with unattached nobility and the courage to sacrifice one's most cherished objects for the benefit of others. In the din of the ritualistic exegesis, the moral ideas of the Vedic corpus concerning the issues of *ṛta, dharma,* righteousness, nobility and just life get obfuscated. The Yajur Veda asks every human being to follow a course of life that is universally righteous: *ṛtasya patha preta.*[7] It is further pointed out that all humanity should steadfastly observe and follow the path of virtue that has been shown by the great souls: *ṛtasya panthā manu paśya sādhuangirasah sukṛto yenayanti.*[8] An action in conformity with *ṛta* in the life of an individual is his *dharma,* whereby a person models his life in accordance with the eternal principles that are constantly working to sustain and uphold the whole creation. Viewed in this light the emphasis of Buddha and Mahāvir on noble conduct and *dhamma* can be seen as a reiteration in their teaching of the basic tenets of the great tradition of the *Sanātan Dharma*.

The Veda declare their fundamental ideal to be the transformation of the whole world into a community of noble and righteous people: *kṛṇvante viśvam āryaṁ*. The goal of human life, according to Gautam Buddha, was to reach the level of nobility of an *ārya*. Buddha claimed to be propagating the *ārya* way of life and allusion to *'ariya dhamma', 'ariya magga'*, etc., are prominently found in the Buddhist canon. Buddha claimed to have followed the ancient way, an ancient *dharma* followed by the awakened ones of the olden times. As such there was no necessity for Buddha to have inserted the idea of a deity in his *dharmic* discourse because a deity is not a paramountly important constituent of *dharma. Dharma* deals more with the way of life of a human being. It was for this reason that when he commenced his task as a teacher and delivered his first sermon, he called it the exposition or turning of the wheel of *dharma—dharmacakrapravartana.* Was Buddha inventing a new *dharma* for himself or was he translating his cultural inheritance into an implementable moral regime for his followers? An analysis of the main ingredients of Buddha's moral teaching vis-v-vis the *dhārmic* injunctions of the *Sanātan* tradition can provide an answer. The chief ingredeint of Buddha's moral regime were *satya, ahiṁsa, aparigraha, asteya* and *dān*. If we compare this with the ingredients of Manu's definition of the morality of *dharma* the similarity would appear too stark:

dṛtiḥ kṣama damo' steyaṁ saucamindriyanigrahaḥ
dhīrvidyā satyamakrodho daśakaṁ dharmalakṣanaṁ.[9]

Buddha's emphasis on *samyak ācar,* right behaviour, finds its echo in Manu's prescription that right conduct is the greatest of all *dharma: ācarah parmo dharmaḥ*. True, that Buddha desisted from entering into metaphysical discussions regarding *Brahman, Ātman, Iśvara,* etc, but his refusal to expatiate on these matters does not entail rebellion or condemnation of these issue; it only expresses his personal disinclination. P.T. Raju says: "It should be noted, however, that they did not reject the Vedic gods. Even superficial acquaintance with Jaina and Buddhist literature shows that the gods were retained, but they were given a secondary place."[10]

It is an undisputed fact that Buddha recognized the importance of the cultural and spiritual message of his heritage and held it in great respect. What he criticised was the profligate and callous interpretations of those messages, prevalent among many philosophical schools of his time, but not the essential message itself. There are references in the Suttanipāt to the effect that the real meaning of *dhamma* can be gained from a fruitful study of the Vedas and a person who carefully learns the message of the Veda becomes steadfast in *dhamma* and does not get affected by the ups and downs of life: *vidvā ca vedehi samecca dhammaṁ na uccāvacaṁ gacchati bhuripañyo*. Suttanipāt further stresses the relevance of the knowledge of Veda and the *Śruti (bahussuto)* for the real understanding of *dhamma* and the inculcation of wisdom:

> *evaṁ pi yo vedagu bhāvitatto bahussuto hoti avedha dhammo*
> *so kho pare nijjhapaye pajānaṁ śotavadhānupani supapanno.*

The principles of *dharma* enunciated in the *Sanātan* tradition have been reinterpreted by various teachers in their own specific ways with emphasis being put on those aspects that were of major importance to a teacher. We have been informed in the Sthānāṅg of the Jaina tradition that there are two aspects of *dharma;* one is the aspect based on spiritual principles derived on the basis of the scriptural texts or *sruti*, and the other is based on moral conduct: *deuvihe dhamme—sūyadhamme ceva carittadhamme ceva.*[11] Some teachers emphasise on the former whereas others emphasise the latter. After all, it is said that various individuals receive the *dharmatattava* differently in accordance with their own predilections: *anusāsaṇaṁ puḍho pāṇi.*[12] The great Jaina thinker, Manibhadra, explains that philosophical systems of India, in the end, conform to each other: *darśanānāṁ paryantaika sārupya*. K. Satchidananda Murty quotes Manibhadra to bring the point of relationship among various schools of *dharma* in a clear focus:

"Buddhism can be heard, Jain dharma performed, Vaidika dharma adhered to, and the supreme Siva meditated upon."[13]

The teachings of Buddha and Mahavira do not incorporate any clear theistic formulations because the two teachers were more concerned about the practical aspects of human life. However, many other saints, poets and teachers of India have devoted themselves to the preaching of the glory and majesty of god in their own special manner. A study of the works of some of these great souls of India would indicate their intimate knowledge of the metaphysical principle of the ancient scriptural texts and their adherence to the fundamental texts of *Sanātan* spirituality and the idea of god. Keeping themselves firmly in the mainstream of *Sanātan Dharma* they translated the original scriptural messages in the light of their own experience. Most of these saints used the local vernacular language for the transmission of their message. These saints converged intellectualism of the Vedic and Upaniṣadic metaphysics with the concerns of devotion, love, charity and universal brotherhood to create a highly successful idiom of religious discourse. The motifs and principle images, however, were taken from the scriptural traditions and infused with the social concern of their times. These saints represented the devotional aspect of apprehension of the Supreme Reality and they have been collectively categorised by modern critical opinion as *bhakti* saints.

The word *bhakti* is derived from the root *bhaj* which means, 'to serve, to dedicate'. A synonymous concept of *upasana,* used interchangeably with *bhakti,* means to 'approcah, go and sit close to'. Essentially *bhakti* and *upāsanā* are concepts that describe a person's attitudinal approach towards god. As we have seen earlier, *bhakti* can be treated as one of the many means of relating to god. Be that as it may, the idea of *bhakti or upāsanā* was not an unknown principle in the corpus of the *Śruti.* It is true that *bhakti* as a strong spiritual perspective, in comparison to the *jñān mārg,* emerged in the sixth or seventh century in the southern parts of India and then kept growing till it reached its most fecund manifestation in the northern parts of the country during the fifteenth century onwards. However, the concept of *bhakti* was well recognized during the epochs that preceded the so-called 'bhakti-period' and the latter did not mark a watershed in India's mainstream spiritual pursuit. The Ṛg Veda recognizes devotion as a possible means to reach god. It characterises god as an object of devotion as mother, father and friend—*tvam hi naḥ pitā vaso tvaṁ mātā satakrato babhuvitha. Adhā te sumnamīmahe.*[14] The Upaniṣads recongize *upāsanā* as a means of attaining the grace of the *Brahman* and encourage the spiritual seekers to follow a path of devotion in order to know the *Parabrahman: sarva khalvida brahma tajjalāniti śānta upāsīta ... mano brahmetyupāsīt.*[15] Even Śaṁkara has highlighted the efficacy of devotional contemplation of the *Brahman: mahate hi falāya brahmopāsanabhiṣyate.*[16] In spite of being a hardcore *advaitin,* Śaṁkara recommended devotional worship as an important means of reaching the reality of god.

Śrimad Bhāgawat enumerates nine possible means of devotion to god:

śravanaṁ kirtanaṁ viṣṇoh smaraṇaṁ pādsevanaṁ
arcanaṁ vandanaṁ hāsyam sākhyamātmanivedanaṁ.[17]

A devotee is free to choose any of these means depending on his own personal preference. In the phenomenal world the *Parabrahman* appears as the fundamental ground and cause of the whole creation and in association with its plentiful spendour and *mahāmāyā* he is known as *Bhagawān or Iśvara:*

suddhe mahāvibhutyakhyeparebrahmaṇi śabdyate
maitreyo bhagavachabdassarvakāraṇ kāraṇe.[18]

In its wordly manifestation god is an object of devotion and worship because he is the creator, sustainer and inner controller of everything that exists. Madhvācārya initates the discussion from the point of god's manifestation as Vāsudeva, and then asserts that the same Vāsudeva is an *avatār of Viṣṇu-Nārāyaṇa,* who is also known as *Brahman* in his absolute nature:

bhagavān vāsudeveti paramātmeti vai hariḥ
viṣṇurnārāyaṇasceti brahmeti śrutayojaguḥ.[19]

In tune with the scriptural position, every incarnate idea of god was treated by the *bhakti* saints as the manifestation of the one supreme *Parabrahman* whose nature and essence has been the subject matter of the Veda, Upaniṣad and other scriptural treatises. These saints created a popular rendition of the classical position and coalesced both the conditioned (*saguṇa)* and the unconditioned (*nirguṇa)* nature of *Brahman* in a system of devotion that included "a unique personal monotheism and image mysticism."[20]

Satchidananda Murty maintains that the *bhakti* saints believed god to be one transcendent and immanent Lord of the universe. They also believed that god actually abides in all his glory and power in the person of *Rāma, Kṛṣṇa*, and other divine *avatārs*, and also in their images at Tirumala, Chidambaram, Pandharpur, etc. These saints were sure that "the incarnation form, the image form and the indweller form is as much god as the transcendent form in Vaikuntha or Kailasa."[21] The Bhakti saints came from all castes and classes of the Indian society but received unstinted reverence and respect of all Indians unhindered by any consideration of their social background. Kallar was a *mleccha* by caste, Meykaṇḍār and Sekkilar were *śudra* but the Periya Purāṇam of the latter is regarded as the fifth Veda by even the greatest of brahmins. Sant Śri Ravidās, a cobbler by birth, was accorded the highest regard and respect by the most learned pandits of Varanasi. Śri Ravidās records his personal experience that even the masters of the four Vedas bow before him: *cāriu veda kiyā panḍauti, jan ravidās karai danḍauti*. The *Sanātan* society provided space to these men to attain their highest spiritual status and then raised them to the level of national sainthood. These saints culled the eternal values of the *Sanātan Dharma* and redefined them in the idiom of their times to strengthen the self-respect and religious confidence of the people in an age that witnessed certain historical forces posing grave challenge to the very fundamentals of Indian spirituality. Yogesh Gupta has rightly pointed out that the preponderance of people from the so called 'lower' castes in the cultural renaissance of India is a result of the fact that the greatest cultural threat was being faced by these same vulnerable sections due to the activities of competing religious groups.[22] Girilal Jain's perception supports this viewpoint that the popular "Bhakti movement was a form of resistance and not an attempt at synthesis or compromise."[23] The Bhakti saints proudly proclaimed the grandeur of their spiritual heritage and their own steadfast commitment to it. In the process they instilled courage and pride in every Indian.

The fundamental themes of the *Sanātan* spirituality are reiterated in the message of these saints who made those themes easily comprehendable for the common man in their own language. The *Alvār* and *Nayanār* saints adopted the *saguṇa* manifestation of the *Parampuruṣa* as *Viṣṇu* and *Śiva* respectively, and created a system of devotion based on these manifestations. Tirumular believed in the fundamental unity of *Ātman and Brahman* and held that god dwelt in the heart of every man. The *Nayanār* saint Appar was of the view that god is the essence, and the upholder of *dharma* and *ṛta*. Prabhudeva was an outstanding philosopher of the Vira Śaiva school. His thoughts recreate the *Sanātan* unity of the self and the phenomenal world with the one supreme reality whom he called *Śiva,* and who was described by him as the ground of all reality that appears in multiple forms in the world. All that existed, however, was the one reality of *Śiva*. Vemana was born in a *śudra* family but rose to become not only the most revered saint of Andhra but of the whole of India. His message stressed the unity of the transcendent with the phenomenal: *paramunādu nindu paripurnataye kadā. Ihamu lone paramu nesaguta kānnavā.*[24] Vemana regarded both *Śiva* and *Viṣṇu* as one divine person and saw their presence infusing every aspect of the world: *anniṭa barikimpa viṣṇuvarayucundu.*[25] He exhorted his disciples to know the reality of their own self, and in a verse reminiscent of the message of the Gita—*ātmānām viddhi*, declared that the knowledge of the self leads to the realization of the *Brahman: tannu dā nerigina tāne po brahmambu.*[26] Potuluri Virabrahman considered the whole world to be permeated by *Brahman*. Lallā Yogeśvari, a saint poetess of Kashmir, considered the individual self and the Supreme self as one. She said, "Lord, that I am thou I did not know, Nor that thou are I, that one be Twain."[27] According to her the world of phenomena is just a manifestation of *Nārāyaṇa*.

Sant Ekanāth of Maharashtra was a devout *Vaiṣṇava* and regarded the unity of the divine person as an article of faith: *eka janārdani nema sarvaṭhāyiṇ purusottama*. The difference between man and god is only apparent and those who understand this non-difference attain liberation: *jani janārdan eka jāne to sutalā niḥśekha*. Nāmdeva propagated the *Bhāgvata* school of devotion throughout India. Many of his verses are included in the Ādi Grantha. His poems express the amalgamation of the *saguṇa and nirguṇa* forms of worship. He believed that whenever god is invoked by the use of a name and form he adopts that name and form as his own. Fundamentally, however, there was only one god whom sages have known as *Rāma, Kṛṣṇa, Śiva, Viṣṇu,* etc.: *ghata ghata antar sarva nirantara kevala eka murāri*. It is the one and only *Parabrahma* who appears as *Rama* and *Kṛṣṇa*:

rāmahibhaj tai rāmahi hoi praṇave nāmā dās kesavā
bacauni
aiye maiye eka ān jiu, pindhi umkale saṁsārā.

It is possible for the one *Nārāyaṇa* to manifest itself in many forms: *praṇave nāmdeu ihu karanā anant rupa tere nārāinā*. This seminal *Sanātan* sentiment is eloquently expressed by Samartha Rāmdās. He believed that god is ever present in the hearts of every created being; some call it *Rāma*, others call it *Kṛṣṇa*: *sarva bhutāṇce hṛdaya, nām tyace rāmrāi*. Rāmdās reiterates the theory of *avatār* that finds mention in the Gītā and sees every divine manifestation as the creative intervention of god in the world to restore *dharma* and righteousness: *dharmasaṁsthāpnece nara, te iśvarāce avatār*.

Sant Ravidās was devoutly immersed in, and proud of, the cultural tradition of the *Sanātan Dharma*. His fundamental world view was that of a *Vedāntin,* but he happily accepted the *saguṇa* nature of *Rāma* and *Kṛṣṇa* as the incarnate manifestation of the *Parabrahman*: *Kṛṣṇa karim rām hari rāghava jab lage eke eka nahiñ pekhya*. He worshipped *Rāma* as his *iṣṭadevatā* with the understanding that *Rāma* is the same *Paramapuruṣa* whose breath is said to be all the Veda and the holy scriptures: *cār veda jāke sumṛtisvāṇsā, bhagati heta gāvai raidāsā*. It is the devotee's earnest call that forces the absolute

Brahman to materialize in the form of a recognizable deity. These saint poets did not lay exclusive store on a single idea of god. To them all manifestations of god and all paths of worship were equally true and venerable. God is under the complete sway of the desire of the worshipper. Whenever a pious heart calls him up god comes running to its succour:

nāham vāsāmi vaikunṭhe yogināṅ hṛdaye na ca
madbhaktā yatra gāyanti tatra tisṭhāmi nārada.[28]

These principles are not confined to the works of the poets cited above but find eloquent expression in the message of nearly all saint poets. Tulasidās seems to have adopted the sentiment of the above mentioned verse in his own inimitable style when he said that the supreme reality is without any name and form in the absolute acosmic perspective, but appears in various forms for the love of its devotees. The difference between an incarnate *Iśvara* and an absolute eternal *Brahman* is only apparent and perspectival and not positivistically real or material. All scriptures and every teacher speak about that one god in their own distinct ways:

sagunahiṅ agunahin nahin kacchu bhedā
gāvahin muni purāna budha bedā
aguna arupa alakha aja joi
bhagat prema basa sagun so hoi.[29]

Tulasidās uses the theory of unity of all manifestations of the divine as a stylistic devise to enliven the dramatic element of his narrative. The story of *Rāma's* life in the Rāmcaritamānas is narrated to *Umā* by Lord *Śiva* himself. *Śiva*, while narrating the story, declared *Rāma*, an *avatār* of *Viṣṇu,* as the incarnate *saccidānanda Brahman: brahma saccidānanda ghana raghunāyaka jaṅha bhūpa*. No insecurity, no ravings regarding his own self-importance and no pathological urgency to secure exclusive worship for himself is to be seen in the nature of *Bhagavān Śiva;* on the contrary he declares *Rāma* to be his own *iṣṭadevatā: soi mam iṣṭa deva raghubīrā*. Similarly, *Rāma* declares that no one can secure his *bhakti* without attaining the benediction of *Śiva:*

saṁkara vimukha bhagati caha mori
so nāraki muḍha mati thori.[30]

The reason is simple: every manifestation of god represents the whole essence of the divine in full measure, therefore, denigration of one would amount to the denigration of god itself. Tulasidās believed that *Brahman* has both conditioned and unconditioned nature—*aguna saguna due brahma sarupā*—and in both forms it is the one *Brahman* that finds expression. Anticipating the question regarding the manifestation of the formless absolute into phenomenal forms he explains the mystery as the non-difference of water and the ice particles floating over it:

jo guna rahit sagun soi kaise
jalu him upala bilag nahin jaise.[31]

Rāma in its *paramārthic*, or absolute, sense is the *Brahman* itself: *rām brahma parmāratha rupā.*

Tulasidās accepts the Vedic and Upaniṣadic metaphysics regarding the indescribability of the Supreme Person, but at the same time he also accepts the certainity of the Supreme Person revealing itself in the world in many forms. All divine manifestations—*Śiva, Viṣṇu, Brahmā,* etc,—emerge from the absolute and eternal nature of the *Brahman:*

neti neti jehi veda nirupā
nijānanda nirupadhi anupā
sambhu viranci visnu bhagwānā
upajahiṅ jāsu aṁsa te nānā.[32]

Tulasidās borrowed the spiritual metaphysics from the hoary *Sanātan* tradition and, in the process of transmitting it, he transcreated a completely novel message of devotion that continues to inspire millions of Indians who may not have been able to read the Veda or the philosophical doctrines but understand the fundamental premise of their spiritual tradition through the words of Rāmacaritamānas. In spite of the seemingly chaotic profusion of deities, there is no doubt in the mind of a *Sanātan dharmi* that supervening over this pantheon of *devatās* and *avatārs* is the one single divine persona that is the ultimate and truthful ground of all appearances. Duality is just plain ignorance. Guru Nānak Dev has said that the one *Parabrahma* appears in many forms to the devotee while itself remaining eternally free:

anik ranga nirguna ik rangā
āpe jalu apahi tarangā
āpahi mandaru āpahi sevā
āpahi pujāri āpahi devā.[33]

Guru Nānak has no doubt in his mind that the supreme *Brahman* is capable of being apprehended in *nirguṇa* and *saguṇa* forms. He was also certain that in both these forms it is the one *Iśvara* who appears to create and sustain this universe: *idhai nirgun udhai sargun kela karata bici suāmi merā.*[34] Suryakānt Tripāṭhi Nirālā has beautifully put this sentiment of the all pervasive reality in his poetic narrative:

eka hi hai dusarā nahiṅ hai kuccha
dvaita bhāva hi hai bhrama.[35]

The divine gurus of the Sikh tradition carried the propagation of the *Sanātan* spirituality in right earnest and imparted to it a new strength that stirred the soul of the entire country with a sense of self respect and courage. All the gurus were steeped into the cultural lore of India and regarded its ancient wisdom as the guiding light for their own devotional path. They treated the Veda and Purāṇa with respect and were deferential to the spiritual practices of their forefathers. The Gurū Grantha Sāhib contains respectful references to the Vedas and their collective wisdom. Veda are regarded as the creation of the *Parambrahman: omkari beda nirmaye.*[36] It is under the desire of god that Veda were created for the benefit of humanity: *hari āgiya hoe beda pāp punna vicāria.*[37] It is said that among the multitude of books the best book to be constantly studied are the Vedas: *asaṁkhya grantha mukhi veda pātha.*[38] And what do the Veda, Purāṇa, Smṛti and Śāstra teach? We are told that they teach the truth of the one supreme *Parabrahman:*

simriti sāstar beda purānā pārbrahma kā karahiṅ
bakhiyān.[39]

In reality, the divine creator and unitary *Parabrahman* manifests itself in many forms. In the manner of the one sun seen differently in different seasons, the Supreme Being is seen in various modes by its worshipper. The Granth Sāhib says: *guru guru eko vesa aneka suraj eko ruti aneka. Nānak karte ke kete vesa.* The unconditioned *Parameśvara* is under the control of the righteous and noble creatures and appears in conditoned form for the benefit of its devotees: *nirguna ramu gunaḥ vasi hoi*. The Veda are said to teach men to fasten their attention towards the one *Paramesvar* and recite its name. The gurus believed that recitation of various names of god is the talisman for salvation and freedom of humanity in the *kaliyuga*:

kala meṅ eka nām kṛpānidhi jāhi jape gati pāve
aur dharam tāke sam nāhan iha vidhi veda batāve.[40]

It would be interesting to examine the names which the gurus used to address and invoke the divine in their prayers, songs and exhortations. The gurus were steadfast in their belief that the Supreme Reality, the primal *Puruṣa* is eternal, unborn, fearless, truthful, and without any fixed form. At the same time the gurus seem to have fondly accepted the cultural history of *saguṇa* manifestations of god found in the *Sanātan* tradition. The principle invocation of the Gurbāni describes god as '*satināmu karta purakhu nirvairu akal murati ajuni'*, but many verses included in the Grantha Sāhib describe this eternal god by the use of such names and devotional allusions that correspond the *nirguṇa parmeśvara* to its *saguṇa* manifestations as *Rāma, Gobind, Hari* etc, and bring their metaphysical viewpoint very close to that of the other saints of that time. The description of the real nature of god in Rāmacaritamānas of Tulasidās is amazingly akin to the description that has found favour with the gurus. Tulasidās says:

brahma anāmaya aja bhagavantā
vyāpaka ajit anādi anantā.[41]

Tulasidās has no doubt in his mind that god's fundamental nature is absolute, unborn, timeless and devoid of all phenomenal attributes: *vyāpaka akāl aniha aja nirguna nāma na rupa*.[42] However, for the benefit of the created world he appears in various forms and performs various deeds in accordance with his *līlā*. The *saguṇa* and *nirguṇa* aspects of god do not pose any problem to these teachers in view of the metaphysical realization of the utter and necessary reconcilability of these two aspects in the nature of god.

The *Sanātan* tradition of India has conflated the idea of an eternal divine truth with the cosmic manifestation of that truth in the person of various incarnations like *Rāma, Kṛṣṇa, Buddha*, etc. The Guru Granth Sāhib, too, profusely uses these cultural motifs to describe with reverential delight the god which is the focus of contemplation of the gurus. The gurus seem to have no doubt in their minds that the *acut, abināsi, akāl* entity of their devotion is none else but the '*pārabrahma paramesur*' who, then, is also identified as having revealed itself in the person of *Kṛṣṇa* and *Rāma*. The Granth Sāhib contains many references that drive this point home:

acut pārbrahma paramesur antarjāmi
madhusudan dāmodar swāmi
rikhikesa govardhan dhāri
murali manohar hari rangā.[43]

mohan mādhava kṛsna murāre,
jagadisur hari jiu asur samghāre.[44]

nā ohimarahi nā thage jāhi
jinke rāmu vasai mana māhi.[45]

Obviously, the '*murali manohar*' and '*ramu*' of the above verses can be none other than the *Kṛṣṇa* and *Rāma* whom Indians knew. The names with which the gurus indicate the nature of god are the names of *Hari, Nārāyaṇ, Rāma* and *Gobinda*. The mythological allusions cited in the Gurbani leaves the reader in no doubt that the *parameśvar* of the gurus can be recongized as the supreme *Hari* who bestowed his saving benediction on Prahlād, Dhruva, the elephant *gaj* and the bandit Vālmiki: *Pāñca barakha ko anātha dhru bāriku hari simarat amar atāreī bālmiku supacāro tariyo badhika tare bicāre ... eka nimakha man māhi arādhiyo gajapāti pār utāre ... kini rakhiya bhagat prahilādai harnākhas nakhahi bidāre.*[46] The *paramesvar* who is credited with the specific saving actions in the above *vacana* can obviously be none else than *Viṣṇu* to whom these action are popularly assigned by *Sanātan tradition.*

Undeniably, many of the *bhakti* saints were not inclined towards the ritual worship of god in a stylized and formal system. The gurus of the Sikh tradition believed in the primacy of the contemplation of god's name and performance of pious deeds over mere ritual and sacredotal practices. This insistence of the gurus was in accordance with the high regard that *Sanātan* tradition has for contemplation, spiritual quest and complete devotion over all other outwardly forms of worship. There are many scriptural references where idol worship and cultic rituals have been described as the devotional practices suited for the purpose of the uninitiated and the novices. Highest form of devotion has always been described as the awakening of the divine truth within a person's own self, and raising that self to a level where it identifies itself with the one and only absolute reality: *uttamo brahmasadbhāvo...* Cānakyaniti says that god does not reside in the wood or the stone that are carved into an image; he resides in the pure feelings of the worshipper. Various images acquire sacredness because of the transfer of that devotional feeling to them:

nā devo vidyate kasṭhe na pāṣāne na mṛnmaye
devo hi vidyate bhāve tasmādbhavo hi kāraṇam.

Images and outward ritual forms are regarded as the devotional tools devised for the benefit of the sophomore:

ajñānaṁ bhāvanarthāyah pratimāḥ parikalpitā.[47]

The true fact of the matter is that the supreme person who exists in its infinite glory cannot be represented by man in any worldly image. The words of the Veda warn man against any simplistic attempts to define the Supreme Person through the medium of an image or a concept or a name: *nā tasya pratimā āsti yasya nām mahad yaśah.*[48] However, Indian teachers, generally, did not take upon themselves the task of condemning, traducing or forcibly proscribing the mode of worship of a human being.

The *Sanātan* premise of one god manifesting in many forms constitutes also the metaphysical core of the message of the *bhakti* saints. In fact, if *Sanatan Dharma* can be said to subscribe to any dogma it would be the dogma of the existence of only one reality that suffuses the spiritual and phenomenal aspects of creation and the possibility of the emergence of that reality in various manifestations. *Sanātan Dharma* has laid greater stress on the principles behind both man and the divine rather than on a particular embodied or personalized form. Phenomenally, a human person and a conditioned god are the logical and causal results of creation; acosmically their duality vanishes and the two converge as one into the deep and conscious being of the one reality that only *is—tad ekam*. When *Rāma* asked *Hanumān* to describe what his real nature was, the latter said that as a living body he is a servant of the former; as an embodied soul he is a portion of the eternal self; but as the Self he and *Rāma* are the same: *deha budhya tu dāsoham, jeeva budhya tvadāṅśakah, ātmabudhya tvamevaham iti may niścita matiḥa.*[49] In the context of a spiritual vision of such grandeur the whole world, the entire human kind and all the deities converge necessarily at one common soteriological point where lie the material, efficient and spiritual source of all existence. Differences of name and form are only perceptional and therefore contingent and apparent. "Therefore let everybody work out his own vision of this universe according to his own ideas. Injure none, deny the position of none…All will come to truth in the long run."[50]

The unconditioned *Brahman* and the conditioned manifestations of god are not dual principles operating in hierarchical segregation, but two perceptions of the same truth seen from the phenomenal (*vyāvahārika)* and the absolute *(paramārthika)* reference points. The perceptions in the phenomenal context can be further diversified depending on time and space and the cognitive capacities of various perceptors. Swami Vivekanand has given a very lucid explanation of the relationship between god, man and the world which can be treated as the summary of the major themes of *Sanātan* spirituality.

He says, "The *jiva* is an individual and the sum total of all *jivas* is Isvara. In the *jiva, avidya* or nescience is predominant, but *Isvara* controls *maya* composed of *avidya* and *vidya*, and independently projects this world of moving and immovable things out of Himself. But Brahman transcends both the individual and collective aspects, the *jiva* and *Isvara*... That part of Brahman in which there is the superimposition of creation, maintenance, and dissolution of the Universe has been spoken as *Isvara* in the scriptures."[51] In the world of phenomena *karma-kānda* and *saguṇa* worship is valid; "images are valid indirectly; ceremonies, forms, everything is valid, only with one condition, purity of the heart. For worship is valid, and leads to the goal, if the heart is pure and the heart is sincere..."[52] Nevertheless, all the categories of the world remain valid only from the viewpoint of the *vyāvahārika* where levels of experiences determine and define the nature of reality that is observed. Ramana Maharshi has clarified the problem beautifully: "Being now immersed in the world you see it as real; get beyond it and it will disappear, and Reality alone will remain... You now think that you are an individual; outside you there is the universe and beyond the universe is god. So there is the idea of separateness. This idea must go. For god is not separate from you and the cosmos..."[53]

Sanātan Dharma believes that not only is god one but the whole cosmos and all created beings are one within the nature of god. Once the unique unitariness and non-duality of god is accepted, respect for every idea of that god shall necessarily flow as a metaphysical imperative. Belief in the existence of one god logically precludes the possibility of a disrespectful denigration of the names of that one god by which other human societies invoke it. If god is one, two men cannot but invoke the same god irrespective of the names that are employed for such invocation. *Sanātan Dharma* is deeply aware of this reality and as a direct entailment of its belief accords equal respect to all phenomenal apprehensions of god. The devotional literature of the *Sanātan Dharma* and its various schools echoes the principle concern of Indian spirituality. Many schools of thought and many traditions of worship developed from the soil of India and each of them created in their own novel manner a distinct idiom of spirituality. But none of the spiritual schools or *sampradāya* of Indian origin ever laid any exclusive claim to truth. Hatred for the deities and practices of other systems of worship does not find mention in any of them. What one finds, instead, is a deep undercurrent of similarity, respect and acceptance of shared values of cultural life. India never developed calumny and terror as means to attain spiritual goals because her *dharma* enjoins her to eschew all means that are unrighteous, violent and prejudicial to the weal of common humanity.

Man has never subscribed to a single idea of god throughout its long history. In spite of the effort of certain religious groups to impose their own version of god on others, mankind has continued to evolve many perspectives to satisfy its innate spiritual needs. A diverse and plural world *a fortiori* would cherish diverse ideas of spirituality and every social group should be entitled equally to hold, respect and observe their devotional practices without any threat from other social groups. A dialogue of cultures can begin not from the standpoint of superiority of one party but from the standpoint of equal respect for the viewpoint of the concerned cultures. A theology that assigns ultimate virtue to its own religious idea has neither philosophical nor metaphysical sanction to back such claim. If a religious group claims to establish its own system of worship and way of life over all other human societies, its attempt would necessarily lead to serious denominational clashes and grave social turmoil. In order to assert the unitary vision of a particular religion all other religions would necessarily have to be trivialized, co-opted, banished or destroyed. And if this is done it would leave untold human misery in its wake.

Ecumenical movements of organized religions are dangerous portends because they begin their march, on the one hand, with the clear proclamation that all other religions but their own are barbarous and on the other hand use strong institutional, commercial, academic and political means to achieve consent of others. Sometimes their efforts succeed, sometimes they lead to violence in a society or a community. Those who reject the god of other peoples also reject the hallowed cultural traditions of those people not on the basis of some objective verifiable fact, but on the basis of a subjectively determined and then collectively enforced group agenda. So long as certain groups proclaim their own version of religion as the only valid version of religion and arrogate to themselves the right to enforce that version on all people, peace among human societies would remain a distant dream. Peace and harmony can only be attained by following the path of love, non-violence and equal respect for all cultural and religious practices: *sarva pantha sambhāva*.

Notes

Religare

1. Paul Tillich, "Dynamics of Faith": New York: Harper & Brothers Publishers: 1957: Page/46
2. G. Van Der Leeuw, "Religion In Essence & Manifestation.": London: George Allen & Unwin Ltd.: London: 1938: page/23
3. Don Cupitt, "The Leap of Reason": London: Sheldon Press: 1976: page/120.
4. John Hick, "God And The Universe of Faiths": London: Macmillan: 1973: Page/22
5. Don Cupitt: op.cit: page/22
6. John Hick: op.cit: Page/101
7. Paul Tillich: op.cit: page/39-40
8. A.C.Bouquet, "Comparative Religion—a short outine": London: Casell: 1961, page/11.
9. Nirad C. Chaudhuri, "Hinduism a Religion to Live By": Oxford University Press: Oxford 1995: Page/2
10. Peter B. Clarke & Peter Byrne, "Religion Defined and Explained": London: St. Martin's Press, 1993; Page/5
11. Edwin A. Burtt, "Man Seeks the Divine": New York; Harper & Brothers; 1957, Page/11
12. Ninian Smart, 'Reasons and Faiths': London: Routledge & Kegan Paul: 1958: Page/7

13. Quoted in Girilal Jain, "The Hindu Phenomenon": New Delhi: UBSPD: 1994: Page/15 [from Rene' Guenon, "Introduction to the Study of the Hindu Doctrines": London; Luzac & Co; 1945, Page/105.]
14. Ibid: Page/15
15. James Wm. MaClendon Jr. & James M. Smith, "Understanding Religious Conviction": Notre Dame: Univ. of Notre Dame Press: 1975: Page/27
16. Keith Ward, "The concept of God": Oxford: Basil Blackwell: 1974: Page/2, quotes, R.B. Braithwaite, "An Empiricist's View of the Nature of Religious Belief": Cambridge University Press; 1955
17. Keith Ward: ibid: Page/7
18. Ibid: Page/7
19. Walter Kaufmann, "Critique of Religion & Philosophy": London; Faber and Faber: 1958; Page/73
20. Ibid: Page/74
21. Ed.L.Miller, "God and Reason": New York: The Macmillan Company: 1972: Page/7
22. Ibid: Page/8
23. Quoted from F.H.Bradley, "Appearance and Reality": London: Sonnenschein: 1893: Page/439 at ibid: Page/8
24. A.C. Bouquet: op.cit: Page/12
25. Andrew Lang, "Myth, Ritual and Religion": New Delhi: Aryan Books International: 1993: Page/3
26. Max Weber, "The Sociology of Religion": London: Methuen & Co. Ltd.: Page/28
27. Quoted in Peter B. Clarke, et.al: op.cit: Page/7
28. Deuteronomy: 6.10-15
29. Joshua: 24.19-23
30. Deuteronomy: 8.20
31. Isaiah: 1.18
32. Isaiah: 34.2-3
33. Hosea: 5:14-15
34. Jeremiah: 12.14-17
35. Hosea: 13.14-16
36. Quran: 3.1
37. Quran: 3.1-4

38. Quran: 2.190-193
39. Quran: 2.193
40. Nirad C. Chaudhuri: op.cit: Page/18
41. Ibid: Page/18
42. E.O. James, "The Beginnings of Religion": London: Hutchinson's University Library: Page/38
43. Quoted in Peter. B. Clarke, et.al: op.cit: Page-153
44. Weston La Barre, "The Ghost Dance: Origins of Religions": London: George Allen & Unwin Ltd: 1972: Page/9
45. Isaiah: 1.18
46. Quoted in James Wm.McClendon Jr., et.al, op.cit: Page/12.

Dharma

1. A.C. Bouquet: op.cit: Page/12
2. Atharva Veda: XII, 1.12
3. Chaturvedi Badrinath, "Dharma, India and the World Order": San Andrew Press: Pahl Rungenstein: 1993: Page/92
4. Ibid: Page/135
5. James R. Ballantyne, "Christianity contrasted with Hindu Philosophy": London: James Madden, 1859, pp-xv-xviii"; quoted by H. K. Kaul in "Traveller's India": Oxford University Press: Delhi: 1979, Page/16
6. Artha Shastra, 13.5/6.7
7. Quoted by S. Radhakrishnan, 'Our Heritage': New Delhi: Orient Paperbacks: 1922: Page/10
8. Chaturvedi Badrinath, op.cit.: Page/3-5
9. Atharva Veda; 19.15.6
10. Mahābhārat: Yuddhaparva.
11. Vaiśeṣika Sūtra; 1.1
12. Quoted by Walter Kaufmann: op.cit: Page/190.
13. Āpastamba Dharmasūtra: 1.2
14. Mahābhārat, Shantiparva
15. Giri Lal Jain: op.cit: Page/16
16. Jina Sūtra
17. Dhammapada: 1.3
18. Quoted by Girilal Jain: op.cit: Page/15
19. Hajime Nakamura, "The Meaning of the terms 'Philosophy' and

'Religion' in various traditions", in Gerald James Larson & Eliot Deutseh (Ed) "Interpreting across boundaries": Motilal Banarsidas Pub. Pvt. Ltd: 1989, Page/147
20. Hajime Nakamura: ibid: Page/148
21. Nirad C. Chaudhrui; op.cit: Page/28-29

Close Encounter With the West

1. William Halbfass,"The Eurocentric Approach to India and the Indian Discovery of Europe", in "The Perennial Tree": Ed. K.S. Murty and Amit Dasgupta: New Delhi: ICSSR: 1996: Page/96
2. J.Talboys Wheeler, "Early Travels in India". Delhi: Deep Publications: 1975: Page/ix
3. Ibid: Page/ix
4. Ibid: Page/ix
5. Ibid: Page/110
6. John McKenzie, "Two Religions" delivered as Croall Lectures in 1948: London: Lutterworth Press; 1950; Page/17
7. J.Talboys Wheeler: op.cit: Page/110
8. Ram Chandra Prasad, "Early English Travellers in India": Delhi, Motilal Banarsidas: 1980; Page/284
9. Fr. Pierre Du Jarric, S.J., "Akbar and the Jesuits", Trans. C.H. Payne; Tubi Publishing House, New Delhi, 1979: Page/230
10. Ibid: Page/233
11. R.C. Prasad: op.cit: Page/130
12. J.T. Wheeler, op.cit: Page/208
13. Ibid: Page/208
14. Ibid: Page/110
15. R.C. Prasad: op.cit: Page/3
16. Ibid: Page/3
17. J.T. Wheeler: op.cit: Page/190
18. Ibid: Page/195
19. H.K. Kaul: "Traveller's Inida An Anthology"; Delhi: Oxford University Press: 1979: Page/3-4
20. Ibid: Page/5
21. J.Talboys Wheeler: op.cit: Page/2
22. Ibid: Page/103
23. Ibid: Page/188,198

24. Ibid: Page/196
25. J.W. Massie, "Continent India": London: Thomas Ward: 1839: Pp.213-214, quoted in H.K. Kaul: op.cit: Page/30
26. Ibid: Page/30
27. McKenzie, op.cit: Page/21
28. Halbfass: op.cit: Page/101
29. Nirad C. Chaudhuri; op.cit: Page/106
30. Quoted in Ibid: Page/110
31. Ibid: Page/109
32. R.C. Prasad; Page/286
33. Quoted in O.P.Kejariwal, "The Asiatic Society of Bengal and the Discovery of India's Past"; Delhi: Oxford University Press, 1988: Page/16
34. Quoted in Ashok V. Chowgule, "Christianity in India the Hindutva Perspective": Hindu Vivek Kendra: Mumbai: 1999: Page/12-13
35. Du Jarric: op.cit: Page/137
36. Ibid: Page/137
37. Quoted in Monier-Williams, "Modern India and the Indians": Delhi: Oriental Publishers: 1971: Page/236
38. S.N. Mukherjee, "Sir William Jones A study in Eighteenth Century British Attitudes in India": Orient Longman: 1987: Page/9
39. O.P. Kejariwal: op.cit: Page/21
40. S.N. Mukherjee: op.cit: Page/10
41. Ibid: Page/11
42. O.P. Kejariwal: op.cit: Page/26
43. O.P. Kejariwal: ibid: Page/41
44. S.N. Mukherjee: op.cit: Page/93
45. Asiatic Researches, Vol.II, quoted in SN. Mukherjee: ibid: Page/96
46. Ibid: Page/80
47. Jones, "On the Gods of Greece, Italy and India," quoted in Kejariwal: op.cit: Page/41
48. Ibid: Page/41
49. Ibid: Page/41
50. Ibid: Page/106
51. Quoted in H.K. Kaul: op.cit: Page/32
52. Ibid: Page/32
53. Ibid: Page/33

54. Quoted by S. Crawford Cromwell, "Ram Mohan Roy": New Delhi: Arnold Heinemann: 1984: Page/24
55. Ibid: Page/24
56. Ibid: Page/24
57. Ibid: Page/25
58. Ibid: Page/27
59. Ibid: Page/27
60. Wilhelm Halbfass, "India and Europe – An Essay in Understanding": Albany: State University of New York Press: 1988: Page/167 quoted by Christophe Jaffrelot, "The Hindu Nationalist Movement in India": Viking Penguin India: New Delhi: Page/3
61. C. Jaffrelot: ibid: Page/14
62. Ibid: Page/11
63. Stephen Hay (Ed), "Sources of Indian Tradition: Penguin Books: 1991: Page/16
64. Ibid: Page/37
65. Quoted by Stephen Hay in ibid: Page/33
66. Cromwell: op.cit: Page/38
67. Ibid: Page/41
68. Ibid: Page/41
69. Quoted in Cromwell: ibid: Page/7
70. Cromwell: ibid: Page/5
71. Ibid: Page/36
72. Quoted in Cromwell: ibid: Page/37
73. Quoted in Cromwell: ibid: Page/37
74. Quoted in Cromwell: ibid: Page/37
75. Quoted in Cromwell: ibid: Page/40
76. Quoted in Cromwell: ibid: Page/41
77. Monier-Williams: op.cit: Page/219
78. Cromwell: op.cit: Page/32
79. Cromwell: ibid: Page/57
80. Stephen Hay: op.cit: Page/39
81. Quoted in Stephen Hay: ibid: Page/44
82. Quoted in Stephen Hay: ibid: Page/49
83. Quoted in ibid: Page/49
84. Quoted in ibid: Page/52
85. Ibid: Page/47

86. Ibid: Page/47
87. Cromwell: op.cit: Page/79
88. Quoted in Stephen Hay: op.cit: Page/60
89. Quoted in Stephen Hay: ibid: Page/60
90. Ibid: Page/60
91. Ibid: Page/61
92. Quoted in Stephen Hay: ibid: Page/80-81.
93. Quoted in Stephen Hay: ibid: Page/81
94. Ibid: Page/81
95. Ibid: Page/74
96. Chaturvedi Badrinath: op.cit: Page/37-38
97. Monier-Williams: op.cit: Page/327
98. Wilhelm Holbfass: op.cit: Page/97
99. Ibid: Page/99
100. Ibid: Page/97
101. R.P. Goldman, "Drinking From Our Father's Well" in "The Perennial Tree": op.cit: Page/148
102. Holbfass: op.cit: Page/98
103. Quoted in Stephen Hay: op.cit: Page/81
104. Monier-Williams: op.cit: Page/166
105. Ibid: Page/175
106. Ibid: Page/215
107. Quoted in Arun Shourie: "Missionaries In India Continuities, Changes, Dilemmas": New Delhi: ASA Publication: 1994: Page/99
108. Monier-Williams: op.cit: Page/226
109. Arun Shourie: op.cit: Page/98
110. Flora Annie Steel quoted in H.K. Kaul: op.cit: Page/34
111. John McKenzie: op.cit: Page/12
112. Ibid: Page/13

I Your Lord Am One

1. Peter B. Clarke: et.al: op.cit: Page/50
2. Ibid: Page/50
3. Rafiq Zakaria: "Discovery of God": Mumbai: Popular Prakashan: 2000: Page/163
4. E.O. James: op.cit: Page/16
5. Ibid: Page/16

6. Ibid: Page/16
7. Van Der Leeuw: op.cit: Page/159
8. Ibid: Page/159
9. Ibid: Page/159
10. Ibid: Page/180
11. E.O. James: op.cit: Page/20
12. Rafiq Zakaria: op.cit: Page/xiv
13. Ibid: Page/xiv
14. Ibid: Page/xiv
15. Quoted in Karen Armstrong: "A History of God": Mandarin: London: 1997: Page/16
16. Quoted in W.T. Stace, "The Nature of the World": Princeton University Press: 1940: Page/45
17. Ibid
18. Yehezkel Kaufmann: "The Religion of Israel": London: George Allen & Unwin Ltd.: 1961: Page/359 [translated and abridged by Moshe Greenberg]
19. Ibid: Page/75
20. Ninian Smart, "Reasons and Faiths": op. cit: Page/14
21. Arnold Toynbee "An Historian's Approach To Religion": London: Oxford University Press: 1956: Page/11
22. Ibid: Page/11
23. Ninian Smart: op.cit: Page/14
24. Karen Armstrong op. cit: 1997: Page/4
25. Weston La Barre "The Ghost Dance: Origins of Religion": London: George Allen & Unwin: 1972, Page/161
26. Ibid: Page/138
27. Ibid: Page/186 (notes)
28. Yehezkel Kaufmann op. cit: Page/227
29. Ibid: Page/130
30. La Barre: op.cit: Page/161
31. Ninian Smart, "The Religious Experience of Mankind': Fontana Library Theology & Philosophy: England: 1974: Page/59
32. La Barre: op.cit: Page/576
33. Y. Kaufmann: op.cit: Page/92
34. Ibid: Page/214
35. Ibid: Page/215

36. Ibid: Page/53
37. Ibid: Page/52
38. Ibid: Page/215
39. Rudolf Otto, "The Idea of Holy": Quoted by Ninian Smart in 'Reasons and Faiths': op.cit: Page/27
40. Weston La Barre: op.cit: Page/35
41. Ninian Smart: "Reasons and Faiths": op.cit.: Page/9
42. Y. Kaufmann: op.cit.: Page/21
43. Ibid: Page/22-23
44. E.O. James: op.cit: Page/77
45. Quoted in A.C. Bouquet: op.cit: Page/58
46. Jack Miles, "God A Biography': Vintage Books: New York: 1996: Page/110
47. Rafiq Zakaria: op.cit.: Page/22
48. Ibid: Page/28
49. Arnold Toynbee: op.cit: Page/51
50. La Barre: op.cit: Pages/569, 580
51. E.O. James: op.cit: Page/81
52. Yehezkel Kaufmann: op.cit: Page/7
53. Karen Armstrong: op.cit.: Page/60
54. Ninian Smart, 'The Religious Experience of Mankind': op.cit.: Page/355
55. Karen Armstrong: op.cit: Page/22
56. Ibid: Page/22
57. Y. Kaufmann: op.cit.: Page/137
58. Exodus: 32.27-29
59. Karen Armstrong: op.cit: Page/28
60. Ibid: Page/28
61. Ibid: Page/35
62. Ibid: Page/63
63. W.F. Albright, 'From Stone Age to Christianity Monotheism and the Historical Process': quoted by La Barre: op.cit: Page/595(notes)
64. Jack Miles: op.cit: Page/20
65. D.S. Margoliouth, 'Mohammad And The Rise of Islam': New Delhi: Voice of India: 1985: Page/19-20
66. E.O. James: op.cit: Page/81
67. Psalm 82.6-7

68. Arnold Toynbee, "An Historian's Approach to Religion": Oxford University Press: London: 1956: Page/11
69. Ibid: Page/33
70. Ibid: Page/135
71. Ibid: Page/137
72. La Barre: op.cit: Pages/24, 12
73. Quoted in Toynbee: op.cit: Page/174
74. Ibid: Page/188
75. MS.111 180: 13.9.1931: in Ashok Vohra "Culture And Value": ICPR: New Delhi: 1998: Page/23
76. Ibid: Page/52
77. Quoted in La Barre: op.cit: Page/329
78. Y.Kaufmann: op.cit: Page/146
79. Ibid: Page/75
80. "The Challenge of Totalitarianism" in "Jews and Christians in a Pluralistic World": Ed.Ernst Wolfgang Bockenforde & Edward Shils: London Weidenfeld & Nicolson: 1991: Page/83
81. Karen Armstrong: op.cit: Pages / 65-66
82. Yehezkel Kaufmann: op.cit: Page/226-227
83. Ibid: Page/91
84. Ibid: Page/337
85. Ibid: Page/134
86. La Barre: op.cit: Pages/19,26
87. Keith Ward, "The Concept of God": Oxford: Basil Blackwell: 1974: Page/135
88. "Reasons and Faiths": op.cit: Page/166
89. Thomas V. Morris, "The Concept of God" (Ed) Oxford University Press: New York: 1987: Page/3
90. La Barree: op.cit.: Page/6
91. Paul Tillich: op.cit: Page/123

The Living God

1. Y. Kaufmann: op.cit: Page/23
2. W.T. Stace: "The Nature of the World": Princeton University Press: 1940.
3. Raffaele Pettazzone: "The Supreme Being: Phenomenological Structure and Historical Development in "History of Religions": Ed.

Mircea Eliade, Joseph M. Kitagawa: The University of Chicago Press: 1959: Chicago: Page/60-61

4. Karen Armstrong: op.cit: Page/68
5. Quoted in Edward Hussey, "Presocratics": Duckworth: 1974: Page/46
6. Ibid: Page/99
7. Ibid: Page/39
8. Ibid: Page/48
9. Ibid: Page/49
10. Robert Oakes: "Does Traditional Theism Entail Pantheism" in Thomas V. Morris: op.cit: Page/57
11. Arnold Toynbee: op.cit: Page/14
12. Wilhelm Hobfass: op.cit: Page/95
13. Quoted in Walter Kaufmann: op.cit: Page/100
14. Ibid: Page/88
15. Karen Armstrong: op.cit: Page/74-75
16. Isaiah: 19:24-25
17. Romans: 8:34
18. Acts: 3:13
19. Romans: 1.3
20. Romans: 3.22
21. Romans: 3.28
22. Romans: 7.6
23. I Corinthians: 2.16
24. II Corinthian: 3:14
25. Galatians: 2.21
26. Galatians: 2:16
27. Romans: 1
28. I Corinthians: 15:12-17
29. James Barr, "Journal of Theological Studies"—39(1998), quoted by Geza Vermes, "Jesus the Jew: Christians and Jewish Reactions", in 'Jews and Christians in a Pluralistic World' Edited by Ernst–Wolfgang Bockenforde & Edward Shils: London: Weidenfeld & Nicolson: 1991: Page/31
30. Ladwig Wittgenstein: 'MS 119 151: 22.10.1937' and MS120.836: 8.9.12.37 quoted in Ashok Vohra: ibid: Page/37
31. Quoted in Ashok Vohra: ibid: Page/38
32. "The Oxford Companion to the Bible" Pp.320-321 quoted by Arun

Shourie in 'Harvesting Our Souls': ASA Publications: New Delhi: 2000: Page/216

33. "Macropaedia", quoted in Arun Shourie: ibid: Page/216
34. "Macropaedia", quoted in Arun Shourie: ibid: Page/216-217
35. Luke: 3.22
36. John: 5.19
37. John: 10:30
38. John: 10:31
39. John: 14: 16
40. Malachi: 3.6
41. Keith Ward: op.cit: Page/47
42. Ibid: Page/48
43. La Barre: op.cit: Page/606
44. Geza Vermes: op.cit: Page/27
45. MS 119 71: 4.10.1937: Ashok Vohra: op.cit: Page/35
46. MS 120: 83 c: 8-9.12.1937: of Ashok Vohra: op.cit: Page/37-38
47. Quoted in Geza Vermes: op.cit: Page/26
48. MS 120 83 c: 8-9.12.1937: Ashok Vohra: op.cit: Page/37
49. Paul Tillich, "Dynamics of Faith": New York: Harper & Brothers Publishers 1957: Page/18,34
50. Karen Armstrong: op.cit: Page/2
51. Ibid: Page/238
52. John: 1.5
53. I Corinthians: 13.9-12
54. I Corinthians: 8:5-6
55. Karen Armstrong: op.cit: Page/120
56. Arnold Toynbee: cp.cit: Page/295
57. Ibid: Page/294
58. Walter Kaufmann: op.cit: Page/129
59. Ibid: Page/128
60. Ed.L.Miller: op.cit: Page/124
61. I Corinthians: 1:22-25
62. Colossians: 2.8
63. Quoted in Ed.L.Miller: op.cit: Page/119
64. II Corinthians: 11.14
65. Walter Kaufmann: op.cit: Page/104
66. Ibid: Page/217

67. Edwin A.Burtt: op.cit:
68. Quoted in Ed.L.Miller: op.cit: Page/127
69. Ibid: Page/127
70. Ibid: Page/130
71. Micah: 4.5
72. Zachariah: 14.9
73. Keith Ward: op.cit: Page/124
74. Ibid: Page/126
75. Ibid: Page/129
76. Ibid: Page/130
77. Ingolf U. Dalferth, "Theology and Philosophy": Basil Blackwell: Oxford: 1968: Page/53
78. Wilbur Marshall Urban, "Humanity and Deity," George Allen & Unwin Ltd.: London: 1951: Page/34
79. Ibid: Page/34
80. La Barre: op.cit: Page/26
81. Ibid: Page/7
82. Ibid: Page/35
83. Walter Kaufmann: op.cit: Page/126
84. Ibid: Page/129
85. Quoted in W.M.Urban: op.cit: Page/78
86. Ibid: Page/78
87. Quoted in Urban: ibid: Page/326
88. Ibid: Page/326
89. Quoted in Urban's ibid: Page/268
90. Quoted in Urban: ibid: Page/214
91. Ed.L. Miller: op.cit: Page/220
92. Quoted by Robert P. Scharlemann in "The Textuality of Texts" in David E. Klemm & William Schweikes (Ed) 'Meanings in Texts and Actions: Questioning Paul Ricoeur": University Press of Virginia: Charlotts Ville: 1993: Page/22
93. Ibid: Page/21
94. Quoted in Ashok Vohra: op.cit: Page/
95. Ingolf U. Dalfreth: op.cit: Page/56
96. J.Wm.McClendon et.al: op.cit: Page/16
97. Quoted by Dalferth: op.cit: Page/44
98. Ibid: Page/6

99. Quoted by Russel Nieli, " Wittgenstein: From Mysticism to Ordinary Language": State University of New York Press: Albany: 1987: Page/9
100. 'Tractatus-7': quoted in ibid: Page/109
101. Ed.L.Miller: op.cit: Page/187
102. Russel Nieli: op.cit: Page/132

To You Your God To Me Mine

1. Schuyler Brown, "The Origins of Christianity: A Historical Introduction to the New Testament": New York: Oxford University Press: 1984: Page/16
2. Ibid: Pages/18-21
3. Joseph M. Kitagawa "The History of Religions in America", in "The History of Religions: Essays in Methodology", Edited by Mircea Eliade and Joseph M. Kitogama: The University of Chicago Press: Chicago: 1959: Page/25
4. Ibid: Page/26
5. "Comparative Religion: "Whither and Why?" in Mircea Eliade, et. al: op.cit: Page/42
6. "Reden", Rede 4: Quoted by Friedrich Heiler "The History of Religions as a Preparation for the Co-operation of Religions" in Mircea Eliade, et.al: op.cit: Page/141
7. Ibid: Page/139
8. W.M.Urban: op.cit: Page/17
9. Ingolf U. Dalferth: op.cit: Page/36
10. Quoted by Friedrich Heiler: op.cit: Page/155
11. Ibid: Page/156
12. Keith Ward: op.cit: Page/3
13. Phrases Taken from Dalfreth: op.cit
14. Don Cupitt , "The Leap of Reasons": Sheldon Press: London: 1976: Page/121
15. P.H. Nowell–Smith, "Ethics": Basil Blackwell: Oxford: 1957: Page/ 169
16. Ibid: Page/169
17. Van Der Leeuw: op.cit: Page/49
18. Walter Kaufmann: op.cit: Page/171
19. P. H. Nowell–Smith: op.cit: Page/169

20. Keith Ward: op.cit: Page/121
21. P.H. Nowell–Smith: op.cit: Page/41
22. R.M. Hare, "The Language of Morals": Oxford University Press: London: 1952: Pages/177.9
23. I.T.Ramsay quoted in James McClendon, et.al: op.cit: Page/18
24. Quran: 48.29
25. John: 17.9
26. Keith Ward: op.cit: Page/107
27. Ibid: Page/137
28. Ibid: Page/146
29. Ibid: Page/150
30. Ibid: Page/152
31. Ibid: Pages/124,126,129
32. Ibid: Pages/126-127
33. Quoted in Arun Shourie: 'Harvesting Our Souls": ASA Publication: New Delhi: 2000: Page/159
34. Ibid: Page/160
35. James Collins, "God in Modern Philosophy": London: Routledge & Kegan Paul: 1960: Page/18
36. Ibid: Page/37
37. Dalferth: op.cit: Page/38
38. Ibid: Page/43
39. Ibid: Page/43
40. Ibid: Page/44
41. Ibid: Page/47
42. Quoted in Dalferth, ibid: Page/56
43. Dalferth: ibid: Page/56
44. Ibid: Page/65
45. Peter B. Clarke, et.al: op.cit: Page/79
46. Ibid: Page/ 79
47. Ibid: Page/83
48. Quoted by Heiler: op.cit: Page/155-156
49. Van der Leeuw: op.cit: Page/180
50. Ibid: Page/181
51. Jean Danielou, "Phenomenology of Religions and Philosophy of Religion," in Mircea Eliade, et.al: op.cit: Page/69
52. Don Cupitt: op.cit: Page/109
53. Ibid: Page/105

In The Mirror of My Heart

1. S. Radhakrishnan, "The Hindu View of Life": New Delhi: Indus: 1993: Page/32
2. S. Radhakrishnan, "Our Heritage": Delhi: Orient Paperbacks: 1992; Page/20
3. P.T. Raju, 'The Concept of Man in Indian Thought' in 'The Concept of Man', Edited by S. Radhakrishnan and P.T. Raju: Indus: New Delhi: 1995: Page/217
4. Ibid: Page/216-217
5. John Gribbin, "In Search of Schrodinger's Cat": London: Corgi Books–Black Swan: Page/3
6. Ibid: Page/208
7. Ibid: Page/211
8. Gauḍapāda: Mānḍukya Karikā 3.19
9. Ibid:
10. Quoted in Stephen Kaplan, 'Hermeneutics, Holography and Indian Idealism': Delhi: Motilal Banarasidas: 1987: Page/132-133
11. Stephen Kaplan: ibid: Page/132-133
12. Brahma Sūtra Śaṁkar Bhāsya (BSSB): 2.1.24
13. Rāmānuj, 'Gitā Bhāsya': 7.14
14. Yoga Vāśiṣtha 4.41.18
15. BSSB: 1.1.1
16. Stephen Kaplan: op.cit: Page/87
17. Mānḍukya Karikā – 2.5
18. Stephen Kaplan: op.cit: Page/9
19. Ibid: Page/10
20. Ibid
21. Gary Zukav, 'The Dancing Wu Li Masters': New York: Bantam Books: Page/75
22. Ibid: Page/79
23. Ibid: Page/79
24. Quoted in Gary Zukav: ibid: Page/114
25. Mānḍukya Karikā 1.7.
26. Gary Zukav: op.cit: Page 222
27. Deepak Chopra, 'How to know God': New York: Rider: Page/30
28. Yajur Veda 40.6
29. Fritjof Capra, 'The Tao of Physics: USA: Bantam Books: Page/116-117

30. Heisenberg, 'Physics and Philosophy', quoted in Fritjof Capra: ibid: Page/125
31. Śivasaṁhitā, 1.1
32. Ibid: 1.35
33. Vedānt Muktāvali, 22
34. Laṁkāvatāra Sūtra, II.36
35. Ṛg Veda, 10.129.4
36. Śaṁkar, 'Vivekacuḍāmaṇi,'13
37. Swami Ranganathananda, 'The Message of the Upanisads': Bombay: Bharatiya Vidya Bhavan: 1993 Page/14
38. Ibid: Page/14
39. Quoted in ibid: Page/14
40. 'Our Heritage': op.cit: Page/34
41. Ibid: Page/36
42. Gītā: 18.63
43. Quoted in 'Our Heritage': op.cit: Page/47
44. Ibid: Page/54
45. Quoted in Ranganathananda: op.cit: Page/13
46. Quoted in Ranganathanand; ibid: Page/21
47. Quoted in Ranganathanand: ibid: Page/37
48. Íśāvāsyopaniṣad, 16
49. Ṛg Veda, 4.60.5
50. Gary Zukav: op.cit: Pages/256, 281
51. Heinz R. Pagels, 'The Cosmic Code': New York: Bantam Books: 1990: Page/82
52. Padma Purāṇa
53. Māṇḍukya Karikā, 1.18
54. Āpastamba Dharmasūtra
55. Ṛg Veda, 3.55.11
56. Ṛg Veda, 8.58.2
57. Śaṁkar, 'Upadesaśahāsri', 1.27
58. Ibid: 1.28
59. Uttaragītā
60. John M.Koller, "The Indian Way": New York: Macmillan Publishing Company: Page/24
61. Ibid: Page/28
62. Ṛg Veda, 10.82.7

63. Usha Grover, 'Symbolism in the Aranyakas and Their Impact on the Upanisads': New Delhi: Guruvar Publication: 1987: Page/25
64. Quoted in Usha Grover; ibid: Page/25
65. Bṛhadāraṇyaka: 2.3.1
66. S. Radhakrishnan, 'Religion and Society': New Delhi: Indus: 1995: Page/120
67. Deepak Chopra: op.cit: Page/8,9
68. Ibid: Page/8
69. S. Radhakrishnan, 'Religion and Society': op.cit: Page/121
70. Madhvācārya., 'Madhvasiddhāntasār' 21
71. Quoted by S. Radhakrishnan, in 'Religion and Society': p.cit: Page/122
72. Īśāvāsyopaniṣad, 6

Ekoham Bahusyam

1. Quoted in Ṛg Ved Samhita', Vol. I: Veda Pratisthan New Delhi: 1977: Pages/100-101
2. Ibid: Page/101
3. "A History of Ancient Sanskrit Literature", Quoted by Swami Prakashanand Saraswati in 'The True History and Religion of India': OSDL: Austin: 1999: Page/243
4. Quoted in 'Ṛg Veda Samhita': op.cit: Page/105
5. Quoted in 'Rg Veda Samhita': ibid: Page/103
6. Quoted in ibid: Page/110
7. Quoted in ibid: Page/128-129
8. Bṛhaddevatā, 1.2
9. Nirukta, 7.1
10. Nirukta, 7.1
11. Nirukta, 7.4
12. Bṛhadāraṇyaka, 3.9.2
13. Ibid: 3.9.8
14. Ṛg Veda, 3.53.8
15. Ṛg Veda, 10.85.16
16. Taittiriya Āraṇyaka, 11.9
17. Taittiriya Brāhmaṇ 2.8.8.5
18. Atharva Veda, 17.1.19
19. Nirukta, 7.5

20. Bṛhaddevata, 1.5
21. Ibid, 1.70
22. Nirukta, 7.5
23. Bṛhaddevatā, 1.97
24. Ibid, 1.106
25. Ibid, 1.71
26. Ibid, 1.77
27. Ibid, 1.122
28. Ibid, 2.2
29. Ibid, 1.96
30. Ibid, 2.18
31. Ṛg. Veda, 2.1.3
32. Ṛg Veda, 2.1.4
33. Ṛg Veda, 2.1.6
34. Bṛhaddevatā, 2.124
35. Ibid, 1.62
36. Ibid, 1.63
37. Ibid, 1.64
38. Ṛg Veda, 1.164.46
39. Bṛhaddevatā, 1.23
40. Ibid, 2.32
41. Ibid, 2.33
42. Ibid, 2.34
43. A.A. Macdonell, 'Vedic Mythology': Edited by G. Buhler, Vol. III, Part 1A: Indological Book House: Varanasi: Page/1
44. Ibid: Page/2
45. Nirukta, 7.4
46. Ibid, 7.4
47. Ibid, 7.4
48. Ṛg. Veda, 1.69.1
49. Atharva Veda Saṁhitā, 13.3.13
50. Nirukta, 7.6
51. Ibid, 7.7
52. Ibid, 7.7
53. A.A. Macdonell: op.cit; Page/2,3
54. Ibid: Page/15.16
55. Ibid: Page/16

56. Ṛg Veda, 5.3.1
57. Ṛg Veda, 1.89.10
58. A.A. Macdonell: op.cit: Page/20
59. Bṛhaddevatā, 3.81
60. Ibid, 3.82
61. Ibid, 3.39
62. Ṛg Veda, 1.115.1
63. Ṛg Veda, 4.53.2
64. Ṛg Ved, 4.26.1
65. Ṛg Veda, 2.30.1
66. A.A. Macdonell: op.cit: Page/71
67. Ṛg Veda: 3.29.11
68. Ṛg Veda: 1.69.1
69. Nirukta, 7.15
70. Jaiminiya Brāhmaṇ, 2.90
71. Śatapatha Brahman, 11.1.6.7
72. Nirukta, 7.1
73. Ṛg Veda, 5.67.4
74. Ṛg Veda, 1.3.9
75. Ṛg Veda, 10.2.3
76. Atharva Veda, 1.1.4
77. Muṇḍaka Upaniṣada, 1.2.1
78. Atharva Veda, 10.7.13
79. Atharva Veda, 10.7.38
80. Ṛg Veda, 10.82.3
81. Yajur Veda, 32.1
82. Atharva Veda, 13.4.4-5
83. Kaivalyopaniṣad
84. Atharva Veda, 13.4.12-13
85. Manusmṛti, 12.123
86. Ṛg Veda, 3.32.8
87. Atharva Veda, 7.41.1
88. Ṛg Veda, 9.102.5
89. Ṛg Veda, 5.67.4
90. Sāyan's Bhāsya on Ṛg Veda
91. Bṛhaddevatā, 7.130
92. Ibid, 2.86
93. Ṛg Veda, 4.50.4

94. Ṛg Veda, 10.114.5

Cosmic Emanation

1. Nirukta, 7.5
2. Ṛg Veda, 8.58.2
3. Ṛg Veda, 10.81.3
4. Ṛg Veda, 10.81.4
5. Taittirīya Brāhmaṇ, 2.8.9.6
6. Atharva Veda, 13.4.11-13
7. Atharva Veda, 13.4.16-17
8. Atharva Veda, 13.4.22
9. Atharva Veda, 13.4.23
10. Atharva Veda, 13.4.25
11. Atharva Veda, 13.4.44-45
12. Yajur Veda, 32.4
13. Ṛg Veda, 6.22.1
14. Ṛg Veda, 8.1.1
15. Atharva Veda, 2.1.5
16. Atharva Veda, 2.2.1
17. Atharva Veda, 2/2/2
18. Ṛg Veda, 10.114.5
19. Aitareya Brāhmaṇ, 1.1
20. Taittirīya Āraṇyaka, 10.16.1
21. Bṛhadāraṇyaka Upaniṣad, 2.5.15
22. Koller: op.cit: Page/27
23. Ṛg Veda, 10.129.1
24. Ṛg Veda, 10.129.2
25. Ṛg Veda, 1.164.30
26. M.L. Gupta, 'The Cosmic Yajna': Bharatput: Samhita Books: 1999: Page/215
27. Ṛg Veda, 10.129.3
28. Ṛg Veda, 10.190.1
29. Koller: op.cit: Page/30
30. 'The Cosmic Yajna: op.cit: Page/218
31. James Wallace, 'Brahman – E=MC2': Allied Publishers Pvt Ltd: New Delhi: 1995: Page/82
32. Ibid: Page/91
33. Ibid: Page/78

34. Ṛg Veda, 1.164.14
35. 'The Cosmic Yajna': op.cit: Page/219
36. Ṛg Veda, 10.190.2
37. Ṛg Veda, 10.129.4
38. Nṛsiṁhapurvatāpāni Upaniṣad, 3.1.1
39. Śrimad Bhāgavat, 7.14.37
40. Bṛhadāraṇyaka Upaniṣad, 14.8
41. Muṇḍaka Upaniṣad, 2.1.10
42. Taittirīya Āraṇyaka, 1.23.9
43. S.K. Ramachandra Rao, 'Rg Veda Darsana – Vol.4 – Purusa Sukta': Kalpataru Research Academy: Bangalore: 1999: Page/22-23
44. Ṛg Veda, 10,90,2
45. Ṛg, Veda 10.90.3
46. S.K. Ramachandra Rao: op.cit: Page/82
47. Ibid: Page/84
48. Kaṭha Upaniṣad: 3.11
49. S.K. Ramachandra Rao: op.cit: Page/85
50. Ibid: Page/111
51. Atharva Veda, 1.1.71
52. Iśa Upaniṣad, 1.1
53. Bhāsya on Taittirīya Upaniṣad, 2.1
54. Śaṁkara's Bhāsya on Brahma Sūtra, 1.1.1
55. Bṛhadāraṇyaka Upaniṣad, 1.2.1
56. Ibid, 1.2.4
57. Ibid, 1.1.2, 1.2.7
58. Ibid, 1.3.11
59. Ibid, 3.1.3
60. Ibid, 3.1.4
61. Ibid, 3.1.5
62. Ibid, 1.3.14
63. Ibid, 1.3.12
64. Ibid, 1.3.22
65. Ibid, 3.1.3
66. Ibid, 1.4.3
67. Ibid, 1.4.3
68. Aitareya Upaniṣad, 1.2.3
69. Aitareya Upaniṣad, 1.2.4

70. Muṇḍaka Upaniṣad, 2.20.11
71. Chāndogya Upaniṣada, 2.14.1
72. Iśāvāsyopaniṣada, 15
73. Bṛhadāraṇyaka Upaniṣad, 2.3.1
74. Chāndogya Upaniṣad, 3.18.1
75. Ibid, 3.18.2
76. Ibid, 3.19.1
77. Ibid, 7.1.15
78. Ibid, 7.15.4
79. Radhakrishnan, 'The Bhagawad Gita'; New Delhi: Indus: 1994: Page/24
80. Śrimad Bhāgavat, quoted ibid; Page/24
81. A.G. Krishna Warrier, 'God In Advaita': Shimla: IIAS: 1977: Page/48
82. Quoted in Warrier: ibid: Page/49
83. Śvetāśvatara Upaniṣad, 3.2.3
84. Śaṁkara Bhāsya on Brahma Sūtra 1.2.14
85. S.K. Ramachandra Rao; 'Rg Veda Darsana, Vol.II; KRA; Bangalore; 1998; Page/221
86. Ibid: Page/222
87. Ānandatirtha, quoted in ibid; Page/223
88. Quoted in ibid; Page/223
89. Viṣṇu Dharmottara Purāṇa, 1.58
90. Quoted by S. Radhakrishnana in 'Upanisadon Ki Bhumika': Trans. Ramanatha Shastri: New Delhi: Rajpal & Sons: 1981: Page/148
91. Kalpataru 1.1.20, quoted in ibid; Page/148

Yo Vai Viṣṇuḥ Sa Vai Rudro

1. Rādhā Upaniṣad, 3.4
2. Vāmana Purāṇa, 3.16.17
3. Quoted by Radhakrishnan in 'The Bhagavadgita': op.cit.: Page/23
4. Chāndogya Upaniṣad; 6.3.2
5. A.G. Krishna Warrier, 'God in Advaita': Simla: IIAS: 1977: Page/134-135
6. Ibid: Page/139
7. Ibid: Page/139
8. Ibid: Page/140
9. Ibid: Page/156

10. Radhakrishnan, 'The Bhagavadgita': op.cit: Page/33
11. Ibid: Page/32
12. Bhagavad Gītā, 4.5
13. Ibid, 4.7
14. Ibid, 4.8
15. Ibid, 4.11
16. Quoted by Radhakrishnan in 'The Bhagavadgita': op.cit: Page/159
17. Atharva Veda, 13.3.7
18. Bhagavad Gītā, 7.12
19. Taittirīya Saṁhitā, 6.1.1.2
20. Ṛg Veda, 4.23.10
21. Ṛg Veda, 3.55.10
22. Ṛg Veda, 1.22.18
23. S.K. Ramchandra Rao, 'Visnu Suktani': Part I: Bangalore: Kalpataru Research Academy: Page/91
24. Ibid: Page/58
25. Ṛg Veda, 1.154.4
26. 'Viṣṇu Suktaāi': op.cit: Page/170
27. Ibid: Page/54
28. Śatapatha Brāhmaṇ, 6.7.4.7
29. Aitareya Brāhmaṇ, 1.1.1
30. Quoted in S.K. Ramachanda Rao 'Visnu Suktani' Part II: KRA: Bangalore: Page/37
31. Ibid: Page/18
32. Ṛg Veda, 1.156.2
33. Ṛg Veda, 1.56.1
34. Viṣṇu Suktāni, Part II: op.cit: Page/75
35. Ibid: Page/75
36. Viṣṇu Purāṇa, 3.1.45
37. Ṛg Veda, 1.156.3
38. Viṣṇu Suktāni, Part II: op.cit: Page/28
39. Viṣṇudharmottara Purāṇa, 1.58
40. S. Radhakrishnan in 'Upanisadon Ki Bhumika; op.cit: Page/152
41. Viṣṇu Purāṇa, 1.2.66
42. Harivaṁsa Purāṇa, 25.131-132
43. Viṣṇu Purāṇa, 3.3.27
44. Śvẹtāśvatara Upaniṣad, 3.2.7

45. Baudhāyan Gṛhya Sūtra, 3.2.16.39
46. Rāmāyaṇa, Balkanda, 45.22
47. Mahābhārata, Karṇa Parva, 24.62
48. Ibid: Anuśāsana Parva, 22,227
49. Ibid, 112.53
50. Vārāha Purāṇa, 25.5
51. Vāyu Purāṇa, 66.108
52. Ibid, 25.21
53. Ibid, 24.109
54. Viṣṇu Purāṇa, 1.9.68
55. Vārāha Purāṇa, 9.7
56. Gaṇeṣa Purāṇa, 1.21-22

Hai Hari Bas Kuch Aisā

1. Ṛg Veda, 7.63.3
2. Ṛg Veda, 1.164.39
3. Ṛg Veda, 8.19.25
4. Ṛg Veda, 2.11.12
5. Bṛhadāraṇyaka Upaniṣad, 4.3.32
6. Ṛg Veda, 4.26.1
7. Yajur Veda, 7.45
8. Atharva Veda, 18.4.3
9. Manusmrit, 6.92
10. P.T. Raju, 'The Concept of Man': op.cit
11. Sthānāṅga, 2.1
12. Suvikṛtāṅga, 1.15.11
13. K. Satchidananda Murty, ' Philosophy in India: Traditions, Teachings and Researches': New Delhi: ICPR: 1985: Page/8
14. Ṛg Veda, 8.98.11
15. Chāndogya Upanisad, 3.14.1 ; 3.18.1
16. Brahma Sūtra Śaṁkara Bhāsya, 1.1.24
17. Śrimad Bhāgavat, 7.5.23
18. Viṣṇu Purāṇa, 6.5.72
19. Brahma Sūtra Bhāsya, 2.2.29
20. Murty; op.cit: Page/56
21. Ibid: Page/56

22. Yogesh Gupta; Sant Kavi Raidas': New Delhi: Hindu Pocket Books: 1989: Page/5
23. Jain: op.cit: Page/5
24. Quoted in Murty: op.cit: Page/75
25. Ibid: Page/75
26. Ibid: Page/76
27. Ibid: Page/78
28. Padma Purāṇa
29. Rāmacaritamānas
30. Ibid
31. Ibid; Bālkanḍa, 115.2
32. Ibid; Bālkanḍa, 143.2
33. Rāga Bilāwal Mahlā 5, Gharu 4
34. Rāga Bilāwal Mahlā 5 Dupade Gharu 8
35. Pancavati; Prasaṅga – 4
36. Rāmkali Mahalā 1 Dakhani Omakru
37. Māruvar Mahlā 5 Dakhane 1
38. Japuji 17
39. Gauda Mahlā 5, Sabad 17
40. Soraṭha Mahalā 9 Sabad 5
41. Rāmacaritamānas, Sundarkānd, 38.1
42. Ibid: Bālkanḍ 119.2
43. Māru Solahe Mahalā 5, Sabad 11
44. Ibid
45. Māru Solahe Mahalā 5, [Japu ji, 37]
46. Māru Mahalā 5, Gharu 2, 2
47. Darśanopanisad
48. Yajur Veda; 32.3
49. Ādhyātma Rāmayāna
50. Swami Vivekanand, Quoted in R. Balasubramanium, 'Primal spirituality of the Vedas': New Delhi: 1996: PHISPC: Page/149
51. Vivekananda quoted in ibid: Page/153-54
52. Vivekanand quoted in ibid: Page/148
53. 'Teachings', quoted in ibid: Pages/183,185-186

Table of Transliteration

अ	a
उ	u
ऌ	ḷ
औ	au
क्	k
च्	c
ट्	ṭ
त्	t
प्	p
य्	y
श्	ś
ळ्	ḷ
आ	ā
ऊ	ū
ए	e
अं	aṁ
ख्	kh
छ्	ch
ठ्	ṭh
थ्	th
फ्	ph
र्	r
ष्	ṣ
क्ष्	kṣ
इ	i
ऋ	ṛ
ऐ	ai
अः	aḥ
ग्	g
ज्	j
ड्	ḍ
द्	d
ब्	b
ल्	l
स्	s
त्र्	tr
ई	ā
ॠ	ṝ
ओ	o
घ्	gh
झ्	jh
ढ्	ḍh
ध्	dh
भ्	bh
व्	v
ह्	h
ज्ञ्	jñ
ङ्	ṅ
ञ्	ñ
ण्	ṇ
न्	n
म्	m